EMOTIONAL AND BEHAVIORAL PROBLEMS
OF YOUNG CHILDREN

The Guilford Practical Intervention in the Schools Series

Kenneth W. Merrell, Founding Editor
T. Chris Riley-Tillman, Series Editor

www.guilford.com/practical

This series presents the most reader-friendly resources available in key areas of evidence-based practice in school settings. Practitioners will find trustworthy guides on effective behavioral, mental health, and academic interventions, and assessment and measurement approaches. Covering all aspects of planning, implementing, and evaluating high-quality services for students, books in the series are carefully crafted for everyday utility. Features include ready-to-use reproducibles, lay-flat binding to facilitate photocopying, appealing visual elements, and an oversized format. Recent titles have Web pages where purchasers can download and print the reproducible materials.

Recent Volumes

Classwide Positive Behavior Interventions and Supports:
A Guide to Proactive Classroom Management
Brandi Simonsen and Diane Myers

Promoting Academic Success with English Language Learners:
Best Practices for RTI
Craig A. Albers and Rebecca S. Martinez

Integrated Multi-Tiered Systems of Support: Blending RTI and PBIS
Kent McIntosh and Steve Goodman

The ABCs of CBM, Second Edition:
A Practical Guide to Curriculum-Based Measurement
Michelle K. Hosp, John L. Hosp, and Kenneth W. Howell

DBT Skills in Schools:
Skills Training for Emotional Problem Solving for Adolescents (DBT STEPS-A)
*James J. Mazza, Elizabeth T. Dexter-Mazza, Alec L. Miller, Jill H. Rathus,
and Heather E. Murphy*

Interventions for Disruptive Behaviors:
Reducing Problems and Building Skills
Gregory A. Fabiano

Promoting Student Happiness:
Positive Psychology Interventions in Schools
Shannon M. Suldo

Effective Math Interventions:
A Guide to Improving Whole-Number Knowledge
Robin S. Codding, Robert J. Volpe, and Brian C. Poncy

Group Interventions in Schools: A Guide for Practitioners
Jennifer P. Keperling, Wendy M. Reinke, Dana Marchese, and Nicholas Ialongo

Emotional and Behavioral Problems of Young Children, Second Edition:
Effective Interventions in the Preschool and Kindergarten Years
Melissa L. Holland, Jessica Malmberg, and Gretchen Gimpel Peacock

Transforming Schools: A Problem-Solving Approach to School Change
Rachel Cohen Losoff and Kelly Broxterman

Emotional and Behavioral Problems of Young Children

*Effective Interventions
in the Preschool and Kindergarten Years*

SECOND EDITION

**MELISSA L. HOLLAND
JESSICA MALMBERG
GRETCHEN GIMPEL PEACOCK**

PRAIRIE STATE COLLEGE
LIBRARY

THE GUILFORD PRESS
New York   London

Copyright © 2017 The Guilford Press
A Division of Guilford Publications, Inc.
370 Seventh Avenue, Suite 1200, New York, NY 10001
www.guilford.com

All rights reserved

Except as indicated, no part of this book may be reproduced, translated, stored in a retrieval system, or transmitted, in any form or by any means, electronic, mechanical, photocopying, microfilming, recording, or otherwise, without written permission from the publisher.

Printed in Canada

This book is printed on acid-free paper.

Last digit is print number: 9 8 7 6 5 4 3 2 1

LIMITED DUPLICATION LICENSE

These materials are intended for use only by qualified professionals.

The publisher grants to individual purchasers of this book nonassignable permission to reproduce all materials for which permission is specifically granted in a footnote. This license is limited to you, the individual purchaser, for personal use or use with individual students. This license does not grant the right to reproduce these materials for resale, redistribution, electronic display, or any other purposes (including but not limited to books, pamphlets, articles, video- or audiotapes, blogs, file-sharing sites, Internet or intranet sites, and handouts or slides for lectures, workshops, or webinars, whether or not a fee is charged). Permission to reproduce these materials for these and any other purposes must be obtained in writing from the Permissions Department of Guilford Publications.

Library of Congress Cataloging-in-Publication Data

Names: Holland, Melissa L., author. | Malmberg, Jessica, author. | Gimpel
  Peacock, Gretchen, author.
Title: Emotional and behavioral problems of young children : effective
  interventions in the preschool and kindergarten years / Melissa L.
  Holland, Jessica Malmberg, Gretchen Gimpel Peacock.
Description: Second edition. | New York : The Guilford Press, [2017] |
  Series: The guilford practical intervention in the schools series |
  Revision of: Emotional and behavioral problems of young children /
  Gretchen A. Gimpel, Melissa L. Holland. c2003. | Includes bibliographical
  references and index.
Identifiers: LCCN 2016034316 | ISBN 9781462529346 (paperback)
Subjects: LCSH: Adjustment disorders in children. | Preschool
  children—Mental health. | Kindergarten. | BISAC: PSYCHOLOGY /
  Psychotherapy / Child & Adolescent. | EDUCATION / Preschool &
  Kindergarten. | SOCIAL SCIENCE / Social Work. | EDUCATION / Special
  Education / Social Disabilities.
Classification: LCC RJ506.A33 G565 2017 | DDC 618.92/852—dc23
LC record available at *https://lccn.loc.gov/2016034316*

About the Authors

Melissa L. Holland, PhD, is Assistant Professor of School Psychology at California State University, Sacramento, and has a private practice specializing in work with children, adolescents, and their families. She previously worked in mental health clinics; community, child, and family agencies; a major medical center; and a Head Start program providing assessment and intervention services to children and their families. Her publications focus on the emotional health of children. Dr. Holland also presents workshops at regional and national conferences on children's mental health and consults in schools on social–emotional learning and the use of mindfulness and cognitive and behavioral strategies with students.

Jessica Malmberg, PhD, is Assistant Professor in the Departments of Psychiatry and Pediatrics at the University of Colorado School of Medicine. She provides outpatient behavioral health services to children, adolescents, and families presenting with a wide spectrum of behavioral health disorders within the Pediatric Mental Health Institute at Children's Hospital Colorado. Dr. Malmberg's research, clinical work, and publications focus on disruptive behavior disorders, parenting interventions, pediatric psychology (particularly chronic pain conditions and functional disorders), and program development pertaining to preventative and transdiagnostic approaches to pediatric behavioral health.

Gretchen Gimpel Peacock, PhD, is Professor and Department Head of Psychology at Utah State University. She served as program director of the School Psychology Program from 1997 to 2009. Dr. Gimpel Peacock's research, publications, and professional presentations focus on child behavior problems and associated family issues, as well as professional issues in school psychology. She serves on the editorial advisory boards of several school psychology and related journals. She is coauthor of *School Psychology for the Twenty-First Century, Second Edition,* and coeditor of *Practical Handbook of School Psychology,* among other books.

Preface

This book is intended to equip child-focused mental health providers with information on how to address common emotional and behavioral problems exhibited by preschool- and kindergarten-age children (ages 3–6). Our main focus is providing practical and effective interventions that can easily be implemented by clinicians working in educational settings, as well as by clinical psychologists and other mental health providers working with children in nonschool settings. In addition, we emphasize working with parents of young children who are exhibiting behaviors of concern. Although some techniques for working individually with children are covered, it is our belief that parents are instrumental in resolving problems young children are experiencing, since preschool children spend much of their days with their parents.

Although preschool and kindergarten children may not be diagnosed with specific disorders or classified according to specific special education categories, they may still exhibit a number of behavioral and emotional problems that cause concern for their parents and teachers. In addition, research has consistently shown that many children who exhibit problems in the preschool years continue to have problems into elementary school, and even later. Thus it is important to provide prevention methods and early intervention to decrease the potential negative long-term effects of these difficulties. This book provides clinicians with interventions that have been shown to be effective with young children based on the current available research evidence.

Chapter 1 begins with an overview of childhood emotional and behavioral problems and how they are likely to manifest during the preschool and kindergarten years. Also discussed in Chapter 1 are correlates of these problems and information related to the continuity of such difficulties. Chapter 2 provides information on assessment methods: norm-referenced assessment measures (rating scales) and other types of assessment methods (interviews, observations) are discussed. This chapter specifically focuses on the use of these measures and techniques with young children and covers diagnostic measures as well as screening and progress monitoring assessment tools. The next three chapters cover interventions for specific areas of concern. Chapter 3 focuses on the treatment of externalizing problems in young children (e.g., attention-deficit/hyperactivity disorder, conduct problems) and extensively discusses parent training. Chapter 4 covers interventions for internalizing problems (i.e., anxiety and depression); treatments for the specific anxiety disorders most likely to be diagnosed in the preschool years are highlighted (e.g., specific phobias, separation anxiety disorder). Chapter 5 reviews the treatment of "everyday problems," such as those involving toileting issues (i.e., enuresis and encopresis), sleeping problems (e.g., frequent night wakings), and feeding problems (e.g., children who are "picky" eaters). Because of the nature of these problems, the interventions discussed in this chapter are focused primarily on working with parents. In Chapter 6, an overview of early academic and emotional–behavioral supports for students in the classroom within a multi-tiered system of support is provided, including response-to-intervention models for early literacy and academic issues, positive behavioral interventions and supports within the preschool and kindergarten classrooms, and social–emotional learning programs for use with preschool- and kindergarten-age children. Finally, Chapter 7 discusses situations in which additional assistance for the child should be considered and summarizes the steps for referral.

Each chapter contains parent handouts, assessment tools, and other reproducible materials. Similar materials appear in other sources, but we have found the versions presented here to be particularly helpful in our work with young children.

This book will be a helpful, practical resource for individuals working with preschool- and kindergarten-age children exhibiting emotional and behavioral problems. Although some of the interventions may seem fairly straightforward, they should be implemented by professionals who have training and expertise in child development and a basic knowledge of therapeutic interventions. Individuals who would likely find this book useful include school psychologists working in preschool and kindergarten settings; psychologists and master's-level mental health professionals in private practice who provide services to young children; pediatricians with a strong background in behavioral interventions; and other professionals with child-focused training. This book would also be a useful resource in graduate child therapy didactic and practicum courses.

Acknowledgments

We appreciate the invaluable support and assistance that so many individuals have provided us in the process of completing this book. We are thankful for the exceptional editorial staff at The Guilford Press, including Natalie Graham, Laura Specht Patchkofsky, Katherine Sommer, and Robert Sebastiano, and many others who helped to bring this work to fruition. We also appreciate the support of our colleagues and students, including those who used the first edition of this book and provided us with helpful feedback. And we are grateful for our supportive families, who were patient with the long days and late nights we often spent writing, including Sophie and Colette Lonchar; Hamilton, Spencer, and Holley Peacock; and Brianna Hawks. Finally, we want to acknowledge the late Dr. Kenneth W. Merrell, who began The Guilford Practical Intervention in the Schools series and encouraged us to write the first edition of this book. We are forever indebted to Ken's mentorship and guidance.

Contents

1. **Introduction to Behavioral, Social, and Emotional Problems of Young Children**   1

   Overview of Disorders   2
   Externalizing Problems   3
   Internalizing Problems   5
   Other Problems   10
   Autism Spectrum Disorder   13
   Summary of Problems   15
   Prevalence of Mental Health Concerns in Young Children   16
   The Impact of Behavioral, Social, and Emotional Problems in School Settings   18
   Stability of Behavior Problems   19
   Predictors of Problems   21
   Predictors of Externalizing Problems   21
   Predictors of Internalizing Problems   23
   Chapter Summary/Purpose of This Book   24

2. **Assessment of Mental Health Issues**   25

   Interviews with Parents and Teachers   26
   Interviews as Screeners   26
   Interviews as Diagnostic/Evaluation Tools   26
   Interviews as Progress Monitoring Tools   32
   Interviews with Young Children   33
   Rapport Building/Initial Information Gathering   34
   Context of the Interview   35
   Rating Scales   36
   Social, Emotional, and Behavioral Scales as Screeners   37
   Social, Emotional, and Behavioral Scales as Diagnostic/Evaluation Tools   38
   Social, Emotional, and Behavioral Scales as Progress Monitoring Tools   47
   Direct Observation   47
   Observations as Screeners   48
   Observations as Diagnostic/Evaluation Tools   48
   Observations as Progress Monitoring Tools   54
   Chapter Summary   55

3. Treatment of Externalizing/Conduct Problems   66

Behavioral Parent Training as an Intervention for Externalizing Problems   67
   Overview   67
   Initial Considerations   68
   Conducting Behavioral Parent Training   71
   Group Behavioral Parent Training   81
Enhancing Behavioral Parent Training through the Use of Acceptance
   and Commitment Therapy   82
   Overview   82
   Values   83
   Cognitive Defusion   84
   Contact with the Present Moment (Mindfulness)   85
   Self as Context   87
   Acceptance   88
   Committed Action   88
   Evidence-Based Clinical Application   89
Social Skills Interventions   90
Prevention and Early Intervention Programs   92
Chapter Summary   96

4. Treatment of Internalizing Problems   110

Anxiety Disorders   110
   Fears and Specific Phobias   111
   Separation Anxiety, Including School or Daycare Refusal   119
Selective Mutism   124
   Causes and Prevention of Selective Mutism   124
   Treatment of Selective Mutism   124
Somatic Complaints   126
PTSD and Traumatic Experience/Abuse   127
   Treatment of PTSD   128
   Prevention of Child Abuse and Neglect   131
Depression   133
   Prevention of Childhood Depression   133
   Treatment of Depressive Symptoms   134
Chapter Summary   140

5. Managing and Preventing Everyday Problems   148

Toileting   148
   Toilet Training   148
   Enuresis   150
   Encopresis   154
Feeding/Eating Problems   156
   Promoting Healthy Eating Habits   157
   Typical Feeding Problems   158
   Pica   160
   Rumination   161
Sleep Problems   161
   Problems Initiating Sleep   163
   Arousal Disorders   167
Chapter Summary   169

6. Academic and Behavioral Interventions and Supports in the Classroom   184

RTI for Early Literacy/Academic Skills   186
    Summary of RTI   189
Positive Behavioral Interventions and Supports   189
    Initial Considerations   190
    Establishing Classroom Rules   191
    Developing a Classroom Schedule   191
    Providing Effective Instruction   192
    Utilizing Selective Attention   192
    Reward-Based Behavior Management Programs   193
    Responding to Behavioral Violations and Severe Problem Behaviors   195
    Summary of PBIS   200
Social and Emotional Learning   200
    Benefits of SEL Programs   201
    Common SEL Programs   201
Chapter Summary   205

7. Referral Issues and Conclusion   207

Referral Procedures   207
Referral Sources   208
    Primary Care Provider   208
    Child Psychiatrist   208
    Master's-Level Therapist   209
    Licensed Clinical Psychologist   209
Hospitalization and Other Inpatient Settings   209
Referral Avenues   210
    Medical Insurance   210
    Primary Care Provider   210
    Therapist Associations and Online Searches   210
    Word of Mouth   211
Conclusion and Best-Practice Recommendations   211

References   213

Index   237

Purchasers of this book can download and print copies of the reproducible forms at *www.guilford.com/holland-forms* for personal use or use with individual students (see copyright page for details).

CHAPTER 1

Introduction to Behavioral, Social, and Emotional Problems of Young Children

An increasing focus on the identification of mental health concerns in children and on prevention and intervention strategies has been accompanied by an increasing interest in the social and emotional development of preschool- and kindergarten-age children. Professionals, researchers, parents, and teachers see the early childhood years as an important period in which to provide prevention and intervention services to children who are exhibiting or are at risk for a variety of social, emotional, and behavioral difficulties. This focus on early intervention and prevention is important given that researchers have shown that many children who exhibit emotional and behavioral problems early in life will continue to have such problems throughout childhood and potentially into adolescence and even into their adult years (e.g., Fergusson, Horwood, & Ridder, 2005; Hofstra, van der Ende, & Verhulst, 2002). The preschool and kindergarten years are a time of tremendous development and change, so some instability in behaviors is to be expected, and professionals should be careful to not overpathologize behaviors. However, prevention and early intervention can be tremendously beneficial and should be provided when needed to help improve the lives of children and the adults with whom they interact.

This book provides an overview of evidence-based interventions (those that have research support or appear promising based on research to date) for use with young children. This first chapter briefly reviews the emotional and behavioral problems that may be exhibited by children during the preschool and kindergarten years, as well as the prevalence and continuity of these disorders and their associated risk factors and predictors. Chapter 2 presents information regarding the assessment of young children suspected of having emotional or behavioral problems. Each of the next four chapters presents detailed information about evidence-based interventions for concerns that are commonly seen in the preschool and kindergarten years. Chapter 3 covers externalizing/acting-out behaviors associated with conduct problems, oppositional behavior, and attention-deficit/hyperactivity disorder.

Chapter 4 covers internalizing problems such as fears, anxieties, and depression. Chapter 5 reviews treatments for everyday problems that are commonly seen in preschool- and kindergarten-age children, including toileting problems, feeding issues, and sleep difficulties. Chapter 6 provides a discussion of classroom-based prevention–intervention strategies that can be implemented in preschool and kindergarten classrooms to support the development of both appropriate social–behavioral skills and early literacy skills, with a focus on positive behavioral supports and response to intervention.

OVERVIEW OF DISORDERS

Emotional and behavioral problems in children are typically divided into two general categories: externalizing and internalizing problems. *Externalizing problems* are outer-directed and involve acting-out, defiant, and noncompliant behaviors. *Internalizing problems* are more inner-directed and involve withdrawal, depression, and anxiety. In addition, young children can be diagnosed with neurodevelopmental disorders, including autism spectrum disorder, and commonly exhibit problems that do not fall within either of these general domains (e.g., difficulties with sleep schedules, eating problems, and toileting challenges). In the sections that follow, brief descriptions of the more common emotional and behavioral problems of the early childhood years are provided. Note that this discussion of disorders and problems is not exhaustive but focuses on the disorders that clinicians are more likely to see in their practices when working with young children. These problems are summarized in Table 1.1.

TABLE 1.1. Common Emotional and Behavioral Problems

Externalizing problems	Other problems
Attention-deficit/hyperactivity disorder	Elimination disorders
Predominantly inattentive presentation	Enuresis
Predominantly hyperactive–impulsive presentation	Encopresis
Combined presentation	Feeding and eating disorders
Oppositional defiant disorder	Pica
Conduct disorder	Rumination
	Avoidant/restrictive food intake disorder
Internalizing problems	Sleep problems
Anxiety disorders	Autism spectrum disorder
Specific phobia	
Separation anxiety disorder	
Generalized anxiety disorder	
Social anxiety disorder	
Selective mutism	
Posttraumatic stress disorder	
Somatic symptom and related disorders	
Depressive disorders	
Major depressive disorder	
Persistent depressive disorder	

Externalizing Problems

There are three generally recognized externalizing disorders: (1) *attention-deficit/hyperactivity disorder (ADHD)*, (2) *oppositional defiant disorder (ODD)*, and (3) *conduct disorder (CD)*. Although each of these disorders can be diagnosed in young children, it is rare for a young child to receive the diagnosis of CD, given its more serious nature. However, as will be discussed later, ODD (often considered a developmental precursor to CD) is one of the more common disorders diagnosed during the preschool and kindergarten years. Each of these disorders is discussed in more detail in the following sections.

Attention-Deficit/Hyperactivity Disorder

Over the past several decades, ADHD has received increasing attention in both the research and popular literature. Much of this attention has focused on school-age children, but increasingly researchers are studying ADHD as a syndrome that can be diagnosed in the preschool and kindergarten years. ADHD is defined as "a persistent pattern of inattention and/or hyperactivity–impulsivity that interferes with functioning or development" (American Psychiatric Association, 2013, p. 61). The fifth edition of the *Diagnostic and Statistical Manual of Mental Disorders* (DSM-5; American Psychiatric Association, 2013) specifies that ADHD is a neurodevelopmental disorder with a childhood onset and requires that "several" symptoms must be present prior to age 12. Additional diagnostic criteria for ADHD include the presence of symptoms across at least two settings and evidence that symptoms interfere with functioning. Obviously, preschool and kindergarten children are, by nature, less attentive and more active than are older children. It is noted in DSM-5 that it can be difficult to differentiate symptoms of ADHD from those of typical young-child behavior prior to the age of 4 and that ADHD is most commonly diagnosed in the elementary school years. However, ADHD certainly is diagnosed in the preschool years, and there are an increasing number of studies on ADHD in preschool children, including the National Institutes of Health-funded Preschool ADHD Treatment Study (PATS) designed to evaluate the use of methylphenidate in preschoolers (e.g., Greenhill et al., 2006; Kollins et al., 2006). In studies specific to preschool children, prevalence rates of ADHD have ranged from approximately 2 to 13% (Bufferd, Dougherty, Carlson, & Klein, 2011; Egger et al., 2006; Lavigne, LeBailly, Hopkins, Gouze, & Binns, 2009; Wichstrøm, Berg-Nielsen, Angold, Egger, Solheim, & Sveen, 2012). In general, these studies have noted a higher rate of ADHD in boys than in girls.

There are three subtypes of ADHD defined in DSM-5: (1) predominantly inattentive presentation (in which the child shows at least six of nine inattentive symptoms but fewer than six hyperactive–impulsive symptoms); (2) predominantly hyperactive–impulsive presentation (in which the child shows at least six of nine hyperactive–impulsive symptoms but fewer than six inattentive symptoms); and (3) combined presentation (in which the child shows at least six symptoms of both inattention and hyperactivity–impulsivity). The factor structure of ADHD and the appropriate classification of subtypes has been a subject of much research for a number of years. Recent investigations into the factor structure of ADHD has taken a hierarchical modeling approach and have found support for a general ADHD factor, as well as the specific factors of inattention and hyperactivity–impulsivity in general and clinical samples of school-age children (Dumenci, McConaughy, & Achenbach, 2004; Martel, Von Eye, & Nigg, 2010; Normand, Flora, Toplak, & Tannock, 2012; Toplak et al., 2012). However, at least one study found that while hyperactive symptoms loaded on the general ADHD factor, they did not contribute to either of the specific factors (Ullebø, Breivik, Gillberg, Lundervold, & Posserud, 2012). This bidimensional aspect of ADHD has been seen not just in U.S. samples but across a variety of countries representing diverse populations (Bauermeister, Canino, Polanczyk, & Rohde, 2010). More limited research has been conducted on the factor structure of ADHD in preschool-age children and it is not clear whether a two-factor model is most appropriate for preschool-age children or whether ADHD is better conceptualized as a unidimensional construct in young children, as has been found in some studies (e.g., Willoughby, Pek, & Greenberg, 2012). Interestingly, Hardy and colleagues (2007) found problems in terms of statistical fit with one-, two-, and three-factor models of ADHD for preschool-age children. For parent ratings, the two- and three-factor models were "marginally acceptable" but for teacher ratings none of the models had acceptable fit using confirmatory factor analysis. Additional analyses did suggest that the two and three factor models were satisfactory—but with cross loadings of items on the factors.

Although the factor structure of ADHD symptoms in preschool children may not yet be clear, it is generally agreed that there is a developmental progression of symptoms. While hyperactive–impulsive symptoms may be more common in young children, over time children with hyperactive–impulsive symptoms are likely to show an increase in inattentive symptoms and therefore be moved to a combined presentation diagnostic category (e.g., Lahey, Pelham, Loney, Lee, & Willcutt, 2005).

Oppositional Defiant Disorder and Conduct Disorder

ODD is defined in DSM-5 as "a pattern of angry/irritable mood, argumentative/defiant behavior, or vindictiveness" (American Psychiatric Association, 2013, p. 462). Individuals must have at least four symptoms across these three categories of behavior, and the symptoms must last for at least 6 months. ODD has been estimated to occur in 2–13% of preschool-age children (Bufferd et al., 2011; Egger et al., 2006; Lavigne et al., 2009; Wichstrøm et al., 2012). In these preschool-age samples, significant gender differences have not been noted, even though in older children ODD is reported to be more common in boys than girls (American Psychiatric Association, 2013). Symptoms of ODD often first appear in the preschool years and, if they occur in just one setting, are most typically seen first in the home setting (American Psychiatric Association, 2013). Although DSM-5 categorizes symptoms in the three areas just noted, there are no subtypes of this disorder. However, increasingly researchers are noting that ODD may be best conceptualized as having multiple dimensions (e.g., Lavigne, Bryant, Hopkins, & Gouze, 2015), and the presentation type may have implications for the pattern of problems seen over time. While ODD has been noted as a precursor to CD for some children (particularly in boys; e.g., Rowe, Costello, Angold, Copeland, & Maughan, 2010), ODD is also linked to internalizing symptoms such as depression and anxiety (Boylan, Vaillancourt, Boyle, & Szatmari, 2007). In particular, researchers have noted that the irritability dimension of ODD may be linked to internalizing problems (Loeber & Burke, 2011; Stringaris & Goodman, 2009). ODD symptoms can be identified in the preschool years and, even at that age, different patterns of symptoms can emerge. Preschool-age children who presented with increasing or persistent levels of irritability were associated with poorer outcomes over time, including an increased risk for internalizing and externalizing problem behaviors (Ezpeleta, Granero, Osa, Trepat, & Doménech, 2016).

CD is defined as "a repetitive and persistent pattern of behavior in which the basic rights of others or major age-appropriate societal norms or rules are violated" (American Psychiatric Association, 2013, p. 469). Symptoms in DSM-5 include 15 specific behaviors across four categories: aggression toward people and animals, destruction of property, deceitfulness or theft, and serious violation of rules. Individuals must have at least 3 of the 15 symptoms over the past year and at least 1 symptom over the past 6 months. As noted in DSM-5, CD can be of the childhood-onset type, where symptoms are first present prior to age 10, or of the adolescent-onset type where no symptoms are present prior to age 10. (DSM-5 also allows for an "unspecified onset" in which it cannot be determined when symptoms were first present.) Although CD can occur during the preschool years, the onset is typically later in childhood (American Psychiatric Association, 2013). However, it is worthwhile for clinicians working with preschool- and kindergarten-age children to have a good understanding of both ODD and CD, given the link between the two. In addition, while preschoolers are unlikely to receive a diagnosis of conduct disorder, they may begin to display symptoms of CD in the preschool years, and these symptoms are predictive of later externalizing problems (Rolon-Arroyo, Arnold, & Harvey, 2014). It is also important to note that researchers and clinicians often use the term "conduct problems" to refer to general externalizing behavior problems, and this term should not be seen as synonymous with CD.

Internalizing Problems

Although prevalence rates for specific internalizing problems in young children are often lower than rates for specific externalizing problems, when rates are collapsed across specific diagnoses within these categories, there tend to be similar rates of "emotional" (internalizing) and "behavioral" (externalizing) disorders (Egger et al., 2006; Wichstrøm et al., 2012), and in one study, rates were much higher for emotional disorders (anxiety and depression) than for behavioral disorders (20% vs. 10%; Bufferd et al., 2011). In addition, many young children may not meet criteria for a specific internalizing disorder but may instead exhibit general symptoms such as anxiety, fearfulness, unhappiness, and so forth. If these symptoms are severe enough (whether or not a formal disorder is diagnosed), treatment should be considered. Some of the more common internalizing problems in children are described in this section. Prior to the presentation of some of the specific internalizing disorders, a general discussion of fears and anxieties is presented.

Fears and Anxieties

The terms *fear* and *anxiety* are often used interchangeably; however, there are differences between the two. *Fear* is typically conceptualized as a set of intense physiological responses (e.g., increased heart rate, sweating, shaking) in response to a specific stimulus that is a normal response to a perceived threat. Fear is generally a protective and adaptive response that alerts a person to danger and thereby helps him or her to survive (Essau, Olaya, & Ollendick, 2013). For example, a child who is face-to-face with a bear would likely experience fear. *Anxiety* is considered to be somewhat more vague and diffuse and is typically not a response to a specific or threatening stimulus. For example, the child who worries about going camping in case a bear is encountered—even though there is no direct threat—may feel tense and apprehensive about the trip (Chorpita & Southam-Gerow, 2006; Morris, Kratochwill, Schoenfield, & Auster, 2008). Fears are a normal part of childhood development as children learn to anticipate danger. The anticipation of danger motivates the child to be cautious, thereby preventing the child from being harmed. For example, as children learn that not all dogs are friendly, they may start being more cautious and asking for permission before petting an unknown dog. However, intense fear, anxiety, or a phobic response to seeing dogs and going out of one's way to avoid dogs would not be adaptive for a child. Thus, it is not necessarily the feeling of worry or fear itself that is problematic but the severity of the response and the associated behaviors.

Children do commonly express some fears (although often not at a clinical level), and particular fears seem to cluster at certain ages. Fears in infancy typically occur as a reaction to the environment, such as fear in response to loud noises and, in later infancy, fear of strangers and separation from caretakers. In the preschool and early elementary school years, fears broaden, often involving natural phenomena such as the dark, storms, and earthquakes, as well as animals, imagined supernatural figures, and loss of caregivers. In the later elementary school years, physical injury and school-related concerns may emerge. As children enter adolescence, concerns about friendships and personal adequacy may become more prominent (e.g., Morris et al., 2008; Warren & Sroufe, 2004). Nighttime fears are particularly prevalent in younger children (Zisenwine, Kaplan, Kushnir, & Sadeh, 2013). Gender differences related to fears seem to be present for some fears and not for others. For example, in one study with children ages 5–16, girls were more likely than boys to have fears of animals, strangers, and the natural environment but not loud noises, the dark, or supernatural figures (Meltzer et al., 2008). There are also age differences in how children express symptoms associated with fear and anxiety. Somatic complaints, including headaches and stomachaches, are commonly seen in preschool- and kindergarten-age children. Whereas older children might talk about feelings of anxiety and distressing thoughts, as noted in DSM-5, younger children more often act out their anxiety through excessive and uncontrollable crying, anger outbursts, tantrums, or clinginess. In addition, children who have experienced some form of trauma, such as abuse, may express their anxiety through repetitive play, a symptom commonly seen in children with posttraumatic stress disorder (American Psychiatric Association, 2013).

Anxiety Disorders

Specific phobias are different from typical childhood fears in that they are more persistent and severe than would be expected for the age and developmental level of the child. As defined in DSM-5, specific phobias involve "marked fear or anxiety about a specific object or situation," and in children this fear can manifest by "crying, tantrums, freezing, or clinging" (American Psychiatric Association, 2013, p. 197). Upon exposure to the object or situation, the person experiences a fear or anxiety response; often the feared object is avoided to prevent the anxiety response. Adults must recognize that their fear is excessive for the diagnosis to apply; however, children do not need to have this realization in order to receive a diagnosis of specific phobia. The fear must also be persistent, lasting for at least 6 months (American Psychiatric Association, 2013). Although fears are common in young children, as we have noted, specific, diagnosable phobias are less common, with prevalence estimates ranging from less than 1% to about 10% in preschool-age children (Bufferd et al., 2011; Egger et al., 2006; Paulus, Backes, Sander, Weber, & von Gontard, 2015; Wichstrøm et al., 2012).

Specific to children, particularly younger children, is anxiety surrounding separation from primary caregivers. Though this is a typical response in very young children starting in the later part of the child's first year, at older ages and when this anxiety is excessive, the child might receive a diagnosis of *separation anxiety disorder (SAD)* (American Psychiatric Association, 2013). SAD involves "developmentally inappropriate and excessive fear or anxiety concerning separation from those to whom the individual is attached" (American Psychiatric Association, 2013, p. 190). Children with SAD exhibit a high level of distress when separated from their caregivers or in anticipation of separation. Children with SAD often fear that harm will come to their caregivers or that something bad will happen to them (e.g., kidnapping). Children with SAD will attempt to avoid separation. They may exhibit "clingy" behavior with their caregivers and may experience sleep difficulties (including nightmares) and have physical symptoms such as headaches or stomachaches when separation occurs or is anticipated (American Psychiatric Association, 2013) and, for children who are in school, there is a high rate of school refusal (Higa-McMillan, Francis, & Chorpita, 2014). Specific DSM-5 criteria require that at least three of eight symptoms be present and that the fear, anxiety, or avoidance be persistent for at least 4 weeks in children (American Psychiatric Association, 2013). Prevalence rates of SAD in preschool children have been estimated to range from less than 1% to 10% (Bufferd et al., 2011; Egger et al., 2006; Franz, Angold, Copeland, Costello, Towe-Goodman, & Egger, 2013; Lavigne, 2009; Wichstrøm et al., 2012), with most studies not indicating significant differences in prevalence based on gender; however, one study showed that girls were more likely than boys to have this diagnosis (Franz et al., 2013).

Generalized anxiety disorder (GAD) involves "excessive anxiety and worry . . . about a number of events or activities" that occurs "more days than not for at least 6 months" (American Psychiatric Association, 2013, p. 222). The focus of the anxiety can change over time, but the anxiety must remain excessive based on intensity, frequency, or duration. DSM-5 lists six specific anxiety symptoms (e.g., irritability, sleep disturbance), and the anxiety/worry must be associated with at least one of these symptoms in children (although for adults, there must be at least three symptoms) (American Psychiatric Association, 2013). Children with GAD may not necessarily have more worries than typical children but the intensity of these worries is greater (Higa-McMillan et al., 2014). The prevalence of GAD in preschool children has been estimated to be less than 1% (Lavigne et al., 2009), to close to 4% (Bufferd et al., 2011; Egger et al. 2006), to as high as 9% in some studies (Franz et al., 2013). Gender differences were not noted in any of these studies on preschool prevalence of GAD. Although GAD can be diagnosed in the preschool years, there is little research on the specific symptom presentation during the early childhood years. DSM-5 notes that children with GAD tend to have excessive worry about school and sports performance (American Psychiatric Association, 2013); however, these issues seem likely to be less relevant for preschool-age children.

Social anxiety disorder (social phobia) involves a "marked, or intense, fear or anxiety of social situations in which the individual may be scrutinized by others" and, in children, this fear must be in peer settings, not just with adults (American Psychiatric Association, 2013, p. 202). These social situations provoke fear or anxiety that, in children, can be expressed by "crying, tantrums, freezing, clinging, shrinking, or failing to speak" (American Psychiatric Association, 2013, p. 202). Symptoms must be present for at least 6 months and must cause some impairment in functioning. Children with social phobia typically have fewer friends than their peers and may be hesitant to join social activities (Higa-McMillan et al., 2014). Social anxiety disorder prevalence rates in preschool-age children range from less than 1% (Wichstrøm et al., 2012) to as high as 7.5% (Franz et al., 2013), with several reporting rates in between these estimates (Bufferd et al., 2011; Egger et al., 2006). Gender differences were not noted in these studies.

Selective mutism involves a "consistent failure to speak in specific social situations in which there is an expectation for speaking (e.g., at school) despite speaking in other situations" (American Psychiatric Association, 2013, p. 195). This disturbance must have lasted for at least 1 month, not be limited to the first month of school, and not be due to a lack of knowledge or comfort with the spoken language required in the social situation (American Psychiatric Association, 2013, p. 195). The onset of selective mutism typically occurs during the preschool years, although it may not be recognized until the child is in a school setting. The course of this disorder may be variable, with some children outgrowing the disorder and others continuing to struggle over time with it or other anxiety disorders (American Psychiatric Association, 2013). Selective mutism has been investigated in fewer prevalence studies than some of the other disorders discussed but has been estimated to have a prevalence of less than 2% (Bufferd et al., 2011; Egger et al., 2006). Differences by gender have not been reported. Prior to DSM-5, selective mutism was not categorized as an anxiety disorder. However, symptoms related to anxiety or actual comorbid anxiety diagnoses have long been noted in studies of children with selective mutism, and some researchers have proposed that selective mutism be considered as an early or special form of social phobia (Muris & Ollendick, 2015). It is important to differentiate selective mutism from other difficulties associated with expressive language, including neurodevelopmental disorders such as autism spectrum disorder and communication disorders, which are likely to be more pervasive. Consultation with parents, as well as referrals to speech–language pathologists, may help rule out some of these other reasons for language difficulties.

Other Internalizing Disorders

Posttraumatic stress disorder (PTSD) is one of several disorders listed in the "Trauma- and Stressor-Related Disorders" chapter in DSM-5. Previously PTSD had been listed with the "Anxiety Disorders," and DSM-5 does note that there is a "close relationship" between trauma/stress disorders and anxiety disorders (as well as several other disorders). New in DSM-5 are criteria specific for children age 6 and younger. PTSD occurs following exposure to a traumatic event either by directly experiencing the event, witnessing the event (especially when directed toward a primary caregiver), or learning about a traumatic event that happened to a parent or caregiver. The traumatic event should involve "actual or threatened death, serious injury, or sexual violence" (American Psychiatric Association, 2013, p. 272). PTSD in young children requires the presence of at least one intrusion symptom (e.g., distressing memories, dreams) and at least one symptom indicative of avoidance (avoiding places or people related to the event) or negative alterations in cognitions (increased negative emotional states; diminished interest in/participation in activities, including play; socially withdrawn behavior; and/or persistent reduction in expression of positive emotions). There also must be changes in arousal and reactivity related to the event with at least two of the following symptoms present: irritable behavior/angry outbursts, hypervigilance, exaggerated startle response, concentration difficulties, and sleep disturbances. (American Psychiatric Association, 2013, pp. 272–273).

The PTSD diagnostic criteria in DSM-5 removed the requirement for "fear, helplessness, or horror." The rationale for the removal of this requirement was that across all ages, it did not seem to improve diagnosis, and for preschool children specifically, their immediate reaction may not be known depending on whether someone was present in the situation (Scheeringa, Zeanah, & Cohen, 2011). Also new in the DSM-5 is the modified criterion for the child to witness or simply learn that a traumatic event occurred to a parent or primary caregiver, instead of only directly experiencing the event him- or herself.

In addition to anxiety and the reliving of the trauma, young children with PTSD often exhibit negative emotional states (e.g., fear, sadness, or confusion), behavioral problems, irritability and angry outbursts, and withdrawal from social contact (American Psychiatric Association, 2013). However, it is important to note that preschool-age children may not always exhibit symptoms consistent with what adults might expect. For example, Scheeringa and colleagues (2011) noted that parents of some children reported a neutral reaction or excitement following exposure to a traumatic event, although anger, sadness, and fear were more common.

The prevalence of PTSD in preschool children is estimated to be less than 1% (Egger et al., 2006). However, higher rates are likely to be found in children who have experienced a traumatic event—at least initially. In an older study, Spence, Rapee, McDonald, and Ingram (2001) reported that while close to 14% of mothers of preschool age children reported their child had experienced a traumatic event, the prevalence of PTSD symptoms was very low, with items reflecting PTSD being endorsed for fewer than 5 of the 65 children who had experienced a traumatic event. In a more recent study of preschool children who had experienced a traumatic event (being burned), PTSD was calculated to be present in 25% of the children at 1-month postinjury and in 10% of the children at 6-months postinjury (DeYoung, Kenardy, & Cobham, 2011) if utilizing modified DSM criteria with only one symptom present in each category. Using DSM-IV criteria resulted in a 5% prevalence rate at 1 month and a 1% rate at 6months. Meiser-Stedman, Smith, Glucksman, Yule, and Dalgleish (2008) also evaluated the use of DSM-IV criteria and modified criteria in the diagnosis of PTSD over time in a sample of 2- to 10-year-old children following a motor vehicle accident. At a 6-month follow-up, 14% of the children met diagnostic criteria using modified criteria and less than 2% met diagnostic criteria using DSM-IV criteria (based on parental report).

DSM-5 includes a new category of disorders, "Somatic Symptom and Related Disorders," replacing the somatoform disorders from the DSM-IV (American Psychiatric Association, 2013). Although children can be diagnosed with somatic disorders, typically they will not meet the criteria for a somatic disorder but, instead, may have somatic symptoms associated with an internalizing disorder, such as anxiety or depression. Although the DSM-IV criteria emphasized that somatic symptoms had no medical explanation, and so were presumed to have a psychological origin, DSM-5 states that it is "not appropriate to give an individual a mental disorder diagnosis solely because a medical cause cannot be demonstrated" (American Psychiatric Association, 2013, p. 309). In addition, it is acknowledged that somatic symptoms can be associated with a medical diagnosis. Somatic symptoms can be common in young children, although such symptoms do not mean that a disorder is present. For example, in a study of 319 kindergarten students, 64% were reported to have had at least one physical complaint in the 2 weeks preceding the study, and 31% were reported to have frequent somatic complaints (Serra Giacobo, Jané, Bonillo, Ballespí, & Díaz-Regañon, 2012). Other studies have had similar findings, with abdominal pain, tiredness, leg pains, headaches, and dizziness among the most frequent complaints of children ages 3–5 (Domènech-Llaberia et al., 2004). In addition, tingling sensations or numbness in the extremities, skin rashes or itching, and breathing problems (e.g., shortness of breath, asthma-type symptoms, or hyperventilation) are also possible (Merrell, 2008b).

Children may be diagnosed with the depressive disorders outlined in DSM-5, including *major depressive disorder* and *persistent depressive disorder (dysthymia)*. Although there are no specific depressive criteria for children, DSM-5 does note that instead of having a "depressed mood," children may exhibit an "irritable mood" (American Psychiatric Association, 2013, p. 160). DSM-5 also notes the symptoms commonly seen in children: irritability, social withdrawal, and somatic complaints. However, young children also can experience the core symptoms of depressed mood, such as loss of pleasure or interest in activities during the day. Other symptoms young children may exhibit include weight loss or gain (including a failure to make expected weight gains in young children), insomnia or hypersomnia, loss of energy, psychomotor agitation, and difficulties concentrating. The child must have had some of these symptoms for at least 2 weeks for the symptoms to be considered a depressive episode. A long-term mild depression (lasting at least 1 year for children) is called persistent depressive disorder (formerly dysthymia), whereas a depressed mood that occurs in response to a specific stressor and resolves usually within 6 months is called an *adjustment disorder with depressed mood* (American Psychiatric Association, 2013). Younger children tend to have low prevalence rates of depression with rates for preschool children estimated at 2% or less (Bufferd et al., 2011; Egger et al., 2006; Lavigne et al., 2009; Wichstrøm et al., 2012). Most studies have not reported gender differences in preschool prevalence rates, although Wichstrøm and colleagues (2012) found that boys had a higher prevalence rate than girls (2.6% vs. 1.5%).

Other Problems

In addition to the disorders that fall within the externalizing and internalizing domains, there are a number of other problems with which children can present for treatment. Some of these more common "other problems" seen in preschool children, including toileting difficulties, feeding problems, and sleeping problems, are reviewed here.

Toileting problems are commonly seen in young children, although many preschool children may be too young to receive a formal diagnosis of one of the elimination disorders. *Enuresis* involves the repeated voiding (whether involuntary or intentional) of urine in one's clothes during the daytime (diurnal enuresis) and/or while sleeping (nocturnal enuresis). To be diagnosed with enuresis, a child must be "having accidents" at least twice a week for at least 3 months, or there must be signs of significant distress or impairment in functioning (American Psychiatric Association, 2013, p. 355). According to diagnostic guidelines in DSM-5, children must be at least 5 years of age to be diagnosed with enuresis. However, there is significant developmental variability regarding the age at which children achieve dryness. For example, daytime dryness is generally accomplished before nighttime dryness and boys tend to achieve dryness at a later age than girls (Silverstein, 2004). Cultural norms have also impacted the age at which children master toilet training. For example, in the 1940s, toilet training commonly started before 18 months of age, while more recent data have shown that training now generally starts between 21 and 36 months of age (Choby & George, 2008). Enuresis is categorized as either primary or secondary. Children with primary enuresis have never achieved continuous bladder control, whereas children with secondary enuresis have been dry for some period of time (generally 6 months to 1 year) but then cease exhibiting bladder control (Baird, Seehusen, & Bode, 2014). Etiological explanations of enuresis are varied and include factors such as heritability, delayed/abnormal physiological development, inadequate nighttime secretion of antidiuretic hormone, difficulty with sleep arousability, and inadequate learning history (Ramakrishnan, 2008). Less common influential factors include emotional difficulties, such as anxiety, environmental and/or family changes, and a history of trauma or abuse.

Prevalence estimates for enuresis vary, with all estimates indicating a decline in prevalence as children age. It is estimated that approximately 15–20% of 5- to 6-year-old children continue to experience occasional nighttime wetting (Silverstein, 2004). At age 7, the estimated prevalence rate of enuresis is 9% in boys and 6% in girls. This rate decreases to 7% in boys and 3% in girls at age 10 (Robson, 2009). In adolescence, the prevalence rate markedly declines, with approximately 1% of individuals meeting diagnostic criteria (Campbell, Cox, & Borowitz, 2009). This decline with age is due, at least in part, to the fact that approximately 5–10% of children who engage in bed-wetting spontaneously remit each year (American Psychiatric Association, 2013). Enuresis is more than twice as likely in boys than in girls (Butler et al., 2005). Nocturnal enuresis is three times more common than daytime wetting (Ramakrishnan, 2008).

Encopresis involves soiling in inappropriate places, such as clothing, at least once a month for at least 3 months. Children must be at least 4-years of age to receive this diagnosis (American Psychiatric Association, 2013). Prevalence rates of encopresis have been estimated at 5–6% in preschool-age children (Egger et al., 2006; Wichstrøm et al., 2012). Encopresis is typically due to severe constipation and is referred to as retentive encopresis. However, a smaller subset of children (approximately 10% of those with encopresis) exhibit nonretentive encopresis (Burgers, Reitsma, Bongers, de Lorijn, & Benninga, 2013). Nonretentive encopresis includes children who were never fully toilet trained, children with fear-related avoidance of toileting, children who receive contingent reinforcement for soiling, and children with irritable bowel syndrome (Boles, Roberts, & Vernberg, 2008). Although children must be at least 4 years old to receive a diagnosis of encopresis, children under this age may exhibit toileting problems, such as refusing to use the toilet. Children who exhibit toileting refusal are at greater risk of developing encopresis due to constipation (van Dijk, Benninga, Grootenhuis, Nieuwenhuizen, & Last, 2007). Children with encopresis are significantly more likely to also exhibit difficult temperaments (e.g. stubborn, defiant), as well as emotional and behavioral problems (Campbell et al., 2009).

Feeding and eating disorders covered in DSM-5 include pica, rumination, and avoidant/restrictive food eating. *Pica* involves eating nonnutritive, nonfood items. These items can include a wide variety of substances including paint, fabric, soil, and so on. It is relatively common for infants and toddlers to eat nonfood substances occasionally. This behavior does not necessarily imply the presence of pica, which should only be diagnosed if the behavior is inappropriate for the child's developmental level and persists for at least 1 month (American Psychiatric Association, 2013, p. 329). *Rumination* involves regurgitation of food that then may be rechewed, reswallowed, or spit out. These behaviors must occur for at least 1 month and cannot be better accounted for by a medical condition (American Psychiatric Association, 2013, p. 332). Children with rumination disorder regurgitate partially digested food into their mouths (with no associated nausea, involuntary retching, or disgust) and then spit out or rechew the food. The disorder is most common in infants but is also diagnosed in older children, particularly those with intellectual disabilities or other neurodevelopmental disorders (American Psychiatric Association, 2013). Rumination is voluntary, and children may give the impression of gaining pleasure or satisfaction by engaging in the behavior. *Avoidant/restrictive food intake disorder* involves a disturbance in eating and a failure to meet nutritional energy needs (American Psychiatric Association, 2013). Although all of these feeding disorders may be diagnosed in young children, more typically young children exhibit problems related to feeding and eating that do not meet criteria for a formal disorder. Children may be "picky eaters" or have other issues related to eating (e.g., behavior problems while eating, such as spitting out food) that are not diagnosable disorders. Although these problems do not meet the criteria for a clinical disorder, they can still be highly problematic for parents, and treatment is often warranted.

General childhood feeding difficulties are considered to be quite common, with up to 45% of young children exhibiting difficulties at mealtimes (Adamson, Morawska, & Sanders, 2013). Many childhood feeding difficulties, such as picky eating, mealtime fussiness, and emotional undereating (i.e., eating less in response to stress/negative emotions), are often related to other behavioral difficulties (e.g. emotional dysregulation, noncompliance, hyperactivity) (Blissett, Meyer & Haycraft, 2011). Many of these difficulties are transitory in nature and resolve spontaneously without clinical intervention. However, a smaller subset of children will develop chronic feeding issues, with approximately 25% of typically developing children and 80% of children with developmental disabilities experiencing clinically significant feeding concerns (Manikam & Perman, 2000). Feeding disorders include an array of behaviors that involve failure to eat a sufficient quantity and/or variety of food resulting in chronic malnutrition, poor weight gain, and/or weight loss. The etiology of these problems is varied and includes medical or physical disorders (e.g. metabolic disorder, neuromuscular problems), developmental delays, and behavioral/psychosocial issues (Blissett et al., 2011; Schwarz, Corredor, Fisher-Medina, Cohen, & Rabinowitz, 2001). While younger children tend to have more feeding problems than older children, the general trend is for early feeding problems to persist; in fact, these feeding problems may predict eating disorders in adolescence and adulthood (Silverman & Tarbell, 2009).

More recently, increased attention has also been given to early childhood obesity, as more than 20% of children ages 2–5 are already overweight or obese (Institute of Medicine, 2011). While it is often assumed children will "grow out of it," childhood obesity tends to persist into later life and can increase the risk of obesity-related disease in adulthood. In fact, research has shown that a child who is overweight at age 3 is nearly eight times more likely to be overweight as an adult in comparison to a 3-year-old who is not overweight (Parlakian & Lerner, 2007). Of the various factors that can contribute to obesity, environmental factors have been heavily implicated. In a large-scale study conducted in 12 countries, Katzmarzyk and colleagues (2015) noted that environmental–behavioral factors were important in predicting obesity in children ages 9–11, with low physical activity, short sleep duration, and high TV viewing being some of the most predictive ones. In a study specific to preschool children, establishing routines such as eating dinner as a family, getting an appropriate amount of sleep, and having limited TV viewing were predictive of a lower prevalence of obesity (Anderson & Whitaker, 2010). Given the importance of such environmental factors, early childhood interventions may provide the best opportunities to alter habits and routines to help promote healthy lifestyles and healthy weights.

Sleep problems are also commonly reported by parents of young children, with estimated rates of sleep disturbances ranging from 25 to 40% (Meltzer & Mindell, 2006), although most of these problems will not meet official DSM-5 criteria for one of the many sleep–wake disorders. The most common sleep problems in early childhood include bedtime resistance and frequent nighttime wakings. Other common problems include nightmares, night terrors, sleep talking, and sleepwalking. This is also the peak age for obstructive sleep apnea due to enlarged tonsils and adenoids (Meltzer & Crabtree, 2015). These problems will be temporary for some children but will persist over time for others. Persistence of sleep problems is particularly likely to occur when children begin exhibiting sleep problems at a young age (Thome & Skuladottir, 2005). The long-term implications of early childhood sleep disturbances have been shown to be significant. Results of an 11-year longitudinal study of 490 children revealed that sleep problems at age 4 predicted behavioral–emotional problems in adolescence and were equally predictive of anxiety, depression, attention problems, and aggression (Gregory & O'Connor, 2002).

Autism Spectrum Disorder

Autism spectrum disorder (ASD) is another disorder that is often first diagnosed in the preschool years, especially with the increased emphasis on screening for ASD at well-child visits during the early childhood years. Due to the complex nature of ASD and the interdisciplinary approach needed to address the behaviors associated with this disorder, the treatment of ASD is beyond the scope of this book. However, given that it is commonly identified at an early age, it is important for clinicians working with young children to have some knowledge of this disorder. Therefore, we provide a brief overview here, as well as some information on the assessment of ASD in Chapter 2. Clinicians interested in reading more about the treatment of ASD may wish to consult several of the recent books in this area (e.g., Chawarska, Klin, & Volkmar, 2010; Prelock & McCauley, 2012). Websites such as those from Autism Speaks (*www.autismspeaks.org*) and the UC Davis Mind Institute (*www.ucdmc.ucdavis.edu/mindinstitute*) can also be sources of further information on ASD.

The definition of ASD changed rather substantially between DSM-IV and DSM-5. In DSM-IV, there were several pervasive developmental disorders, which included autism, along with Asperger's disorder (now termed Asperger syndrome), childhood disintegrative disorder, Rett's disorder, and pervasive developmental disorder not otherwise specified. In DSM-5, there is one disorder: autism spectrum disorder. All DSM-IV disorders, except Rett's disorder, are subsumed under DSM-5's ASD diagnostic category. Rett's disorder is seen as a separate genetic condition; individuals with Rett's may qualify for an ASD diagnosis if they meet all of the ASD criteria, but they should not be diagnosed with ASD solely because they have Rett's disorder (American Psychiatric Association, 2013).

Criteria for ASD are divided into two primary categories. Children must show "persistent deficits in social communication and social interaction across multiple contexts" and "restricted, repetitive patterns of behavior, interests, or activities" (American Psychiatric Association, 2013, p. 50). For each of these domains, a severity indictor must be provided: Level 1—requiring support, Level 2—requiring substantial support, and Level 3—requiring very substantial support. There are three criteria listed under the social deficit category, and children must exhibit all three to receive an ASD diagnosis. These are deficits in the following areas: social–emotional reciprocity; nonverbal communication behaviors used in social interactions; and developing, maintaining, and understanding relationships (American Psychiatric Association, 2013, p. 50). Four types of restricted/repetitive behaviors are listed, and children must exhibit two of these four: (1) stereotyped or repetitive motor movements, use of objects, or speech; (2) insistence on sameness, inflexible adherence to routines, or ritualized patterns of verbal or nonverbal behavior; (3) highly restricted, fixated interests that are abnormal in intensity or focus; (4) hyper- or hyporeactivity to sensory input or unusual interest in sensory aspects of the environment (American Psychiatric Association, 2013, p. 50). Symptoms of ASD must be present in the "early developmental period."

The Centers for Disease Control and Prevention (CDC) funds the Autism and Developmental Disabilities Monitoring (ADDM) Network, which provides data on the prevalence of ASD in the United States. The current estimate of the prevalence of ASD is 1 in 68 children (14.6 per 1,000) as evaluated by medical and special education records of 8-year-old children in 2012). This estimate is almost identical to that from 2010 (14.7 per 1,000) but higher than estimates from 2008 (11.3 per 1,000) as well as other previous years dating back to 2000, when the estimate rate was 6.7 per 1,000 (Christensen et al., 2016). The ADDM Network report notes that ASD is more common in boys than in girls, with 1 in 42 boys having an ASD diagnosis and 1 in 189 girls having a diagnosis. When looking at differences by race/ethnicity, non-Latino/a, Caucasian children were more likely to receive an ASD diagnosis than were non-Latino/a African American children and Latino/a children. There were no gender or race/ethnicity differences in the average age of first diagnosis (50 months). However, a greater percentage of non-Latino/a Caucasian children received evaluations at or before the age of 36 months than did Latino/a and African American children. There were also differences in prevalence rates by geographic region. Of the 11 states included, the highest prevalence rates were in New Jersey (24.6%), Maryland (18.2%), Utah (17.3%), and North Carolina (16.9%), and the lowest rates were in Wisconsin (10.8%), and Colorado (10.8%) (Christensen et al., 2016). (Although it should be noted that in states with data from health and educational records, rates were higher than in states with only health records. In Maryland, which had rates calculated both ways, the rate was 8.2% with just health records.)

The causes and risk factors for ASD are complex and likely multifaceted, and a great deal of ongoing research in this area attempts to better identify them. Researchers have noted that ASD likely has a genetic/biological component, and various other factors such as prenatal/perinatal and environmental factors can lead to increased risk of ASD (Chaste & Leboyer, 2012; Durand, 2014). Although there has been much discussion about the potential connection between childhood vaccines and ASD, this link has been disproven (e.g., Parker, Schwartz, Todd, & Pickering, 2004; Taylor, Swerdfeger, & Eslick, 2014), and it is important for parents and clinicians to be aware of this fact.

Children with ASD are at higher risk for other disorders with high rates of comorbidity noted in several studies. For example, Salazar and colleagues (2015) evaluated comorbidity rates in a sample of 101 children ages 4–9 who had an ASD diagnosis and found that 90.5% of these children had another DSM diagnosis. The most common comorbid diagnoses were GAD (66.5%), ADHD (59.1%), and specific phobia (15.1%). These findings are consistent with an earlier study of 10- to 14-year-old children (Simonoff et al., 2008), in which 70.8% of the sample had a least one comorbid disorder. In this sample, the most common comorbid disorders were social anxiety (29.2%), ADHD (28.2%), and ODD (28.1%). In addition, a study with 9- to 16-year-old children with Asperger syndrome or high-functioning autism, also showed very high comorbidity rates (Mattila et al., 2010). Of this sample, 74% met criteria for a current comorbid disorder and 84% met criteria for a lifetime comorbid disorder, with the highest comorbidity rates for ADHD (38%), specific phobia (28%), and tic disorders (26%).

As should be clear from this discussion, ASD is a complex disorder and although there are core characteristics that every child needs to have to receive a diagnosis, actual presentation in terms of severity and comorbid disorders can vary widely. While early intervention for ASD seems to be critical, the research on evidenced-based interventions for ASD still leaves many unanswered questions about long-term outcomes, the specifics of what interventions are the most effective, and what interventions work for very young children (Rogers & Vismara, 2008). In a recent overview of five meta-analyses conducted on early intensive behavioral interventions (EIBIs) for ASD, the authors concluded that the effects of EIBIs were "strong and robust," while also noting the importance of a better understanding of the moderating factors on treatment, as well as a better understanding of what specific treatment components are most important and how EIBIs are being implemented outside of treatment studies (Reichow, 2012).

Summary of Problems

There are a number of social–emotional–behavioral problems that young children may exhibit. Although the review of disorders was organized around DSM categories, as noted throughout, many preschool and kindergarten children who are referred for emotional and behavioral problems will not receive a diagnosis of a specific disorder. In many instances, a full diagnostic assessment may not be needed or warranted. For example, a clinician may choose not to attach a diagnosis to a preschool or kindergarten child who is exhibiting general acting-out behavior problems. Instead the clinician may complete an assessment (e.g., parent interview, rating scale) to gather information on the nature of the problems but not tie the assessment results to a formal diagnosis if it is not required for treatment purposes (e.g., insurance reimbursement, access to services). In other situations, a full diagnostic assessment may be undertaken, and the child may not meet the criteria for a formal diagnosis, although the child may still exhibit sufficient problems of concern to the parent or teacher to warrant intervention. It is important that clinicians not fall into the trap of thinking that a diagnosis is necessary in order for treatment to be provided. Although a formal diagnosis may help guide treatment selection, it is typically more important to identify specific behaviors of concern to address in treatment than to assign a DSM-5 diagnosis.

PREVALENCE OF MENTAL HEALTH CONCERNS IN YOUNG CHILDREN

In the previous section, we cited several studies that examined the prevalence estimates of disorders in preschool-age children. Until the past decade or so, the data regarding the prevalence of specific emotional and behavioral problems in young children were scarce. However, as interest in this population has grown, and clinicians and researchers have realized that young children can meet criteria for specific disorders, the number of studies related to the epidemiology of preschool disorders has increased. As diagnostic tools with young children have improved, epidemiological studies examining DSM diagnoses with preschool-age children have also increased. For example, a number of recent studies (e.g., Bufferd et al., 2011; Lavigne et al., 2009; Wichstrøm et al., 2012) have utilized the Preschool Age Psychiatric Assessment (PAPA; Egger & Angold, 2004) or the Diagnostic Interview Schedule for Children—Young Child (DISC-YC; Lucas, Fisher, & Luby, 1998). Both of these are diagnostic interviews (conducted with parents) developed for the evaluation of symptoms in preschool-age children.

Tools based on the DSM are certainly not without controversy. Arguments against the use of the DSM with young children include the following: (1) the symptoms are too subjective, (2) the symptoms do not apply to preschool- and kindergarten-age children, and (3) the reliability and validity of the diagnoses have not been established with young children. Increasingly researchers are finding support for the same structure of symptoms in preschool-age children as in older children. For example, Sterba, Egger, and Angold (2007) found that internalizing symptoms in preschool-age children followed patterns similar to those noted in older children with emotional symptoms, based on three factors: social phobia, social anxiety, and major depression/generalized anxiety. A three-factor model was also the best fit for disruptive symptoms, with the factors being oppositional disorder/conduct disorder, hyperactivity–impulsivity, and inattention. Strickland and colleagues (2011) obtained similar results in their study but found that a four-factor model (with major depression and generalized anxiety as separate factors) fit better than did the three-factor model.

However, contrary to these findings, Olino, Dougherty, Bufferd, Carlson, and Klein (2014) found that a two-factor model representing internalizing and externalizing symptoms best fit their data. They also found that all symptoms except phobic ones loaded on one common general factor. In a study specific to anxiety disorders (and based on DSM-IV diagnoses), researchers found support for differentiation among anxiety disorders, with GAD, obsessive– compulsive disorder (ODD), SAD, and social phobia emerging as separate factors and fitting the data better than one undifferentiated model (Mian, Godoy, Briggs-Gowan, & Carter, 2012). Given the limited number of studies in this area and the lack of clear consensus, it is likely that more research will be needed to help clarify the structure of symptoms in young children.

Several recent studies that have been conducted on the prevalence of DSM disorders in preschool children are briefly reviewed here. They include all those cited in the earlier discussion of the prevalence rates of individual disorders. In this section, a broader overview is provided. Studies specific to individual disorders are not included in this summary.

Wichstrøm and colleagues (2012) utilized the PAPA to evaluate the presence of disorders in a large sample of Norwegian children. Parents of all children born in 2003 or 2004 in one Norwegian city were invited to participate. Initially 2,475 children were screened utilizing the Strengths and Difficulties Questionnaire (SDQ), and a subset of the parents ($n = 995$) of these children (representing children across the spectrum of SDQ scores) were administered the PAPA. A total of 12.5% of children met criteria for at least one disorder. Encopresis was the most common disorder reported (6.4%). When this disorder was removed, the overall prevalence of disorders was 7.1%, with no single disorder having a prevalence rate over 2%. Overall, more boys evidenced problems than did girls, with ADHD, depression, and sleep disorders being more common in boys. Differences in prevalence were also noted for parental socioeconomic status (SES), with much higher rates of disorders in children from lower SES families (12.8% for any disorder except encopresis) than higher SES families (4.7% for any disorder except encopresis). Significant differences based on family SES were noted for ADHD, CD, ODD, dysthymia, depression, and SAD.

Lavigne and colleagues (2009) utilized the DISC-YC as well as the Child Symptom Inventory (CSI) checklist to examine the prevalence of disorders in a sample of 796 4-year-old children from the Chicago area. Using the DISC scores and any impairment level (incorporating any child who met minimum criteria for a disorder), ADHD (12.8% for any type) and ODD (13.4%) were considerably higher than those noted by Wichstrøm and colleagues (2012). Rates of internalizing symptoms (anxiety and depression) were lower, under 1%. Results utilizing the CSI were similar, although there were higher rates for anxiety disorders (GAD was 2.1% and SAD—not measured with the DISC—was 3.9%) and ADHD (15.5%), but lower rates for ODD (5.2%). In this sample, gender differences were noted only for ADHD, with more boys than girls displaying symptoms of ADHD. No significant differences were noted by racial/ethnic groups when SES and the number of analyses conducted were controlled for.

Bufferd and colleagues (2011) utilized the PAPA in evaluating 541 3-year-old children residing in the Stony Brook, New York, area. Overall, 27.4% of children met the criteria for at least one disorder. ODD (9.4%) and specific phobia (9.1%) were the most common diagnoses. SAD (5.4%) was the only other disorder with a prevalence rate over 5%. Depressive disorders (1.8%), selective mutism (1.5%), and panic disorder (0.2%) were the least commonly reported diagnoses. The authors reported that diagnoses were not associated with demographic variables such as SES, sex, or race/ethnicity, with a couple of exceptions (e.g., specific phobias were more common in lower SES families).

In an evaluation of the reliability of the PAPA, Egger and colleagues (2006) reported on the prevalence of disorders in a sample of 307 children ages 2–5. Youth in this study were drawn from a pediatric outpatient clinic in Durham, North Carolina. Because one of the purposes of the study was to evaluate the PAPA, researchers administered the measure twice to all participants with test–retest intervals ranging from 3 days to 1 month. The overall prevalence of any disorder (excluding elimination disorders) was 16.2% at time 1 and 14.1% at time 2. In general, the prevalence of disorders at time 2 was lower than at time 1, although the difference was significant only for SAD, GAD, and CD in terms of the specific disorders assessed.

Although having the estimates of prevalence rates can be helpful for clinicians, it is important to keep in mind that the interventions discussed here are not designed specifically for any one DSM disorder but, rather, are directed at treating the *specific set of symptoms* the child is exhibiting. This is in line with the more recent focus on transdiagnostic approaches to intervention in which treatment approaches are not tailored to a specific disorder but can be used across diagnostic categories to address common core mechanisms or processes. This approach may be particularly valuable in children given the comorbidity of problems as well as changing nature of symptoms over the time (Ehrenreich-May & Chu, 2014).

THE IMPACT OF BEHAVIORAL, SOCIAL, AND EMOTIONAL PROBLEMS IN SCHOOL SETTINGS

Problem behaviors in children can have significant and adverse outcomes on a variety of variables, including those related to the school setting. While it may not seem as though problems in the preschool and kindergarten years would adversely impact future school performance, this is not the case. In fact, data indicate that prekindergarten (PreK) children in state-funded programs are expelled at 3.2 times the rate of K–12 students, with approximately 10% of sampled teachers reporting expelling at least one child over a 12-month period (Gilliam, 2005). There were notable differences by state (e.g., Kentucky reported no expulsions for PreK children and New Mexico reported 21.10 per 1,000 students), as well as age (older PreK children were more likely to be expelled), gender (more boys were expelled), and race/ethnicity (more African American children were expelled), which may indicate different applications of standards across different settings and groups. On a positive note, access to a mental health consultant was related to lower expulsion rates.

Social and behavioral problems in the early childhood years may have a sustained impact in the later grades. Researchers looking at both externalizing and internalizing problems in young children found that elevated levels of both of these types of problems were predictive of academic problems in first grade (Bub, McCartney, & Willett, 2007). In a longitudinal study that followed children from grades 1–6, researchers found that children with externalizing and internalizing problems in first grade had lower academic achievement and social competence in sixth grade than students without problems (Henricsson & Rydell, 2006). In another study, child aggression (but not general externalizing behaviors) in the early years (ages 2–3) predicted increased academic difficulties at age 7 (Brennan, Shaw, Dishion, & Wilson, 2012). Other researchers have found that inattention in the toddler years uniquely predicts reading problems in second grade (Gray, Carter, Briggs-Gowan, Jones, & Wagmiller, 2014). These behavioral issues at the classroom level (in addition to the individual child level) can have an adverse outcome on school readiness. For example, similar to other studies, Bulotsky-Shearer, Dominguez, and Bell (2012) found that both "overactive" and "underactive" behaviors in the preschool setting were predictive of more cognitive, social, and motor difficulties in the classroom setting. They also found that high classwide levels of underactive behaviors were associated with lower school readiness. Other researchers have looked both at behavioral problems and behavioral competencies (noting that these are not necessarily mutually exclusive) and found that behavior competence predicts positive academic functioning even after taking into account externalizing problems and background characteristics (Kwon, Kim, & Sheridan, 2012). This finding is consistent with other research findings that suggest child competencies mediated the relationship between problem behaviors in the preschool years and academic and social competence in first grade (McWayne & Cheung, 2009). These studies suggest that a sole focus on problem behaviors (without looking at positive behaviors too) may provide incomplete information regarding a child's trajectory.

In addition to the negative impact that child behavior problems can have on individual child outcomes, they can also have a negative impact on classroom and teacher outcomes. Friedman-Krauss, Raver, Morris, and Jones (2014) found that classroom-level behavioral problems in the fall predicted increased teacher stress in the spring. In a longitudinal study from preschool to third grade, researchers found that child externalizing problems were related to teacher–student conflict and this relationship was bidirectional (Skalická, Stenseng, & Wichstrøm, 2015). Similarly, findings from a study with preschool-age children showed a bidirectional relationship between child externalizing problems and teacher–child conflict (Zhang & Sun, 2011).

STABILITY OF BEHAVIOR PROBLEMS

An increasing body of literature has made it clear that behavior problems in preschool and kindergarten children are often (although not always) stable over time. An often-cited early review on the continuity of problems noted that of children who are identified as having externalizing problems during the preschool years, approximately 50% will continue to have behavior problems over time (Campbell, 1995). As discussed in more detail below, more recent studies have also indicated that many children who first evidence problems in the early childhood years will continue to struggle with emotional–behavioral concerns as they grow older.

Much of the research on the stability of specific disorders diagnosed in the preschool years has been focused on externalizing disorders. While many studies have short-term follow-up periods, longer-term follow-ups are important in knowing of implications beyond the preschool years. In a study specific to ADHD, children initially diagnosed at ages 3–5 were followed for 6 years (Riddle et al., 2013). Researchers administered both the parent and teacher versions of the Conners Rating Scales at 3-, 4-, and 6-year follow-up periods. Although symptoms showed a decrease from baseline to the 3-year follow-up, symptoms remained relatively stable over the following 3 years, and parent-rated scores tended to remain in the clinical range (although the same was not true for teacher ratings, with these falling below clinical cutoffs at follow-up periods). When looking at diagnosis stability, 76% met the criteria at year 3 and 77% at year 6 (regardless of medication status). When taking into account behaviors while not on medication, diagnostic rates were higher (90% at year 6). A comorbid diagnosis of ODD/CD substantially increased the likelihood of an ADHD diagnosis at year 6.

When specifically looking at internalizing disorders in later years, preschool-age children with anxious-fearful behaviors as well as hostile-aggressive behaviors, as measured by parent-report questionnaires, were at increased risk for emotional difficulties at ages 10–12 (Slemming et al., 2010). In a large longitudinal study on the stability of anxiety initially diagnosed in the childhood years (although not necessarily in the preschool years), there was a good degree of diagnostic consistency over time, with the highest consistency found for phobic and social anxiety disorders (Carballo et al., 2010). Bosquet and Egeland (2006) also noted the moderate stability of anxiety symptoms over time from the preschool to adolescent years based on correlations between symptoms at different ages.

In a study not specific to diagnoses, in which Pihlakoski and colleagues (2006) followed a community sample of children from ages 3 to 12 using the Child Behavior Checklist (CBCL) and Youth Self-Report (YSR), approximately 30% of children who were in the clinical range on the CBCL at age 3 were also in the clinical range on the CBCL at age 12, with approximately 20% in the clinical range on the YSR. When looking at specific syndrome scales, the aggressive behavior and destructive behavior scales were predictive of later problems across a variety of subscales.

Better understanding of not just diagnoses but the stability of symptoms and symptom clusters is also important. In particular, given that preschool children are not known for their behavioral and emotional regulation skills, understanding what behaviors may be more normative and not predictive of later problems and what behaviors may be more of a cause for concern is important. In a recent study, Hong, Tillman, and Luby (2015) used diagnostic interviews (including the PAPA) to evaluate children in the preschool years (ages 3–5) and again in the early school years (ages 6–9). Behaviors that were not predictive of continuing problems included losing one's temper, low-intensity property destruction, and low-intensity deceitfulness/stealing. In contrast, high intensity of property destruction, deceitfulness/stealing, argumentative/defiant behaviors, and peer problems, as well as both low- and high-intensity aggression toward people and animals, were predictive of later school-age conduct problems.

In a group of children who were identified as having CD at age 5, not only were they more likely to continue to display symptoms consistent with CD at age 10 (compared to controls without CD), they were also more likely to have poor academic performance, have a greater need for special education services, and require more teacher effort (Kim-Cohen et al., 2009). Even in the group of children who no longer qualified for a CD diagnosis at age 10 (62.5% of the initial CD sample), they continued to have significantly higher scores than controls on multiple CBCL subscales (more by parent report, less by teacher report) and were more likely to require special education services.

Given these research findings, it seems likely that many children who are identified as having emotional and behavioral problems during the preschool years will continue to exhibit problem behaviors beyond preschool. Therefore, the preschool years are an ideal time to intervene. Although not all young children identified as having problems continue to have problems at later ages, certainly the substantial number of children who do so warrants more attention to treatment for this age group. If interventions are successful with preschool- and kindergarten-age children, the number of children in need of interventions later in life and the complexity of the interventions needed should be reduced.

PREDICTORS OF PROBLEMS

With the mounting evidence that many preschool- and kindergarten-age children who are identified as having behavioral problems continue to have such problems, researchers have begun to investigate the factors that mediate long-term outcomes. If the factors that lead to initial and continued problems and those that contribute to a decrease in later problems can be determined, then it would be easier to develop interventions targeted to the populations that would benefit the most. In the following sections (and in Tables 1.2 and 1.3), the factors that have been noted to predict problems over time are summarized.

Predictors of Externalizing Problems

Many of the factors identified as contributing to both the initial expression of behavior problems, as well as their long-term stability, are related to characteristics of the child's family. Parenting behaviors are probably the most studied of these factors and have consistently been related to child behavior problems. Gerald Patterson is perhaps the best known for developing models in this area, and Patterson's coercive parenting cycle model is cited extensively as a predictor of child externalizing problems (Patterson, 1982). Many of the family-based interventions for child behavior problems are based, in large part, on this

TABLE 1.2. Predictors of Externalizing Problems in Young Children

Parent characteristics	Child characteristics
Parenting behaviors (e.g., coercive parenting, negative discipline strategies)	Insecure attachment
	Difficult temperament/poor self-regulation
Parental stress	Physiological regulation
Parental psychopathology	
Family dysfunction	Demographic variables
	Low socioeconomic status
	Low birthweight
	High violent TV viewing

model. In the coercive parenting pattern, parents make repeated requests of their children, who do not comply with these requests. Eventually the parent backs down from the request, due to the negative or aggressive behaviors exhibited by the child. Thus the parent negatively reinforces the child by withdrawing the aversive command or request. The parent, in turn, is negatively reinforced by the discontinuation of the aversive behaviors the child was exhibiting. Typically, there is an escalation in this pattern, with parents eventually resorting to more severe methods of discipline in attempts to obtain compliance. The use of these severe methods is often reinforced by the child stopping his or her negative behaviors only once the severe methods are used. In this pattern, both the parent and child tend to escalate their use of negative and aggressive behaviors. These parenting patterns are likely evident from an early age, with a number of studies noting a link between parenting behaviors in the preschool years and later externalizing problems (e.g., Heberle, Krill, Briggs-Gowan, & Carter, 2015).

Parental stress and family dysfunction are important factors in predicting both the initial onset of problems, as well as the continuation of such problems. Preschool children whose parents experience significant distress are more likely to develop externalizing problem behaviors (e.g., (Heberle et al., 2015; Miller-Lewis et al., 2006), although this effect may be mediated by ineffective parenting practices (e.g., Heberle et al., 2015). The presence of parental psychopathology in children's preschool years has also been linked to the presence of externalizing problems (Breaux, Harvey, & Lugo-Candelas, 2014).

Although much of the research on predictors of externalizing behavior problems has focused on parent characteristics, more recent research has examined child-focused factors that may contribute to the expression of externalizing problems. Child temperament and self-regulation are two child-focused factors that may be linked to later difficulties. Low levels of inhibitory control have been linked to externalizing problems across samples representing different ethnic/cultural groups (e.g., Olson et al., 2011). Child temperament has also been linked to later externalizing problems when the temperament is characterized as more inflexible and less persistent (e.g., Miller-Lewis et al., 2006). Physiological regulation (as measured by respiratory sinus arrhythmia which is involved in heart rate variability) in the early preschool years has also been noted to be related to later externalizing problems, with greater physiological regulation at age 3 associated with a decreased risk for later externalizing problems (although such a relationship was not seen at ages 4 and 5; Perry, Nelson, Calkins, Leerkes, O'Brien, & Marcovitch, 2014).

Attachment has also been evaluated as a child factor that may be related to the development of externalizing problems, with several studies noting a link between insecure types of attachment in the preschool years and the development of externalizing problems (e.g., Fearon, Bakermans-Kranenburg, van IJzendoorn, Lapsley, & Roisman, 2010; Moss, Cyr, & Dubois-Comtois, 2004). In addition, one study noted that a secure attachment may moderate the association between harsh parenting and child aggression (Cyr, Pasalich, McMahon, & Spieker, 2014) in that a secure attachment can serve as a protective factor when harsh parenting practices are in place. Interestingly, researchers have noted that preschool-age children who have a less secure attachment with their mothers but have a high-quality relationship with their teacher do not show an increased risk level for behavior problems when compared to youth with a secure attachment to their mothers (Buyse, Verschueren,

& Doumen, 2009). Thus, the relationship between attachment and problem behaviors may be more complex than it appears based solely on the parent–child attachment relationship.

Demographic variables also have been related to externalizing behavior problems. For example, SES has often emerged as a predictive factor, with low SES related to high levels of externalizing problems (Piotrowska, Stride, Croft, & Rowe, 2015). Another predictor that has been linked to a potential increase in externalizing problems includes low birthweight (Bohnert & Breslau, 2008). Interestingly, higher rates of television viewing have also been correlated with reports of increased inattentive/hyperactive behaviors, as well as antisocial behaviors in young children, although the relationship with antisocial behavior seems to hold true mostly for television content that is violent in nature (Christakis & Zimmerman, 2007), while for inattention problems the association was more broadly with "noneducational" content rather than specific to a type of content (Zimmerman & Christakis, 2007).

As research methods and statistical analysis have become more sophisticated over time, researchers are increasingly able to examine the possibilities of more complex relations between some of these factors. For example, Barnes, Boutwell, Beaver, and Gibson (2013) examined poor parenting practices (spanking, specifically), externalizing problems, and self-regulation in a sample of twins. Their results suggest that shared genetic influences may account for some of the relationship between parenting practices and externalizing problems, as well as between self-regulation and externalizing problems. It is likely that in the future, nuances of the various predictive factors mentioned here (and potentially others not mentioned) will become clearer.

Predictors of Internalizing Problems

Although researchers have been examining predictors of externalizing disorders for many years, historically they have been less focused on internalizing disorders. It does appear that there are some similarities across these clusters of problem areas. Ineffective parenting practices and parental stress/distress during the preschool years may lead to an increased risk of internalizing problem behaviors for children in later years (e.g., Heberle et al., 2015). Parental psychopathology has also been found to be a risk for internalizing, as well as externalizing, problems (e.g., Breaux et al., 2014; Marakovitz, Wagmiller, Mian, Briggs-Gowan,

TABLE 1.3. Predictors of Internalizing Problems in Young Children

Parent characteristics	Child characteristics
Ineffective parenting practices	Difficult temperament
Parental stress	Behaviorally inhibited temperament
Parental psychopathology	Negative emotionality
Low social support	Insecure attachment
	Delayed language
	Demographic variables
	Low socioeconomic status
	Low birthweight
	Low parental education

& Carter, 2011). Social support has been noted to be a protective factor for children, with those with greater supports being less likely to develop internalizing problems at school age even if parenting practices are ineffective (e.g., Heberle et al., 2015).

Child characteristics such as temperament, including behavioral inhibition and negative emotionality, as well as delayed language development, have also been examined as predictors of internalizing problems. Researchers have examined the role of inhibition in predicting future problems. High inhibition in the preschool years has been linked to later internalizing problems (e.g., Hastings et al., 2015; Hirshfeld-Becker et al., 2007; Marakovitz et al., 2011). Negative emotionality in preschool has also been linked to later internalizing problems (e.g., Davis, Votruba-Drzal, & Silk, 2015; Marakovitz et al, 2011; Shaw, Keenan, Vondra, Delliquadri, & Giovannelli, 1997), although this variable may interact with parenting factors; at least one study notes that negative emotionality was a stronger predictor of later internalizing problems when mothers exhibited high levels of parental warmth (Davis et al., 2015). Delayed language in the preschool years has also been linked to internalizing problems in later childhood and early adolescence even when controlling for other variables (e.g., maternal intelligence, SES) that may impact these factors (Bornstein, Hahn, & Suwalsky, 2013). While an insecure attachment style has also been linked to internalizing problems, the relationship is not as strong as that with externalizing problems (e.g., Groh, Roisman, van IJzendoorn, Bakermans-Kranenburg, & Fearon, 2012).

Demographic factors, including lower SES, have also been linked to an increased risk for later internalizing problems (e.g., Carter et al., 2010; Hastings et al., 2015), and this link has been shown to exist in studies within and outside of the United States (e.g., van Oort, vam der Ende, Wadsworth, Verhulst, & Achenbach, 2011). Lower parental education levels have also been linked to an increased risk for internalizing problems in several studies (e.g., Burlaka, Bermann, & Graham-Bermann, 2015; Carter et al., 2010). Specific to the child (rather than family characteristics), low birthweight has been linked to an increased risk of internalizing problems (Bohnert & Breslau, 2008).

CHAPTER SUMMARY/PURPOSE OF THIS BOOK

Social, emotional, and behavioral problems during the early childhood years are clearly a real concern with potentially adverse long-term outcomes. Given that the problems identified during the preschool and kindergarten years put children at an increased risk for later problems, prevention and intervention efforts in the preschool and kindergarten years can be important in mitigating their potential to have long-lasting effects. A number of evidence-based psychosocial treatments support their use with young children or show particular promise for use with this age group. The purpose of this book is to provide a review of, and implementation guidelines for, these evidence-based psychosocial interventions. Clinicians should be able to use the information and materials provided to develop assessment strategies and treatment plans for most of the disorders commonly seen during the preschool and kindergarten years.

CHAPTER 2

Assessment of Mental Health Issues

As noted in Chapter 1, children who exhibit emotional or behavioral problems during the early childhood years often do not simply "outgrow" their symptoms. Youth exhibiting both externalizing and internalizing problems may continue to struggle with those difficulties in later years. Mental health professionals have realized that by the time a child reaches school age, he or she may have missed vital interventions that could have thwarted later, more serious problems. Changes in education policy beginning several decades ago pushed the concept of early intervention into the forefront of our awareness and subsequent practice (Shonkoff & Meisels, 1990). In order for early intervention to occur, there must be adequate assessment measures for screening young children for the potential presence of social–emotional–behavior problems and for accurately identifying young children with mental health problems and other special needs. Equally important, once a child begins to receive interventions, progress monitoring should occur to help determine if the child is making progress.

Though challenges exist in the assessment of young children, including limited measures and variability in behavior, encouraging developments have emerged over the last several decades. An increasing number of behavior rating scales, designed specifically for the assessment of preschool- and kindergarten-age children, have become available. In addition, as research on observations and interviews of preschool- and kindergarten-age children has increased, historic beliefs that useful information could not be obtained from young children have been challenged and revised. This chapter provides an overview of these measures and techniques, highlighting those that have the best reliability and validity for preschool and kindergarten populations. Each section explores assessment methods, including screening, diagnostic/evaluation, and progress monitoring tools. The screening tools as discussed in this chapter can be used for universal, Tier 1 screening at the classwide or schoolwide level and also used as brief measures to determine if further assessment of an individual child is warranted. Progress monitoring tools, as referred to in this chapter, are those that can monitor children's responses to treatment and interventions. Progress monitoring tools are often used at regular intervals (e.g., weekly) over the course of treatment.

INTERVIEWS WITH PARENTS* AND TEACHERS

Parent and teacher/daycare worker interviews are crucial to gaining a comprehensive understanding of the young child. The chief request and referral for services almost always comes from the adults in the child's life, such as parents or teachers. Therefore, an important element in the assessment of the young child is to clarify who has concerns about the child and what specifically these concerns are. Conducting an interview with key adults is the primary way of gathering this information.

Interviews as Screeners

Interviews with parents, teachers, and daycare providers are usually the first step in determining if further assessment of problem behaviors is warranted. At different intervals throughout the year, teachers, can be asked if there are any children that they have concerns about in their classrooms that may warrant further attention. This informal screening can often be useful in identifying those children that may need extra supports. Typically, when concerns are first noted in the school setting, parents are contacted to gain an understanding of the history of the concern and breadth of the problem. Additionally, parents are always contacted before considering a more formal assessment to discuss the concerns and determine if further measures are necessary. Informal interviews/conversations, touching upon the concerns of the referring party, can help to determine whether or not further action must be taken, including an additional assessment of the child.

Interviews as Diagnostic/Evaluation Tools

More in-depth interviews are frequently used as part of a comprehensive evaluation of a child. The most common informants to interview about the functioning of a young child are his or her parent(s), teacher(s), and/or daycare provider(s). The following section overviews the components to include in interviews used for the purposes of a comprehensive child assessment.

Parent Interviews

The parents' consent, cooperation, and participation are critical in the assessment of young children. The parent is often the best source of information regarding the child's history, current difficulties, and outside factors that may be impacting the child's behavior, such as family problems, a death in the family, or a recent move. In addition, the parent is an invalu-

---

*To simplify wording throughout this book, we refer primarily to *parents*, with the understanding that this usage also includes nonparent caregivers.

able resource for connecting the clinician with other key adults in the child's life so that the interviewer can gather as much information as possible about the child. The parent can also provide the clinician with the necessary consents so that he or she can consult with other providers. An example of a consent form is provided in Form 2.1.*

The first task in the parent interview is to build rapport. To help put the parent at ease, the clinician should introduce him- or herself and discuss the purpose of the interview and assessment. Any questions the parent has about the assessment process should be answered. It is important to empower parents by letting them know the clinician is there to help them and their child, and that the parents are crucial to the process because they are the "experts" on their child. In addition, clinicians should be aware that, even for parents who initiated the referral for evaluation or treatment, the testing situation may be a potential threat to a parent's self-esteem/self-efficacy. Parents may struggle with guilt surrounding their child's problems, blaming themselves for their child's difficulties. For many parents, the idea that their child may have a disability can also be quite traumatic, evoking a sense of failure or loss for the parents (Frick, Barry, & Kamphaus, 2010). An effort should be made to support the parents through the process and reframe the situation by reinforcing the fact that the parents are intervening in their child's difficulties at an early age, which can be helpful in preventing later problems.

During the interview, the clinician gathers information about the referral question or presenting problem behaviors. Reviewing the child's symptomatology, asking the parent to describe the child's behavior, and understanding both the meaning and the function of the behavior in relationship to the child's family are important (American Academy of Child and Adolescent Psychiatry, 2007). It is common for parents, caregivers, teachers, and other adults in the child's life to differ in how they perceive the problem behavior. These differences may be related to a variety of factors, including the amount of time the adult spends with the child, the circumstances surrounding the time spent with the child, the ideas each adult has about developmentally appropriate childhood behaviors, and how each adult interacts with the child. In addition, children often exhibit different behaviors in different settings, depending on the expectations in each setting. For example, a child with few structured activities or demands at home may not exhibit many problem behaviors with his or her parents, whereas in the structured preschool setting the child may have difficulty staying seated or attending to the teacher. It is up to the interviewer to determine the factors involved in these differences by conducting careful interviews with all key adults in the child's life and through observations of the child.

In addition to identifying specific problem behaviors, one primary purpose for interviewing parents is to obtain a report of relevant background information on the child (Merrell, 2008a). Background and developmental information is necessary to provide a detailed history of the child's physical and cognitive development, as well as his or her social, emotional, and behavioral history and development. Other caregivers, such as foster parents or legal guardians, can still provide a meaningful account of the child's relationship with others or of important events that may have helped shape the child's development (American Academy of Child and Adolescent Psychiatry, 2007). Core areas to be included in an

---

*All reproducible forms appear at the ends of chapters.

interview with parents are discussed in the next sections (American Academy of Child and Adolescent Psychiatry, 2007; Mazza, 2014; Merrell, 2008a). A summary of these areas is provided in Table 2.1, and an example of an intake form (either to be used by the clinician to help structure the interview or to be given to the parent to complete before the initial appointment) is included in Form 2.2.

FAMILY RELATIONSHIPS

How the child relates to family members, including parents, siblings, and extended family, should be covered in the interview. Attachment to parents/guardians should be explored. Changes within the family system, such as birth of siblings, deaths, divorce, removal from the home, and changes in caretaking arrangements, such as custody and visitation, also should be noted. In addition, clinicians should inquire about the child's compliance with family rules and parental disciplinary practices. It is important when assessing these areas to take into account the sociocultural context of the family's beliefs and values (Clark, Tluczek, & Gallagher, 2004).

CULTURAL BACKGROUNDS AND BELIEFS

The cultural background of the family and how it affects the way the parents perceive their child's behaviors, as well as what kind of help they may or may not be seeking, also needs to be explored. Using strategies to promote this level of understanding, such as asking the family questions about their background, cultural beliefs, and values, is important, especially when working with a family from a culture other than the interviewer's. Asking the family about their culture is preferable to adhering to preconceived notions or stereotypes, which can lead to bias and erroneous conclusions. If necessary, interpreters should be used when there is a language barrier. In addition, it may be useful to meet with parents on several occasions and perhaps away from the school in order to foster trust and a better understanding of their values and beliefs (Ferguson, 2005).

COGNITIVE AND SCHOOL FUNCTIONING

The parents' understanding of their child's cognitive strengths and weaknesses, along with his or her academic progress (if applicable) and school/daycare functioning, should be

TABLE 2.1. Areas for Inclusion in a Clinical Interview with Parents or Caregivers

- Family relationships
- Cognitive and school functioning
- Peer relationships
- Physical development
- Child medical and psychiatric history
- Family medical and psychiatric history
- Social–emotional development and temperament
- Interests and talents
- Strengths
- Unusual/traumatic circumstances
- Prior testing

addressed. Areas to be explored include the child's ability to separate from the parent to attend school or daycare; the child's verbal, attentional, and organizational skills; the child's motivation to learn (if in a school setting); and the child's relationships with school staff and teachers. If records of past school-related services (e.g., early intervention programs) are available, the interviewer should request copies from the parent or obtain consent from the parent to contact the appropriate organization for these records.

PEER RELATIONSHIPS

The interviewer should inquire about the child's friendships with other children his or her age in daycare, school, church, or neighborhood settings. He or she should also explore social skills and deficits, such as the child's level of self-control, empathy toward others, and social communication via language and nonverbal behavior (e.g., smiling appropriately, give-and-take conversation, and eye contact). The type of play the child is engaging in with other children his or her age should also be discussed (e.g., has the child progressed from side-by-side or "parallel play," which is common in toddlers, to associative or cooperative play, such as sharing toys, communicating verbally, and playing together?).

PHYSICAL DEVELOPMENT

Asking parents about the child's developmental history, including prenatal history, is critical. Important areas to include are prenatal exposure to alcohol, illicit substances, or medications; pregnancy or birth complications; prematurity of the child; and if the child required an extended hospital stay after birth. The interviewer also should inquire about developmental milestone achievements, such as ages at which the child walked and was toilet trained. The child's language acquisition, including when the child first babbled, said his or her first words, and spoke in sentences, is crucial to overview. Any concerns around the child's speech patterns and how the child uses language in a social context should also be discussed.

CHILD AND FAMILY MEDICAL AND PSYCHIATRIC HISTORY

A medical and psychiatric history of the child and his or her family of origin can provide information relevant to the child's current behaviors. Inquiries about hospitalizations, allergies, health problems, sensory problems (such as vision or hearing loss), injuries (including head injuries), and operations, as well as the child's reactions to these illnesses and events, can provide important developmental information. The interviewer also should obtain any psychiatric records that may exist for the child, including reports from previous evaluations and/or therapy sessions. In addition, family medical and psychiatric history should be explored to help determine if there is a familial pattern of any mental health problems. Parental mental illness or stress affects children's mental wellness; therefore, inquiry into parental mental health is important (Bluth & Wahler, 2011; Sameroff, Seifer, & McDonough, 2004; Tonge et al., 2006).

SOCIAL–EMOTIONAL DEVELOPMENT AND TEMPERAMENT

This category includes information about the child's personality, style of attachment to caregivers, temperament, present and past mood regulation, and adaptability to novel or difficult situations, including the child's ability to regulate mood and self-soothe. The assessment of mood should cover the past and current presence of moodiness or irritability, excessive tearfulness, anxiety or fearfulness, temper tantrums, somatic or bodily complaints, and other psychologically relevant symptoms.

INTERESTS, TALENTS, AND STRENGTHS

In addition to obtaining information about the problem behaviors the child is exhibiting, the interviewer also should inquire about the child's areas of strengths, interests, and talents. Important areas to cover include activities the child likes to do for fun at home and school, any proficiencies the child has in a particular developmental area, and the parents' perceptions of the child's strengths. A parent's report of the child's strengths, or lack thereof, can give the clinician further information about the quality of the parent–child relationship.

TRAUMATIC CIRCUMSTANCES

Unusual or traumatic circumstances include events such as child physical abuse, sexual abuse, neglect, family violence, natural disasters, or exposure to other traumatic events. The interviewer should determine if any such events occurred and, if so, the impact of the exposure should be explored, along with reviewing any related medical, psychological, and/or social service records. This data can be helpful in piecing together information about the severity and effects of the situation on the child.

PRIOR TESTING

As previously mentioned, any past psychological testing should be obtained in order to aid the interviewer in the child's present assessment. For example, some children have had developmental assessments conducted when they were toddlers, or have had screening assessments administered when entering preschool, such as Head Start. This information can be useful in determining prior functioning and the young child's foundational skills.

Teacher/Daycare Worker Interviews

Teachers, daycare workers, and other important adults in the child's life can provide a wealth of information about the child outside of the home setting. The teacher/daycare provider interview is conducted somewhat differently from the interview with the parent, in that the teacher/daycare provider likely will not have much background or developmental information on the child. Instead these sources would provide information about the child's relations with peers and adults, the child's mastery of beginning key concepts and academic skills, and the child's ability to meet expectations of the school or daycare setting. Any related supports or interventions that are being used with the child, along with the child's response to those supports, should be discussed. In addition, the clinician should inquire about the child's strengths and talents at school and daycare.

During the interview, it is important to build rapport and gain the cooperation of the teacher/daycare worker in order to gather as much information as possible regarding the child's problems and strengths. Before conducting this interview, the clinician, if operating outside of the school setting, should ensure he or she has a signed release-of-information form from the parent (see Form 2.1). It is important to be aware of the laws and policies in the state wherein the clinician works and also in the school district wherein the child resides (if applicable) in order to best understand confidentiality and release of information requirements (McConaughy, 2013).

The teacher/daycare worker should be approached as a member of a team and as someone who can help remediate problems in the school or daycare setting and facilitate the child's experience of success. It is important that the teacher/daycare worker be respected for both his or her knowledge about the child and also for his or her time limitations. Eliminating all but the most essential work for the teacher/daycare provider, scheduling meetings or phone calls during his or her planning times or the children's nap time, and always personally thanking the teacher/daycare provider for his or her involvement in the evaluation are simple, yet important rapport building strategies (Frick et al., 2010).

Areas to include in the teacher/daycare worker interview are summarized in the next section and are listed in Table 2.2. Of course it would be important to select topic areas and questions that meet the concerns about that particular child (McConaughy, 2013).

GENERAL INFORMATION ABOUT THE CHILD

General information about the child should be obtained, including the overall impression the teacher or daycare provider may have about the child. Because the teacher/daycare provider sees the child in a different context than the parent does, this portion of the interview may produce different information (Mazza, 2014).

SCHOOL/DAYCARE BEHAVIOR PROBLEMS

Once the interviewer has gathered general information from the teacher/daycare provider, the focus can be turned to any problem behaviors in the school or daycare setting. Specifically, information on how long the behavior has been occurring, what interventions have

TABLE 2.2. Areas for Inclusion in a Clinical Interview with Teachers or Child Care Workers

- Concerns about the child
- School/Day care behavior problems
- Academic performance, if applicable
- Social skills
- Strengths and talents

been tried, along with the child's response to those interventions, are essential to cover. Antecedents and consequences of the behavior should also be assessed (McConaughy, 2013).

ACADEMIC PERFORMANCE, IF APPLICABLE

When working with a teacher, the child's academic performance/mastery of beginning skills should be overviewed. Any intervention, along with the child's response to the intervention, should be noted. Follow-up questions to determine if learning issues are due to ability deficits or performance issues are important (Mazza, 2014).

SOCIAL SKILLS

Clinicians should inquire about the social skills and peer relationships of the child. Relationships with classmates, types of play in which the child engages, and any aggressive behaviors should be explored. Assessing for any social skills deficits is important, as this could also help to guide intervention.

STRENGTHS AND TALENTS

The teacher's/daycare provider's understanding of the child's areas of strengths and talents is important to include. Areas such as activities the child likes to do for fun at school, any proficiencies in a particular developmental area, and his or her perceptions of the child's strengths are all relevant. As with the parent's report of the child's strengths, inquiring about the teacher's/daycare provider's impressions of the child's strengths can give the clinician further information about the quality of the teacher/daycare provider–child relationship.

Interviews as Progress Monitoring Tools

In addition to being used as part of screening and diagnostic evaluations, interviews can be useful progress monitoring tools in determining the utility of home, school, and/or daycare interventions. Checking in with those adults that are key in the care of the referred child can help determine if the interventions used are successful or need adjustment. A simple call home to inquire how the parent perceives progress, or lack thereof, for the child is commonly used as a way of tracking intervention progress. Regular contacts with teachers and daycare providers can also provide valuable information as to how the child is progressing in those settings. Through such interviews and information gathering, adjustments can be made to the intervention, depending on what is working. Questions such as, "How often do you notice your child having a tantrum since the last time we checked in?" or "Have you seen any changes in your daughter's aggressive behaviors over the last week?" can be ways of using interviews for monitoring progress. Though often used for research purposes, standardized interviews, such as the Diagnostic Interview for Children and Adolescents–IV (DICA–IV; Reich, Welner, & Herjanic, 1997), could also be used to evaluate pre- and post-outcome data for interventions.

INTERVIEWS WITH YOUNG CHILDREN

A variety of theories and ideas regarding the usefulness of interviewing young children have been expressed over the years. Young children are often viewed as illogical and unable to distinguish reality from fantasy. The work of developmental theorists has added some support to these beliefs. For example, in Piaget's theory of cognitive development, it is assumed that, although children between the ages of 2 and 7 are able to represent thoughts with words, they lack the ability to engage in logical reasoning (Piaget, 1983). Such theories have led some to believe that important information cannot be reliably obtained from young children. Although the type of information one can obtain from young children in an interview is limited, young children are capable of producing higher-quality self-report information than was previously considered possible (Marchant, 2013; Merrell, 2008a). In fact, children may be one of the most important sources of information, particularly in cases of abuse or when the child is exhibiting more internalizing symptoms (Angold & Egger, 2004). However, because of the limitations associated with interviewing young children, it is recommended that any information obtained from a young child through an interview be combined with other relevant information, such as parent and teacher interviews, rating scale data, and clinical observations, to achieve the fullest possible clinical picture of the young child. Of course, in some cases a child interview would not be indicated. If an interview with the child would not glean any insight into the situation or if the child is exhibiting primarily behavioral issues (e.g., aggression, tantrums, noncompliance), the clinician would work instead with the parent and/or school staff to identify the problem areas and develop any needed interventions.

When interviewing a young child, it is important to keep in mind key developmental issues. Young children are often shy and timid in initial interviews and likely will have difficulty verbalizing thoughts and feelings (Sattler, 1998). Preschoolers typically define other people in concrete, inflexible terms, such as thinking someone is all good or all bad, without understanding that the person can exhibit both qualities (Keith & Campbell, 2000; Sattler, 1998). In addition, because preschool- and kindergarten-age children are typically unable to sustain attention on any one task for a long period of time, they may need to be interviewed over several sessions. Seeing a child multiple times also can prove beneficial for rapport building. Young children are typically more active and impulsive than older children, creating, at times, a challenging situation for the interviewer. Children must be attentive before they can participate in an interview process (Greenspan & Greenspan, 2003). Redirection is often helpful to refocus the child, as is simply saying the child's name frequently during the conversation. Giving the child frequent reinforcers (such as stickers or candy) for staying on task also can be helpful. However, it is important that the child does not perceive that he or she is being rewarded for a certain type of answer. Such an impression could influence the child to change his or her response set (e.g., when the interviewer asks about fears, the child says that he or she is afraid of daycare when he or she actually likes daycare). It also can be helpful to use statements such as "Let's put our ears on for these questions," or, to validate the child's feelings about the questions, "I know this question might be hard to answer, but I need you to think about it and give me an answer." These statements can help the child focus and respond to the interviewer's inquiries. Finally, young children have limited verbal capabilities, including a small emotional vocabulary (Knell, 2000), making it necessary for the interviewer to pay attention to other aspects of the child's presentation, along with the child's words. The clinician should attend to the child's depth and style of personal relatedness, and his or her mood, gestures, themes covered in play or conversation, range of emotions expressed, and contact with the clinician (Greenspan & Greenspan, 2003).

Despite the difficulties of conducting interviews with young children, such interviews can provide valuable information that may not be available from other sources, such as the level of the child's distress, any thought distortions that may exist, anxious and depressed symptoms, and "secrets" that are detrimental for the child to keep. The interviewer therefore must be attuned to what the young child is expressing in the interview setting, as well as to the factors that may be affecting the quality of the information obtained. In addition to the limited cognitive capacity of preschool- and kindergarten-age children, factors such as the level of rapport established, the context of the interview, and the motivation of the child are important in determining the validity of the interview.

Rapport Building/Initial Information Gathering

The initial step in any interview with a young child is to put him or her at ease. The young child may have difficulty separating from his or her parents (Marchant, 2013). If this is the case, the best practice is to invite the parent and child into the office together, so that the child will feel more comfortable with the situation and setting. Once the child is comfortable, the interviewer can ask the parents, in a matter-of-fact manner, to go into another room if the interviewer would like to see the child individually (Merrell, 2008a). Most likely, this sequence will be all that is needed for the child to feel at ease with the process. If the child becomes upset, the clinician can reassure the child that the parent is right outside the office and that he or she will be able to see his or her mom or dad when finished. Obviously, if the child becomes extremely upset, the interview may need to be discontinued and rescheduled for another time. However, parents can remain in the office, unless the parents' presence is affecting the interview process (e.g., the child refuses to engage with the interviewer with the parent in the room).

Interviewers at times make the mistake of attempting to get a child to verbalize before the child is fully attending to the interviewer and the situation (Greenspan & Greenspan, 2003). Building rapport by sitting at the child's level on the floor or in a smaller chair (McConaughy, 2013) and engaging in child-directed play activities are important steps. The 2009 position statement of the National Association of School Psychologists (NASP) on *Early Childhood Assessment* specifically lists the use of structured and unstructured play periods as a means of gathering information, monitoring progress, and informing decision making for the school psychologist. The clinician should have available toys appropriate to the child's developmental level, as well as toys that will facilitate communication. Drawing materials, dolls, play-dough, clay, or other nondisruptive manipulatives can be useful for engaging the child. Complex board games or other activities that would require a great deal of mental effort should be avoided. When building rapport, the clinician should focus on describing the child's activities, as well as attending to the child's verbalizations (which may be minimal), and refrain from probing too much for information.

Once the clinician begins to ask the child questions, other play-based methods also can be helpful in facilitating the interview process. Puppets can be quite useful when asking children questions that may feel threatening to them (McConaughy, 2013). For example, the examiner can ask the child's puppet the questions, request that the puppet "find out" the answer from the child, and allow the puppet to respond. To help determine the validity of the responses, the examiner can ask the puppet several nonthreatening questions about the child, to which the examiner can validate the answers (e.g., the child's hair color or name).

Context of the Interview

As mentioned previously, young children's behaviors can vary widely across time and settings, making it difficult to accurately perceive what the young child may be experiencing. Therefore, the context of the interview must be taken into account, including both the immediate assessment situation and the broader background context of the child (Garbarino, Stott, & Faculty of the Erikson Institute, 1992).

Many elements related to the situation in which the assessment takes place can affect the way a young child responds to the interviewer. For example, the child may respond differently if he or she knows the interviewer than if the interviewer is a stranger. Because young children are often shy and timid in new settings (Hirschland, 2008), it is likely the young child would be apprehensive initially with someone who is unknown, taking a longer time to establish rapport. With an interviewer the child knows, the child may answer questions according to what the child thinks the interviewer would want to hear and based on past experience with that person.

The way the questions are asked also can have a significant impact on what type of information is obtained. If leading or closed-ended questions are used, it is likely that the young child will respond in a way he or she thinks would please the interviewer, potentially giving inaccurate or false reports of what happened. This is particularly likely with preschool-age children, who are more inclined to please adults than are older children (Hughes & Baker, 1990). Note the difference between the following two examples:

Leading (closed-ended) question: "Your stomach hurts when you feel scared, right?"
Nonleading (open-ended) question: "How does your body feel when you feel afraid?"

However, it can be difficult to obtain information from a preschool-age child simply through the use of nonquestioning statements such as "Tell me about your friends." Thus it is recommended that a combination of short, probing (but nonleading) questions designed to clarify statements, open-ended questions, and statements designed to encourage the child to talk (e.g., "Uh-huh," "I see") be used with preschool-age children (McConaughy, 2013).

The setting in which the interview is conducted is another element that may affect the way a child responds. The young child may respond differently if he or she is in an unfamiliar office than in a place where the child already feels comfortable and safe, such as the school setting. The interviewer may not be able to change some of these elements, but it is important to recognize their potential impact of these factors on the child. Allowing the child to hold a personal item, such as a favorite doll, blanket, or stuffed animal, can help put the child at ease.

In addition, the perceived outcome of the interview may influence a child's motivation to participate or the responses the child provides. For example, the abused child who has been threatened with harm if he or she talks about the abuse would likely be motivated either to not talk to the interviewer or to deny that abuse occurred. The use of rapport-building techniques, combined with simple reassurance and keen observation, is necessary to gather information in these cases. If the child gives any leads, such as "My daddy is mean," it is best to restate the phrase into a question, "Your daddy is mean?" and then ask more about this statement, such as "Tell me how your daddy is mean" (Sattler, 1998).

Broader issues related to culture and educational and familial history should also be considered (Garbarino et al., 1992). Cultural differences between the interviewer and the child can impact the process in several ways. First, cultural differences may be misinterpreted as pathology or as disrespect. For example, in some Native American cultures it is considered disrespectful or aggressive to engage in direct eye contact (LeBeauf, Smaby, & Maddux, 2009), whereas in the mainstream American culture, absence of eye contact could indicate a lack of respect or that the person is lying or anxious. These culturally based differences must be investigated further if they do arise, so that the child is not needlessly pathologized. Consulting with a person from the same cultural background as the child can help the interviewer obtain further information about that culture and its associated practices. One could also ask the parent or caregiver about his or her cultural background to get a better understanding of the family's beliefs, practices, and value system.

Another form of cultural influence that can affect the interview process involves children acquiring, through contact with their parents or community, a general "cultural mistrust" of persons not of their culture. The child who mistrusts outsiders may give only limited information in an interview or may lie to protect family members. It could be helpful to interview the child's parents or other family members to gain a better understanding of the familial beliefs before talking with the child. Children from families who have frequent negative contact with law enforcement or social service agencies may have learned to be distrustful and to not share information with others. It is important for the interviewer to be clear on the reasons for the interview and the possible benefits and help to be gained by the child after the assessment has been conducted.

RATING SCALES

Rating scales, which require parents, other caregivers, and/or teachers to indicate how often a child performs a variety of behaviors, have several advantages over other types of assessment procedures, particularly for young children:

1. Rating scales permit the collection and quantification of data regarding the occurrence of infrequent behaviors likely to be missed by observations (Barkley & Murphy, 2006).
2. They foster objectivity and clarity from different individuals who are responsible for the care and management of the child in different settings (Frick, Barry, & Kamphaus, 2010).

3. They usually have normative data available to establish the significance of the child's behavior relative to peers (Merrell, 2008a).
4. They are time efficient and cost effective (Frick et al., 2010).

Rating scales can provide reliable and valid data particularly with young children, whereas other procedures, such as child interviews, may not. Rating scales can also be an effective tool both for screening for initial concerns and for progress monitoring.

Although rating scales have a number of advantages that make them particularly well-suited for use with kindergarten- and preschool-age children, their limitations should be taken into account. For example, rating scales are not designed to measure behaviors per se, but to assess perceptions of behavioral and emotional characteristics that have been formed over time by the rater (Merrell, 2008a). Therefore, informant characteristics and other factors can impact the ratings of the child's behaviors. Parental distress, for example, may influence parent reports of child symptoms (Frick et al., 2010). Error variance, including *temporal variance* (the tendency of behavior ratings to be only moderately consistent over time), *setting variance* (the situational specificity of behavior), *source variance* (the objectivity, or lack thereof, of the rater), and *instrument variance* (slight variations among rating scales purportedly measuring similar constructs) also may affect ratings. Additionally, response bias, including *acquiescence* (the tendency of some test takers to answer true/false or yes/no items consistently in one direction), *social desirability* (referring to test takers, either consciously or unconsciously, endorsing items in a socially desirable direction), *faking* (the deliberate attempt by the test taker to distort or manipulate his or her responses to create a particular impression), and *deviation* (the tendency to answer test items in unconventional or unusual ways) are present in varying degrees in all behavior rating scales and may decrease the accuracy of the ratings (Merrell, 2008a). Finally, assessing internalizing symptoms, such as anxiety and depression, is challenging as these problems are not as readily observable as externalizing behaviors (Merrell, 2008a) and, therefore, may be missed by the rater. However, despite these challenges, rating scales are still considered a primary assessment tool when assessing emotional and behavioral problems of young children. By obtaining aggregated information, in which rating scales are used as part of a multimethod, multisource, multisetting assessment, these types of problems should be minimized, especially when taking into account another source's ratings, interview information, and observations (Merrell, 2008a).

Over the past several decades, rating scales for young children have increased in number. Most of these scales have involved downward extensions of existing scales (e.g., the preschool versions of the CBCL), although some were developed specifically for this population (e.g., the Preschool and Kindergarten Behavior Scale). This section provides an overview of psychometrically sound behavior rating scales designed for use with the preschool and kindergarten population. Rating scales that can be used for screening and progress monitoring, in addition to diagnostic assessment, are also addressed.

Social, Emotional, and Behavioral Scales as Screeners

Increasingly publishers are developing scales to be used specifically for screening emotional, behavioral and social concerns. These screeners can be used to evaluate multiple children in a setting to determine the incidence of problem areas and to help identify children for additional services and/or evaluation. Several of these screeners are discussed briefly next.

The BASC-3 Behavioral and Emotional Screening System (BASC-3 BESS; Kamphaus & Reynolds, 2015) was developed for use by schools, clinics, and researchers to screen for a variety of behavioral and emotional disorders. It includes 25–30 items on the form and has a preschool (ages 3–5) version. The factor structure of the prior version (the BESS-2) has been supported by research (Harrell-Williams, Raines, Kamphaus, & Denver, 2015), with the preschool version of the BESS-2 found to be highly correlated with outcomes such as social and emotional development for young children (Dowdy, Chin, & Quirk, 2013).

The Social Skills Improvement System Performance Screening Guide (Elliott & Gresham, 2008) is a universal screening measure for children ages 3–18 for academic and social–behavioral difficulties, and can also be used as a progress monitoring tool to help guide intervention. This measure can be used as a classroomwide assessment tool and has good psychometric properties, as does the standard version of the SSIS discussed in the section "The Social Skills Improvement System Rating Scales."

The Systematic Screening for Behavior Disorders, Second Edition (SSBD-2; Walker, Severson, & Feil, 2014), is a multistep screening measure completed by the teacher. First, select students from the class are identified and rank ordered based on their display of either internalizing or externalizing disorders. Second, the teacher completes two measures on the top three ranked students: the Critical Events Checklist and the Combined Frequency Index. If any students exceed normative criteria on these measures, stage three is initiated, which involves the child being observed by a trained school professional (i.e., school psychologist). Though the manual states good psychometrics, to date there is little outside research on this screening measure. However, the original edition of the SSBD three-stage model evidenced strong reliability and validity (Feil, Walker & Severson, 1995), although multiple screening steps can make assessment more complex.

The Modified Checklist for Autism in Toddlers, Revised with Follow-Up (M-CHAT-R/F; Robins, Fein, & Barton, 2009) is a screening tool completed by parents of children ages 16–30 months to assess risk specifically for ASD. This tool is most often used by those working in pediatric health care settings and can be administered to parents at the child's medical well-child visits. Children receiving at-risk scores after follow-up had a 47.5% risk of later being diagnosed with an ASD (95% confidence interval) and a 94.6% risk of any developmental delay or concern (95% confidence interval). The total score has been found to be more effective in determining risk than alternative scores when screening for ASD (Robins et al., 2014).

Social, Emotional, and Behavioral Scales as Diagnostic/Evaluation Tools

The following sections overview several rating scales that may be used as part of a more comprehensive child assessment. The scales selected for this section have evidenced good psychometric properties when assessing young children for overall social, emotional, and behavioral functioning.

Broadband Rating Scales

One advantage of using broadband rating scales as an initial measure in an assessment is that they can identify concerns across internalizing and externalizing domains. If these measures reveal clinically significant areas of concern, a more comprehensive assessment and/or intervention of the problem area may then be warranted.

BEHAVIOR ASSESSMENT SYSTEM FOR CHILDREN

The Behavior Assessment System for Children, Third Edition (BASC-3; Reynolds & Kamphaus, 2015), is a comprehensive rating-scale system designed to assess problem behaviors in children and adolescents. The BASC includes both parent and teacher scales, with separate forms available to assess children in three age groups: 2–5, 6–11, and 12–21. The Parent Rating Scale—Preschool version (PRS-P; normed on 600 children) and the Teacher Rating Scale—Preschool version (TRS-P; normed on 500 children) are highlighted here (see Table 2.3). In addition, there is a Parenting Relationship Questionnaire—Preschool Version (BASC-3 PRQ) that is available to assess such areas as Attachment, Discipline, Involvement, Parenting Confidence, and Relational Frustration.

The PRS-P contains 139 items, and the TRS-P contains 105 items. All items are rated as occurring *never, sometimes, often,* or *almost always*. Both scales have empirically derived composite scores and subscale scores that address a wide array of emotional and behavioral problems, including both internalizing and externalizing disorders.

Reliability and validity are moderate to strong, as reported in the BASC-3 manual (Reynolds & Kamphaus, 2015). Coefficient alpha reliabilities are similar across the general and clinical samples, ranging from .77 to .93. On the BASC-3, test–retest reliabilities ranged between .79 and .94 across raters on the preschool forms and interrater reliabilities ranged between .56 (Internalizing Composite) to .83 (Adaptive Composite). Because this scale is so new, little outside research is available on this measure. However, research on the BASC-2 conducted by Myers, Bour, Sidebottom, Murphy, and Hakman (2010) found that the BASC-2 PRS-P was a reliable measure of hyperactive and attentional problems in

TABLE 2.3. BASC-3 PRS-P and TRS-P Scales

Externalizing Problems	Other Problems
Hyperactivity	Atypicality
Aggression	Withdrawal
	Attention Problems
Internalizing Problems	
Anxiety	Behavioral Symptoms Index
Depression	
Somatization	Adaptive Skills
	Adaptability
	Social Skills
	Functional Communication of Daily Living[a]

[a]Located only in Parent Version.

young children, consistently providing an overall composite level of problem behaviors, and thereby having fairly good classification abilities. However, correlations between internalizing subscales were lower, which is consistent with what the BASC-3 manual reports for the latest version.

New to the BASC-3 are probability indices geared toward determining the probability that a child will continue to have challenges in specific areas. On the BASC-3 PRS-P and TRS-P these indices include a General Clinical Probability Index, measuring a variety of general challenges in behavior and social functioning, and a Functional Impairment Index, measuring interactions with others, mood, or performing age appropriate tasks. In addition to measuring broad behavioral constructs such as hyperactivity, social skills, and adaptive functioning, the BASC-3 includes a Developmental Social Disorders (DSD) content scale that evaluates the presence of behaviors, such as self-stimulation and withdrawal and poor socialization, that are commonly associated with ASD. No outside research to date has been completed on the BASC-3 DSD scales. However, in a study of the BASC-2 DSD scale conducted by Bradstreet, Juechter, Kamphaus, Kerns, and Robins (2016), adequate sensitivity and specificity values were found when classifying children with ASD from those without any diagnoses, but not when differentiating between children with ASD and those with other diagnoses. Lane, Paynter, and Sharman (2013) conclude that parent raters of children with ASD tend to rate greater impairment in their child's adaptive behaviors on the BASC-2 than teachers do. They recommend, therefore, when using the BASC-2 for assessing challenging behaviors for children with ASD that both parent and teacher perspectives be obtained, if available.

CHILD BEHAVIOR CHECKLIST AND TEACHER'S REPORT FORM

The CBCL (Achenbach & Rescorla, 2001) is a widely used measure for the assessment of problem behaviors in children. This scale and its school-version counterpart, the Teacher's Report Form (TRF; Achenbach & Rescorla, 2001), are often used as broad-band measures to determine areas in which children are exhibiting problem behaviors. Normative data are available for children ages 6–18 on the CBCL and the TRF. The CBCL and TRF are among the most widely used rating scales designed for parents and caregivers to assess problem behaviors of children. These scales have been found to be psychometrically sound, with good reliability and validity (Achenbach & Rescorla, 2001). Downward extensions of the CBCL and TRF have been developed specifically for preschool-age children. These include the Child Behavior Checklist for Ages 1.5–5 and the Caregiver–Teacher Report Form for Ages1.5–5 (CBCL 1.5–5 and C-TRF; Achenbach & Rescorla, 2000). The CBCL 1.5–5 (normed on 700 children) and C-TRF 1.5–5 (normed on 1,192 children) both have 99 items that are geared more specifically to reflect problem behaviors toddlers and preschoolers tend to exhibit. All items are rated on a 3-point scale: *not true, somewhat or sometimes true,* and *very true* or *often true*. The CBCL 1.5–5 and C-TRF 1.5–5 have identical subscales, with the exception of the Sleep Problems subscale, which is only on the CBCL 1.5–5 (see Table 2.4). In addition to the syndrome scales, there are three composite scores (Internalizing, Externalizing, and Total Problems) as well as DSM-oriented scales, which include items that were rated by psychologists and psychiatrists as being consistent

TABLE 2.4. CBCL and C-TRF 1½–5 Scales

Total Problems	DSM-Oriented Scales
Internalizing Problems	Depressive Problems
Externalizing Problems	Anxiety Problems
	Autism Spectrum problems
Emotionally Reactive	Attention-Deficit/Hyperactivity Problems
Anxious/Depressed	Oppositional Defiant Problems
Somatic Complaints	
Withdrawn	
Attention Problems	
Aggressive Behavior	
Sleep Problems (CBCL only)	

with DSM-5 diagnostic categories. These DSM-oriented scales include Affective Problems, Anxiety Problems, Autism Spectrum Problems, Attention-Deficit/Hyperactivity Problems, and Oppositional Defiant Problems. The CBCL 1.5–5 also includes a Language Development Survey (LDS) to aid in the identification of language delays. The CBCL is available in multiple languages, as is a Multicultural Supplement to the manual that incorporates data obtained with the CBCL 1.5–5 scales on samples of children living in different cultural societies and geographic areas (Achenbach & Rescorla, 2009).

According to the manual, both the CBCL and C-TRF 1.5–5 have strong psychometric properties, and supporting research suggests adequate reliability and validity, including factorial validity (Achenbach & Rescorla, 2000; Pandolfi, Magyar, & Dill, 2009; Tan, Dedrick, & Marfo, 2006). Cross-informant ratings across scales were moderate (.61 between home raters, .65 between school raters, and .40 between home and school raters), whereas test–retest reliability was high (r = .80s–.90s for most scales; Achenbach & Rescorla, 2000). In addition, the CBCL 1.5–5 has been shown to be effective in diagnosing emotional and behavioral problems in young children with ASD when used in conjunction with other clinical data (Pandolfi et al., 2009).

CONNERS RATING SCALES

The Conners Rating Scales, currently in their third edition (Conners-3; Conners, 2008), have been used for years to detect problem behaviors in children and adolescents. The Conners-3 long form includes screener items for depression and anxiety, in addition to assessment of attentional and behavioral issues. The short form can also be used as a screener if the rater is limited on time (Connors, 2008). A new addition to the Conners assessments is the Conners Early Childhood (Conners EC; Conners, 2009). The Conners EC assesses behavioral, social, and emotional problems for young children ages 2–6, along with measuring whether or not the child is appropriately meeting major developmental milestones (Adaptive Skills, Communication, Motor Skills, Play, and Pre-Academic/Cognitive; see Table 2.5). It has a multi-informant format (parent/guardian, teacher, and childcare provider), allowing for easy comparison of scores across raters. Parents, teachers, and childcare providers are asked to consider the child's behaviors during the past month and rate their occurrence on a 4-point

TABLE 2.5. Conners Early Childhood Rating Scales

Behavior Scales	Developmental Milestone Scales
Inattention/Hyperactivity	Adaptive Skills
Defiant/Aggressive behaviors	Communication
Social functioning/atypical behaviors	Motor Skills
Anxiety	Play
Mood and affect	Pre-Academic/Cognitive
Physical symptoms	
	Oppositional
	Cognitive Problems/Inattention
	Hyperactivity
	ADHD Index

scale (*not at all true, just a little true, pretty much true,* or *very much true*). In addition, just like the version for older children, it has full-length and short forms. The Conners EC has excellent reliability and validity, according to the manual, though the validity information is primarily extracted from the other, more extensively validated Conners measures. High levels of internal consistency (.86–.93) and test–retest reliability (.87–.95) were found with the Conners EC, with interrater correlations among parents being a bit lower (.72–.84; Conners, 2009).

PRESCHOOL AND KINDERGARTEN BEHAVIOR SCALES

The Preschool and Kindergarten Behavior Scales—Second Edition (PKBS-2; Merrell, 2003) is a 76-item behavior rating scale that measures social skills and social–emotional problem behaviors in children ages 3–6. This instrument can be completed by parents, teachers, daycare providers, or others who are familiar with the child's behavior. The PKBS-2 items were designed specifically to reflect the unique social and behavioral aspects of the preschool and kindergarten developmental period. The items on the PKBS-2 comprise two separate scales: a 34-item Social Skills Scale and a 42-item Problem Behavior Scale. The subscales on the Social Skills Scale include Social Cooperation, Social Interaction, and Social Independence. The Problem Behavior Scale assesses both externalizing and internalizing problems, with five supplementary problem behavior subscales. The PKBS-2 is a useful tool for assessing general problem behaviors and social skills in young children, particularly those exhibiting the typical problems seen in daycare, preschool, and other childcare settings. For assessing children with severe problem behaviors of lower frequency, such as those exhibited by children in clinical settings, a scale such as the CBCL, Conners, or BASC may be more appropriate. The PKBS-2 was developed with a national normative sample of 3,317 children and has good psychometric properties, including adequate reliability and validity (Merrell, 2003). The original version of the PKBS, when used as a screener for preschool children with and without developmental delays, was found to adequately identify social deficits and problem behaviors, with the children in the comparison group having statistically significantly fewer deficits and behaviors than those children who were delayed developmentally (Merrell & Holland, 1997). These findings have not been replicated with the second edition.

Narrow-Band Rating Scales

The rating scales included in this section measure specific areas of social, behavioral, and emotional functioning, as opposed to the broad-band scales that give an overview of the child's functioning in multiple areas. These scales may be used as either screeners or as a part of a more in-depth assessment in the areas of social, behavioral, and emotional health. As with broad-band scales, narrow-band scales should be used as only one piece of information in a thorough assessment. Scales for assessing behavior challenges, social development, emotional functioning, ADHD, and ASD are overviewed. Rating scales for ASD can be used in conjunction with interviews, medical evaluations, and standardized observations, such as the Autism Diagnostic Observation Schedule, Second Edition (ADOS-2; Lord, Rutter, DiLavore, Gotham, & Bishop, 2012), as the best practice in identifying children with this disorder.

EYBERG CHILD BEHAVIOR INVENTORY

The Eyberg Child Behavior Inventory (ECBI; Eyberg & Pincus, 1999) is a parent rating scale used with children ages 2–16 to assess the frequency and severity of disruptive behaviors. The items reflect common behavior problems seen in children. Parents are asked to rate each item on a 7-point scale to indicate how often each behavior occurs. They also indicate with a "yes" or "no" rating whether each behavior is a problem for them. The ratings of behavior frequency are summed to create an Intensity Score, and the "yes" responses are summed to create a Problem Score. Sometimes discrepancies can exist between the Intensity Score and the Problem Score. A high Problem Score and a low Intensity Score may indicate that the parent/caregiver has a low tolerance for normal child misbehavior, may have unrealistic expectations of the child, or may be overwhelmed by childrearing. Conversely, if the Intensity Score is high and the Problem Score is low, the parenting style may be overly permissive. In either case, the clinician should investigate possible reasons for the discrepancy, as this can help direct intervention approaches.

The ECBI is simple and quick to use and is helpful in identifying children with externalizing behaviors (Weis, Lovejoy, & Lundahl, 2005). The scale has been found to have adequate reliability and validity (Funderburk, Eyberg, Rich, & Behar, 2003; Gross et al., 2007), though due to a more limited standardization sample ($n = 798$) and the fact that not all ages were represented in the sample, some caution is recommended. The ECBI has been found to be accurate in screening for conduct problems (Levitt, Saka, Romanelli, & Hoagwood, 2007). A teacher version of this instrument (the Sutter–Eyberg Student Behavior Inventory [SESBI]; Eyberg & Pincus, 1999) contains items rated in the same manner as those on the ECBI, but these items have been reworded so that they are more appropriate for a school setting.

AGES AND STAGES QUESTIONNAIRES: SOCIAL–EMOTIONAL

The Ages and Stages Questionnaire: Social–Emotional (ASQ:SE-2; Squires, Bricker, & Twombly, 2015) is a rating instrument to be completed by parents of children ages 2 months to 5 years of age for both screening and assessment purposes. This low-cost and simple screening instrument evaluates social and emotional competencies and problems of children at 9 different age levels (2, 6, 12, 18, 24, 30, 36, 48, and 60 months). The items for each age-level questionnaire were created to be developmentally specific, measuring seven behavioral areas: Self-Regulation, Compliance, Social-Communication, Adaptive Functioning, Autonomy, Affect, and Interaction with People. The technical manual reports good psychometric properties, including validity and reliability, with test–retest reliability at 89% (Squires et al., 2015). Because this scale has been recently revised, few independent studies have been conducted. Some evidence suggests that the former version, the ASQ:SE, has adequate psychometric properties when used cross-culturally (Heo & Squires, 2012). However, at very young ages the ASQ:SE had been found to be less valid in the detection of psychosocial problems, with alphas from .46 at 6 months to .66 at 14 months (de Wolff, Theunissen, Vogels, & Reijneveld, 2013). More research is necessary to investigate these technical properties of the ASQ:SE2.

DEVEREUX EARLY CHILDHOOD ASSESSMENT

The Devereux Early Childhood Assessment for Preschoolers, Second Edition (DECA-P2; LeBuffe & Naglieri, 2012), is a strengths-based, nationally standardized measure to assess the social and emotional health of children ages 3–5. Aimed at promoting resiliency, the testing kit comes with rating forms and a guide for parents and teachers highlighting research-based strategies and tips to enhance children's social and emotional health, as well as tips for improving the overall quality of preschool programs. Little external data are currently available on its psychometric properties; however, the manual claims adequate reliability and validity (LeBuffe & Naglieri, 2012). Research on the first version of the DECA found strong support for its overall validity (Nickerson & Fishman, 2009) and reliability for examining social–emotional skills and behavioral concerns for preschoolers, including those from culturally diverse or impoverished backgrounds (Crane, Mincic, & Winsler, 2011).

SOCIAL SKILLS IMPROVEMENT SYSTEM RATING SCALES

The Social Skills Improvement System Rating Scales (SSIS-RS; Gresham & Elliott, 2008) is a comprehensive social skills assessment system that includes parent and teacher rating forms for use with children ages 3–18. The SSIS-RS includes a variety of age ranges and assessment instruments; however, only the preschool forms are reviewed here. Good psychometric properties of the SSIS-RS have been found (Frey, Elliott, & Gresham, 2011; Gresham & Elliott, 2008). Both parent and teacher versions include empirically derived subscales, making it easy for cross-comparison of scores. Subscales include Social Skills (Communication, Cooperation, Assertion, Responsibility, Empathy, Engagement, and Self-Control), Competing Problem Behaviors (Externalizing, Bullying, Hyperactivity/Inattention, Internalizing, and Autism Spectrum) and Academic Competence (Reading Achievement, Math Achievement, and Motivation to Learn). Standardization was based on a nationwide sample matched to the U.S. population estimates for race, region, and SES. Gresham, Elliott, Cook, Vance, and Kettler (2010) investigated agreement across informants for problem behaviors and social skills and found them to be weak to moderate (0.15–0.38), with convergent validity coefficients stronger than discriminant validity correlations. High internal consistency and validity have been found across raters when using the SSIS in elementary and secondary populations (Gresham, Elliott, Vance, & Cook, 2011).

ATTENTION DEFICIT DISORDERS EVALUATION SCALE

The Attention Deficit Disorders Evaluation Scale—Fourth Edition (ADDES-4; McCarney & Arthaud, 2013a, 2013b) and the Early Childhood Attention Deficit Disorders Evaluation Scale (ECADDES; McCarney, 1995a, 1995b) are behavior rating scales designed to assess ADHD symptoms. To date, there has been no update on the ECADDES.

The ADDES-4 measures ADHD symptoms in childhood and adolescent populations (ages 4–18). The ADDES-4 has a home (46 items) and a school (60 items) version, both of which contain Inattentive and Hyperactive–Impulsive subscales. The items from these two scales are summed to create a total score. Parents and teachers rate the child on a 5-point Likert-based scale, ranging from 0 ("Does Not Engage in the Behavior") to 5 ("Behavior Occurs One to Several Times per Hour"). The reliability and validity of both the home and school ADDES-3 versions are adequate, including internal consistency at .99 for the total scale, test–retest reliabilities at or above .91, and interrater reliability of the subscales ranging between .85 and .90, as reported in the manuals.

The ECADDES (McCarney, 1995a, 1995b) also has a home (50 items) and school (56 items) version and was designed specifically to assess ADHD symptoms in young children ages 2–6. The format of the scale resembles that of the older-age version, in which parents and teachers rate the child on a 5-point Likert-based scale. The ECADDES also contains two subscales, Inattentive and Hyperactive–Impulsive, in addition to a Total Score. Overall there appears to be adequate technical support for the scale included in the manual, with an internal consistency at .99 for the total scale and test–retest reliabilities exceeding .89 (McCarney, 1995a, 1995b), although there is a great deal of overlap between the two subscales, as evidenced by the factor analysis reported in the manual.

ADHD RATING SCALE–5

The ADHD Rating Scale–5 (DuPaul, Power, Anastopoulos, & Reid, 2016) is an 18-item rating scale based on DSM-5 criteria for ADHD. Separate forms and norms for home and school raters are available for both the child version (ages 5–10) and the adolescent version (ages 11–17). The ADHD Rating Scale–5 contains both an Inattention Scale and a Hyperactivity–Impulsivity Scale, which are summed to obtain a Total Score. The scale was normed on 2,069 parent ratings and 1,070 teacher ratings of children between the ages of 5 and 18. The authors of the ADHD Rating Scale–5 report good to adequate test–retest reliability, ranging between .80 and .93 across Total Score and Inattention and Hyperactivity subscales for both parent and teachers, although teacher ratings had greater stability. Coefficients were lower for impairment ratings across parent and teacher sources (ranging between .62 and 90). Internal consistency reliability was found to be high across all subscales on both versions. Adequate predictive ability when using combined parent and teacher ratings was evident, although it was lower if just parent ratings were used. Because the ADHD Rating Scale–5 is so recently developed, independent research evaluating this scale is limited. However, research on the prior ADHD Rating Scale–IV was found to have acceptable psychometric properties, including internal consistency, factor structure, convergent and divergent validity, discriminant validity, and responsiveness (Zhang, Faries, Vowles, & Michelson, 2005).

A preschool version of the ADHD Rating Scale–IV (Dupaul, Power, Anastopoulos, & Reid, 1998), is available, although more research needs to be conducted in order to further validate its psychometric properties. The scale is a modified version of the prior form, with the original 18 items adjusted to account for the developmental level of preschool children. Parent ratings were collected on 902 children and teacher ratings were collected on 977 children. Preliminary data suggest good internal consistency, test–retest reliability, and concurrent validity (McGoey, DuPaul, Haley, & Shelton, 2007).

CHILDHOOD AUTISM RATING SCALE

The Childhood Autism Rating Scale—Second Edition (CARS-2; Schopler, Van Bourgondien, Wellman, & Love, 2010) was developed to help screen for and identify children ages 2 and older with ASD and to distinguish them from children with developmental delays who do not have ASD. Ratings on the CARS are intended to be completed on the basis of direct behavioral observations of the child. The ratings are based on frequency of behaviors, as well as behavior intensity, peculiarity, and duration. The items included on the CARS-2 are similar to those on the original version, with high agreement found between the original CARS items and DSM-IV criteria, evidencing low false positives (Rellini, Tortolani, Trillo, Carbone, & Montecchi, 2004). The CARS-2 is purported to be more responsive to individuals on the high-functioning end of the autism spectrum (those with average or higher IQ scores, better verbal skills, and more subtle social and behavioral deficits). The Questionnaire for Parents or Caregivers, an unscored scale that can be used to gather information for making Standard and High Functioning ratings, is also available. The CARS-2 manual touts good technical properties, including reliability and validity (Schopler et al., 2010), with external research supporting its use as a well-validated and reliable screener (Vaughan, 2011).

GILLIAM AUTISM RATING SCALE

The Gilliam Autism Rating Scale—Third Edition (GARS-3; Gilliam, 2013) is a behavior rating scale to be used by teachers, parents, and professionals in screening for and helping to identify ASD in individuals ages 3–22. The 56 items are based on definitions of ASD provided by DSM-5 and the Autism Society of America. The items are grouped into six subscales that reflect the core symptoms of ASD: Restrictive/Repetitive Behaviors, Social Interaction, Social Communication, Emotional Responses, Cognitive Style, and Maladaptive Speech. The test is designed both as a screener, assessment measure and a progress monitoring tool, as noted by the authors. The test manual includes data that show adequate evidence of reliability and validity (Gilliam, 2013). External research suggested that the previous version, GARS-2, may have underestimated the presence of autism symptoms, evidencing low diagnostic validity (Norris & Lecavalier, 2010; Pandolfi et al., 2009). However, more research is needed on the GARS-3 to determine diagnostic validity with this version.

Social, Emotional, and Behavioral Scales as Progress Monitoring Tools

Not only do these previous rating scales demonstrate usefulness as screeners and primary assessment tools, they have also been found to have utility as progress monitoring tools. Most scales can be used, and often are, as pre–post measures to determine treatment effectiveness, whereby the screener becomes the outcome measure (Hess, Pejic, & Castejon, 2014). When using cognitive-behavioral interventions, for example, it is commonplace to use a pre–post rating scale to screen for initial areas of concern and to evaluate treatment outcomes (Plotts & Lasser, 2013). In addition, some rating scales, which we discuss briefly next, have specifically been designed as monitoring tools.

The Connors-3 (Connors, 2008) touts efficacy as an intervention tool, including a four-step guide for developing and monitoring treatment effectiveness (Step 1: Identify and prioritize treatment targets; Step 2: Create specific treatment goals; Step 3: Develop individualized strategies to reach each goal; Step 4: Tracking progress; regularly reviewing and revising goals). According to the author, the Connors scales can be used before, during, and after intervention has been implemented in order to track intervention efforts. The BASC-3 BESS (Kamphaus & Reynolds, 2015) was developed for use as a screener and progress monitoring tool. It takes only 5–10 minutes to complete and requires no formal training for raters, allowing for progress monitoring from multiple sources. In addition, the BASC-3 Flex Monitor (Kamphaus & Reynolds, 2015) is an Internet- based tool that can be used to track and monitor the effect of a behavioral intervention implemented by a professional (e.g., school psychologist) in the school setting. It provides a bank of behaviorally or emotionally based items that can be selected to create a customized form that can both monitor progress and enable scores to be compared to a nationally representative population sample. Although these measures are designed for progress monitoring purposes, to date little independent research is available as to their efficacy.

DIRECT OBSERVATION

Observation is one of the most valuable tools in the assessment of young children. Because young children communicate more through behavior than through words, observation serves as a cornerstone of psychological assessment when evaluating the social, emotional, and behavioral functioning of this age group. In order to observe behavior in a manner that leads to useful information, the "target behavior," or the behavior to be evaluated, must be identified prior to the observation period. Broad constructs—such as "aggressive," "hyperactive," "poor social skills," "anxious," and "friendly"—must be operationally defined so that the observer and others have a clear understanding of what constitutes the specific behaviors (Kazdin, 2012). For example, if a child is described by his or her preschool teacher as being "hyper" in the classroom, the observer must interview the teacher more thoroughly to understand what behaviors specifically mean "hyper" to that teacher. Once the observer gathers specific descriptors of that behavior from the teacher (e.g., "out of seat during seat time," "climbing on chairs," "fidgeting in seat," "throwing classroom materials"), then the observer can track those behaviors more precisely and accurately.

Observations as Screeners

Observations of problem behavior in the home or school setting are usually what brings awareness to the fact that there is a concern regarding the child. Parents or other key adults in the child's life notice that there may be a problem behavior or other symptom of concern. The child's behavior may be informally compared to the other children living in the home or attending school or daycare to determine if these behaviors are out of proportion to the demands and expectations of the setting. These observations are then shared with key adults in the child's life, including parents, teachers, and other caregivers. A common first step in screening for the problem behavior is to begin to observe and track those times when the behavior occurs, identifying problematic and nonproblematic activities and times of day (Wacker, Cooper, Peck, Derby, & Berg, 1999). Some form of intervention may be implemented at this point (e.g., redirection, reinforcement, reassurance) to try and ameliorate the behavior. If the child does not respond to the initial interventions, or if the problem behavior is more complicated or worsens, an informal, structured observation method, such as the SSBD (Walker, Severson, & Feil, 2014; refer to the section "Social, Emotional, and Behavioral Scales as Screeners"), may be used to further assess the problem.

Observations as Diagnostic/Evaluation Tools

The following sections overview the use of both structured and unstructured observations when used in the context of an assessment of a child.

Informal, Structured Observations

Structured observations, including formal and informal coding systems, can be helpful in identifying and tracking problem behaviors in the school, home, or daycare setting. For the purposes of this book, *informal observation* means that a child was not observed through a formal, published observational system, although coding charts or other aids may have been used. Given that the behaviors of young children are often variable for different settings, times, and individuals, the observer should watch the child at different times of the day and while the child is engaged in different activities. The observer should attempt to see the child as many times as necessary to observe a representative range of behaviors and affective states. In addition, the child should be observed interacting with different peers and/or adults across multiple settings (Benham, 2000).

Naturalistic observations—observing the child in his or her natural environment, such as at school or daycare—offer advantages over other observational methods. In naturalistic observations the child is able to engage in normal daily activities in which his or her targeted behaviors naturally occur. Naturalistic observations also provide the observer with the opportunity to determine *antecedents* (what happens right before the behavior occurs) and *consequences* (what happens right after the behavior occurs) that may be maintaining the child's behaviors (see the "Functional Assessment" section later in this chapter). During this type of observation, it is important that the observer remain as unobtrusive as possible so that the child is not influenced by his or her presence (Merrell, 2008a).

In addition to observing the child's behavior, it is important to pay attention to setting variables that may be related to the behaviors of concern. Important elements of the setting to observe include: (1) the adult's interactions with the children, (2) possible distractions or outside noises, and (3) the physical setting the child is in, including the amount of space available to the child, the child's proximity to other children throughout the day, and the materials available in the setting.

After completing the observation, the observer should talk with the teacher/daycare worker about his or her perceptions of the child's behaviors during the observation period. In particular, the observer should ask the teacher/daycare worker if the behaviors exhibited by the child during the observation are representative of his or her usual behaviors in that setting. The observer also should note whether the teacher/daycare provider seems to be especially lenient or critical of the child and if his or her observations match the observer's.

DATA RECORDING METHODS

A variety of recording methods have been identified and summarized (Kazdin, 2012; Merrell, 2008a). Here we review those most likely to be used when observing young children. A summary of these selected techniques is provided in Table 2.6. To illustrate each of these techniques, the example of a child screaming in class (e.g., raising his or her voice above peers and/or what is expected in that particular classroom setting) is used.

Using the *event* or *frequency recording* procedure, the observer records the number of times a specific behavior occurs over the length of the observation—in our example, the number of times the child screams in class during a 20-minute observation session. The advantages of this procedure are that it is easy to use (the observer makes checkmarks or uses a simple counter to track when the behavior occurs), and it can be used to determine antecedents and consequences of the child's behavior (see the upcoming "Functional Assessment" section). A disadvantage of this procedure is that it cannot easily be used with behaviors that do not have a clear beginning and end (e.g., fidgeting could be difficult to record with this technique, as it often does not have a clear beginning or end).

Using the *duration recording* procedure, the observer records the length of time a behavior occurs. Both total duration (total time the child screamed during the observation period; e.g., 6 of the 20 minutes) and duration per event (the length of time for each time the child screamed; e.g., one scream that was 1 minute, and another that was 5 minutes) can be calculated. The duration recording procedure has the advantage of being simple to conduct using a wall clock or stopwatch, although it is not helpful for behaviors without a clear beginning or end (e.g., fidgeting in seat) and may be less useful for behaviors that last only a short time.

TABLE 2.6. Observation Coding Procedures

Technique	Definition	Example
Event/frequency recording	Record the number of times the specific behavior occurs over length of the observation	Record number of times the child screams
Duration recording	Record the length of time a behavior occurs	Record length of time the child screams
Interval recording		
Partial-interval recording	Record the behavior if it occurred at any point during the interval	Record screaming if the child screams at any time during the interval
Whole-interval recording	Record the behavior only if it occurred during the entire interval	Record screaming only if the child screams throughout the entire interval
Momentary time sampling	Record the behavior at exact intervals in time	Look at child every 15 seconds; if the child is screaming at that instant, record as screaming

An observer using the *interval recording* procedure records the presence or absence of a given response within a certain time interval. In our example, the 20-minute observational period would be divided into short intervals of, perhaps, 30 seconds each, and the behavior would be recorded if the child screams (1) at any time during the interval (*partial-interval recording*) or (2) during the entire interval (*whole-interval recording*). The Interval recording procedure is a good choice for behaviors that are not clearly discrete or for behaviors that occur at a moderate but steady rate (e.g., thumb sucking). A disadvantage is that it requires the observer's complete attention to the child. Therefore, the procedure is more difficult to use reliably and would be particularly difficult for a teacher or other staff member to do if he or she also had to attend to other matters in the classroom. Figure 2.1 presents an example of a completed interval recording form, with a blank copy provided in Form 2.3.

The *momentary time sampling* procedure is a type of interval recording, but it does not require the observer to monitor the whole interval. Using this procedure, the observer divides the observation session into equal intervals, as with the interval recording methods. However, the behavior would be counted as occurring only if it is emitted at the moment the interval terminates. For example, with a 15-second interval, the behavior would be recorded as occurring or not occurring once every 15 seconds. In our example, the child would be recorded as screaming in class only if the behavior occurred at the moment the interval (e.g., 15-second period) ended. This technique requires only one observation per interval and is useful for behaviors that are apt to persist. However, some important, lower-frequency behaviors may be missed when using this procedure.

Once the observer has completed his or her observations of the child, it is important to evaluate the significance of the data. Obviously, if the child's behaviors are dangerous

Behavior or Interval Recording Form

Child's name: Jane Smith　　　　　　　　　　　　　　Date: August 7th
Observer: Joe Jones　　　　　　　　　Location observed: Kindergarten
Activity observed: Story Time and Rug Time　　Start/stop time: 9:30–9:45 A.M.
Interval length/type: 30 seconds/partial interval recording

Interval	Screaming	Out of area	Hitting others
1	X		
2		X	X
3		X	
4	X		
5	X		
6			
7			
8			
9		X	
10		X	
11			
12			
13			
14			
15	X		X
16			
17			
18			
19			
20		X	
21		X	
22	X	X	
23			
24			
25			
26	X		
27	X		
28			
29			
30		X	

TOTAL _____

FIGURE 2.1. Example of a completed interval recording form.

or significantly disruptive, they would be considered problematic and would require some form of immediate intervention. However, because other behaviors, such as difficulty staying seated or fidgeting, are common among preschoolers and kindergartners, the observer should determine if these behaviors are atypical in comparison to his or her peers or problematic given the requirements of the setting in which the child was observed. To help determine the severity of a child's behaviors in relation to that of his or her peers, the observer should also record the same behaviors of several randomly selected peers from the child's class, daycare, or other setting. The observer could choose to rotate observing different children over the interval period, could observe all children at once, or could observe children at different times.

Informal Observations by Parents or Teachers

Often a clinician will ask parents or teachers to keep track of behavior problems they are seeing in the home or classroom. These observations may be somewhat structured (e.g., a recording form is used) but are often less structured than those the clinician would do him- or herself. These observations can be particularly helpful in the home setting. Rarely does a clinician go into the home to observe behaviors, primarily due to logistics and also because of obtrusiveness and reactivity toward having the observer in the home (Merrell, 2008a). Having a parent track behaviors in the home can provide valuable information about how often the behaviors of concern are occurring in this setting. When asking parents or teachers to track behaviors, a simple frequency count method is typically used. Form 2.4 is an example of a "behavior log" that could be used by parents to track the occurrence of some of the more common disruptive behaviors seen in the home environment. This method can be useful both for an initial assessment of the problematic behavior and also for progress monitoring (e.g., if fewer behaviors are noted over the course of treatment, this could indicate the effectiveness of that intervention).

Functional Assessment

A functional assessment of behavior, which typically includes observation as a key component, involves determining the "purpose" of the problem behavior in terms of what is reinforcing and maintaining it. By determining the function of a behavior and matching interventions to this function, the effectiveness of interventions should be increased. Researchers have noted that problem behaviors generally serve one of several functions: children receive social attention from peers or teachers (positive or negative); children are able to escape or avoid a task; sensory reinforcement is provided; or access to a tangible reinforcer is obtained (Gresham & Lambros, 1998; Steege & Watson, 2009). When assessing the child, the full range of these reinforcements must be considered, in addition to understanding that a single behavior may have multiple functions (Steege & Watson, 2009). Knowing the function of the behavior can help prevent the problem behavior from being inadvertently reinforced. For example, if a functional assessment determines that a child misbehaves to escape participating in story time, sending the child to time-out in this situation would not be appropriate and would likely reinforce the misbehavior because it allows the child to escape the story time. Instead, inappropriate behaviors can be ignored, and the child can be positively reinforced for engaging in story time.

Although observational methods are often used to obtain the information needed for a functional assessment, interviews with parents and teachers also help identify the antecedents and consequences of the behavior (e.g., ask the parent what he or she does after the child misbehaves), as can asking parents and teachers to use an ABC (antecedent–behavior–consequence) log (such as the one in Form 2.5) to record what happens before and after the problem behavior occurs. When conducting an observation to identify the possible function of a targeted behavior, the observer would document the antecedents of the misbehavior (e.g., screaming), or what happens right before the child begins to scream (e.g., the child is engaged in a solitary activity), as well as the consequences of the child's screaming (e.g., the child gets attention from the teacher and the screaming stops). In this example (assuming this pattern is consistent across time), it appears that the child's behavior is being maintained by attention, so the intervention should focus on decreasing attention for screaming and increasing attention for appropriate behaviors in this situation, such as making a request in a normal tone of voice or playing quietly with toys. Sometimes functional assessments are complicated by seemingly multiple explanations for a behavior. For example, the child who is screaming may be reinforced for this behavior both by the delivery of teacher attention and the escape from an aversive activity.

Functional assessment techniques are most frequently used to evaluate externalizing behavior problems. Such techniques may be less applicable for internalizing problems as identifying internal thoughts and feelings may be more difficult, particularly in young children. However, increasingly functional assessment techniques are being applied to internalizing problems. For example, school refusal and selective mutism often are maintained by environmental factors, and the use of functional assessment methods can be useful in identifying maintaining factors for these disorders (Kearney & Spear, 2013).

While functional assessment techniques can be valuable in identifying the direct environmental contingencies associated with a problem behavior, there are often less-proximal factors that should also be taken into account. For example, communication problems, family issues, modeling of inappropriate behaviors by others, and frustrations in the learning environment may also be additional confounding factors that contribute to a problematic behavior (Merrell, 2008a). Therefore, although functional assessment can be a valuable tool, particularly for understanding externalizing behaviors, it should be used as only one approach in the social, emotional, and behavioral assessment of the young child, and should occur within a multisetting, multimethod, multisource design whenever possible (Steege & Watson, 2009).

Formal Observations

Although there are numerous formal observational systems that provide information about children's behaviors in naturalistic settings (e.g., home, school, or daycare), few focus specifically on the young child. One measure that does include observations of preschool and kindergarten children is the Early Screening Project (ESP; Walker, Severson, & Feil, 1995). The ESP includes observations of young children's behaviors through its Social Behavior

Observations component. The ESP observations are designed to provide information on children's social behaviors and, in particular, children's social interactions with peers and adults. A duration recording procedure is used to record the amount of time the observed child is engaged in *prosocial behaviors,* such as playing well with others; *negative social behaviors,* such as verbal misbehaviors, disobeying rules, or throwing tantrums; or *nonsocial behavior,* such as solitary play. Normative data are available, enabling the observer to compare the child being observed with other children his or her age to determine if the problem behaviors are significant. In research studies, significant differences were found between children who did and did not exceed the ESP's normative referral criteria (Feil, Severson, & Walker, 1998).

In addition, the ADOS-2, frequently referred to as the "gold standard" for measuring autism spectrum behaviors in children, is a semistructured observational assessment measure of the communication, social interaction, and play behaviors of individuals suspected of having ASD or other pervasive developmental disorders. There are five modules included in the ADOS-2, each designed to assess children ages 12 months to adulthood, with differing developmental and language levels, from nonverbal to verbally fluent. The Toddler Module is designed specifically for children between ages 12 and 30 months who do not consistently use phrase speech. The examiner selects the module that is most appropriate for the child being assessed depending on the child's expressive language level and chronological age. Within each module are structured and semistructured activities and relevant behaviors that take approximately 40–60 minutes of total administration time to observe and code (Lord et al., 2012).

Observations as Progress Monitoring Tools

Observations are a commonly used tool to determine intervention effectiveness in the home or school setting. Checking with key adults in the child's life about their observations of how the child is improving can provide helpful information regarding the efficacy of the intervention. Adjustments to the interventions can then be made based on these observations.

Typically, in school settings, informal, structured observational measures are used. These often include daily charts, behavior logs, or home–school notes (see Chapter 6 for a discussion of a home–school note) that are examined daily or weekly to assess whether progress has been made in the targeted area of concern. In the home setting, behavior record cards (BRCs), or behavior logs, are commonly used by parents to monitor and record a child's progress in meeting behavioral goals (Nadler & Roberts, 2013; see Form 2.4). When using behavioral logs as progress monitoring tools, parents are taught to count their child's discrete problematic behaviors. Parents can also be encouraged to record their use of certain behavior management strategies, as record keeping can assist parents in becoming more mindful and accountable in consistently using effective behavior management strategies. Continued observations and check-ins with parents and teachers can ensure that the interventions continue to be successful. Once progress has been noted, or the goal has been reached, the interventions (and progress monitoring) can be phased out. If the problem behavior reoccurs, or worsens once the intervention has been phased out, these observations can inform practice and the interventions can be put back in place.

CHAPTER SUMMARY

The social and emotional assessment of young children is becoming a well-researched domain. Recent advancements have included the development of behavior rating scales designed specifically to assess the problem behaviors of young children and research on observational methods and interviewing techniques for use with the preschool- and kindergarten-age child. In general, the best practice for assessing the young child involves integrating information from various sources and measures in order to gain the most complete and accurate diagnostic picture of the child without stigmatizing or overpathologizing normal childhood behaviors.

FORM 2.1

Consent to Obtain or Release Confidential Information

Identified Client Information

Name: _____ Date: _____

AKA, if any: _____ Date of birth: _____

I hereby authorize and request the exchange of information and/or release of psychiatric and/or medical treatment and/or school records accumulated during the period beginning (month/day/year) _____ through (month/day/year) _____ between: _____.

Name of Releasing Individual, Title: _____

Agency, Address, City, State, Zip: _____

and

Name of Requesting Individual, Title: _____

Agency, Address, City, State, Zip: _____

For the purpose of:

Evaluation _____ Treatment Planning _____ Other (specify) _____

Information to be released/exchanged (specify):

_____
_____
_____
_____
_____
_____
_____

This consent can be revoked by the undersigned grantor at any time. If not revoked earlier, it shall terminate at the end of: ____ 3 months ____ 6 months ____ 12 months

Parent or Guardian Signature: _____ Date: _____

Witness Signature: _____ Date: _____

Professional Signature: _____ Date: _____

Date release mailed: _____ Date materials mailed: _____

From Melissa L. Holland, Jessica Malmberg, and Gretchen Gimpel Peacock. Copyright © 2017 The Guilford Press. Permission to photocopy this form is granted to purchasers of this book for personal use or use with individual students (see copyright page for details). Purchasers can download additional copies of this material (see box at the end of the table of contents).

FORM 2.2

Child Intake Form

Identified Client Information

Name: _____ Male/Female: _____ Date: _____

Date of birth: _____ Birthplace: _____ Age: _____

Address: _____ Ethnicity: _____

Siblings (names/ages and brief statement on the child's relationship with the person)

1. _____
2. _____
3. _____
4. _____
5. _____
6. _____

Person to call in emergency: _____

Telephone: H: _____ W: _____ Cell: _____

Parent(s) Information

Name(s): _____

Marital status (circle one):   Married   Divorced   Separated   Living together (never married)

Other (describe): _____

Past and present marriage(s) (years together, names and statement about the nature of the relationship(s), e.g., friendly, distant, physically/emotionally abusive, loving, hostile):

_____
_____
_____
_____

Education (highest level completed):

Mother _____ Father _____

(continued)

From Melissa L. Holland, Jessica Malmberg, and Gretchen Gimpel Peacock. Copyright © 2017 The Guilford Press. Permission to photocopy this form is granted to purchasers of this book for personal use or use with individual students (see copyright page for details). Purchasers can download additional copies of this material (see box at the end of the table of contents).

Child Intake Form (page 2 of 6)

Current employment:

Mother _____

Father _____

Home schedule of:

Mother _____

Father _____

Child's relationship with primary caregiver(s): _____

_____

Presenting Problem

Describe the problem behavior (Be as specific as you can: when did it start, how does it affect your child, how does it affect you?) _____

_____

_____

_____

_____

Estimate the severity of the above problem: Mild _____   Moderate _____   Severe _____

Very severe _____

What types of things have you tried that have been helpful in working with your child's problem?

_____

_____

What types of things have you tried that have not been helpful in working with your child's problem?

_____

_____

What is your primary goal for treatment? _____

_____

_____

Past and Current Treatment

Medical doctor(s) (name /phone): _____

_____

(continued)

Child Intake Form *(page 3 of 6)*

Past/present medical care (major medical problems, surgeries, accidents, falls, illness): _____

_____

_____

_____

Developmental history:

Were there any concerns during pregnancy or at birth (prenatal exposure to alcohol, illicit substances, or medications; pregnancy or birth complications; prematurity; extended hospital stay after birth; etc.)?

_____

_____

_____

At what age did your child first:

Sit alone _____   Crawl _____   Walk _____

Talk (one word) _____   Talk (sentences) _____

Does your child have any current health problems?   Yes _____   No _____

   If yes, what? _____

_____

What time does your child typically wake up? _____

What time does your children typically go to bed? _____

Note any sleeping difficulties your child has: _____

Is your child currently on any medications?   Yes _____   No _____

   If yes: Medication and dose: _____

_____

        For what was it prescribed? _____

        How long has child been on it? _____

        Who prescribed it? _____

        How does it affect behavior? _____

Any past medications: _____

Any hospitalizations?   Yes _____   No _____

   If yes, list: _____

Any ER episodes?   Yes _____   No _____

   If yes, list: _____

Any significant illnesses?   Yes _____   No _____

   If yes, list: _____

(continued)

Child Intake Form *(page 4 of 6)*

Any problems with:

Vision _____   Hearing _____   Speech _____

Any medical conditions that run in the family (e.g., diabetes, thyroid problems, cancer)?

Yes _____   No _____

If yes, describe: _____

_____

Any family history of mental illness, alcoholism or violence (including suicide, depression, hospitalizations in mental institutions, abuse, etc.): _____

_____

_____

_____

Any traumatic experiences for the child (child physical abuse, sexual abuse, neglect, family violence, natural disasters, or exposure to other traumatic events): _____

_____

_____

_____

Any concerns around cognitive or school performance, if applicable: _____

_____

_____

_____

Describe your child's adjustment and functioning at school/daycare, if applicable: _____

_____

_____

_____

_____

_____

Describe your child's temperament and information about your child's emotional development:

_____

_____

_____

_____

_____

(continued)

Child Intake Form *(page 5 of 6)*

Friendships, Community, and Spirituality (describe quality, frequency, activities, etc.):

_____
_____
_____
_____
_____
_____
_____
_____

Past/Present Psychotherapy for Child (specify month year(s) [beginning–end], estimated no. of sessions, name, degree, phone and address, initial reason for therapy, individual/family, medication, brief description of the relationship and how helpful it was, and how/why it ended):

1. _____
_____
_____

2. _____
_____
_____

3. USE THE OTHER SIDE OF THE PAGE FOR MORE INFORMATION ABOUT PSYCHOTHERAPISTS.

Has your child ever had a psychological assessment/evaluation (testing)?   Yes _____   No _____

If yes, who did the evaluation and what were the results? _____

_____
_____
_____
_____

Describe your child's childhood in general (relationships with parents, siblings, others, school, neighborhood, relocations): _____

_____
_____
_____
_____
_____

(continued)

Child Intake Form

What talents does your child have (things your child does best/strengths)? _____

_____
_____
_____
_____
_____
_____

Please write below any other information you would like me to know about your child and your situation.

FORM 2.3

Behavior or Interval Recording Form

Child's name: _____ Date: _____

Observer: _____ Location observed: _____

Activity observed: _____ Start/stop time: _____

Interval length/type: _____

Interval	Screaming	Out of area	Hitting others
1			
2			
3			
4			
5			
6			
7			
8			
9			
10			
11			
12			
13			
14			
15			
16			
17			
18			
19			
20			
21			
22			
23			
24			
25			
26			
27			
28			
29			
30			

TOTAL _____

From Melissa L. Holland, Jessica Malmberg, and Gretchen Gimpel Peacock. Copyright © 2017 The Guilford Press. Permission to photocopy this form is granted to purchasers of this book for personal use or use with individual students (see copyright page for details). Purchasers can download additional copies of this material (see box at the end of the table of contents).

FORM 2.4

Behavior Log

Child's name: _____

Behaviors should be recorded for at least 3 days during the time between dinnertime and bedtime. If no problem behaviors occurred on a certain day, make sure to indicate so by writing either a "0" or "no behaviors" in the appropriate column. In the "Hours" column, record the number of hours for which you recorded behaviors.

Behavior 1: _____ Examples of Behavior 1: _____
Behavior 2: _____ Examples of Behavior 2: _____
Behavior 3: _____ Examples of Behavior 3: _____

Date	Hours	Noncompliance	Physical Aggression	Temper Tantrums
Example: 1-1-15	Example: 3	Example: III	Example: 0	Example: IIII

From Melissa L. Holland, Jessica Malmberg, and Gretchen Gimpel Peacock. Copyright © 2017 The Guilford Press. Permission to photocopy this form is granted to purchasers of this book for personal use or use with individual students (see copyright page for details). Purchasers can download additional copies of this material (see box at the end of the table of contents).

FORM 2.5

ABC Log

Behavior: _____   Child's name: _____

Date	Time	Antecedent: What happened before behavior occurred (place, situation, others involved)?	Description of Behavior	Consequence: What happened after the behavior occurred?

From Melissa L. Holland, Jessica Malmberg, and Gretchen Gimpel Peacock. Copyright © 2017 The Guilford Press. Permission to photocopy this form is granted to purchasers of this book for personal use or use with individual students (see copyright page for details). Purchasers can download additional copies of this material (see box at the end of the table of contents).

CHAPTER 3

Treatment of Externalizing/Conduct Problems

Children who exhibit externalizing problems, such as noncompliance, tantrums, and aggression, comprise the largest source of referrals to children's mental health services in the United States (Wolff & Ollendick, 2010) and are the most common problems mentioned to pediatricians by parents during pediatric exams (Arndorfer, Allen, & Aliazireh, 1999; Cooper, Valleley, Polaha, Begeny, & Evans, 2006). However, many preschool- and kindergarten-age children with disruptive behaviors do not receive a formal DSM diagnosis. For some children these behaviors are a normal and temporary part of childhood; however, for other children, mild forms of disruptive behaviors function as developmental precursors to more significant and long-term problems. Children who continue to engage in persistent and high rates of disruptive behaviors may be assigned a DSM-5 diagnosis, such as ODD or CD. Although numerous predictors of problem behavior stability have been identified, those involving parenting and family factors have been the most heavily implicated (Duncombe, Havighurst, Holland, & Frankling, 2012; Parent et al., 2011; Patterson, 1982). For example, parenting behaviors that involve warmth and clear limit setting are more likely to lead to prosocial behaviors in children, whereas negative, inconsistent, and controlling parenting practices are more likely to lead to behavioral difficulties in children (Combs-Ronto, Olson, Lunkenheimer, & Sameroff, 2009; Scaramella & Leve, 2004).

Given the important mediating role of parenting in the development of childhood behavior problems, developing effective parenting interventions has received significant attention. Of the various interventions available, behavioral parent training is considered to be the current best practice in treating childhood conduct problems (Eyberg, Nelson, & Boggs, 2008). Overwhelming empirical research supports the use of behavioral parent training as an intervention for conduct problems in children of varying ages (Kaminski, Valle,

Filene, & Boyle, 2008; Michelson, Davenport, Dretzke, Barlow, & Day, 2013). A growing body of research supports the use of both individual and group parent training for families of preschool-age children who have disruptive behavior disorders (Maughn, Christiansen, Jensen, Olympia, & Clark, 2005; Michelson et al., 2013). Studies have also supported the use of behavioral parent training for young children with ADHD (Fabiano et al., 2009). In addition to improving parenting skills and reducing child disruptive behaviors, behavioral parent training programs may lead to other positive changes in parent and family functioning. For example, marital satisfaction scores and parental depressive symptoms have both shown significant improvements after participation in a parent training intervention (Barlow, Smailagic, Huband, Roloff, & Bennett, 2014; Ireland, Sanders, & Markie-Dadds, 2003).

This chapter begins with a discussion of factors to consider when initiating behavioral parent training and how the utilization of motivational interviewing techniques can assist with engaging families in treatment. Next, a comprehensive overview of behavioral parent training methods is provided, followed by a review of techniques that have been shown to enhance traditional behavioral parent training, including acceptance and commitment therapeutic concepts and child-focused social skills interventions. The chapter ends with a discussion of comprehensive early intervention and prevention programs that have been implemented in an attempt to alter the developmental trajectory of childhood conduct problems and ameliorate their long-term negative effects.

BEHAVIORAL PARENT TRAINING AS AN INTERVENTION FOR EXTERNALIZING PROBLEMS

Overview

Behavioral parent training programs are heavily rooted in behavioral theory, particularly reinforcement and punishment procedures based on operant conditioning (McMahon & Forehand, 2003), as well as social learning theory (Patterson, 1982). Operant conditioning procedures involve modifying antecedents (e.g., giving effective commands) and consistently applying effective consequences. Consequences that function as reinforcers will increase the likelihood of that behavior recurring, while punishers will decrease the future likelihood of that behavior recurring. For example, a child who offers to share his or her toys is praised; a child who grabs toys from a playmate is sent to time-out. These training programs assume that childhood conduct problems are generally related to interactions the child has with significant others, most often parents, who provide important cues and consequences for their child's behavior (Maughan et al., 2005). Thus, treatment gains are achieved by having parents consistently implement behavior modification strategies that they are taught in treatment sessions. Although the child is typically present in most sessions, the clinician does not work individually with the child because parents are considered the primary change agent.

Many prominent behavioral parent training programs now utilized are based on the operant two-stage parent-training model originally developed by Hanf (1969). The first stage emphasizes the development of parental attending skills and the use of differential attention to enhance the parent–child relationship and increase appropriate child behaviors. These skills are typically taught in a play-based context. After mastering the positively based behavior management skills, parents are taught to give effective commands and implement effective and consistent methods of discipline (typically time-out). Empirical evidence that guides the order in which treatment components are taught is limited. Although at least one study has indicated that order does not influence treatment outcomes (Eisdenstadt, Eyberg, McNeil, Newcomb, & Funderburk, 1993), most behavioral parent training programs continue to adhere to the original ordering of the Hanf model. Consideration of the coercive nature of the parent–child relationship found in this population provides theoretical support for teaching parents positive attending skills first, as these strategies will create a more positive social context and increase the likelihood of cooperative behavior (McMahon & Forehand, 2003).

Active training methods are used to teach parenting skills. Skills are first taught didactically. Handouts that describe the skills and their application are typically given to parents. Skills are then modeled in each session by the clinician. Most commonly this is done with the referred child present, although videotape models also may be used. For example, parents may be shown a videotape of one parent using the skills appropriately and another in which the skills are used inappropriately, so that they can observe the difference in the application of the skills, as well as the response of the child. Following the initial modeling, parents practice the skills in session and receive feedback from the clinician. Parents are also assigned homework in which they practice the new skills in the home environment and monitor their progress. The feedback or coaching aspect of behavioral parent training is critical in helping parents learn how to use the skills effectively. When learning a new skill, parents may apply the skills inappropriately, or they may have difficulties with their application that were not anticipated prior to practice. This observation and coaching can help address these problems as they arise. In addition, directly observing the parent using the skills assists the clinician in obtaining an accurate picture of the parent's skill level. When providing feedback, it is important that the clinician provide positive responses regarding what parents are doing well, in addition to providing corrective feedback.

Initial Considerations

Although behavioral parent training is often an effective intervention for families whose child displays disruptive and noncompliant behaviors, it is not appropriate for all families. Before deciding to use behavioral parent training, several factors must be considered. Often an initial consideration is the age of the child. Behavioral parent training programs can be used with parents of children of varying ages, although most programs are focused on parents of younger children, rather than adolescents. The preschool age range is typically considered the ideal time to intervene, as early childhood misbehaviors are less complex and more transitory in nature. Additionally, coercive parent–child interactions are less heavily ingrained, making these behaviors more malleable overall (Lavigne et al., 2010). Thus, many behavioral parent training programs are geared specifically toward the parenting of preschool and early elementary school-age children (Kaminski et al., 2008; McCart, Priester, Davies, & Azen, 2006).

Parent-related factors such as socioeconomic status, marital conflict, parental psychopathology, and psychosocial stressors (e.g., social isolation, single-parent household, limited family resources) have all been found to influence the effectiveness of behavioral parent training programs (Shelleby & Kolko, 2015). Thus, the clinician should ask about such factors as part of a comprehensive intake assessment (see Chapter 2). Providing additional services that more completely address identified needs may be appropriate for some families. For example, if a parent is experiencing depression or a couple is having marital problems, it would be appropriate to refer these families for additional therapeutic services. Conversely, behavioral parent training programs can be enhanced to include therapeutic components to address other family problems (e.g. parent enhancement therapy; Griest at al., 1982). Children may also require additional services, such as programs targeting academic difficulties or medications. Comprehensive services targeting both parent and child issues may address the needs of the family more completely and thereby increase the overall effectiveness of behavioral parent training (Barkley, 2013; Chacko, Wymbs, Chimiklis, Wymbs, & Pelham, 2012; Shaw et al., 2014).

Parental motivation also plays a key role in the outcome of behavioral parent training programs and should be assessed prior to beginning treatment. Some parents react negatively to parent training because of its focus on working with the parents rather than with the child. When parents initially seek services, they may expect the clinician to meet with their child individually, and they may not expect to be extensively involved in the intervention. Some parents may perceive behavioral parent training as an insult to their parenting skills. Other parents may simply not have the time or energy to devote to parent training. Often, giving parents a rationale for the use of behavioral parent training (subsequently described) can resolve some of these issues and help prevent confusion about services (which will hopefully reduce dropout rates).

Motivational interviewing has been shown to effectively address more significant parent resistance and/or low motivation (Shaw et al., 2014). Motivational interviewing is a goal-directed counseling approach that utilizes a broad collection of techniques to help people explore and resolve ambivalence about behavioral change (Lundhal, Kunz, Brownell, Tollefson, & Burke, 2010). The clinician's role in using motivational interviewing is to increase a client's awareness of the implications of changing and/or of not changing their behavior through a nonjudgmental and collaborative approach. The four central tenets of motivational interviewing include (1) expressing empathy, (2) developing discrepancy, (3) rolling with resistance, and (4) supporting a client's self-efficacy (Lundahl et al., 2010). Four specific therapeutic skills support these principles, including (1) open-ended questions, (2) affirmations, (3) reflective listening, and (4) summarizing (Suarez & Mullins, 2008). If, for example, a clinician was working to develop discrepancies with a parent presenting with low motivation, the clinician might say, "You have mentioned that you know learning effective discipline strategies is the best choice for your child but that attending sessions won't fit your hectic schedule. What are some of your concerns about fitting sessions into your current schedule?" If a parent continues to present as highly resistant during a conversation, a clinician can "roll with resistance" by making the following type of statement: "It's okay if you don't feel like any of these ideas will work for you. If you'd like to share what you've tried, perhaps together we can find something that could work for you."

Although motivational interviewing originated in the early 1980s, it has only recently begun to be evaluated as a therapeutic tool with pediatric populations. A review of outcome studies evaluating behavioral health interventions and motivational interviewing techniques with pediatric populations offers initial evidence of its promising impact (Suarez & Mullins, 2008). Although most studies have focused on interventions involving physical health (e.g., diabetes, obesity), child behavior management interventions have also been discussed. For example, one study compared a motivational enhancement technique with a treatment-as-usual control group. The motivational enhancement technique consisted of 5–15 minutes of motivational interviewing interventions delivered in three doses during the first few therapy sessions and addressed the importance of attending and adhering to treatment. Results showed that caregivers in the motivational enhancement group attended more sessions, reported higher treatment motivation, and demonstrated greater treatment adherence, as rated by both the caregiver and the therapist (Nock & Kazdin, 2005).

The Family Check-Up is a unique ecological, family-centered prevention program for reducing child conduct problems that employs motivational interviewing techniques to stimulate parents to modify ineffective parenting practices (Chang, Shaw, Dishion, Gardner, & Wilson, 2014). The Family Check-Up is a two-to-three session intervention that involves completing a comprehensive multimethod, multi-informant ecological assessment and providing feedback that emphasizes parenting and family strengths, as well as drawing attention to the family's unique challenges and areas of possible change (Smith, Stormshak, & Kavanagh, 2015). The clinician takes into account the family's needs and motivation to change and then develops an individually tailored treatment plan based on an ecological parent management training perspective. A seminal study evaluating the Family Check-Up showed that mothers who received motivational interviewing demonstrated significantly higher levels of maternal involvement. Children in the Family Check-Up group showed significantly reduced aggressive behaviors at 12-month follow-up, compared to the control group, although no significant differences were noted between the groups at 24-month follow-up (Shaw, Dishion, Supplee, Gardner, & Arnds, 2006). A similar intervention, the Classroom Check-Up, has also been developed as a classroom-level consultation model within the schools (see Chapter 6 for more details).

Once a family has committed to participate in treatment, it is important to provide a rationale for behavioral parent training. Clinicians should emphasize that such training can be very effective in managing their child's conduct problems, and that early intervention is central to preventing the problems from worsening over time. It is important to link the parents' behavior with the child's behavior without blaming the parents for the child's conduct problems. Explaining to parents that their behaviors can influence their child's reactions, and that by changing their own behaviors they can improve their child's behavior, is often effective. Children with conduct problems usually have different behavior patterns from those of other children, and thus, parents need to learn different ways to interact with their child in order to help decrease the negative behaviors and increase the positive ones. In addition, it should be acknowledged that parenting can be stressful, and that parenting a child with conduct problems is even more so. Normalizing how this added stress can cause parents to react with frustrations is often helpful, while also noting that these reactions only serve to increase negative child behaviors. Parents can be empowered by emphasizing that by changing their parenting behaviors, the result will likely be a reduction in negative child behaviors, less parental stress, and a more positive parent–child relationship.

Conducting Behavioral Parent Training

A typical behavioral parent training program is outlined in the following sections. This program is very similar to behavioral parent training programs discussed by others (e.g., Barkley, 2013; McMahon & Forehand, 2003; McNeil & Hembree-Kigin, 2011; Webster-Stratton, 2011). As mentioned earlier, many of today's prominent behavioral parent training programs are based on the operant two-stage parent-training model for noncompliant children developed by Hanf (1969). The first stage emphasizes the development of parental attending skills and use of differential attention in an attempt to enhance the parent–child relationship, while the second stage focuses on the effective implementation of consequences for misbehavior. An outline of the steps involved in the program is provided in Table 3.1.

Explaining Behavioral Principles

As previously mentioned, behavioral parent training is based on social learning and operant conditioning principles. By teaching parents the scientific principles upon which specific parenting skills are based, parents are more likely to have an understanding and appreciation of why they are implementing a skill in a certain way (Patterson, Chamberlain, & Reid, 1982). In addition, parents are better able to problem solve as they encounter new behavior problems, by flexibly applying the behavioral principles they have previously learned. Finally, there is an increased likelihood that parents will continue to implement the skills after therapy services are terminated. Obviously, too much theoretical detail may be overwhelming for parents, but a brief explanation of key behavioral principles can be quite helpful. Parents should be given a handout (see Form 3.1) that contains succinct explanations of behavioral principles such as reinforcement, punishment, and extinction. The clinician should go over this handout with parents and attempt to elicit examples of their child's behavior to help illustrate these principles. It is often helpful for the clinician to provide an example and then ask the parent for an additional example, using an interaction the parent has recently had with his or her child.

TABLE 3.1. Outline of Behavioral Parent Training Treatment Components

- Explanation and overview of behavioral terminology
- Using strategic attention
- Implementing child's game
- Effective commands
- Discipline techniques for inappropriate behaviors
    Time-out
    Use of privileges
- Managing behaviors in public places (generalization of skills)
- Maintenance phase (e.g., booster sessions)

Using Strategic Attention

In the first stage of behavioral parent training, parents are taught to use their attention strategically by attending to and praising appropriate behaviors exhibited by their child (e.g. "catching their child being good"; see Form 3.2). By attending to appropriate behaviors, parents (1) increase the likelihood that these behaviors will increase in frequency and (2) help teach their child which behaviors he or she *should* do rather than focusing solely on what the child should *not* do. This positive component of behavioral parent training can help set the stage for a more positive and enjoyable parent–child relationship overall. In addition, positive feedback may help increase the child's self-esteem, which is a common concern for parents.

Parents of children with behavior problems are oftentimes so overwhelmed by the need to monitor (and attempt to decrease) their children's negative behaviors that they neglect to notice the appropriate behaviors. This type of one-sided interaction can lead to the coercive parenting cycle described in Chapter 1. In order to form a positive parent–child relationship and increase the likelihood that their child will engage in appropriate behaviors, parents should focus on striking a balance between providing positive attention and implementing consistent discipline. During phase one of treatment, the clinician should speak with parents about the "magical ratio" regarding the number of positive versus negative interactions they should have with their child (e.g., the 5:1 rule). Specifically, for every one time they provide negative attention or discipline their child, they need to find five opportunities to interact with their child in a positive manner. This ratio creates a powerful contrast between which behaviors are desirable and which are inappropriate. Although this "magic ratio" was originally based on research with couples engaged in conflict resolution (Gottman & Levenson, 1992), it has been applied broadly to educational and family contexts (Armstrong & Field, 2012; Flora, 2000). However, it is worth noting that currently there is no empirical literature supporting an optimal ratio (e.g., 5:1 vs. 4:1) when parenting a young child.

In addition to teaching parents to offer positive attention for their child's appropriate behaviors, they should also be taught how to use planned ignoring. Children frequently engage in inappropriate behaviors to obtain their parent's attention. These attention-seeking behaviors may include whining, pouting, complaining, and crying. Parents may be inclined to respond to these behaviors by reprimanding, scolding, or using other discipline methods. Unfortunately, this response is frequently reinforcing the child's undesirable behaviors, as it results in the child obtaining the parent's attention (albeit negative attention). Planned ignoring can be a very helpful strategy for reducing these types of behaviors. This strategy involves providing no attention (e.g., no eye contact, no physical response, and no verbal response) for this attention-seeking behavior. It is critical that the clinician prepare parents to expect that their child's behavior may briefly worsen when first using this strategy (e.g., extinction burst). Parents should be informed that if they give in to their child's behavioral escalation, this will likely result in a worsening in behavior, as they have taught their child that if he or she escalates, they will eventually receive reinforcement. The importance of persistence should be emphasized, and parents should be given reassurance that these behaviors will eventually improve.

Implementing Child's Game

In addition to modeling and prompting parents to use their attention strategically during the natural interactions that take place within a session, positive attending skills should also be taught and practiced in the context of child-focused play situations, often referred to as "Child's Game" or "Time-In." A few different types of age-appropriate toys that promote constructive, interactive play should be available for this activity. Legos, wooden blocks, Tinker Toys, Lincoln Logs, and drawing materials are commonly used. Toys that should be avoided are those that do not allow for spontaneous interactions between the child and parent, games that have structured rules or expectations (e.g., board games, Legos specific to a building set), and those that have the potential to promote aggressive play. During this positive playtime, the parent's attention should be focused completely on the child, and the child should be allowed to lead the play. In order to keep the play child focused, parents are told to refrain from asking questions, giving commands, or being critical. They are also instructed to ignore instances of minor misbehavior; however, for major misbehaviors, parents are instructed to end playtime. During this playtime, parents are told to (1) describe what the child is doing (e.g., "You're putting the yellow block on top of the blue block."), (2) reflect verbal statements the child makes (e.g., after the child says, "I like blue," the parent might say, "You like blue. I do too. Blue is a pretty color."), (3) imitate/join their child's play (e.g., if their child is building a block tower, the parent is also building a block tower), and (4) praise the child for appropriate behaviors. Parents should be encouraged to use a combination of specific, labeled praise statements (e.g., "Thank you for handing me the block I needed. You shared very nicely."), as well as general, unlabeled praise ("Great job!"). Labeled praise statements are helpful in letting the child know specifically what it is the parent likes, so parents should be encouraged to incorporate such praise statements when interacting with their child.

When teaching parents to use these positive, child-directed skills, the clinician explains the activity to the parents and provides a rationale for its use. Parents are also given a handout (see Form 3.3) that contains a detailed description of Child's Game and the pertinent skills that parents should be using during this activity. Once this activity has been explained to parents, the clinician should model the skills with the referred child, so that the parents can see how the skills are put into practice. Although this activity sounds relatively easy to do, it is important to acknowledge that parents often feel silly doing this at first (especially in the presence of the clinician), and that many parents find that avoiding questions is particularly difficult when first learning this "game." Because asking questions is a common way for adults to interact with children, parents often ask why they need to refrain from asking questions during this positive playtime. The clinician should explain that the purpose of this play activity is for parents to overlearn positive attending skills and that anything that takes away from the child-directed nature of the activity should be avoided. Since questions tend to lead play (e.g., "Why don't you paint a picture of our family?") and conversation (e.g., "What color are those blocks?") and make the activity become parent directed, they are to be avoided during this time. However, parents should be assured that there is nothing wrong with asking questions of their child in their everyday interactions.

Once the clinician has modeled the skills, the parent should be encouraged to gradually join in the play. Eventually the clinician should allow the parent to take over the play with the child, and the clinician should coach the parent on his or her use of the child-directed skills. For example, if the parent asks a question (e.g., "These are colorful blocks, aren't they?") but does not realize the error, the clinician would point it out to the parent (e.g., "Oops, that was a question. Try just saying, 'Those are colorful blocks you're playing with' "). If the parent is having difficulties knowing what to say (i.e., there are long periods of silence), the clinician should encourage the parent to provide a description or praise statement (e.g., "Now would be a good time to tell Ella you like how she's sharing her crayons with you"). As just mentioned, the clinician should also give the parent positive feedback when the parent uses a skill well (e.g., "Nice job praising Sammy for sharing with you").

In addition to coaching the parent on what he or she is saying to the child, the parent should also be coached on how the statements are delivered. Parents often sound unenthusiastic when first engaging in this activity and have little inflection in their voices. It is crucial that clinicians model enthusiasm when they are interacting with the child, and that they coach parents to be more enthusiastic if needed. Parents who are unenthusiastic or do not appear genuine will often have problems keeping their child engaged and interested in this activity because children will pick up on their parents' lack of interest.

For homework, parents are instructed to practice these skills for at least 5–15 minutes per day and to track their practice, as well as note any problems they encountered (see Form 3.4). If there are multiple children in the household, the parents should practice with only one child at a time. Parents are encouraged to use these skills with children other than the referred child, but each child should have his or her own time. If there are two parents in the household, it is ideal to have each parent practice these skills, although they should do this independently.

These skills are practiced in session until parents have mastered their use. Some behavioral parent training programs have specific guidelines for determining when mastery of these techniques is achieved. For example, in parent–child interaction therapy (one of the specific training programs available), parents are considered to have mastered these skills when they can provide 10 labeled praise statements, reflective statements, and behavioral descriptions, as well as 3 or fewer commands, questions, or criticisms within a 5-minute period (McNeil & Hembree-Kigin, 2011).

Giving Effective Commands

After parents have mastered the use of positively based parenting skills, they should be taught to give effective, appropriate commands before implementing discipline strategies. Parents often give commands that make it difficult or impossible for the child to comply. For example, parents may provide a long string of different commands without giving the child time to comply in between commands, or they give vague commands that do not contain enough information about what the child is expected to do. Parents also frequently phrase commands as questions (e.g. "Can you pick up the blocks?"), which inadvertently conveys to the child that compliance is optional. In addition, parents often phrase statements as commands but fail to follow through with a consequence if the child does not comply, which only serves to reinforce the child's noncompliance.

Parents should be mindful to give only developmentally appropriate commands and to ensure that the child is physically capable of completing any command given (Schroeder & Gordon, 2002). Before giving a command, the parent should make sure that he or she has the child's attention. Saying the child's name, standing in front of the child, and making eye contact are possible ways to establish a connection with the child. Commands should be given one at a time. If a parent would like the child to complete a multistep task, the parent should break the task down into smaller steps. For each step, the parent should (1) give a command, (2) wait for the child to comply/not comply, and (3) provide an appropriate consequence. Parents should also make sure that their commands are stated as directives, rather than as questions or suggestions. Statements such as "It would be nice if you would clean up your toys" do not tell the child that the toys *must be cleaned up immediately*. If the parent wants this task to be completed, a more appropriate command would be "Please pick up the toys on your bedroom floor and put them in the toy chest." Commands should be as specific as possible, so that there is no doubt as to what is expected from the child.

If a task involves a choice, parents can include the choice in their command. For example, if a mother is directing her child to put on her shoes—but the child can wear either her sneakers or her boots—the mother might say, "Addie, we're ready to go to the park now. Please put on either your white sneakers or your brown boots." Rationales for commands should be brief and presented either before the command (as in the previous example) or after the child complies. For example, after complying with the command from the previous example the parent might say, "Thank you for putting on your boots as I asked. I wanted you to put on your shoes because we're ready to go to the park now." Preschool children do not need lengthy rationales; they often *ask* for rationales (i.e., "Why?") simply to delay complying with the command.

Parents should be instructed to only give commands when they plan to follow through with an appropriate consequence for compliance or noncompliance. A conversation regarding the importance of "picking your battles" can be completed with parents, and the pitfalls of intermittent use of consequences can be highlighted. Using the metaphor of "playing the slot machines" can be helpful in describing how children will "gamble" (i.e., be noncompliant) with the hopes of "winning the jackpot" (i.e., not having to complete the task assigned and not receiving a consequence). Parents are encouraged to be mindful that the "house should always win" (i.e., parents must consistently follow through with a consequence for each act of noncompliance). By (1) reducing the commands given to those that are most important to parents, (2) always providing a consequence, and (3) phrasing commands appropriately, parents can expect to see an increase in their child's compliance. These guidelines for giving appropriate commands are discussed in session with parents, and they are given a handout (see Form 3.5) that summarizes the use of commands.

Using Appropriate Discipline Techniques

After learning how to give appropriate commands, parents are taught to use specific disciplinary techniques for those occasions of noncompliance. It is very important that parents continue to use the positive parenting skills previously mastered as they learn new disciplinary skills. Parents should continue to engage in the structured play activity (i.e., Child's

Game) on a regular basis and should be attuned to opportunities throughout the day to positively attend to their child's appropriate behaviors. Additionally, parents should always provide positive reinforcement as soon as their child complies with a given command.

The discipline technique of choice with preschool- and kindergarten-age children is time-out. Most parents have had some experience with time-out and often insist that it "does not work" for their child. Thus, one of the first tasks a clinician faces is "selling" the parents on the use of a technique they may not be inclined to use. When time-out does not work, it is typically because parents do not use it in an appropriate manner. An effective time-out involves removing the child from all reinforcers. Many parents continue to talk to their children while they are supposedly in time-out. Although the content of what is said may be negative (e.g., "Sit down. You need to learn to behave or you'll never get out of time-out"), the attention that the child is receiving is typically reinforcing. Thus, in such instances, the child is not truly experiencing a time-out.

Parents often leave their children in time-out for excessively long periods of time. The general rule of thumb is that children should be in time-out for 1 minute per year of age, not to exceed 5 minutes. Extensive time-outs can be difficult to enforce, and they deny children learning opportunities. The time-out should be brief so that children can reenter the situation, engage in negative or positive behaviors, and receive appropriate consequences. Repeated instances of (1) the child performing an inappropriate behavior and being sent to time-out and (2) the child performing an appropriate behavior and receiving positive reinforcement help the child learn which behaviors are appropriate and which are not. Parents also may believe that time-out does not work because the child will not automatically stay in the time-out location. Parents may become frustrated that their child is continually leaving the time-out and, because they are unsure what to do, they simply let the child end his or her own time-out. In such situations, the child learns that he or she can escape with no consequence, and consequently, time-out becomes ineffective.

Time-out is explained to parents in session, and they are given a handout (see Form 3.6) on its use. Any information the parents have provided to the clinician about their previous use of time-out should be acknowledged and addressed. Parents are initially taught to use time-out in response to noncompliant behavior. After giving a command (e.g., "Please put on your coat"), parents are instructed to wait 10 seconds for the child to comply. Parents are encouraged not to count out loud, as children will learn to ignore the command and delay the initiation of compliance until their parent reaches a certain number. If the child does not comply within that time period, the parent repeats the command and tells the child he or she will go to time-out if the child does not comply (e.g., Please put on your coat or you will go to time-out"). Again, the child is given 10 seconds to begin to comply. If the child still does not comply, the parent should immediately send the child to time-out (e.g., "You didn't put on your coat, as I instructed, so you need to go to time-out").

Of course, most children will not willingly go to time-out, so the parent will often need to lead the child to the time-out location. If the child will not walk with assistance to time-out, the parent should physically guide or pick up the child from behind and place him or her in time-out, making one brief, directive statement such as "You need to sit and be quiet until I tell you to come out." While the child is in the time-out location, all verbalizations and activities by the child are ignored. It is extremely important that the parent understand why he or she should ignore the child during the time-out period; that is, that attending to the child is reinforcing and defeats the purpose of placing the child in time-out. If the child leaves the time-out location, he or she should be placed back in time-out immediately, while the parent continues to actively ignore (e.g., no verbalizations). Initially, the parent may have to stand very close to the time-out location so that he or she can promptly return the child to time-out.

While the put-back method is generally sufficient, a back-up room may be required for some children who persist in their refusal to stay in time-out. When using this approach, the parent should first be supported in identifying an appropriate space in their home for the back-up room. This room should have a door that can be closed, is well lit, and has ample room to move around, and all items that could be considered entertaining (e.g., toys) or dangerous (e.g., medications, breakables, heavy furniture) should be removed. Once the back-up room has been established, the parent should be instructed to implement the following back-up room procedure. If the child leaves the time-out chair, the parent should say, "Because you left the time-out chair, you have to go to the back-up room." The child should then be physically guided or carried to the back-up room. The parent should close the door and hold it shut as necessary but should not lock it. After 1 minute, the parent should take their child back to the time-out chair. This procedure can be repeated as necessary. A child should not be given "credit" toward his or her time-out time during this procedure. If a child requires a third trip to the back-up room during any given time-out, the child's time-out should then be completed in the back-up room. If this occurs, all previously discussed requirements for ending time-out should be met (e.g., time expired, child is quiet). Alternatively, parents can choose to use a room as the primary time-out location. The necessary characteristics of a time-out room are identical to that of a back-up room (e.g., well-lit, ample room, all reinforcing items removed). In this case, the parent would place the child in the time-out room at the onset of the time-out and allow him or her to leave the room once requirements for ending time-out have been satisfied (e.g., time expired, child is quiet). It should be noted that if a child engages in significantly destructive and/or self-injurious behavior during time-out, parents are encouraged to discontinue use of time-outs until these concerns can be discussed further with a mental health professional.

When time-out is first used, children can often take a long time to quiet down and stop crying. Thus, initially parents may be instructed to let the child out of time-out as soon as he or she is quiet for a very brief period of time (e.g., 10 seconds). Gradually, this time would be increased, so that the child remains in time-out for the appropriate length of time (i.e., 1 minute per year of age, with a maximum time of 5 minutes). Ultimately, the child should be required to complete the full length of the time-out and should be let out of time-out once he or she has been quiet for at least 15–30 seconds. In this way, the parent avoids inadvertently reinforcing any misbehavior that might be occurring when the time has expired. Additionally, this process allows a parent to support the child in developing appropriate emotional self-regulatory abilities, as the child's release from time-out becomes contingent on his or her ability to calm down (Shelleby et al., 2012). When the child has been quiet for the appropriate length of time, the parent should let the child out of time-out with the explanation, "You're being quiet, so you may come out of time-out now." Once the child is released from time-out, the parent should repeat the original command and provide the appropriate consequence (i.e., praise for compliance, another time-out for noncompliance). It is very important that parents complete this last step of reissuing the original command; otherwise, children may come to view time-out as a way of escaping a task they did not want to complete.

The location of the time-out should be discussed with parents in session. Parents sometimes have difficulty enforcing time-outs because they place the child in locations they cannot see (e.g., at the end of a hallway) or near something the child can reach and destroy (e.g., placing a child near a lamp he or she can reach and knock over). Parents are often instructed to use an adult-sized straight-back chair for time-out. Ideally, the child's feet should not reach the floor. The chair should be located in an area where the parent can see the child, but not where the child can access any potential reinforcers (e.g., the child should not be able to see the TV). In addition, the chair should be in an area in which there is nothing within reach of the child. Although a chair can be easiest for parents to use, other defined spaces (e.g., a bottom step, a small rug placed on the floor) can also work for time-out locations.

Although many parents use timers to track the length of time the child is in time-out, the use of a timer can present a problem, specifically, that parents and children may come to view the sounding of the timer as an indicator that time-out is over. It should be stressed that it is *the parent* (not the timer) who releases the child from time-out and that the child is let out *once he or she is quiet* (not once the timer sounds). If a parent uses a timer, he or she should make it clear to the child that he or she will not be dismissed from time-out until the parent indicates it is time. Timers are typically most helpful for parents who might "forget" that their child is in time-out. However, given that parents should be taught to monitor their child during time-out so that they can (1) immediately return the child to time-out if the child escapes and (2) release the child from time-out once the child is quiet, many believe that timers are not needed and may actually create problems for parents. Therefore, the use of timers is generally discouraged.

Given the potential problems that arise when using time-out, it is extremely helpful if parents have an opportunity to practice it in a therapy session. Once the clinician has explained the use of commands and time-out to the parent, the parent is coached on his or her application of it in session. This phase begins by asking the parent to interact with his or her child in a play context. Gradually the parent begins to give commands to the child. At first these commands should be relatively easy for the child to comply with (e.g., "Please hand me the red block" in reference to a block the child is not currently using), but gradually the parent should make the commands more demanding in an attempt to elicit noncompliance in session (e.g., "Please put the blocks away."). The clinician should coach the parent on his or her use of commands to ensure that the parent is phrasing them appropriately. When the child complies with a command, the parent should always praise the child for compliance (e.g., "Thank you for handing me the red block like I asked you to do."). If the child does not comply, the parent is coached through the process of putting the child in time-out and ignoring him or her for that time period. Initially, it can be very difficult for parents to ignore their child during a time-out. Many young children scream and cry vigorously and may use hurtful words in their attempts to secure their parents' attention (e.g., "You don't really love me," or "I hate you."). Or some young children may express a need to go to the bathroom while sitting in a time-out. This scenario should be discussed with parents and a plan should be preemptively created so that parents are consistently approaching this situation in an identical manner. Two possible options to consider using in this situation include (1) ignoring the child's request until the time-out is over (even if the child has an accident) or (2) allowing the child to go to the bathroom and then immediately returning the child to time-out. If parents use the second option, clinicians should stress the importance of providing minimal attention to their child during this interaction.

Once time-out has been covered in session, parents are instructed to begin using it at home and tracking the results, as well as any problems they encounter (see Form 3.7). After parents have implemented the use of time-out for noncompliance, the clinician helps the parent identify some "house rules," which, if broken, will result in an immediate time-out for the child. Parents should be encouraged to set a limited number of house rules (two or three is a good number to begin with when working with young children) and save these rules for behaviors that are most important (e.g., "Keep hands and feet to yourself"). When the child fails to follow a house rule, he or she is immediately sent to time-out. No warning is given in this situation.

Additional Reinforcement/Discipline Methods

Although time-out is the discipline method of choice for young children, alternative methods, such as contingency contracting, may also be used. Contingency contracting may involve a comprehensive token economy system, in which poker chips or points (that can be exchanged for tangible reinforcers) are given to the child for appropriate behavior and taken away for inappropriate behavior. However, token economy systems can get quite complex and cumbersome for parents. Using privileges (instead of tokens or points that must be exchanged) is often easier for parents. When using privileges to manage behavior, parents should begin by listing the privileges their child can earn for appropriate behaviors and those that will be taken away for inappropriate behaviors (see Forms 3.8 and 3.9). The privileges that the child can earn by exhibiting positive, prosocial behavior would be extra privileges that the child receives, in addition to his or her everyday privileges (e.g., watching an hour of TV). The privileges that are removed for inappropriate behaviors would be those everyday privileges that the child automatically receives; when a rule is broken or an expected task not performed, the child loses one of these everyday privileges. Tangible reinforcers can be used in addition to privileges in this system.

Parents can also set up a positive reinforcement system in which a child earns points toward a specific reinforcer. For example, if a child wants to see a certain movie, the parents could create a chart that has a picture of a character in this movie at the end of a "road." Each time the child engages in an appropriate behavior, he or she is able to move a marker down the road and one step closer to the movie character. When the child's marker reaches the character, he or she earns the reinforcer (e.g., going to the movie). When this method is used with young children, they should be able to earn the reinforcer quickly. If they must wait for several days or weeks, the delay between the behavior and the reinforcer will be too long and the intervention will be unsuccessful. If the delay is longer, parents should consider giving small reinforcers along the way. For example, if the child cannot earn the movie reinforcer for at least 2 weeks, parents could move the marker along the "road" on the chart and provide a small reinforcer for each move (or every other move). This small reinforcer should be something that can be delivered immediately (e.g., playing a game with a parent, a small treat).

Generalization and Maintenance of Skills

Initially the skills previously described are taught and practiced with the home setting in mind. Obviously, though, it is crucial for parents to learn to generalize these skills to behaviors in settings outside the home, such as grocery stores, restaurants, and department stores. Before attempting to apply the skills outside the home, the clinician should ensure that parents can easily use the skills in session. Parents who are still struggling with giving appropriate commands or using discipline skills in a consistent manner in the home will have added difficulties applying the skills in public places. Teaching parents to generalize skills to other settings is typically the last component of behavioral parent training. See Form 3.10 for the handout explaining this step.

When parents first practice these new skills outside the home, they should begin with relatively brief "training trips" that are not necessary to complete. For example, a parent may take a training trip to the grocery store to pick up just a few items that he or she does not have to obtain that day. Before embarking on this trip, the parent should set up some rules with the child. For example, rules for appropriate grocery store behavior might include: (1) stay within arm's reach of the cart, (2) do not take items off the shelf unless told to do so, and (3) talk in your indoor voice. A discussion of the consequences associated with failure to follow the rules should also be conducted.

Once in the store, the parent should make sure to praise the child for following the rules and for any other appropriate behaviors. The parent may want to engage the child in the shopping experience by directing him or her to take certain items off the shelf and put them in the cart. The parent should also consider setting up a reward program for complying with the rules. For example, when the child follows the rules or engages in other appropriate behaviors, the child can be given a token. If the child has a certain number of tokens by the end of the shopping trip, he or she can exchange the tokens for a reinforcer (e.g., a candy bar, a movie to watch at home, a special trip to the park with a parent).

For inappropriate behaviors, parents can use time-out in the store if they are comfortable doing so. The child should be required to sit or stand in an out-of-the-way section of the store. The child should not have access to any preferred items, and no attention should be given to him or her. Typically, the regular time-out period is shortened, and time-out can be terminated once the child is quiet for 15–30 seconds. If the child refuses to complete the time-out in the store (e.g. tantrums excessively, refuses to stay seated), a parent can also choose to walk the child to a more private time-out location (e.g., the car, the bathroom). The clinician should stress that the child always be returned to the original setting after a time-out, as immediately going home might encourage future misbehavior.

For some parents, using a community time-out may not always be feasible and may feel too uncomfortable. Instead, parents can add a response–cost component to the reward system in which the child loses tokens for inappropriate behaviors. If the child begins to throw a tantrum in the store, parents should be instructed not to give in to the behavior, however embarrassing. For example, if the child tantrums because his or her mother will not give the child the candy he or she wants, it is imperative that the mother not give the child the candy just to stop the tantrum. Doing so would only serve to teach the child that a long enough or loud enough tantrum will get him or her what he or she wants. In this situation, the child should be completely ignored. If this is too difficult for the parent to ignore the child while remaining inside the store, the child should be taken outside. However, clinicians should stress to parents that they should never leave their child unattended. Children should never be taken to the car and simply left there. As just discussed, once the child has stopped tantruming, the parent should be encouraged to return with the child to the original setting before going home.

In addition to learning how to generalize skills to situations outside the home, parents also need help in planning for generalization in situations in which they are not present (e.g., preschool), especially if their child is having problems across settings. The clinician could consult with the preschool teacher (along with the parent) and set up a similar behavior management program in school. Another option would be to use a home–school note system (e.g., Barkley, 2013; described in more detail in Chapter 6).

Ensuring that skills are maintained over time is also important. Unfortunately, treatment gains are often reduced at follow-up compared to gains immediately following intervention (Lundahl, Risser, & Lovejoy, 2006). While there is little empirical research regarding the best way to promote maintenance of treatment gains (Eyberg et al., 2008), several different approaches have been proposed. The most commonly used approach involves providing "booster sessions" for parents (Kolko & Lindhiem, 2014). Such sessions might involve brief (e.g., 30–60 minutes) monthly meetings, wherein skills are reviewed and practiced and any problem areas discussed.

Group Behavioral Parent Training

Conducting behavioral parent training in a group setting is an option clinicians may want to consider if they do not have the time or resources to implement individual parent training. Group behavioral parent training is conducted in the same manner as the individualized format. However, the child is typically not present, and the parents do not have the opportunity to practice skills in session with their children. Instead, parents typically engage in role playing with other parents and then practice the skills at home with their children. Because children are not present, group behavioral parent training programs often make use of videotaped models so that parents can see the application of the skills with actual children.

Possibly the best known and most researched group behavioral parent training program is The Incredible Years videotape-based program (Webster-Stratton, 2011). Employing strategies based on the Hanf model (consistent with the basic format discussed earlier), this program emphasizes positive parenting and teaching parents to replace maladaptive parenting strategies with more effective ones. In addition, this program works to improve collaboration between parents and teachers to ensure consistency across settings. Skills are modeled in session through the use of videotaped vignettes. The vignettes depict parents modeling both the appropriate and inappropriate use of the skills. The vignettes then serve as a stimulus for group discussions, problem solving, and collaborative learning. The use of these models seems to be a critical component in the program. Webster-Stratton and Hancock (1998) have noted superior effects of their program when the videotaped models are used in comparison to when they are not used. The program teaches specific strategies, including enhancing positive relationships between parents and children through child-directed interactive play, praising the child for desirable behaviors, and incentive programs. Parents are then taught appropriate disciplinary strategies such as effective commands, ignoring, monitoring, and time-out.

A recent meta-analytic review of The Incredible Years behavioral parent training program revealed that this program is effective and is viewed favorably by parents (Menting, de Castro, & Matthys, 2013). When the program is used with Head Start preschool parents, significant improvements in parenting skills have been observed, including a reduction in harsh disciplinary practices, as well as increased nurturing and provision of emotional support to their children (Hurlburt, Nguyen, Reid, Webster-Stratton, & Zhang, 2013). In other research, improved parenting practices and reduced childhood conduct problems were evident several years after termination of the parent program (Posthumus, Raaijmakers, Maassen, Engeland, & Matthys, 2012). A meta-analytic review involving 50 studies that used the Incredible Years Parent Program found it to be effective overall, namely reducing child disruptive behaviors, with the greatest results found in those children with more significant initial problem behaviors (Menting, Orobio de Castro, & Matthys, 2013).

In addition to developing the basic behavioral parent training program, Webster-Stratton has created an add-on program that addresses other parenting needs. This includes additional vignettes that focus on parental self-control, communication skills, collaborative problem-solving skills, and strengthening social support and self-care. Research has demonstrated that participation in an add-on program results in additional improvements beyond those obtained in the basic parent training intervention in the clinically targeted areas (e.g., improved communication), maternal depression, and a child's problem-solving abilities and social skills (Webster-Stratton, 2011).

Group parent training seems to be as effective as individual parent training (Menting et al., 2013) and is clearly more cost-effective (Chronis, Chacko, Fabiano, Wymbs, & Pelham, 2004). However, there are some potential disadvantages to using the group format. Although parents in a group may benefit from sharing knowledge and experience with one another (Webster-Stratton, 2009), this format, which encourages the sharing of personal information, may be uncomfortable for some parents. Parents with more significant skills deficits, psychopathology, and/or severe psychosocial stressors may need more individualized attention than can be provided in a group setting. Individual behavioral parent training allows the clinician to address the specific needs of the family and to pace the treatment program so that it is most appropriate for the family.

ENHANCING BEHAVIORAL PARENT TRAINING THROUGH THE USE OF ACCEPTANCE AND COMMITMENT THERAPY

Overview

Although behavioral parent training is considered the most widely empirically supported treatment for young children with conduct problems (Eyberg et al., 2008), recent research evaluating the added utility of incorporating acceptance and commitment therapeutic techniques into treatment with this population has been conducted (Coyne & Murrell, 2009). Acceptance and commitment therapy (ACT) is a therapeutic approach that emphasizes compassionate acknowledgement and acceptance of experiences, through the use of mindfulness and behavior change strategies, in order to increase psychological flexibility (Hayes, Strosahl, & Wilson, 2012; see Figure 3.1). Psychological flexibility is described as having contact with the present moment and changing or persisting in behaviors in the service of chosen values (Hayes et al., 2012). Clinicians can promote these ACT principles when working with parents through use of specific exercises, metaphors, and behavioral tasks discussed in the following sections. Our intention is not to provide an exhaustive review of ACT or discuss the applicability of these principles when working directly with a child; rather, it is to provide a brief overview of several key ACT principles and offer practical suggestions for how to incorporate these principles into treatment with parents.

Values

Values are the principles that give our life's meaning, direction, and chosen purpose. Values are different from goals, which are tasks or achievements to accomplish. By identifying their values, individuals are provided with a purpose for facing unpleasant sensations/experiences and engaging in value-driven behaviors. For example, parents may find it easier to commit to implementing a time-out procedure, which can be time intensive and emotionally aversive, by reminding themselves of their parenting values (e.g., raising an emotionally well-adjusted child). When ACT principles are integrated into treatment, a clinician should

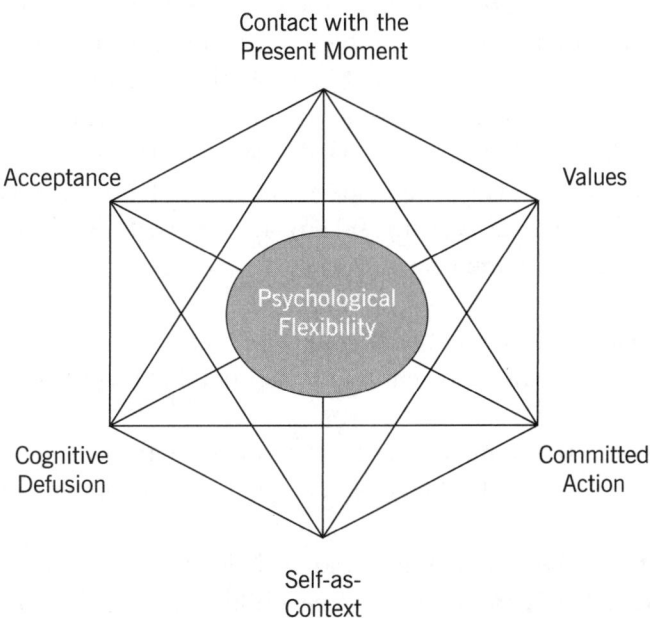

FIGURE 3.1. Acceptance and commitment therapy (ACT) core processes. From Hayes, Strosahl, and Wilson (2012). Copyright © 2012 The Guilford Press. Adapted by permission.

first spend time working with parents on values clarification. Values clarification involves asking parents to step back from their everyday struggles and identify what gives their life meaning. Many different exercises have been proposed to assist with this process, including using an assessment measure (such as the Personal Values Questionnaire), a card identification task (parents choose from cards with pregenerated values written on them), or the "eulogy exercise" (Hayes et al., 2012).

An alternative to the card identification task is providing parents with 16 small pieces of paper and instructing them to write a different value on each piece of paper (this can be related to parenting specifically or could be broadened to encompass other life values). After writing down 16 values, parents would be asked to discard four values that they could do without. Repeat this step until parents are left with their four top values. At the conclusion of this exercise, clinicians should discuss parents' experiences in completing this exercise (e.g., "Did anything surprise you about the values with which you are left? Were there any values that were easy to discard? Any values that felt really difficult to discard?"). In the eulogy exercise, a parent would be asked the following question: "Imagine you had died and could attend your own funeral. What would you hope to hear people say about you during their eulogy?" Other variations of this exercise could include prompting parents to imagine the content of a speech given by their child at their 50th wedding anniversary or at their 80th birthday party.

Cognitive Defusion

In ACT, the power of language is heavily emphasized. As verbal beings, people have developed verbal rules that are used when interacting with the world. These rules are often helpful because they allow us to efficiently process and respond to information presented. However, these rules can also become problematic when they are rigidly followed and/or when they provide an inaccurate representation of what is actually occurring. Cognitive fusion refers to a person's tendency to become overly focused on the content of his or her thoughts, which results in failure to acknowledge and incorporate other useful sources of behavioral regulation (Luoma, Hayes, & Walser, 2007). The following passage," An Adapted Zen Koan for Parents" (Coyne & Wilson, 2004, p. 470), powerfully illustrates how cognitive fusion can negatively impact parenting.

> *Question* 1: What is the sound of one hand clapping?
> *Answer*: The sound of one hand clapping is the sound of one hand clapping.
>
> *Question* 2: What is the sound of one child misbehaving?
> *Answer*: The sound of one child misbehaving is the sound of one child misbehaving.
>
> *Question* 3: What is the sound of my child misbehaving?
> *Answer*: The sound of "I cannot control my child," the sound of "I should be able to," the sound of "I am a bad parent," the sound of "I don't know what to do," the sound of "I hate this child," the sound of "I should not feel this way," and the sound of my failure.

When using an ACT approach, it should be emphasized that it is not the content of thoughts that is problematic; rather, parenting practices may be negatively impacted because of how parents *relate* to their thoughts. For example, a parent that has the thought "I cannot control this child," and, as a result, struggles to initiate effective discipline practices because of perceived ineffectiveness would be considered more cognitively fused. In contrast, a parent that has the same thought and acknowledges it as just a thought, and nothing more, would be less cognitively fused and would be more likely to utilize effective discipline practices.

Parents can be supported in learning more effective ways of relating to their thoughts through the use of cognitive defusion techniques. Cognitive defusion involves learning to view thinking as an ongoing behavioral process and to view thoughts as thoughts, rather than fusing to what these thoughts are implying (Luoma et al., 2007). Instead of attempting to change the content of thoughts, a clinician works with parents to alter the context that relates the undesirable thoughts to undesirable behaviors. A frequently used cognitive defusion exercise is the "milk exercise" (Hayes et al., 2012, pp. 71–72), in which parents are asked to imagine a glass of milk for a few moments. Next, they would be asked to repeatedly say the word "milk" out loud for at least 60 seconds. As this word is repeatedly spoken, parents will find that it begins to lose some or most of its meaning. They may also notice that other functions of this word become more dominant (e.g., the way the word sounds). This exercise can then be repeated with a more emotionally salient and difficult word for parents such as "failure."

Another commonly used cognitive defusion exercise is "leaves on a stream" (Hayes et al., 2012, p. 245). This exercise aims to support parents in looking *at* thoughts rather than *from* thoughts. Through engagement in this exercise, parents are better able to recognize the difference between having a thought and owning a thought. It also helps parents to recognize that they are constantly having thoughts, despite the fact that they may be largely unaware that this is occurring. To start, a clinician should begin by describing how a person's mind is constantly narrating, often without conscious awareness. Parents are then encouraged to get into a comfortable position, close their eyes, and spend time noticing any internal narration that might be occurring. The clinician should emphasize that they are to simply notice any thoughts they have including any opinions, comments, or questions. Encourage parents not to judge or attempt to change these thoughts but to simply notice them. Next, parents are asked to visualize a gently flowing stream with leaves floating along the surface of the water. The clinician should then encourage parents to spend the next few minutes identifying thoughts as they enter their mind, placing them on a leaf, and letting the thoughts float down the stream. At the conclusion of this exercise, the clinician can discuss parents' experience and then should encourage regular practice.

Contact with the Present Moment (Mindfulness)

Behavioral parent training programs largely focus on purposefully changing operant contingencies that are contributing to the presence of a child's disruptive behaviors. Unfortunately, for some families, these operant contingencies, particularly those implicated in the parent–child coercive cycle, have become automatized and highly resistant to change

(Dumas, 2005). Given the central role of negative reinforcement in developing and maintaining the parent–child coercive cycle, clinicians may wish to enhance traditional behavioral parent training with ACT strategies that address parents' own experiential avoidance. Experiential avoidance is a term used to describe a person's attempts to avoid or suppress unwanted physical sensations, thoughts, and/or feelings. Experiential avoidance can lead to using inflexible parenting strategies, being inconsistent with behavior management strategies, withdrawing from interactions with their child, and causing parents to overreact to their child's negative emotions and/or behaviors (Coyne & Murrell, 2009).

Mindfulness-based parenting strategies have been developed in an effort to target parents' experiential avoidance, particularly as it interferes with their ability to successfully implement effective behavior management strategies and promote a more effective pattern of parent–child interactions. Mindfulness refers to focusing one's attention on what is occurring in the present moment in an open and nonjudgmental fashion (Kabat-Zinn, 1994). More specific to parenting, mindfulness-based strategies encourage parents to be present-focused and nonreactive and to embrace an open, accepting attitude of their parenting thoughts, feelings, and behaviors, as well as their child's behaviors (Coatsworth, Duncan, Greenberg, & Nix, 2010). Research has demonstrated that parents who are less likely to use mindfulness are more likely to use harsh punishment strategies, particularly if they are coping with numerous stressors (Shea & Coyne, 2011). In research conducted by Neece (2013), parents of 2½- to 5-year-old children with developmental delays who participated in a mindfulness-based stress reduction program reported significantly less stress and depressive symptoms, as well as greater life satisfaction when compared with wait-list-control parents. Additionally, children whose parents participated in the program were reported to have fewer behavior problems following the intervention, specifically with regard to ADHD symptomatology. These findings are consistent with those found in other research (Singh et. al., 2007). Furthermore, mothers of young children with autism who were trained in the use of mindfulness reported increased satisfaction with their parenting skills and interactions with their children, as well as reductions in their children's levels of aggression, self-injury, and noncompliance (Singh et al., 2006).

Many parents may find mindfulness to be a relatively easy concept to grasp but will find it difficult to use in their daily interactions with their child. Parents should be made aware that mindfulness is a skill that requires cultivation through regular practice and often does not come easily to people. Clinicians are encouraged to identify exercises that can be easily integrated into a parent's daily life such as mindful breathing, mindful walking, and mindful eating. Identifying activities that parents can engage in daily should increase the likelihood that parents will practice mindfulness more regularly.

Mindful breathing is one example of a structured mindfulness exercise that can be introduced and practiced during a therapy session (Bogels & Restifo, 2014). In this exercise, parents are asked to get into a comfortable position, close their eyes, and draw their attention to their breath. Parents should be instructed to continue breathing regularly, not attempting to change or control their breath. If parents find that they are attempting to control or change their breath, simply encourage them to notice these efforts and let them go. Parents should be prompted to continue breathing at their regular pace for several minutes.

During this time, parents should continue focusing their attention on their breath, noticing any sensations that may be occurring throughout their body (e.g. the way their chest/stomach change, the temperature of the air as it enters/exits, the way their body feels). The clinician should comment that if parents notice that extraneous thoughts arise, as they inevitably will, they should acknowledge these thoughts and then gently bring their attention back to their breath.

The concept of mindfulness can also be readily applied when parents are engaged in strategies taught in behavioral parent training (e.g., strategic attention, Child's Game). Not only should this help parents further develop their ability to be mindful, it will also likely increase parents' effective use of these strategies. Parents who are more mindful during interactions with their child are also more likely to consistently respond to and provide contingent consequences for their child's appropriate and inappropriate behaviors. When discussing mindfulness within the context of Child's Game, a parent would be encouraged to notice, without judgment, everything that happens during this interaction with his or her child, which may include noticing what the child is doing and saying, as well as any thoughts, feelings, and emotions the parent may be experiencing. By engaging in Child's Game mindfully, parents are more likely to be able to successfully use the descriptive, reflective, and praise statements required during this special playtime (Coyne & Murrell, 2009).

Self as Context

Over the course of an individual's life, a largely unconscious process happens wherein we learn to develop coherent stories about who we are, what we do, and how our internal experiences influence and justify our behaviors (e.g., "I am a professional," "I am worthless"). In ACT, this is known as *self-as-content* (Hayes et al., 2012). More specific to parenting, a parent will develop a conceptualized self of who he or she is as a parent based upon past experiences (e.g., "I am a bad parent"). Through mindfulness and cognitive defusion, individuals can begin to recognize that they are not the sum total of their physical sensations, thoughts, and emotions; rather, there is a *stable self* that is doing the observing. From this perspective, parents can learn to let go of unhelpful self-evaluations, while retaining their sense of self. This ACT process is known as *self-as-context*.

One commonly used metaphor that helps make the distinction between a conceptualized self and self-as-context involves imagining a chessboard (Coyne & Murrell, 2009; Hayes et al., 2012). The stable self is the chessboard, while the conceptualized self are the chess pieces. The black pieces are unwanted thoughts and emotions, and the white pieces strive to refute these negative internal experiences. When a parent becomes fused with a thought and believes that thought is true and represents the sum total of who he or she is, he or she is up on the board in the middle of the battle between the pieces. When a parent is able to engage in cognitive defusion and mindfulness, he or she becomes the board, which is stable and unchanging, and allows the parent to observe this battle from a distance. While this battle may be unpleasant, the mind is able to recognize it as harmless and separate from the stable self, which allows a parent to let go of unhelpful negative self-evaluations and continue to engage in value-based actions.

Acceptance

As discussed earlier, experiential avoidance occurs when a parent attempts to avoid or suppress unwanted physical sensations, thoughts, and/or feelings, which then can result in engagement in ineffective parenting strategies (e.g., withdrawal, punitive/controlling, inconsistent). In ACT, acceptance is presented as an alternative to experiential avoidance. Acceptance involves being aware of and embracing one's internal experiences without making any efforts to change them (Hayes et al., 2012). By encouraging parents to become more accepting of their internal experiences, they will then be better able to purposefully choose to engage in value-based actions.

When introducing acceptance, it is helpful to first support parents in acknowledging the futility of emotional control and avoidance. Providing psychoeducation about the relationship between experiential avoidance and parenting styles will likely be helpful. A clinician can describe how an experientially avoidant parent may become overly permissive and/or authoritarian in his or her parenting approach. The negative effect of these parenting approaches on a child's disruptive behaviors should be emphasized (Rinaldi & Howe, 2012). Acceptance can then be introduced as an effective alternative to experiential avoidance. Numerous metaphors have been developed to assist with this process (Hayes et al., 2012). Simple examples that highlight the futility of "the struggle" (i.e., experiential avoidance) may include getting caught in a riptide or quicksand, a tug-of-war, or a Chinese finger trap. In each of these examples, the clinician should stress that the more an individual struggles in these situations, the worse they become. Alternatively, the pink elephant exercise can be used. In this exercise, parents are instructed not to think about a pink elephant, which inevitably causes the parent to think about a pink elephant.

Once parents have begun to recognize the ineffectiveness of experiential avoidance, acceptance should be introduced as a viable and helpful alternative. A clinician should explain to parents that by letting go of the struggle with their negative thoughts and feelings, they will have the energy and focus to engage in value-based actions. To help illustrate the concept of acceptance, a clinician should consider using the passengers on the bus metaphor (Hayes et al., 2012). In this exercise, parents are encouraged to imagine that they are bus drivers, and the bus is their life. On this bus are passengers, which represent our thoughts, feelings, and memories. Parents want to drive their bus in a certain direction (i.e., value-based actions), but there may be times when the passengers become angry and begin to demand that the bus be taken in a different direction. The bus driver may argue with the passengers or may strike a deal that he or she will drive the bus wherever they want, so long as they sit back and stay quiet. This interaction highlights the concept of experiential avoidance. In contrast, parents should be challenged to consider the benefits of simply acknowledging the passengers, while continuing to drive the bus in the direction they would like to go.

Committed Action

A final ACT principle that can be used to enhance behavioral parent training is committed action. Committed action involves purposefully choosing to engage in behaviors, even those that are difficult, in order to move in a direction that is consistent with previously identified values. This phase of treatment incorporates more traditional behavior change techniques, while continuing to employ other components of ACT. Committed action involves taking four specific steps:

1. Pick a high-priority valued domain and develop an action plan for behavior change.
2. Commit to actions that are linked to values.
3. Attend to and overcome barriers to action with other ACT techniques (e.g., mindfulness, cognitive defusion).
4. Return to step 1 and generalize to larger patterns of action, other domains of living, other areas of psychological flexibility, and so forth (Luoma et al., 2007).

Engaging parents in a conversation about committed action may be particularly worthwhile when discussing consistently using behavior management strategies, particularly those that may result in a child's behavioral and/or emotional escalation (e.g. planned ignoring, time-out). For example, parents may have previously identified that they hold the value of raising a respectful child. A clinician could work with the parents to make commitments to refrain from engaging in experiential avoidance (e.g. withdrawing command, giving in to a tantrum) when their child begins misbehaving, and instead, utilize mindfulness and cognitive defusion techniques. In other words, parents are committing to consistently engaging in effective behavior management strategies, despite anticipated behavioral and/or emotional escalations displayed by their child, in order to move forward in a valued direction.

Evidence-Based Clinical Application

To date, there is limited published research on ACT-enhanced behavioral parent training. Several studies have been conducted in which a combined group curriculum involving ACT principles and parent training strategies were evaluated (Brown, Whittingham, Boyd, McKinlay, & Sofronoff, 2014; Whittingham, Sanders, McKinlay, & Boyd, 2014), although it should be noted that these studies specifically targeted children with chronic medical conditions (e.g., cerebral palsy, traumatic brain injury). This combined curriculum involved two sessions discussing ACT principles, followed by six sessions of training in specific parenting strategies. In each of these studies, results demonstrated that an ACT-enhanced parent-training curriculum was associated with more significant improvements in targeted parent (e.g., overreactivity and verbosity) and child variables (e.g., ECBI intensity score) in comparison to standard parent-training interventions.

Coyne and Wilson (2004) described how to use ACT principles in conjunction with parent–child interaction therapy (PCIT) when working with a typically developing young child with conduct problems (e.g., noncompliance and aggression). In this illustrative case example, the child's mother was initially engaged in several sessions wherein ACT principles were discussed, including values identification, mindfulness, cognitive defusion, and acceptance, before participating in PCIT coaching sessions focused on parenting skills acquisition. Values identification was used to increase treatment engagement, and committed action exercises were incorporated to facilitate participation in the PCIT coaching sessions. Previously learned ACT principles were then flexibly incorporated into the PCIT coaching sessions throughout treatment, as needed. For example, when the mother learned planned ignoring, she encountered difficulties with adherence due to experiencing negative thoughts about her own incompetence and imagined a terrible future for her child. Mindfulness and cognitive defusion techniques were practiced (such as those described earlier), which resulted in increased feelings of competence and improved parenting skills.

Taken together, clinicians are encouraged to consider how these ACT principles can be used to enhance behavioral parent training by targeting relevant parental processes (e.g., avoidance, cognitive fusion, parental disengagement) that may be hindering new skill acquisition. Based upon the current literature, it is likely worthwhile for clinicians to allocate some time at the beginning of treatment to orient parents to ACT principles. Once this foundation has been established, clinicians can then flexibly integrate ACT principles into behavioral parent training sessions when any barriers are encountered.

SOCIAL SKILLS INTERVENTIONS

As discussed in earlier chapters, the preschool years are often the time that social problems develop or first become apparent. Two general types of approaches have been used to teach social skills and social competence to children. The *structured learning approach* to teaching social skills focuses on the step-by-step teaching of actual skills (e.g., how to start a conversation). The *social problem-solving approach* focuses more on teaching problem-solving skills that can be applied in social situations (e.g., deciding on an appropriate course of action when feeling left out of a playground game). Research has demonstrated that social skills training interventions often produce small but meaningful short-term gains; however, thoughtful development and implementation of these interventions is critical, as these gains are often cancelled out by problems with social validity, maintenance, and generalization (Merrell, 2008a).

There are a variety of social skills programs that use the structured learning method of training, all of which involve the following components: (1) introducing and defining the skill through didactic means, (2) modeling the skill, (3) overseeing student rehearsal of the skill, and (4) providing performance feedback on how effectively the student performed the skill in the rehearsal/role play. Programs that use this method are based on a group-training format, including small pull-out groups of four to eight children or a whole class of students. With young children, in particular, it is often recommended that the classroom approach be used. For example, the widely used Skillstreaming program recommends that training take place in the classroom, as well as in other locations in which social skills are important (e.g., playground, lunchroom; McGinnis, 2011). For younger children who are not yet enrolled in a typical school classroom, an appropriate setting could also be in preschool or daycare. One of the difficulties with teaching social skills is the lack of generalization that occurs from training settings to real-life settings. Utilizing a classroom approach, in which the teacher is one of the trainers, allows for reinforcement of appropriate social skills throughout the day (not just during the training session), which is considered key to promoting generalization and maintenance of the social skills.

The first step in teaching social skills in the structured learning method involves having the clinician introduce and define the skill. Typically the clinician generally describes the skill and then specifies the steps involved in completing it. For example, the skill of following directions, as defined by the Skillstreaming program (McGinnis, 2011), includes the following steps: (1) listen, (2) think about it, (3) ask, if needed, and (4) do it. After teaching these steps to the students, the skill is modeled by the group leader so that the children can see how the skill is actually used. Children then take turns practicing the skill through role plays and receiving feedback from peers and group leaders. Children receive positive reinforcement for appropriate use of the skill and corrective feedback for inappropriate use. Following the session, children are assigned homework to practice the skill in real-life settings.

Since children often do not use the skill appropriately at first, feedback from parents and teachers is advisable. If social skills are taught in a pull-out group format, the teacher should be kept apprised of the skills the children are learning so that he or she can assist with the training in real-life settings. In addition, parents should be involved by reviewing homework sheets the child brings home or through ongoing contact with the group leaders.

In addition to following these steps, clinicians need to establish basic group rules and behavioral contingencies for appropriate and inappropriate behavior during group meetings. For example, children who are actively participating should earn points or tokens that can then be exchanged for tangible reinforcers at the end of the group meeting. If children are talking out of turn or engaging in aggressive behavior during meetings, they should lose points or tokens.

Problem-solving skills training is the other main type of intervention that has been used with children in an attempt to decrease aggressive behaviors and increase prosocial behaviors. Such programs teach children to go through a series of problem-solving steps when they are faced with a problem (see Table 3.2). Children are first taught to define the problem (e.g. wanting to play with other kids at the playground but not knowing how to approach them). Next, children are taught to brainstorm and identify multiple solutions to the problem. At this stage, the focus is purely on identifying as many solutions as possible, and these solutions will typically include prosocial, as well as antisocial solutions. Teachers and parents should be coached to refrain from evaluating suggested solutions at this stage, as they are often tempted to dissuade any antisocial solutions that are offered. Some solutions children may generate in response to the problem of wanting to join a group on the playground may include asking to join in, throwing a ball at the group, and asking the teacher to tell the group to let other kids play too. After such a list of solutions has been generated, each solution is evaluated (e.g., "If I have the teacher ask if I can play too, the other kids might think I'm a teacher's pet"), and the most appropriate solution is chosen

---

TABLE 3.2. Problem-Solving Steps

- What is the problem?
- What are possible solutions to the problem?
- What would happen if . . . ? [Evaluate outcomes of each possible solution.]
- Which option should I choose?
- How did my chosen option work out?

and implemented. Following the implementation of the solution, the child evaluates the outcome of the chosen solution (e.g., "I was scared to ask at first, but they said 'sure,' so it was great").

Problem-solving programs have had some positive effects for older children (ages 7–13), both as stand-alone interventions and in combination with other approaches. For example, a recent literature review on the efficacy of problem-solving skills training, parent training, and a combination of the two found that the combined intervention generally yielded more positive outcomes than either intervention alone (Kazdin, 2010). Research on the use of problem-solving skills with young children, however, is still limited. In a study with young children ages 4–8 that compared the efficacy of parent training; child training (using problem-solving skills training); teacher training; child and teacher training; parent, child, and teacher training; or no treatment, positive treatment effects were shown in all treatment combinations. Although the interventions involving parent training produced greater positive changes in child behavior problems, the child-focused intervention did lead to better problem-solving skills for the children and fewer negative peer interactions. Furthermore, adding teacher training to parent training and/or child training improved treatment outcomes for child misbehavior in the classroom (Pidano & Allen, 2015).

The lack of research on social skills programs targeted to young children is not unique to the problem-solving approach. Although some social skills programs have been developed specifically for preschool-age children (e.g., the preschool version of the Skillstreaming program), much of the outcome research with young children has focused on children with developmental delays, rather than on typically developing children. In general, the outcome literature on social skills training is not extremely positive. As mentioned previously, social skills interventions have demonstrated limited generalizability and poor social validity (Merrell, 2008a). In order for a social skills intervention to be most effective, these programs must have social validity, be taught and practiced in real-life settings, be coordinated and reinforced across settings, and be evidence based.

PREVENTION AND EARLY INTERVENTION PROGRAMS

As noted in Chapter 1, preschool-age children who exhibit externalizing symptoms are at risk for continuing to display problem behaviors throughout childhood and adolescence. Unfortunately, young children with conduct problems represent a chronically underserved population, with approximately 70% not receiving any treatment and even fewer receiving treatment that is empirically supported (Webster-Stratton & Reid, 2003). Some children will eventually receive services, but these services may come too late. Given the serious consequences associated with the early display of conduct problems, effective prevention and early intervention programs must be initiated long before the child reaches school age (Campbell, 2002). The longer a child and family go without treatment, the more difficult it becomes to make meaningful change.

Given the substantial advances that have been made in identifying the risk and protective factors associated with developmental pathways leading to conduct problems, increased attention has been paid to developing preventative and early intervention programs for children with externalizing behavior problems. Preventative work has primarily focused on selective and indicated prevention programs. That is, children who are targeted for treatment are at risk of or already exhibiting conduct problems at an elevated rate and oftentimes at a clinical level. For example, targeted children may meet the criteria for ODD but not as yet for CD. Many prevention programs involve multiple interventions across multiple settings, combining many of the interventions previously reviewed into a comprehensive package. These programs typically target parenting skills (through behavioral parent training), child social competence (through social skills/social competence training), and general aggressive/disruptive behaviors (through home- and school-based behavioral interventions). Other risk factors associated with conduct problems in children, such as poor academic skills, are also sometimes targeted. Furthermore, these programs often work to improve collaboration between parents, teachers, peers, and the broader community to ensure consistency across settings. As each of the main intervention components have been previously described in this chapter, we have not outlined a prevention program, per se, instead choosing to briefly review the literature on some of the existing prevention programs.

The Fast Track program is a comprehensive early intervention/prevention program that incorporates parent-focused treatment, classroom interventions, and child-focused interventions. In this program, all children at targeted schools were provided with a classwide intervention that included training in emotional understanding, friendship skills, self-control skills, and social problem-solving skills. In addition, for children identified as "high risk," parenting interventions, social skills training, and academic tutoring were offered. In an evaluation of the program after the first year (at the end of first grade), some significant positive effects were noted for the high-risk students (e.g., increased social problem solving, increased positive peer interactions, and decreased parental physical punishment). However, on many of the variables related to disruptive behavior (e.g., CBCL and TRF externalizing scores), there were no significant improvements (Conduct Problems Prevention Research Group [CPPRG], 1999a). For the non-high-risk children who received the classroom prevention component, significant positive effects were reported for peer-rated aggression and hyperactive-disruptive behaviors, and intervention classrooms were rated as more positive. However, there was no improvement in teacher ratings of child behaviors (CPPRG, 1999b). A longitudinal analysis completed after the third year of the program continued to show modest positive effects, including reduced aggression and increased prosocial behavior (by both teacher and peer report) and improved academic engagement (by teacher report; CPPRG, 2010). Of note, peer-reported effects were only significant for boys, stronger intervention effects were shown in less disadvantaged schools, and effects on aggression were larger for those who showed higher baseline levels of aggression (CPPRG, 2010).

Barkley and his colleagues have also investigated early intervention programs. They compared a comprehensive school-based early intervention program to a home-based program and a combined (school and home intervention) program. Children who participated were identified prior to kindergarten entry as having high levels of disruptive behaviors. The comprehensive school-based treatment program included social skills training (incorporating structured learning of social skills, following the Skillstreaming model, and self-control and anger-control training); a classroom token system, including a response–cost component; and other behavioral contingency interventions. The home intervention was a standard 10-week group behavioral parent training program. Outcomes indicated that the school-based interventions were effective and led to improvements in children's disruptive behaviors, social skills, and self-control, whereas behavioral parent training was not effective. The authors attributed the lack of significant results for the behavioral parent training, at least in part, to the fact that a large percentage of parents did not attend and that these parents did not actively seek out services (Barkley et al., 2000). Although the school-based program was initially beneficial, these gains were not maintained at a 2-year follow-up (Shelton et al., 2000).

The Triple P—Positive Parenting Program (Triple P; Sanders, 1999) is a multilevel model program, consisting of five levels of intervention on a tiered continuum of increasing strength and narrowing reach. This program was originally designed for children from birth to age 12, and has recently been extended to include youth ages 12–16. Classified as universal prevention, level 1 involves disseminating parenting strategies to the entire population through the use of media sources, tip sheets, and videotapes. Level 2 is a one-session, 20- to 30-minute consultation with a primary health care provider for mild behavioral concerns, who provides and discusses tip sheets outlining ways of solving common child management and developmental problems. Level 3 is a four-session, 20-minute consultation program conducted by a primary health care provider wherein parents are taught appropriate parenting skills designed to address mild to moderate conduct problem behaviors. Level 4 provides individual or group therapy for children with severe behavioral difficulties, and Level 5 offers intensive supports for families with serious difficulties (e.g., partner conflict, child maltreatment). These services are provided by a trained mental health professional and treatment is longer in duration (typically a minimum of 10–12 sessions; Sanders, 2010). To date, emphasis has been given to the two upper levels of the program (Levels 4 and 5), with these levels constituting standard clinical treatment using behavioral parent training principles.

In a randomized controlled trial of families and their 3-year-old children, Level 4, Level 5, and a wait-list control group were compared. At posttreatment, both treatment groups reported reduced child conduct problems, although significant improvements were only observed in the Level 5 group. Moreover, parents in the treatment groups reported reductions in the use of aversive parenting practices, although there were not significant group differences on observational measures. At 1-year follow up, treatment gains were maintained (Bor, Sanders, & Markie-Dadds, 2002). More recently, efforts have been made to universally disseminate Triple P Level 4 to preschool-age children and their parents. In one study, 186 families were randomly selected from local preschools to participate in a group-based Triple P prevention program. Significant reductions in dysfunctional parenting behaviors and child behavior problems were reported at postintervention. At 4-year follow-up, improvements in dysfunctional parenting behaviors were maintained; however, there was no evidence of long-term effects on child behavior problems (Heinrichs, Kliem, & Hahlweg, 2014). In general, all forms of Triple P have been shown to have moderate-to-large effects for both child and parenting behaviors, with the exception of Level 1 Triple P, which has been shown to have small effects (Thomas & Zimmer-Gembeck, 2007)

Webster-Stratton, who has examined group parent training extensively, extended the application of The Incredible Years program from one of intervention to one of prevention.

In one such study (Reid, Webster-Stratton, & Baydar, 2004), mothers of Head Start children participated in 8–12 weekly 2-hour group behavioral parent-training sessions that used videotaped modeling. In addition, Head Start teachers received 2–6 days of inservice trainings that consisted of the same material taught to the parent groups (e.g., positive behavior management and appropriate discipline techniques). Results demonstrated differential program effects depending on the child's initial levels of problem behaviors and the mothers' use of ineffective parenting strategies at baseline. Children exhibiting high levels of conduct problems at baseline and mothers who were initially highly critical and using ineffective parenting strategies benefited the most from the program.

More recently, The Incredible Years program, as well as other behavioral parent-training curriculums, has been evaluated as a prevention program when embedded in a medical setting. The utilization of prevention programs in primary care pediatric settings addresses a number of barriers to accessing adequate and appropriate care. For example, Reedtz, Handegard, and Morch (2011) evaluated a shortened version of The Incredible Years Program when working with a nonclinical community sample in a public health care center. This study was conducted to determine if a shortened parent training program could reduce certain risk factors related to the development of childhood behavior problems (e.g., harsh parenting, parents' sense of competence, positive parenting). The shortened intervention differed from the standard program in length (6 vs. 12 parent sessions) and only covered content related to positive disciplinary strategies (play, praise, and rewards), while choosing not to cover topics related to limit setting, ignoring, and time-out. Parents of children between 2 and 8 years of age (mean age = 3.88 years) were randomly assigned to the treatment or control group. Results from this study demonstrated that there were significant differences between the treatment and control group regarding reductions in harsh parenting and children's behavior problems, while strengthening positive parenting and parents' sense of competence.

Other research has also sought to examine the utility of early identification and intervention with young children in primary care. One such study (Berkovitz, O'Brien, Carter, & Eyberg, 2010) screened children using the ECBI within a pediatric primary care setting. They targeted children that scored greater than 1 standard deviation from the normative mean and had mothers who indicated wanting help for their child's behavior. Children were randomly assigned to one of two conditions, both which were an abbreviated version of PCIT for use in pediatric primary care: (1) a four-session therapist-led group intervention or (2) written materials describing basic PCIT concepts and guidelines for practice. Both groups demonstrated moderate-to- large effect sizes with regard to decreases in child problem behaviors and ineffective parenting strategies.

Taken as a whole, current evidence reveals modest positive effects for prevention and early intervention programs on outcomes of child and parent behaviors, although these positive findings are not consistently produced and are not always maintained at follow-up. These results may be due, in part, to the fact that most prevention programs continue to target children who are already demonstrating clinically concerning levels of disruptive behaviors. The literature indicates that relatively younger children are more likely to experience treatment success and their families are more likely to complete treatment (Lundahl et al., 2006). Given the substantial advances that have been made in delineating the developmental pathways leading to the onset of externalizing behavior disorders, additional efforts should be made to intervene earlier in the developmental trajectory of these children. As more research is conducted on conduct problems and their treatment and prevention, it is hoped that specific skills, as well as program process variables (e.g., parental involvement, treatment setting), will be identified and will clearly lead to more positive and enduring outcomes.

CHAPTER SUMMARY

This chapter has presented an overview of the more common and empirically supported techniques for working with young children who demonstrate externalizing behavior problems. Due to the potential for long-term adverse outcomes for these children, it is important to identify these problems early on and implement appropriate interventions. By far the intervention with the most empirical support for conduct problems is behavioral parent training. Thus, this intervention should always be considered when a child presents with disruptive behaviors. However, as recent studies have shown, combining multiple interventions that target functioning in different settings may produce a wider array of positive outcomes. Thus, clinicians should consider using a multifaceted intervention that targets the child's behavior at home, school, and daycare.

FORM 3.1

Behavior Basics

Knowing some basic behavioral principles can help you understand why your child behaves the way he/she does. Applying skills based on these principles will help you increase your child's good behaviors and decrease his/her negative behaviors.

ABCs of Behavior

A = **Antecedent:** What is happening <u>before</u> a behavior occurs.

B = **Behavior:** The actual behavior that occurs.

C = **Consequence:** What happens <u>after</u> the behavior occurs. If the consequence is desirable, the behavior is more likely to happen again; if the consequence is undesirable, the behavior is less likely to happen again.

Let's look at the ABCs using a couple of examples.

Example 1:
<u>Antecedent ("A")</u>: A child in a store sees candy in the checkout aisle.
<u>Behavior ("B")</u>: The child pesters his/her mother to buy the candy.
<u>Consequence ("C")</u>: The mother buys the child candy.
<u>Long-term consequence</u>: The child will be more likely to pester his/her mother in the future when he/she wants something since it "worked" for him/her before.

Example 2:
<u>Antecedent ("A")</u>: A child in a store sees candy in the checkout aisle.
<u>Behavior ("B")</u>: The child pesters his/her mother to buy the candy.
<u>Consequence ("C")</u>: The mother ignores the pestering and does not buy the child the candy.
<u>Long-term consequence</u>: The child will be less likely to pester his/her mother in the future since this behavior did not "work" for him/her.

Positive Reinforcement
- Providing a desirable consequence (a reinforcer) to increase a behavior. Reinforcers can include toys, privileges, attention, and praise.
    o Some unpleasant things can also be reinforcers. For example, since children are often reinforced by parental attention, even negative attention (e.g., yelling) may increase behaviors.
    o For reinforcers to be most effective, they must be provided immediately after a behavior.

Escape
- Also known as negative reinforcement. This involves removing something unpleasant to increase a behavior.
    o For example, a child may be allowed to leave the dinner table ("escape") after trying several bites of food.

(continued)

From Melissa L. Holland, Jessica Malmberg, and Gretchen Gimpel Peacock. Copyright © 2017 The Guilford Press. Permission to photocopy this form is granted to purchasers of this book for personal use or use with individual students (see copyright page for details). Purchasers can download additional copies of this material (see box at the end of the table of contents).

Behavior Basics (page 2 of 2)

- o Sometimes things we think are punishing actually reinforce a child's behavior. For example, if a child who doesn't like to sit at the dinner table is told she will have to leave unless she behaves appropriately, she may then act up more to leave the table.

Differential Reinforcement
- Reinforcing a desirable behavior, while ignoring an undesirable behavior.
  - o For example, if your child is throwing toys (in an effort to get your attention), ignore the throwing behavior and once he/she does **any other** appropriate behavior, reinforce him/her for it immediately.

Extinction
- When you stop reinforcing a behavior that was previously reinforced. This is a way to **decrease behavior.**
  - o For example, if you no longer purchase a candy bar for your child when he/she begins pestering you at the checkout line, this behavior will decrease.

Extinction Burst
- When a behavior is placed on extinction, it **may initially cause the behavior to worsen** before it gets better.
  - o This reaction is very common and will eventually stop if you are persistent. **Persistence is critical**. If you initially ignore a behavior but eventually give in once the behavior has escalated, you have now taught your child that if he/she escalates, he/she will eventually receive reinforcement. In other words, the problem will become worse! That is why you must be committed to using extinction before you initiate use of this strategy.

Punishment
- Implementing a consequence to decrease a behavior. This may involve adding an aversive consequence (e.g., extra chores) or removing something desirable (e.g., loss of privileges). Generally speaking, removing something desirable is the most effective type of punishment.

FORM 3.2

Using Your Attention Strategically

"Time-In"

The first step in effective parenting is the establishment of positive parent–child interactions (i.e., "time-in"). "Time-in" helps promote a positive parent–child relationship and helps create a critical balance between providing attention to children for appropriate behavior and discipline for inappropriate behavior. Encouraging children with well-planned physical contact and verbal praise helps them develop appropriate social behaviors that lead to high levels of self-confidence and self-esteem.

The 5:1 Rule

The use of "time-in" coupled with consistent discipline creates a powerful contrast between what behaviors you want your child to engage in and those you do not want your child to engage in. It is the balance between "time-in" and consistent discipline that is critical. There is thought to be a "magical ratio" regarding the number of positive versus negative interactions you should have with your child. For every 1 time that you have to "get after" or discipline your child, try to find 5 ways to be positive. In other words, strive to maintain a ratio of 5 positive interactions for every 1 negative interaction.

Catch Your Child Being Good

Disciplining your child for inappropriate behaviors only provides information about what *not to do*. Verbally praising or giving attention to your child for appropriate behavior ("catching your child being good") teaches your child what *to do*. We often ignore our children when they are quiet and engaging in appropriate behaviors. You don't have to wait until your child does something extraordinary to provide praise and attention. For example, if your child does not interrupt you while you are on the phone and you do not praise him/her, your child will learn that if he/she behaves, this positive behavior is ignored.

Ways to Provide Positive Attention

When you see your child engaging in desirable behaviors, **immediately** tell him/her that you like that behavior. When you praise your child, **be specific about what is desirable.** For example, "I really like when you play quietly with your toys." You can also use special activities as a reward, but do not make all fun activities between you and your child dependent on good behavior. Additional examples of praise are:

Physical	Verbal
Hugs	"I like it when you . . ."
Pats on head or shoulder	"Thanks! That was terrific when you . . ."
Smiles, kisses, eye winks	"Great! Nice going! Excellent job! Super! Fantastic!"
High fives	"Just for behaving so well, you and I will . . ."
Thumbs up	"I am very proud of you when you . . ."

(continued)

From Melissa L. Holland, Jessica Malmberg, and Gretchen Gimpel Peacock. Copyright © 2017 The Guilford Press. Permission to photocopy this form is granted to purchasers of this book for personal use or use with individual students (see copyright page for details). Purchasers can download additional copies of this material (see box at the end of the table of contents).

Using Your Attention Strategically (page 2 of 2)

Be sure to avoid insincere compliments. For example, avoid statements such as, "Thanks for playing nicely with your sister. Why can't you do that all the time?" Praising your child should make him/her feel good about what he/she just did, not remind him/her of inappropriate behaviors from the past.

Planned Ignoring

There are certain "attention-seeking" behaviors such whining, pouting, complaining, and crying that many children display. Parents often respond to these behaviors with scolding or reprimanding. Unfortunately, this response may reward your child, as some attention (even if it is negative) is better than no attention.

Planned ignoring can be a helpful strategy to reduce these behaviors. This involves providing no attention (e.g., no eye contact, physical response, or verbal response) for the attention seeking behavior. When using this strategy, the behavior often gets worse before it gets better (extinction burst). If this happens, **don't give in** and know that persistent ignoring is key to improvement. When using this strategy, it is critical to respond with positive attention to the first instance of your child's appropriate behavior.

FORM 3.3

The Child's Game

In order to increase your child's good behaviors, it is important to reinforce these behaviors by paying attention to them. The best way to practice this is in a play setting. This type of interaction also helps with parent–child bonding and can increase the positive relationship between a parent and child. Below are guidelines for conducting these play sessions.

1. **Select a time.** Select a 5- to 15-minute time period each day to play with your child.
2. **Interact with just one child.** During this playtime, you should play with only one child at a time. You can engage in this activity with all of your children, but make sure to play with each child separately. Work to minimize distractions and avoid multitasking.
3. **Select appropriate toys.** Select three to four different toys you can use during this playtime. These toys should be constructive, unstructured, and nonviolent in nature (e.g., blocks, Legos, Lincoln Logs).
4. **Use child-directed statements.** As you begin playing with your child, use the following types of verbalizations and interactions:
   a. **Praise.** Provide your child with praise for appropriate behaviors. Use specific statements when possible and praise effort (rather than outcomes). All praise should be genuine and enthusiastic.
      - Examples:
        o "I like how still you're sitting in your chair!"
        o "Good job with your tower. You are being so careful stacking those blocks."
   b. **Descriptions.** Describe specifically what your child is doing. Be genuine and enthusiastic. Think of these verbalizations as a "play-by-play" of your child's activity.
      - Examples:
        o "You put the blue block on top of the red block"
        o "You have a green crayon, and you're drawing a circle."
   c. **Reflections.** Reflect back the basic message your child is communicating to show you are listening.
      - Examples:
        o *Your child says:* "I'm gonna draw a monster." *You say:* "You're going to draw a monster. I can't wait to see it!"
        o *Your child says:* "Green is my favorite color." *You say:* "You like green. That is a nice color."
   d. **Joining in/imitation.** Play with your child and/or imitate your child's play.
      - Example:
        o If your child is building towers with blocks, you should too.
5. **Avoid directive statements.** During your playtime, you should refrain from the following:
   a. **Asking questions:** For example, "What are you drawing?" or "What color is this?"
   b. **Giving commands:** For example, "Why don't you draw a picture of our house?"
   c. **Being critical:** For example, "That's not a very good picture of our house—our house is white, not red."
6. Occasionally during this playtime, your child may misbehave. If this misbehavior is minor, simply ignore it. When your child begins to behave appropriately again, reengage in play with him/her. If the misbehavior is severe, end the playtime.

From Melissa L. Holland, Jessica Malmberg, and Gretchen Gimpel Peacock. Copyright © 2017 The Guilford Press. Permission to photocopy this form is granted to purchasers of this book for personal use or use with individual students (see copyright page for details). Purchasers can download additional copies of this material (see box at the end of the table of contents).

FORM 3.4

Homework Sheet for the Child's Game

Child's name: _____

Date	Did you practice? (Yes or No)	Comments

From Melissa L. Holland, Jessica Malmberg, and Gretchen Gimpel Peacock. Copyright © 2017 The Guilford Press. Permission to photocopy this form is granted to purchasers of this book for personal use or use with individual students (see copyright page for details). Purchasers can download additional copies of this material (see box at the end of the table of contents).

FORM 3.5

Giving Effective Commands

Providing strategic attention to your child's appropriate behaviors is very important but does not guarantee desired behavior. Children thrive under conditions that provide structure, clear expectations, and predictability. Giving effective instructions is a critical part of teaching children how to behave appropriately. Below are some simple and important guidelines for improving your child's compliance.

1. **Pick your battles.** Only give commands in situations in which it is important that a command be given and at times when you can follow through. It is critical that you are consistent in providing consequences for noncompliant behaviors.

2. **Get your child's attention.** Prior to giving a command, make sure you have your child's attention. Make eye contact, say your child's name, move closer to your child, etc. You should always be in the same room as your child when giving a command and you should reduce potential distractions (e.g., turn off the TV).

3. **Only give commands your child can complete.** Tasks involving activities that are too difficult for your child to understand or complete adequately should not be given.

4. **Make commands direct and simple.** Use a simple, direct instruction (e.g., "Pick up your shoes") and use a firm tone. Do not use a question when you want your child to do something (e.g., "Can you go put your shoes on?"). Using a question implies a choice and you must be willing to accept "no" for an answer.

5. **Give one command at a time.** Children often have difficulties following through with multistep commands. Give one command at a time, with a consequence for compliance/noncompliance after each command.

6. **State commands positively.** Instead of telling your child what *not* to do (e.g., "Don't jump on the couch"), tell your child what *to do* (e.g., "Please sit down").

7. **Make limited use of explanations.** Often children ask for explanations or rationales simply to avoid complying with a command. Providing an explanation after giving a command also takes away the focus from the command. If a rationale is provided, it should be given before the command (e.g., "We're going to visit Grandma and it's cold outside. Please go put on your coat now") or after the child has complied (e.g., "Thanks for putting your coat on like I asked; we're going to visit Grandma and it's cold outside").

8. **If possible, give choices.** When children are offered choices, it oftentimes leads to increased compliance. If the child can make a choice, let him/her know that in the command (e.g., "Please put on your red coat or your blue coat").

From Melissa L. Holland, Jessica Malmberg, and Gretchen Gimpel Peacock. Copyright © 2017 The Guilford Press. Permission to photocopy this form is granted to purchasers of this book for personal use or use with individual students (see copyright page for details). Purchasers can download additional copies of this material (see box at the end of the table of contents).

FORM 3.6

Using Time-Out Effectively

Time-out is an effective method to reduce your child's inappropriate behaviors. However, it should always be used in combination with other positively based techniques you have already learned. Make sure you are positively attending to appropriate behaviors and using effective commands. Never give a command that you do not intend to back up and always provide praise when your child complies with a command. To effectively use timeout with your child, follow the guidelines below.

1. **Give a simple and direct command.** Always give appropriate commands in a firm, neutral voice (see Form 3.5).

2. **Wait 10 seconds.** After giving a command, be silent for 10 seconds and wait for your child to comply. You may want to count silently to yourself (don't count out loud).

3. **Praise compliance.** If your child begins to obey the instruction within 10 seconds, immediately praise him/her.

4. **If no compliance, restate the command.** If your child does not make any effort to obey within 10 seconds, repeat your instruction and include a time-out warning (e.g., "If you don't _____ [repeat the command], then you will go to time-out"). After giving this warning, wait another 10 seconds for compliance.

   Note: When you are using time-out for something other than compliance (e.g., breaking a household rule, such as hitting a sibling), send your child to time-out immediately and do not use this warning statement

5. **Praise compliance.** If your child obeys a warning, immediately praise him/her.

6. **If no compliance, send/take child to time-out.** If your child does not comply with your command within 10 seconds, send/take your child to time-out. Say, "Since you did not do as I asked, you must go to time-out." Your child should not be allowed to argue, belatedly comply with the command, etc. Initially, you may need to use physical guidance to get your child to the time-out location. Try gently guiding your child to the time-out location. If necessary, pick your child up from behind and carry him/her to the time-out location. Once your child is in the time-out location, say firmly, "Sit here and be quiet until I tell you to come out."

7. **Do not attend to your child.** Do not give your child any attention while he/she is in time-out. Do not talk to your child. Continue what you were doing but keep an eye on your child so that you can put him/her back in time-out if he/she leaves time-out without permission. When your child has remained in the time-out quietly for the appropriate amount of time (see below), return to your child and say, "Because you are quiet, you may come out of time-out now."

8. **Restate the command.** After your child is released from time-out, repeat the original instruction your child disobeyed. Repeat steps listed above as needed.

(continued)

From Melissa L. Holland, Jessica Malmberg, and Gretchen Gimpel Peacock. Copyright © 2017 The Guilford Press. Permission to photocopy this form is granted to purchasers of this book for personal use or use with individual students (see copyright page for details). Purchasers can download additional copies of this material (see box at the end of the table of contents).

Using Time-Out Effectively *(page 2 of 2)*

Frequently Asked Questions about Time-Out

How long should my child stay in time-out?

The general rule of thumb is that children should remain in time-out for about 1 minute per year of age, not to exceed 5 minutes. However, when initially using time-out, this time frame is typically too much to expect, so plan on working up to it. When time-out is first used, it is common for children to cry, whine, scream, etc., for long periods of time. If this behavior occurs, postpone releasing your child from time-out until he/she has been quiet for 15–30 seconds. Do not use a timer during time-out but keep your eye on the clock.

Where should my time-out location be?

Time-out in a chair is the preferable method. The chair should be an adult-size dining-room-type chair. The chair should be placed far enough away from all objects (including walls) so that your child cannot kick or hit anything while in the chair. There should be nothing reinforcing that your child has access to from the chair (e.g., TV, toys). The time-out chair should be placed in a location that you can observe (e.g., in a hallway, not in a closet or bathroom).

What if my child leaves the time-out chair?

It is not uncommon for children to test the limits when parents first begin to use time-out. Children who squirm, bounce, roll around, etc., in the chair should not be considered out of time-out. This behavior should simply be ignored. Children will often leave the chair and may do so immediately after being placed in time-out. It is important that, if this happens, you immediately return your child to time-out but remain silent. When first using time-out (when it is most likely your child will leave the chair), it is a good idea to stand right next to the chair (but do not look directly at your child or do anything to give your child attention). That way, you can immediately put your child back in time-out as soon as he/she leaves the time-out chair. If your child persists in leaving the time-out chair, talk with your therapist about other options.

What should I do if my child says he/she needs to get out of the chair?

Your child is not to leave the time-out chair to use the bathroom or get a drink until his/her time is up and he/she has completed the task that was asked of him/her. If your child is permitted to leave time-out following a certain demand, he/she will come to use this demand as a means of escaping from time-out on each occasion he/she is placed in the chair. Simply ignore all requests your child makes.

FORM 3.7

Homework Sheet for Time-Out

Child's name: _____

Date	Time	Length of Time-Out	Comments (describe any problems)

From Melissa L. Holland, Jessica Malmberg, and Gretchen Gimpel Peacock. Copyright © 2017 The Guilford Press. Permission to photocopy this form is granted to purchasers of this book for personal use or use with individual students (see copyright page for details). Purchasers can download additional copies of this material (see box at the end of the table of contents).

FORM 3.8

Using Privileges to Manage Behavior

Privileges can be used to reinforce your child for appropriate behaviors and to discipline him/her for inappropriate behaviors. This method may be used when it is not possible to use time-out or as an addition to time-out for specific behaviors.

Providing Privileges for Appropriate Behavior

1. With your child, make up a list of privileges he/she can earn. These should include extra-special privileges (e.g., getting a new toy, going out to eat with a parent) as well as other, common privileges (e.g., 15-minute later bedtime, extra dessert, watching an additional TV show).

2. Make a list of behaviors and chores that your child can do to earn privileges. Make sure that you do not place unreasonable expectations on your child. Good examples of chores/tasks for young children are: picking up toys, helping set the table, putting away clean clothes, helping feed the dog, etc.

3. When your child completes a chore or behavior on your list, give him/her one of the privileges, making sure to praise your child for completing the behavior/chore. For example, when your child earns the privilege of watching an extra TV show, you might say, "Thanks for taking your toys out of the living room. Because you did such a good job cleaning up, you may watch one extra TV show today." Provide your child with the common extra privileges on a regular basis and occasionally give him/her one of the extra-special privileges.

4. Provide lots of reinforcement, especially initially. When beginning the program, look for opportunities to give your child privileges for appropriate behaviors, and remember that you can reward your child for good behaviors that are not on the list you have made. Parents often expect too much at once and wait for "big" behaviors to occur before providing reinforcement. This makes it less likely that the program will be successful because the child will rarely have access to the privileges.

Taking Away Privileges for Inappropriate Behavior

1. Make a list of privileges your child automatically receives on a daily basis. These privileges are those your child does not need to do anything special to obtain but are the everyday privileges you allow your child (e.g., an hour of TV, unlimited access to all toys, inviting a friend over).

2. Make a list of behaviors/chores that your child must do in order to keep these automatic privileges. This list should be relatively short and should include only those chores or tasks your child is expected to complete on a daily basis (e.g., getting dressed, brushing teeth at night).

3. Make a list of inappropriate behaviors that you will not tolerate from your child (e.g., hitting siblings, spitting out food at the dinner table).

4. As long as your child completes the daily tasks identified in step 2, he/she is allowed to keep his/her automatic privileges. If these daily tasks are not completed, or your child exhibits one of the inappropriate behaviors identified in step 3, then take away certain automatic privileges. It may be easiest to pair each negative behavior with a specific privilege that will be lost. Go over this list with your child so that he/she knows what is expected of him/her and what will happen when he/she does not complete a daily task or engages in an inappropriate behavior.

It is important to understand that you are not bribing your child. Many parents feel their children should obey house rules simply because it is their responsibility. Remember, though, that you get paid for working at a job. In the same sense, obeying house rules is your child's job, and he/she should be able to earn privileges in the same way you earn a paycheck.

From Melissa L. Holland, Jessica Malmberg, and Gretchen Gimpel Peacock. Copyright © 2017 The Guilford Press. Permission to photocopy this form is granted to purchasers of this book for personal use or use with individual students (see copyright page for details). Purchasers can download additional copies of this material (see box at the end of the table of contents).

FORM 3.9

Privileges Worksheet

Earning Privileges for Appropriate Behaviors

Extra/Optional Behaviors and Chores
1. _____
2. _____
3. _____
4. _____
5. _____
6. _____
7. _____
8. _____
9. _____
10. _____

Extra Privileges
1. _____
2. _____
3. _____
4. _____
5. _____
6. _____
7. _____
8. _____
9. _____
10. _____

Special Extra Privileges
1. _____
2. _____
3. _____
4. _____
5. _____

Removal of Privileges for Inappropriate Behaviors

Expected Behaviors and Chores
1. _____
2. _____
3. _____
4. _____
5. _____
6. _____
7. _____
8. _____
9. _____
10. _____

Automatic Privileges
1. _____
2. _____
3. _____
4. _____
5. _____
6. _____
7. _____
8. _____
9. _____
10. _____

Inappropriate Behaviors
1. _____
2. _____
3. _____
4. _____
5. _____

From Melissa L. Holland, Jessica Malmberg, and Gretchen Gimpel Peacock. Copyright © 2017 The Guilford Press. Permission to photocopy this form is granted to purchasers of this book for personal use or use with individual students (see copyright page for details). Purchasers can download additional copies of this material (see box at the end of the table of contents).

FORM 3.10

Managing Behavior Problems in Public Places

After your child has learned to comply with rules and commands at home, it will be easier to teach him/her to behave as expected in public places, such as stores and restaurants. When out in public, it is important to praise appropriate behaviors and provide consequences for inappropriate behaviors, just as you would do at home. Below are guidelines to help you.

- **Take practice trips.**
    - Take 15 to 20-minute practice trips where you practice the guidelines below.
- **Set up the rules for expected behaviors beforehand and review these rules with your child.**
    - Have a maximum of three to four rules.
        - Example: If you are taking your child grocery shopping, your rules might be: "Stay within arm's length of the cart, do not take any items off the shelves, and talk in your indoor voice."
- **Praise your child for good behaviors.**
    - Provide your child with positive reinforcement for appropriate behaviors.
    - Use specific labeled praise when your child follows rules.
        - Example: "Thank you for staying next to the cart."
    - Consider providing a special reward after the trip.
    - Consider using a point or token system in which the child is able to earn points/tokens (items that can later be exchanged for special reinforcers) for appropriate behaviors.
- **Set up consequences for misbehavior.**
    - Establish predetermined consequences and explain these to your child ahead of time.
    - If using a point or token system to reinforce your child, you can also add a response–cost component in which you take away points/tokens for inappropriate behaviors.
    - Consider using a modified time-out in public if you have used it successfully at home.
        - Require your child to sit or stand in one location for a brief period of time (e.g., 30–45 seconds of quiet).
- **Give your child something to do.**
    - Talk to your child frequently and provide him/her with small tasks.
        - Example: If you are grocery shopping, you might ask your child to reach for the items on the lower shelves (only after you have pointed the items out to the child).
- **If your child throws a tantrum—*do not give in.***
    - Ignore your child's tantrum behaviors.
    - If necessary, leave the store, restaurant, etc., until your child calms down. (*Note:* Never leave your child alone—you should always accompany your child when it becomes necessary to leave the public place.)
        - Once your child is calm, you should always return to the original activity. Otherwise, your child will learn that tantruming is an effective way to escape a situation.

From Melissa L. Holland, Jessica Malmberg, and Gretchen Gimpel Peacock. Copyright © 2017 The Guilford Press. Permission to photocopy this form is granted to purchasers of this book for personal use or use with individual students (see copyright page for details). Purchasers can download additional copies of this material (see box at the end of the table of contents).

CHAPTER 4

Treatment of Internalizing Problems

As discussed in Chapter 1, internalizing disorders are characterized by a wide spectrum of symptoms, including depression, anxiety, somatic complaints, and social isolation. These disorders are often more difficult to detect than overt or externalizing behavior disorders, particularly in young children. Due to the complexities involved in both the detection and treatment of these symptoms, internalizing problems are often misdiagnosed and left untreated. In addition, clinicians working with young children with anxiety or depression need to be aware that they often have a different symptom presentation than do older children. This chapter provides an overview of the prevention and intervention methods for young children with anxiety, selective mutism, somatic complaints, and depression. A section that reviews working with young children who have been exposed to traumatic situations/abuse is also included. The chapter concludes with a discussion of mindfulness interventions and a sampling of some techniques with children who exhibit internalizing disorders.

ANXIETY DISORDERS

As previously noted, there are a wide array of anxiety disorders in young children, but all involve fear and anxiety that are out of proportion to what would be expected based on the setting and the child's developmental level. Minimizing a child's fears and anxieties by telling the child that he or she is "silly" or "stupid" is countertherapeutic. Instead the child's feelings should be validated as concerning and upsetting to the child. Although there may be a tendency to assume that a child's anxiety will dissipate by itself, or that the child is just being "difficult" or "attention seeking," there is evidence that some anxiety problems can persist from early childhood into later childhood and even into the adult years (Merrell,

2008b). Thus if a child's fears or worries have become extreme and/or more intense than is expected, it is important that interventions be implemented.

Once an anxiety problem has been identified and the specific symptoms have been defined through an assessment (see Chapter 2), a treatment plan can be developed. Different disorders and symptom constellations often call for similar, though uniquely different, interventions. Outlined here are treatment plans and interventions for common anxiety problems in young children, including specific phobias and separation anxiety. See Form 4.1 for a parent handout on anxiety interventions.

Fears and Specific Phobias

Prevention of Specific Phobias

Several steps can be taken in order to prevent childhood fears from escalating into phobic responses. Once again, it is important to avoid belittling the child's fears in a misguided attempt to reduce them. Statements such as "That is ridiculous, there are no monsters outside of your window" may only make the child feel that he or she cannot talk with adults about the fear—a far cry from depotentiating the fear, as was intended. A better approach is to validate the child's fear without confirming that the fear is real. For example, a parent might state, "I understand, Eli, that the trees make scary shadows outside of your window and that you feel afraid. I know that you know those are just trees outside, but they do move around a lot at night, don't they?" Such a response allows the child to feel understood while, at the same time, helping him or her to make sense of the stimulus that is causing the fear (Garber, Garber, & Spizman, 1992).

While belittling the child's fear should be avoided, it is also advisable to avoid inadvertently reinforcing it. Fears and phobias can be learned, sustained, and intensified by having another person, often an influential person in the child's life, instruct the child to be afraid. For example, if the child is fearful of dogs, it would only reinforce his or her fear to avoid dogs, perhaps commenting to the child, "There is a dog, Matthew. I know you are afraid of dogs, so we will walk the other way to get away from it." This strategy may be a tempting one, as the parent may want to calm the child, but in the long run, this type of response will likely only intensify the fear (Ollendick, Davis, & Muris, 2004).

Treatment of Fears and Specific Phobias

Treatment of fears and phobias typically involves behavioral techniques such as desensitization, modeling, and contingency management, as well as cognitive techniques such as using positive self-talk. Mindfulness exercises have also recently been used successfully with younger populations, and will be overviewed later in this chapter. Empirical support for the efficacy of these techniques in the preschool- and kindergarten-age population has been growing, and many techniques that can be used with elementary-age children and adolescents have been found to work with younger children, as long as the clinician ensures that explanations and procedures are adapted to the cognitive level of the young child.

SYSTEMATIC DESENSITIZATION

Systematic desensitization involves a gradual exposure to the feared stimulus, combined with a response that is considered to be incompatible with anxiety (e.g., relaxation). Children first identify different situations in which they may encounter the feared object and rate the level of fear associated with each of these situations. These items are organized into a "fear hierarchy" (in which fears are listed from least to most feared), and the child is then exposed to the feared stimuli while simultaneously using an anxiety-relieving technique, such as progressive muscle relaxation. This exposure can occur either *in vivo* (in the real-life setting) or through an imagined experience. This technique is one of the most commonly used, as well as one of the most efficacious, interventions for fears and phobias in children (Morris et al., 2008; Ollendick et al., 2004). The use of deep breathing and progressive muscle relaxation techniques in working with the young child has been found to be successful (Friedberg et al., 2011).

An example of a phobia of spiders, presented in a dialogue between a clinician and a child, is used in this section to illustrate the use of systematic desensitization. Sophie was referred to the clinician after she began to have extreme reactions to spiders, such as running away, crying, and screaming. This phobia was interfering with her functioning because she refused to engage in certain activities (e.g., playing in the yard with friends) for fear she would encounter a spider.

> CLINICIAN: So, Sophie, tell me about spiders.
>
> SOPHIE: Spiders are scary . . . I hate them.
>
> CLINICIAN: What about spiders makes them scary?
>
> SOPHIE: They're brown and hairy and have big legs and they eat people.
>
> CLINICIAN: Uh-huh, and what else?
>
> SOPHIE: I saw a movie where a kid got stuck in a web, and the spider bit him and ate him.
>
> CLINICIAN: And what do you do when you see a spider?
>
> SOPHIE: I run away and scream. One time I saw one at my preschool, and I hid in the bathroom.

Allowing the child to talk freely about what makes the stimulus scary for him or her and what he or she does when exposed to it is helpful in gathering more specific details about the child's phobia that can be used to help create the fear hierarchy. Often, though, young children have difficulty elaborating on their phobias and their associated behaviors. Typically, the child's parents need to assist in identifying the child's reactions to the feared object, as well as in constructing the hierarchy. The fear hierarchy should begin with an item that produces little fear in the child (e.g., looking at a picture of a spider in a book) and end with the item that produces the most fear (e.g., touching a spider). The number of items included on the hierarchy are dependent upon the complexity of the child's fear.

Each of the items on the fear hierarchy should be rated by the child to determine the associated level of fear. For young children, it is often helpful to use a visual rating system, such as the one depicted in Form 4.2, while asking the child "how full of fear" he or she is. The child might say that he or she is "full up to my knees" to indicate some fear, "full up to my stomach" to indicate a moderate amount of fear, or "full up to my head" to indicate more severe fear. It can be helpful to ask children a series of questions about their fear to understand under what circumstances they are the most fearful. The following conversation between the clinician and Sophie is an example of this kind of questioning.

CLINICIAN: Sophie, I think I understand how scary spiders are for you. Using our system for how to rate your fear, how scary would you say you feel with us just talking about spiders?

SOPHIE: Up to my knees.

CLINICIAN: OK, and how about when you see a picture of a spider in a book?

SOPHIE: Up to my stomach. (*Points to her stomach.*)

CLINICIAN: OK, and how scary is it to see a TV show about spiders?

SOPHIE: Up to my shoulders.

CLINICIAN: I see. And how about when you actually see a spider on the wall?

SOPHIE: All the way up my neck. (*Points to her chin.*)

CLINICIAN: And to hold a spider?

SOPHIE: Past my head! (*Points to the ceiling.*)

Using this type of questioning, the clinician is able to develop a hierarchy of stimuli to work on with Sophie, such as the example provided in Table 4.1. It is important to note that creating such a list may make the child anxious and typically takes place over several sessions. As noted earlier, parents of young children typically are involved in the creation of the hierarchy. They can be asked to identify what objects/situations their child avoids on a regular basis and what stimuli lead to anxiety reactions (e.g., crying, clinging).

TABLE 4.1. Hierarchy of Fears

Most fearful

Seeing a spider on the table next to me
Seeing a spider on the wall
Seeing a spider in a movie
Seeing a picture of a spider in a book
Saying the word *spider*

Least fearful

Once the fear hierarchy has been constructed, the clinician can begin to pair the items with a response that is incompatible with fear. Typically, relaxation is used as this incompatible response. Here are summaries of some relaxation techniques commonly used with children.

DEEP BREATHING

Stress tends to affect the bodies of adults and children alike in many ways. For example, people tend to take shorter, shallower inhalations when they are anxious, in addition to taking fewer breaths ("forgetting to breathe"). A technique helpful to adults and children is learning the art of deep breathing. To practice deep breathing with a child client, pick a quiet, private place to start. Both the clinician and the child should lie on their backs. The child should be instructed to put one hand on his or her stomach and one hand on the chest. When breathing correctly, the hand on the stomach should move up and down, but the hand on the chest does not. The clinician can model for the child the correct way to breath, instructing him or her to "fill up your stomach with air, like a balloon." Feedback is often necessary (e.g., "Do not arch your back or push out your stomach"). Clinicians should let the child know that it can take a lot of practice to "belly breathe" and encourage the child to practice the skill every day. The clinician should also instruct the parents to praise the child when he or she does so and to practice the skill with the child, when able. Once the skill has been mastered lying down, the child can practice the skill sitting down and standing up, as well as in different situations and contexts (Friedberg, Gorman, Hollar Witt, Biuckian, & Murray, 2011). More breathing techniques are offered in the section "Mindfulness" later in this chapter.

SLOW BREATHING

Once deep breathing has been mastered, the next step is to help the child slow down his or her breathing. A common technique is to count to four as the child breathes in, have the child hold his or her breath for four counts, breathe out for four counts, then hold the exhalation for four counts. The number of counts can be modified depending on the age and lung capacity of the child. Again, the clinician should model for and practice with the child to aid him or her in the acquisition of the skill. More information on breathing, along with variations for the young child, can be found also in the "Mindfulness" section.

PROGRESSIVE MUSCLE RELAXATION

When people are "stressed" or anxious, their muscles often tighten, leading to many physical complaints, such as headaches, backaches, leg aches, and stomachaches. Children tend to have many somatic, or physical, complaints when they are upset. Progressive muscle relaxation is one technique designed to relieve these physical symptoms—which, in turn, reduces the feelings of anxiety. Progressive relaxation is based on a principle of muscle physiology, wherein if you create tension in a muscle, and then release the tension, the muscle has to relax.

The first step of progressive muscle relaxation is to have the child sit comfortably or recline slightly in a comfortable chair. The techniques of deep and slow breathing can be practiced with the child to aid in initial relaxation. The clinician should let the child know that he or she will be doing a variety of different exercises to help relax muscles. It is preferable that the clinician does the exercises along with the child, modeling the correct postures and discussing the benefits of each pose. To add to the ease of implementing these techniques, a sample script is often used (see Form 4.3). This script should be adapted, as needed, to fit the age and developmental level of the child. Slow, deep breathing should be used in between each exercise.

Imagery and fantasy may also be incorporated into a systematic desensitization protocol, as described next:

IMAGERY

Imagery may be used in conjunction with deep breathing and/or progressive muscle relaxation. The child can be instructed to imagine him- or herself engaged in an activity or at a location that is fun and relaxing. If the child cannot think of any, the clinician may suggest images such as swinging on a swing, playing at a playground, or visiting the beach. Touch, scent, and sounds can be introduced in addition to the visual imagery of the child engaged in a pleasurable activity. For example, for the child imagining him- or herself swinging, the clinician can suggest how the child might feel the wind in his or her hair, hear the sounds of the playground, smell the sweet grass, and experience the tickle he or she may feel in the stomach when swinging really high.

EMOTIVE IMAGERY

This technique involves identifying one of the child's superheroes and then incorporating this hero into a fantasy story involving the child. The use of fantasy tied to a child's personal hero can heighten the child's interest and commitment in the treatment (King, Heyne, Gullone, & Molloy, 2001). The child is asked to close his or her eyes and to imagine and describe the hero in a story that arouses positive emotion. Once the story is created, the clinician introduces the lowest item on the fear hierarchy into the narrative, thereby pairing the positive emotions with the feared stimulus. This story is then used as a relaxation technique, while the clinician supports the child in working through the fear hierarchy. The clinician should be alert to any nonverbal signs that the child is anxious in order to not progress too quickly.

Although relaxation and/or imagery are the most common "incompatible responses" used in systematic desensitization, it may not be feasible to use relaxation techniques with some preschool children. Distraction techniques are good alternatives to use with younger children. This may include having the child bring his or her favorite toys to the session and, while exposing the child to the anxiety provoking items on the hierarchy, encouraging the child to play with the favored toys. Allowing the child to interact with a favorite person, or engaging the child in something funny to evoke laughter, can also be effective alternatives to relaxation techniques (Schroeder & Gordon, 2002).

Once the child has practiced and mastered relaxation (or an alternative incompatible response has been chosen), the clinician can begin the next step of systematic desensitization by pairing the items on the fear hierarchy with the relaxation (or other similar) response, starting with the first item on the hierarchy. Using the example of Sophie, she would say the word *spider* (see Table 4.1). Before and after she says the word, the clinician would practice the relaxation skills with her, being sure to focus on the skills that she finds the most relaxing. The premise behind this pairing is that a child cannot be anxious and relaxed at the same time (i.e., it is physiologically impossible). Therefore, having the child confront his or her phobias or fears while relaxed will disinhibit, or "turn off," the anxious response and make him or her feel more in control and less fearful of those objects or situations. This process typically takes time and often has to occur over the span of multiple sessions. The process should not be rushed; the clinician should allow ample time for the child to feel masterful over the first few items on the list before proceeding to the more feared items. The example in the following dialogue highlights the integration of these skills.

CLINICIAN: OK, Sophie, you did a great job of belly breathing and relaxing your muscles. You said that your fear feelings are at your "feet" right now, using our system of rating fear. Now I want you to say the word *spider*. Take in a deep breath, and as you breathe out, say the word *spider*, like this. (*Does the exercise.*)

SOPHIE: (*Takes in a deep breath.*) Spider.

CLINICIAN: Good. Now take in a few more deep breaths and let them out. (*Models the deep breathing.*) Now I want you to tell me how much fear you have using our system. Is it at your feet, your knees, your stomach, your shoulders, your neck, or your head?

SOPHIE: My knees.

CLINICIAN: OK, let's take in a few more deep breaths and relax some muscles (*Proceeds to engage in some of the progressive muscle relaxation exercises.*) Now how would you rate your fear feelings?

SOPHIE: My feet.

CLINICIAN: OK, good. Let's have you take in another deep breath and let it out. Now, I want you to take in one more deep breath and say the word *spider* while you breathe out, like this. (*Models.*)

SOPHIE: (*Takes in a deep breath.*) Spider.

CLINICIAN: Good, now let's do another deep breath and let it out. Now where would you rate your fear feelings?

SOPHIE: My feet.

CLINICIAN: Good, Sophie. Let's have you take in another deep breath, and as you let it out, again say "spider."

As this example illustrates, the clinician does not automatically proceed up the fear hierarchy but instead continues to focus on one area, until Sophie feels comfortable with it. Once mastery in one area is attained, the clinician would introduce the next item on her hierarchy, "Seeing a picture of a spider in a book," and combine such a picture with the same relaxation techniques. At each session, the clinician would start with the beginning items on the hierarchy and work up, so that the child is not flooded at the beginning of the session. Praise and positive reinforcement should be given for any progress made; these concepts are discussed further in the subsequent section "Contingency Management."

The use of exposure-based treatments, including systematic desensitization, have proved to be one of the most efficacious treatments for anxiety when working with children (Higa-McMillan, Francis, Rith-Najarian, & Chorpita, 2016). As mentioned earlier, exposure can be either *in vivo* (graduated real-life exposure to the feared stimulus) or imaginal (having the child imagine the feared stimulus). Although *in vivo* exposure has some practical limitations, it has been found to be more efficacious in reducing phobic reactions for children than imaginal exposure. Results of studies examining *in vivo* exposure as compared to imaginal exposure found that for children ages 3–10, *in vivo* exposure was more effective than no treatment or imaginal exposure modalities (Cowart & Ollendick, 2013; Ollendick & King, 1998). In our example, Sophie would likely benefit more from gradual exposure to her feared stimulus (spiders) through books, photographs, plastic spiders, and real spiders, coupled with relaxation exercises, than if she imagined the items.

Parents also should be involved in this treatment process with young children. They should be taught the incompatible response being used in treatment with their child so that they can help their child implement the technique at home when he or she is faced with anxiety-provoking stimuli. Although parents can assist with exposure exercises, they should be instructed to avoid "rushing" the fear hierarchy. Parents should work with the child on what has been covered in therapy sessions at home and/or in the community. For example, a child with a dog phobia who has mastered looking at a picture of a dog in session should be allowed to practice this skill at home by looking at dog books and receiving praise for this accomplishment from his or her parents.

OTHER INTERVENTION TECHNIQUES FOR FEARS AND PHOBIAS

As noted previously, although systematic desensitization is the most commonly used technique for fears and phobias, other techniques have also been found to be effective. Some of these other techniques (which are reviewed next), or a combination of techniques may also be used.

Cognitive Approaches. Cognitive-behavioral therapy (CBT) techniques, including positive self-talk, have become well-established interventions for children with anxiety. Although more complex CBT techniques would be avoided when working with younger children, simpler cognitive techniques can be successfully used. In a study by Hirshfeld-Becker and colleagues (2010), children ages 4–7 who were assigned to a parent–child CBT intervention evidenced significant improvement over controls on social phobia/avoidant disorder (effect size = 0.95) and specific phobia (effect size = 0.78), with these gains maintained at a 1-year follow-up. In a large scale review of the literature of anxiety treatments for children and adolescents ages 3–18, CBT was found to be an effective intervention for anxiety, evidencing large overall effect sizes (1.19) across studies (Higa-McMillan et al., 2016).

The use of positive self-statements can be an excellent tool for young children with anxiety or depression to help them feel more positive and self-assured in a variety of situations. The clinician can, with the child's help, make a list of positive statements the child can make about him- or herself or the situation. For each negative thought or statement, a positive thought should be developed. These could be referred to as "worry erasers" for the young child. For example, for a child who is afraid to go to preschool, the child could say to him- or herself, "I am not afraid," "I will be OK until my daddy picks me up," or "I am brave and will make friends." It is important to have the child practice the positive self-talk often. Have the child begin by saying the statements out loud, then try to switch the child to internal self-talk before he or she goes into the social situation (e.g., saying the statements in his or her head or softly to him- or herself).

Modeling. Modeling is a well-researched and frequently used technique that has been found, through a systematic review of the literature, to be very efficacious when working with children ages 2–16 with anxiety (Higa-McMillan et al., 2016). This approach allows the child to observe an individual interacting with the feared stimulus in a nonfearful manner. For example, a child with a dog phobia may watch another child pet a dog. Modeling can either be live or symbolic. In live modeling, the child observes an actual person interacting with the feared stimulus. In symbolic modeling, the model is either presented on video or the child imagines the model. Participant modeling, in which the child engages in the behavior with the model (e.g., the child also begins to pet the dog), also can be used. Often other techniques, such as positive self-talk and deep breathing, are used along with modeling, wherein negative or maladaptive thoughts are addressed through adaptive coping strategies and cognitive restructuring (Dasari & Knell, 2015; Schoenfield & Morris, 2009). For example, in participant modeling, the model may begin to approach the dog, saying, "I'm feeling kind of scared, but it's going to be okay. I know I can get a little closer to the dog." Following this, the child would be encouraged to approach the dog, using similar coping/positive self-talk statements. Modeling is most effective when the model's exposure to the threatening stimuli is gradual (Morris et al., 2008).

Research with children ages 3–5 years has shown that children in a group format, in which models approached the feared stimulus while the fearful children watched, had significantly less fear and more approach behaviors to the stimulus than children who were exposed to the feared stimulus without a model (Ollendick & King, 1998). Both filmed modeling and live modeling have been found to be efficacious procedures for treating excessive fears and phobias. Participant modeling has been shown to be even more effective than either symbolic or live modeling without a guided participation component (Cowart & Ollendick, 2013; Ollendick & King, 1998). Although same-age peers are typically used as models, parents, teachers, and other adults also can serve as models by allowing the child to observe them coping in a nonfearful way with the feared stimulus.

Contingency Management. Contingency management is another popular method for working with children who display phobic behaviors, and includes shaping and positive reinforcement as the most commonly used techniques to reduce phobic behaviors in young children, often combined with parent training in such techniques (Cowart & Ollendick, 2013; Lewin, 2011). Shaping involves reinforcing successive approximations toward the target behavior through positive reinforcement. For example, in the case of the child who has a dog phobia, he or she would be reinforced first for being in the same room with the dog, then reinforced for approaching the dog, and finally reinforced for petting the dog. Positive reinforcement, such as praise and/or tangible reinforcers (e.g., small toys or stickers), would be used to strengthen and maintain any gains made. Using a variety of reinforcers works best to keep the interest of the child (Friedberg et al., 2011). Charts can be helpful in visually demonstrating the child's accomplishments in combating the fear. For example, for the child with the dog phobia, a winding road could be drawn on a piece of poster board, with different accomplishments noted along the road (e.g., looking at a dog in a book, being in the room with a dog, approaching the dog, petting the dog) and a small marker moves along the road as the child accomplishes these steps. Extinction protocols should then be put into place, wherein the avoidance behaviors are no longer reinforced (Morris et al., 2008; Ollendick et al., 2004), meaning that the parents or other caregivers no longer pay attention to or give in to the avoidant behaviors or give excessive reassurance in response to the avoidant behaviors.

In a review of the research on the use of contingency management techniques, Ollendick and King (1998) concluded that reinforced practice (gradual exposure with reinforcement) was shown to be more effective than no treatment and superior to live modeling and verbal coping skills treatment modalities. Contingency management methods may be particularly useful with preschool- and kindergarten-age children who may have difficulties with some of the other techniques (e.g., positive self-talk, systematic desensitization) that have a more cognitive component.

Separation Anxiety, Including School or Daycare Refusal

At one time or another, almost all children experience some form of anxiety when separated from their primary caregivers. In fact, this separation anxiety is developmentally appropriate during the toddler years (18–24 months). Toddlers often cry, cling, and have temper tantrums when they are about to be separated from their parents. Some children, however, will continue to have these anxiety symptoms beyond this developmental stage, or in excess of what would be expected beyond toddlerhood, warranting clinical attention (Huberty, 2010). As discussed in Chapter 1, the essential feature of separation anxiety is an excessive anxiety concerning separation from the home or from those adults to whom the child is attached, beyond that expected for the child's developmental level, and lasting for a period of at least 4 weeks (American Psychiatric Association, 2013).

The initial separation that occurs when children begin daycare or school can be stressful for all children. The unfamiliar surroundings and people, along with the separation from their parents, results in initial feelings of uneasiness for many children. Most children overcome their feelings of anxiety and quickly begin to enjoy their new setting. For those children who continue to exhibit symptoms of separation anxiety at the time of separation or in anticipation of separation, intervention is imperative. The following sections outline how to prevent and treat such problems. Although the interventions described in this section are contextualized for the school or daycare setting, many of these techniques also can be used when a child displays anxiety about being left with a babysitter or unfamiliar relative or when entering any new situation about which the child is fearful.

Prevention of Separation Anxiety

The prevention of separation anxiety in young children can be challenging for mental health providers because these patterns may be present before a child enters school or other care setting, where the symptoms may be first noticed or evidenced. Therefore, prevention may need to focus on preventing the worsening of problems and related consequences of the anxiety (Huberty, 2008). However, before their child enters a new setting, parents can take steps to help prevent significant anxieties from forming. Obviously the parents must first feel comfortable with the upcoming situation. Parents should carefully select the daycare or preschool setting their child is to attend, ideally visiting several different settings to evaluate which type is best for both the parent and the child. Interviewing the daycare providers/teachers and observing a "typical" day in the new setting can give parents a feeling of security and comfort, which in turn helps the child to begin to feel confident. If the child is anxious about having a new babysitter, it is often a good idea for the babysitter to visit with the child while the parents are in the home to help familiarize the child with the new person. Likewise, parents should consider taking their child to a new daycare or school setting in advance to familiarize the child with the new surroundings. A weekend or evening trip to see the building and the yard area and help ease the child into the new setting can be helpful.

Parents should convey a genuinely positive attitude about the new setting or situation to their child. Discussing some of the exciting things that take place in that environment (such as games, art projects, and field trips) with their child can be helpful. The teacher's, babysitter's or daycare provider's name should be used in these conversations to familiarize the child with the new adult.

On the "big day," the parent should accompany the child to the new setting and stay with the child for a short while so that he or she does not feel abandoned. If the parent is having difficulties letting go, arranging to have another adult with whom the child is familiar accompany him or her may be a helpful source of support for the parent. The parent can encourage the child to engage in the initial activities of the day. If the child shows no difficulty joining in, the parent should let the child know that he or she will return to pick up the child at the end of the day. The parent should make certain that he or she is not late picking up the child, particularly during the first several days. Even if the child shows hesitation about joining in or begins to tantrum when the parent leaves, the parent should still separate from the child after a brief time at the daycare, school, or other care setting. Daycare providers and preschool/kindergarten teachers are typically quite accustomed to these behaviors and can help the child transition to the school activities.

After the day spent at daycare, school, or with the new sitter, the parent should allow some time for the child to discuss his or her day in the new setting or situation, responding with enthusiasm to the information the child shares. The parent should be encouraged to praise the child for his or her accomplishments and place any materials and art projects the child has brought home on the refrigerator door or in a scrapbook to "show off" the child's achievements.

Treatment of Separation Anxiety

The first indication of a separation anxiety disorder, as related to daycare or school, is often a child's refusal to go to daycare/preschool. The child may state this refusal directly by indicating that he or she does not want to go to the new setting any longer and that he or she would prefer to stay home with the parent. Often, though, the child's anxiety may be communicated in a more indirect manner. The child may complain of stomachaches or headaches in the morning or throw temper tantrums when the parent is getting the child ready for daycare/preschool. Typically the child also becomes quite clingy when the parent attempts to leave the child at the new setting. If the child does voice specific concerns about the daycare/preschool setting, it is important for the adult to listen carefully and determine the validity of these concerns. If a child notes, for example, that his or her daycare provider is "mean," the parent should ask the child to describe "mean." For instance, the parent could say to the child, "Serena, it sounds like you feel Ms. Thompson is mean. What does she do that is mean?" This can aid the adult in ruling out any maltreatment that is occurring in the setting. If necessary, the parent could make unannounced visits to the setting to observe how the adults interact with the children and to determine if anything seems unusual. Although rare, maltreatment can occur in daycare and school settings and, if it is suspected, it is essential to investigate further and, if necessary, place the child in a different setting. Most often, though, the child is simply having anxiety about the setting, and this anxiety must be addressed before it becomes more serious.

However, not all cases of school refusal are due to separation anxiety. If the child's worry is centered on something specific occurring in a daycare setting, such as teasing from other children (as opposed to anxiety about separating from the parent), this child may be exhibiting a school or social phobia. Children with a school or social phobia usually have fears associated with a specific concern, whereas children with separation anxiety have worries focused primarily on separation from the parent. It is important to look for reinforcing factors for staying home, such as escaping aversive social or evaluative situations; if the child is able to pinpoint a specific concern he or she is having at the setting, the parent should address the concern with the daycare provider or teacher as soon as possible (Huberty, 2011; Kearney, 2006). It is also possible that the child is simply reinforced for staying home where the child receives parental attention and/or other reinforcements (e.g., TV access) when not attending school or daycare.

The physical complaints that are typical in young children may initially be mistaken for real physical problems. Although obviously many children do catch colds and other illnesses, parents should determine, as soon as possible, if the child is feigning illness. Clues parents can look for include (but are not limited to): frequent sickness complaints before leaving for school or daycare, then miraculously "getting better" once he or she is allowed to stay home; no physical signs of illness, such as a runny nose or fever; frequent complaints of illness during the weekdays or before returning to the avoided setting, but no illness reported during the days spent with the parent; and pleas from the child that he or she feels ill just before returning to the daycare or school setting, when previously the child seemed fine. A visit to the pediatrician to rule out any medical illness is an appropriate step a parent can take. If there is no medical reason the child should be absent, the child should be returned to the daycare or school setting. More interventions for somatic complaints are highlighted later in this chapter. Parents and other adults are strongly advised not to reinforce the child's anxious and avoidant behaviors. Allowing the child to stay home often inadvertently worsens the child's anxiety and, therefore, it is critical that the child be quickly brought back to the avoided setting, at least for part of the day, and no longer be allowed access to the reinforcements (e.g., TV) if the child is at home during school time. The child should be reinforced for attending school via positive reinforcement (e.g., praise), and parents should ignore behaviors the child engages in to attempt to avoid going to school (e.g., crying, whining). In addition, parents may want to set up a system in which the child can earn tangible reinforcers for going to school without exhibiting negative behaviors. See Form 4.4 for a parent handout detailing the treatment of separation anxiety disorder.

The following steps, presented in a case example of Colette, a child who was refusing to attend kindergarten, are used to illustrate the treatment for separation anxiety.

1. The night before Colette was to return to school, her mother told her that tomorrow she would be going back to school. Her mother ignored Colette's cries, tantrums, and pleas to stay home.
2. The next morning, her mother got Colette up, helped her dress, fed her breakfast, and told her, in a matter-of-fact manner, that she would be dropping her off at the school on her way to work. Again, all pleas for not going to school by Colette were completely ignored.
3. Colette was given a "transitional object" to help her feel safe in the school setting. A transitional object is an item given by a primary attachment figure to remind the child of the caregiver. Examples include a locket with photograph of the parent in it, a "lucky penny," a "power ring," or a note or picture drawn by the parent to help the child feel special, loved, and powerful. Colette's mother gave her a lucky penny to keep in her pocket to help her feel "strong" and "happy" throughout her day, until they could see each other again that night.
4. Colette's mother had forewarned her teacher about her separation anxiety, and the teacher helped to comfort Colette that day. Even though Colette cried frequently that day and isolated herself from other children, she was able to stay in the classroom for the whole day. When she played a game with the other children, the teacher praised her.
5. Colette's mother picked Colette up after her school day and spoke with the teacher about how Colette had managed. Colette's mother reinforced Colette that evening for her day at school. She told Colette that she knew it was hard for her to have gone to school, but that each day it would get easier. With some effort, Colette's mother was able to ignore the tantrums and pleas Colette engaged in that evening about not wanting to attend school again.

6. The next morning Colette launched into the same behaviors of screaming, crying, and refusing to go to school. Colette's mother continued with the routine she had implemented the day before, and, once again, dropped Colette off at school. Upon picking Colette up from school, her teacher told her mother that Colette had been able to join the rest of the children more that day than the previous day. Colette's mother reinforced this accomplishment by taking Colette out to her favorite restaurant that night.
7. It took several weeks of this routine before Colette began to attend school without argument and with a positive attitude. Colette had conquered her separation anxiety and was able to have a positive kindergarten experience.

As this case example shows, parental consistency was key to Colette's returning to the school setting. For children whose parents have allowed them to stay out of school for a long time because of their anxiety symptoms or for children with severe anxiety symptoms, a more gradual exposure to the school setting may be necessary. For example, the child might first go to school for an hour each day and gradually work up to staying for the whole school day. Skill building before fully integrating back into the classroom, including cognitive techniques and social skills building and relaxation skills, may be warranted in more severe cases (Doobay, 2008). However, in most cases an immediate and full return to school is appropriate. Returning the child to the avoided setting is the primary intervention used in the treatment of separation anxiety disorder, along with the use of cognitive-behavioral techniques (American Academy of Child and Adolescent Psychiatry, 2007). In a study evaluating a parent–child CBT intervention (including child-focused interventions such as skill building and exposure, as well as parent skills training and anxiety management strategies) with children ages 4–7, children with separation anxiety disorder demonstrated a meaningful decrease in anxiety symptoms (effect size = 0.82) compared to a wait-list control group, with these gains maintained at a 1-year follow-up (Hirshfeld-Becker et al., 2010). Other techniques that may be used in addition to returning the child to the school setting include the following:

Technique	Examples
Relaxation techniques	Deep and slow breathing techniques Progressive muscle relaxation Guided imagery
Positive self-talk	"I can do it." "I am brave."
Sticker charts	Sticker for each school day attended; once a certain number of stickers is obtained, the child earns a special reinforcer (e.g., going out for ice cream after school with Mom)
Contracts	A written agreement that if the child attends school without throwing a tantrum in the morning, he or she can watch an hour of TV after school

SELECTIVE MUTISM

Selective mutism can be challenging to treat, once it reaches the awareness of the mental health professional, because the behaviors have already been supported and reinforced by the child's environment, making it less malleable to change. Therefore, both the prevention and treatment of selective mutism must involve helping to also shape the reactions and behaviors of those adults in the child's environment.

Causes and Prevention of Selective Mutism

Explanations for the causes of selective mutism vary, though it is likely that the child has been reinforced for his or her silence through negative reinforcement (i.e., the child is allowed to escape or avoid an aversive task by not talking), thereby making the behavior highly resistant to intervention. For example, peers in the child's class may begin to "interpret" the mute child's needs to others, the child may receive special attention (i.e., positive reinforcement) for not speaking, and the teacher may withhold making requests of the child if the requests seem to upset or bother him or her (Kehle, Bray, & Theodore, 2010). Thus, to help prevent selective mutism, adults should require that the child answer on his or her own; if the child does not, adults should ensure that he or she is not receiving special attention or being allowed to escape a task because of a failure to talk. Anxiety has also been implicated as playing a significant role with those children who become selectively mute, now being included in DSM-5 as an anxiety disorder, and, therefore, the underlying anxiety must be examined and treated as well (Manassis, 2013). Often selective mutism is not fully recognized until it has become a significant problem.

Treatment of Selective Mutism

School is the most common setting in which children exhibit selective mutism. Obviously a child who does not speak at school poses a significant educational problem, and treatment should be implemented promptly. The most effective treatments for selective mutism are behaviorally based interventions implemented in the school environment. Hence, school psychologists are likely to be the targeted professional for educating parents and teachers about the disorder and designing the intervention strategies. Parent education about the treatment of selective mutism is necessary in order for progress to be supported in the home setting (Luby, 2013).

The most common treatment for selective mutism is the shaping and generalization of speaking behaviors (Manassis, 2013). Shaping refers to the positive reinforcement of successive approximations to the target behavior—in this case, audible speech. Positive reinforcement strategies may include verbal praise, attention given to the child, a sticker, a small toy, or other reward. The successive approximations that may be reinforced include the child responding to a question (1) with one-word answers, (2) with several-word answers, and (3) by spontaneously offering an answer. For example, at the initial stages of treatment, the teacher may ask the child, "What color crayon would you like to draw with?," and then provide the crayon and verbal praise when the child answers "Red." Later the child may be asked more complex questions that require more wordy responses.

In addition to initially requiring the child to use limited speech, intervention programs also may involve the use of select peers at the beginning stages of treatment. For example, instead of having the child speak in front of the whole classroom, the child may initially be prompted to speak in small-group activities. Once the child begins to speak comfortably in a small group, more children are gradually added to the group.

Self-modeling, wherein the child is videotaped responding to parental requests but the tape is edited to appear as if the child is responding to teacher requests, also shows promise for treating selective mutism. The videotape is shown to the child in school on several occasions. The child can also be reinforced by earning small rewards for watching the video. Additionally the video can be shown to the child's peers in order to promote peer expectation for appropriate speech (Kehle et al., 2010).

As described previously, it is important to eliminate any reinforcement the child receives for not speaking. The child should not be allowed to point or make other signals for things he or she wants; indeed all nonverbal attempts to communicate should be ignored. This should be the case both at home and at school. Other students in the class or siblings should not be allowed to "speak for" the child; instead, the child's peers should be told that the child must now speak for him- or herself.

As the child begins to speak more frequently and in the presence of more people, the prompts and reinforcers that were previously used are gradually "faded out." It is important to continue with the reinforcement of verbal behaviors and the consistent ignoring of nonverbal attempts at communication until the child demonstrates verbal fluency and appears to find spoken language reinforcing, in and of itself (e.g., others respond to the child's verbal requests; the child appears to be making friends; the teacher positively responds to the child's answering of a question).

Another supplemental strategy that can be used involves having the child invite a school friend to his or her house over a weekend, with the parents reinforcing verbal communication or play between the two of them. It is hoped that the child will then begin to be verbal with this peer in the school setting as well. If the child is verbal with his or her siblings, the teacher can invite the siblings into the classroom after school and allow the child and the siblings to play a game. Assuming the previously mute child becomes verbal during the game, the teacher can then begin to include some of the child's classmates in the game (Kehle et al., 2010).

At times the child's parents may not be aware of the full extent of their child's difficulties in the school setting because the child converses freely at home. Volunteering in the child's classroom can help parents see the extent and pervasiveness of the child's problem and form a collaborative connection with school personnel. Parents should only reinforce verbal behaviors and encourage their child to speak for him- or herself in different settings (Kehle et al., 2010).

Although these techniques are often successful, implementing them takes time and considerable energy on the part of the teacher, other students, parents, and professionals working with the child. It is extremely important that, once established, the intervention techniques continue until the child's selective mutism has resolved. Inconsistency likely will only reinforce the problem.

SOMATIC COMPLAINTS

As mentioned in Chapter 1, somatic symptoms may be common in young children—although rather than forming a specific somatic disorder these symptoms may co-occur with internalizing disorders such as anxiety and depression. It is important to rule out a medical problem as the sole reason for somatic concerns. Thus, if a child with somatic symptoms has not recently seen his or her primary care provider, such a referral would be an appropriate first step.

The type of intervention used to treat somatic symptoms is partially dependent on the origin of the symptoms. For example, the child could be experiencing separation anxiety and having somatic symptoms as a result. The child could also be feeling depressed; somatic complaints are common among young children who have depression. Alternatively, the child could be focused on his or her body as a result of parental stress or somatic symptoms. In a study by Wolff and colleagues (2010), maternal stress and maternal somatic symptoms were particularly related to the development of somatic symptoms in young children. Therefore, in this case, treatment of family stress and parental somatic issues would be necessary to best help the child.

Many treatments for somatic concerns are those that can be effectively used for depression and/or anxiety. The Treatment for Anxiety and Physical Symptoms (TAPS; Warner et al., 2006) is a treatment protocol that addresses nonmedical somatic complaints and incorporates CBT methods with family psychoeducation. Although the protocol was developed for elementary and secondary students and has not yet been evaluated for children under the age of 8, it can be adjusted for working with younger children. The child sessions begin with some brief psychoeducation, followed by feelings recognition, in which the child is helped to communicate feelings as opposed to somatically experiencing them. Next, physical responses to anxiety and pain are overviewed, and diaphragmatic breathing is practiced along with the use of a Likert scale to track physical discomfort. Cognitive restructuring is introduced, in which negative thinking is examined and replaced with healthier thoughts. An exposure hierarchy is also used to gradually expose the child to situations that may be making him or her feel anxious. Relaxation techniques and positive self-talk can be added as well. Parent sessions are also incorporated to help parents understand their child's somatic complaints and associated anxiety, in addition to teaching them how to reinforce progress (Reigada, Fisher, Cutler, & Warner, 2008). For the young child who is not able to engage in cognitive restructuring, focusing on rehearsing positive self-statements and relaxation techniques, as opposed to using thought rejection and replacement, may be indicated. The TAPS program has been found to be efficacious, with 80% of children aged 8–16 in the treatment group experiencing a reduction in somatic discomfort and anxiety following intervention as compared to no improvement in the wait-list control group, and continuing to maintain these gains 3 months following treatment (Warner et al., 2011). Even though these results are promising, and modified CBT programs have been found to be efficacious with young children (Hirshfeld-Becker et al., 2010), more research is needed when using this program with younger children.

PTSD AND TRAUMATIC EXPERIENCE/ABUSE

As described in Chapter 1, PTSD is a disorder that emerges when a child has been exposed to some form of trauma. Not every child exposed to a traumatic event will develop PTSD symptoms or eventually meet the full criteria for PTSD; however, it is common for children to develop some PTSD symptoms (including reexperiencing the trauma, avoiding the stimuli associated with the trauma, or experiencing negative alterations in cognition and unpleasant symptoms of increased arousal; American Psychiatric Association, 2013) following abuse, as well as other traumatic events.

The most common forms of trauma to which young children are exposed include abuse and neglect, witnessing domestic violence, and witnessing community violence, natural disasters, and accidents (Nickerson, Reeves, Brock & Jimerson, 2009). It is difficult to prevent PTSD symptoms, due to the typically uncontrollable/unpredictable nature of these types of stressors. Different children respond differently to stressors as a result of past learning, physiological makeup, available social supports, and coping strategies. A child who has been exposed to a traumatic stimulus and evidences symptoms of PTSD should receive immediate intervention to decrease the severity of the symptoms. Left untreated, PTSD can have an impact on subsequent social, academic and psychological functioning, potentially leading to greater problems later in development (Nickerson et al., 2009).

In the United States (including the District of Columbia, American Samoa, Guam, the Northern Mariana Islands, Puerto Rico, and the U.S. Virgin Islands) state statutes identify persons who are legally required to report abuse to the appropriate child protective agency. In most of these regions, mental health clinicians, teachers, and other professionals are specifically named as reporters, if there is a reasonable suspicion that abuse has occurred (Child Welfare Information Gateway, 2014). Most states have a strong immunity against liability for the reporter if the report of abuse is made in "good faith." Failure of a professional to report suspected abuse could result in various actions, such as fines, revocation of licenses, and/or incarceration. The professional should review the relevant child-abuse reporting laws in his or her state to determine the specifics of when and how to fill out a report.

Additionally, the clinician who works with children should be aware of any relevant cultural practices or approaches to disciplining children. Different cultures have differing parenting practices; terminology surrounding those practices and the cultural heritage and religious beliefs of the family should be explored and taken into consideration when working with the child (Bornstein, 2013). For example, if a child reports that he or she is "whooped" at home, it is important to try to determine whether this means (1) spanked with an open hand occasionally when misbehaving, (2) hit with a closed fist, (3) hit with an object, or (4) hit on different parts of the body. It is important to reiterate, however, that if abuse or neglect is suspected, a child-abuse report is mandated, regardless of the mitigating circumstances surrounding the event. It is not the clinician's duty to make sense of the surrounding circumstances; it is the clinician's duty to report any suspected abuse so that the appropriate authorities can investigate the situation.

Often with preschool- and kindergarten-age children the best "window" into the child's world is through observing the child's behaviors. Children rarely verbally report abuse, particularly if the perpetrator is the child's parent. However, if a child does verbalize allegations, it is essential to fill out and submit a child-abuse report.

The psychological and emotional effects of abuse are often more difficult to detect than the physical effects. Unfortunately, the psychological effects also often cause more long-standing difficulties for the child and may lead to mental health problems well into adulthood (Nickerson et al., 2009). Therefore, detection and treatment are imperative. Children who have been abused can exhibit a wide array of psychological difficulties; however, there is no set pattern of symptoms that is typical of all children who have been abused. Young children who have been physically abused frequently have problems with attachment and engage in aggressive behaviors. In addition, they may be withdrawn or anxious. Children who have been sexually abused may have some of the same symptoms (e.g., behavior problems, anxiety) in addition to sexual acting-out behavior, or even oversexualized behavior—one of the symptoms unique to sexual abuse. Young children (age 2–6) who have been sexually abused may engage in inappropriate levels of sexual behavior (e.g., excessive masturbation), may know sexual terms most children their age do not, may show their genitalia to others in public or without shame, or otherwise exhibit high levels of sexualized behaviors (Lowenstein, 2011).

Although the majority of abused children will experience some psychological distress, not all children who have been abused may have psychological symptoms. In some children who are initially asymptomatic, these symptoms may be noted later (a phenomenon known as the "sleeper effect"), whereas other children may never experience psychological effects. Children who never show any symptoms may have a number of resiliency factors (e.g., supportive family members, good social skills), and/or the abuse may not have been traumatic enough to the child to produce harmful psychological effects (Saywitz, Mannarino, Berliner, & Cohen, 2000).

Treatment of PTSD

The initial step in the treatment of PTSD is to ensure the safety of the child and to make certain that the child is no longer being exposed to the traumatic circumstances. It is almost impossible to attempt to treat a child for trauma when he or she continues to be traumatized in his or her environment. Obviously, psychological safety also is important.

Despite the limited empirical evidence to support the use of traditional play therapy with children as a sole means of intervention, play-based techniques can be used initially when establishing a rapport with the child, thus increasing the child's feeling of comfort in the therapy, and setting parameters for the work to be done. Play allows the child to externalize thoughts, images, and feeling states and accompanying sensations that are frequently impossible to put into words (Gil, 2010). Play-based approaches with children were shown through a meta-analytic review of 93 treatment-control comparisons for a variety of childhood disorders to have a treatment effect size of 0.80, indicating some support for their use (Bratton, Ray, Rhine, & Jones, 2005). A more recent meta-analysis that used more rigorous methods (Lin & Bratton, 2015) reported a moderate effect size of 0.47 for child-centered play therapy approaches with a greater effect size for studies with full parental involvement (0.59) than for those with limited or no parental involvement (0.33).

Some common toys used in play-based techniques are puppets, doll families and dollhouses, crayons/paints and paper, clay, dinosaurs and other animal figurines, play food and dishes, sand trays, and baby dolls. Reviewing the rules of the playroom, along with the role of the therapist, can be helpful (see Figure 4.1). Repetitive play can help children who have experienced some form of trauma to reenact the trauma via therapeutic and developmentally appropriate means while working through it. Aggressive behaviors and even physical attacks exhibited by the traumatized child in play, while often disturbing to teachers and new clinicians, can offer a way for the child to replace feelings of fear with feelings of control, safety, and power (Gil, 2010). If the child engages in aggressive behaviors outside of the therapeutic environment (e.g., in the school or daycare setting), however, further interventions, such as those discussed both in this chapter and in Chapter 3, should be considered. In sum, play-based techniques used in conjunction with PCIT or CBT modalities, can provide an effective means of increasing comfort in the therapy sessions and help establish the therapeutic alliance.

Cognitive behavioral therapy (CBT) has the most empirical support for addressing symptoms of PTSD in children. Many trauma-focused CBT programs have treatment components for both the child and the parent. A review of the literature supports the dual use of CBT when working with PTSD symptoms (Higa-McMillan et al., 2016; Nickerson et al., 2009). With young children, in particular, this combined parent and child treatment approach likely will be the most efficacious.

Parents may be involved in interventions in several ways. Many parents will need some basic information regarding childhood PTSD, including the diagnostic criteria and childhood presentation of the disorder, as well as a description of the course of treatment. If applicable, it also may be helpful to educate parents about normal childhood physical, sexual, and emotional development, in order for typical behaviors to not be pathologized, and

> "My name is Kelly. I am someone children come and play with or talk to about things that are bothering them. Sometimes in here we will talk about things, sometimes we will play. You can play with whatever you want to in here. We will meet each week for about 45 minutes. There are only three rules in here. The first rule is that you cannot hurt yourself, the second rule is that you cannot hurt me, and the third rule is that you cannot hurt the toys. Also, all of the toys stay here in this room; you cannot take toys home with you. Other than that, we can do what you would like in here. Everything that you do in here and talk about in here will stay between you and me. I won't tell anyone about it, unless you are going to hurt yourself or hurt someone else, or if someone else is hurting you. If one of those things is happening, I will have to tell someone to make sure that you are safe. We can talk about it if any of those things come up. Do you have any questions about anything I just said?"

FIGURE 4.1. Sample dialogue between therapist and child: Introductory play session.

about ways in which they can help their child feel personally safe. In addition, many parents of traumatized children often need psychological assistance themselves, as they frequently experience some emotional distress due to their child's trauma. Specific interventions for these parents, such as cognitive strategies to decrease self-blame and exposure techniques related to their thoughts and feelings about their child's experiences and symptoms, may be beneficial (Cohen, Mannarino, Berliner, & Deblinger, 2000; Yule, Smith, Perrin, & Clark, 2013). Parent training (as discussed in Chapter 3) also may be part of a CBT program to help them address aggressive, acting-out behaviors exhibited by their child, as well as reinforce appropriate behaviors and provide positive, child-directed time at home (King et al., 2000). Because harsh discipline or punishment can worsen a traumatized child's feelings of low self-esteem and insecurity, parents should be advised that disciplinary methods be executed in a patient and nonpunitive manner (Yule et al., 2013). Family therapy also may be indicated along with CBT intervention (James & Mennen, 2001). Last, making home and school activities more structured, including establishing routines and reducing unstructured time, can help reduce the child's anxiety. Overall, inclusion of the parents in treatment has been found to lead to more efficacious outcomes when working with children with trauma (Sharma-Patel et al., 2011).

Child-directed components that may be part of a CBT intervention package are psychoeducation, coping skills training, social skills training, and gradual exposure. Psychoeducation often includes age-appropriate information on personal safety and, if the child has been sexually abused, information on sexuality and sexual abuse to assist children in avoiding (to the extent possible) future abuse incidents. Coping skills training includes interventions that assist children in dealing with the distressing, dysfunctional thoughts and feelings related to the trauma. The techniques used may include relaxation training (as discussed earlier in this chapter), as well as cognitive coping skills similar to those used with children who have depression or anxiety disorders. These techniques, which have been used with some success with children with PTSD, include replacing negative, maladaptive thoughts with more positive, coping thoughts, and addressing self-blame and cognitive distortions (Cohen et al., 2000; Yule et al., 2013). Relaxation techniques, including mindfulness work (see the section "Mindfulness"), can be useful in decreasing any physical symptoms of arousal the child continues to experience (Catani et al., 2009). Because children often evidence increased aggressive behaviors and/or problematic social behaviors following instances of trauma, including abuse, some training in social skills/social problem solving (discussed in Chapter 3) may be beneficial (King et al., 2000).

Gradual exposure, a key component in CBT interventions for PTSD, is considered by many to be the most important part of a successful treatment program for this disorder. Children construct an anxiety hierarchy composed of aspects of the trauma with items that are less anxiety provoking (e.g., interactions with the abuser at times he or she was not abusing the child) at the bottom, and items that are extremely anxiety-provoking (e.g., specifics about the abuse event) at the top. The clinician gradually takes the child through the hierarchy of items. Exposure to the items may be attained by talking about them, drawing, storytelling, playing, or any other method that is appropriate for the child's age and developmental level. As part of the gradual exposure, relaxation training and positive self-talk may be used as mechanisms for coping with the anxiety (King et al., 2000).

Young children who are still in the grip of reliving their trauma also often have nightmares and difficulties with sleeping and eating. The content of the child's dreams may not be recognizable to the child, except for the fact that the dream was anxiety provoking. Reading soothing bedtime stories, engaging in regular bedtime and mealtime routines, and frequent comforting and reassurance by the parent are recommended. If the child is able to recognize the content of his or her nightmare, the clinician can work with the child to develop an alternate narrative for the dream, such as the inclusion of a superhero to have it conclude in a positive way; this outcome can be cognitively rehearsed and depicted in a drawing on paper by the child throughout the day. By rehearsing the new outcome, the ending may change at night (Yule et al., 2013). Communication between the child's clinician and parents is very helpful in monitoring and treating these related symptoms.

Prevention of Child Abuse and Neglect

Considerable effort has been directed toward preventing child abuse and neglect, which can have long-term negative consequences if left untreated. Ideally, prevention measures should be based on an understanding of the risk factors that can lead to child abuse and neglect, and they ought to be provided for families before the abuse begins. Common risk factors for abuse and neglect are reviewed here, along with an overview of available family services.

Primary prevention—that is, determining the common risk factors and intervening before any abuse has occurred—is often conducted by teachers, daycare providers, and other professionals who work closely with the young child on a daily basis and have the opportunity to make frequent observations. These risk factors often co-occur and are cumulative; no single risk factor is indicative of a potentially abusive situation, although several risk factors could render the family more vulnerable to abusive events. Common risk factors include premature birth of the child, depressive symptoms and anxiety in the mother, a single-parent household, families who experience divorce or significant marital discord, coercive discipline, and poverty and its associated factors (such as low education levels, substance use, criminal activity, and crowded conditions) (Crossen-Tower, 2014; Juntunen, 2013).

If several of these risk factors are present, professionals should consider intervening by connecting the parents or family with the appropriate social services. For example, if coercive discipline is used, the parent could be (1) given resources (such as handouts and books) for positive parenting skills or (2) encouraged to attend classes in effective disciplinary tactics for young children. In many situations, it also is appropriate to offer parents individual parent training (as discussed in Chapter 3) to help them break the coercive parenting cycle. Parent training programs, such as those discussed in Chapter 3, can arm parents with specific strategies for intervening and managing their child's behavior, as well as increasing positive interactions and strengthening the parent–child relationship. Parents who appear to have mental health needs should be encouraged to seek individual treatment. Parents going through a difficult divorce or experiencing frequent marital discord should be directed to the appropriate resources for marital or family therapy services or linked with legal services to aid in the separation process. Social services can offer assistance to families experiencing financial hardship and other stressors related to financially impoverished situations, such as the need for food, jobs, and appropriate housing.

Helping these at-risk families make positive connections with other people, including increasing their approach to helping resources, may also reduce the risk of child abuse and neglect (Crossen-Tower, 2014). Social connections provide outlets for ongoing frustrations, offer families resources and alternative perspectives during stressful times, and keep families from feeling isolated. Anyone can make a connection with a family in need—teachers, social workers, daycare providers, friends, physicians and nurses, therapists, and school psychologists. Individuals who have made a connection with a family could then suggest additional resources, such as becoming involved in a service or program that could address the family's specific needs.

Protective factors, or conditions that increase resiliency and resistance to conditions of adversity, can be identified and reinforced. Such factors may be child-related, such as innate intelligence or talents, or parent-related, such as having appropriate disciplinary skills or adequate social support (Crossen-Tower, 2014). Protective factors, just like risk factors, are cumulative; the more coping skills and resiliency the family has, the less likely it is that the family will engage in abuse. Helping the family to draw on their resiliency and positive coping styles during times of crisis can thwart the occurrence of abuse. Many preventive resources already exist in communities to aid families at risk for abuse and neglect. Obviously the type of resource that would be most beneficial to a particular family would depend on that family's specific needs. Table 4.2 contains a list of resources available in many areas; in addition, the professional should familiarize him- or herself with the specific resources available in the area in which the family resides. Other recommended resources include those provided by the family's church or synagogue, such as counseling groups, food pantries, and financial assistance; those offered by local universities and law schools, such as low- to no-cost counseling services; medical services (through an affiliated training hospital) and legal advice; and services offered to the public by local media, such as food or clothing drives and other programs.

TABLE 4.2. Preventative Resources for Families at Risk for Abuse

- Parents Anonymous
- National Center for Child Abuse and Neglect
- Alcoholics/Narcotics Anonymous
- Child protective services
- Social services (city/county/state)
- Head Start
- Crisis nurseries and short-term emergency child placements
- Emergency housing shelters and services
- County mental health services
- Child development centers
- Various parenting or crisis hotlines
- School psychologists or counselors

Other methods of prevention are directed more specifically at the child, and have been linked to overall decreased rates of abuse, increased self-disclosure about abuse, and the prevention of negative outcomes, such as guilt or shame, if abuse has occurred (Finkelhor, 2007). For example, some Head Start programs use a prevention program for child sexual abuse, in which the child watches a video on good and bad forms of touching, then discusses the video and what action to take (e.g., say "no," leave, and tell a trusted adult about it) if anyone touches them in a private way. This type of prevention, using videos and/or books, also could be taught in daycare, preschool, or therapy settings, or at home.

Obviously not all programs and services will benefit all families, in part due to the heterogeneity of children and parents within a risk group. Prevention programs are most effective when they are based on prior knowledge of a child's and family's risk factors (Beckwith, 2000).

DEPRESSION

Feeling sad or depressed at times is a normal occurrence for both children and adults. An occasional depressed mood can occur at any age and can have a variety of causes. Most young children who experience a depressed mood recover quickly, with the sadness lasting for only a brief period of time. No intervention is likely warranted for these children. However, some children have a more pervasive depressed mood that does not remit and interferes with daily living activities, including interpersonal relationships and decreased school and home functioning. Children with this symptom presentation may meet the criteria for one of the depressive disorders discussed in Chapter 1 and may warrant intervention.

Prevention of Childhood Depression

The prevention of chronic childhood depression begins with early recognition of the signs and symptoms of depression. Teachers, parents, daycare workers, and other adults in the child's life can all play an integral role in identifying when a child appears depressed. The young child typically has difficulty understanding or verbalizing his or her thoughts and feelings. It has been shown, however, that children as young as the age of 3 can accurately identify their emotions, and children by the age of 5 are able to verbalize their feelings instead of acting upon them (Luby, 2000).

Increasing the support to the child and paying attention to the factors that could be contributing to the child's change in functioning are important. For example, if the child is being bullied by another student at school, the teacher should intervene in the classroom, as well as alert the child's parents about the bullying. Signs and symptoms of child abuse, as just discussed, are also important factors to consider. Because maternal depression has been found to be a risk factor for children becoming depressed, family therapy or parent therapy may also be indicated. Finally, establishing regular routines in the home and increasing positive activities for the child can help to prevent depression or be used as an early intervention for the child who begins to evidence depressive symptom signs.

Treatment of Depressive Symptoms

The treatment for depression in adolescents and adults typically includes a variety of cognitive-behavioral techniques. Studies have begun only recently to examine the treatment of depression in preschool- and kindergarten-age children, although data from some studies suggest that developmentally adjusted forms of CBT, in addition to PCIT work, appear to be effective (Luby, 2013). Given the cognitive component of these techniques, implementing them with young children may be challenging and may require some modification. In general, a multifaceted approach, which includes parent education and family systems work, along with individual treatment, is often recommended (Lenze, Pautsch, & Luby, 2011; Luby, 2013).

Establishing an effective therapeutic alliance with the parents early on is important in maintaining the involvement of the family and child in treatment. A good way to foster this alliance is to educate the parent on childhood depression, its course, and treatment. Parent education often leads to a discussion of issues that could be maintaining the child's depression, such as family problems or parental depression. Children whose parent is depressed may be more likely to exhibit depressive symptoms themselves (Lewis, Rice, Harold, Collishaw, & Thapar, 2011). If parent psychopathology is an issue, individual treatment for the parent should be recommended in addition to treating the child's depressive symptoms. In addition, a poor parent–child relationship or general family dysfunction can contribute to a child's depressive symptoms and would likely need to be directly targeted in treatment (Merrell, 2008b).

The type of treatment used with the young child largely rests on what types of symptoms the child is exhibiting and what situation seems to be maintaining the depression, and depends on a careful assessment by the clinician. The clinician also should determine how the young child is currently feeling via the use of pictures or feelings charts. An example of a feelings chart is provided in Form 4.5. In addition, Form 4.6 depicts a chart that may be used on a daily basis (with the parent assisting the child) to track the child's moods over time.

If the young child appears to have many negative thoughts and low self-esteem, these thoughts need to be challenged supportively and replaced by more positive thoughts (i.e., cognitive restructuring). Gentle questioning about different topics may reveal where the child's faulty thinking lies. Often the child is repeating to him- or herself a negative statement told to him or her by a peer, sibling, or parent. The following example illustrates this technique of challenging and replacing negative faulty thinking. This example involves Tim, a 5-year-old who has been saying that he is "stupid" while in session with his clinician.

TIM: I can't do this puzzle. I'm stupid.

CLINICIAN: You think that you are stupid? What makes you think that?

TIM: We had to do puzzles at school, and I couldn't do that puzzle either.

CLINICIAN: Yeah, some puzzles can be pretty tricky.

TIM: All puzzles are tricky for me because I'm dumb.

CLINICIAN: I also know that different people are really good at different things, and not so good at other things. It does not mean that people are stupid, it just means that they might be better at something else.

TIM: Yeah, but I'm not good at anything.

CLINICIAN: Didn't you just tell me that you learned to ride your bike over the weekend and that you were good at that? I also remember that clay dog you made in here last week and how good that was. You brought that in for show-and-tell yesterday, right?

TIM: Yeah, everyone said it was really good.

CLINICIAN: So I guess you aren't stupid, you're just good at different things besides puzzles. If you ever think to yourself "I am stupid," you need to say to yourself, "I'm not stupid, I'm good at lots of things." Then tell yourself what you are good at doing. Let's practice saying that. "I'm good at doing a lot of things like . . ."

TIM: I'm good at doing lots of things, like riding my bike.

CLINICIAN: Great job, Tim.

If the young child appears agitated and restless, deep breathing and other relaxation techniques can be useful for him or her to practice both in and out of session. Examples of these techniques were described earlier in this chapter. Mindfulness (more fully explored later) has also been found to be a promising tool in the treatment of depression with children and teens (Raes, Griffith, Van der Gucht, & Williams, 2014; Semple, Lee, Rosa, & Miller, 2009). Training the parents to model the use of these techniques for their child at home is another way to encourage the child to practice these techniques.

As noted earlier, it may be difficult to implement techniques such as cognitive restructuring because of the young child's cognitive level. However, some interventions actively involve parents and therefore may be more appropriate for preschool- and kindergarten-age children. Scheduling pleasurable activities, including exercise or other physical activity, is a frequently recommended intervention for depression whereby parents are instructed to engage their child in a number of active and fun endeavors (Brown, Pearson, Braithwaite, Brown, & Biddle, 2013). For example, parents can involve their child in a physical activity, such as tag or bike riding, or suggest that the child invite a friend from school or daycare over to the house for several hours on a weekend or after school. Involving peers is a particularly appropriate strategy if the child is socially isolated in the home (e.g., no siblings around the child's age and no neighborhood peers). Engaging the child in a fun activity or craft—instead of watching TV—also can be useful, especially if a significant adult in the child's life can help out with, or join, the activity and can give positive reinforcement and praise to the child for participating in the activity. Other activities parents could encourage include drawing, singing, dancing, playing with clay, simple board games, painting, riding a tricycle, or other outdoor physical activities. Anything that the child finds fun and enjoyable (or previously found to be so, if the child has demonstrated a decreased interest in activities as part of his or her depressive symptoms) should be encouraged.

Parents should provide a great deal of positive reinforcement to their child during these activities. The reinforcement should be focused on the child's specific behaviors around his or her engagement and effort (e.g., "I like how you are blending those colors together with paint"), as opposed to more general praise about things that the child has no control over (e.g., "You are so smart," "Good job," or "You are pretty"). Parents should also look for opportunities to praise and encourage other appropriate nondepressive behaviors. In addition, if the parent hears the child make a self-critical statement, the parent can gently and supportively challenge that statement (Saklofske, Janzen, Hildebrand, & Kaufmann, 1998). For families in which there is a poor parent–child relationship that may be contributing to the depression, setting up a structured positive play activity (such as that described in Chapter 3) or fully engaging in behavioral parent training may be beneficial for both parent and child. Although studies focusing on the use of parent training programs for depression are still limited, there is some support for their use. For example, an adapted version of PCIT led to a significant reduction in child depression severity scores in a study of preschoolers with depression (Lenze et al., 2011). While standard methods of parent training were utilized in this study (e.g., positive child-directed time and appropriate discipline), a module specific to emotional development competencies was added, including relaxation techniques, understanding triggers for strong emotion, and empathy training. Because a lack of structure may contribute to depression in children, it is also important that the parent maintain a regular routine for the child, including at mealtimes, bedtimes, and activity times. Minimizing changes within the family as much as possible and talking with the child about impending changes before they occur also may help to reduce the child's distress.

Teachers and daycare workers can assist the child with depression in several ways: (1) allowing the child to sit next to friends or potential friends during rug time, lunch, or class time; (2) avoiding situations in which the child could be socially isolated (e.g., when students choose teams for group projects or games) and focusing on improving social skills and interactions with others; (3) giving frequent praise and positive reinforcement for effort in class; and (4) helping the child focus on the positives instead of the negatives (Huberty, 2013; Saklofske et al., 1998). Teachers can also model coping statements. For example, if the child with depression states, "I can never do anything right" as he or she crumbles up the art project, the teacher can state, "This project is tricky, and a lot of my students have had a hard time with it. Let's see if we can try and do it together." This approach allows the child to "save face"—after all, the project has been perceived as "tricky" by other students—while still providing an opportunity for the child to succeed in the project. Once the child has successfully completed the project, the teacher should praise him or her; when other similar projects come up, the teacher can remind the child of the great work he or she did on the last project.

Mindfulness

Mindfulness is a way of attending to the present moment in a reflective and nonjudgmental fashion and has been found to be useful in the treatment of anxiety and depression in children and adults (Vollestad, Nielson, & Nielson, 2012; Zelazo & Lyons, 2012). There are many techniques and practices as related to mindfulness, including deep breathing, acceptance of thoughts or circumstances, meditation, and yoga, and, as discussed in Chapter 3, mindfulness, including ACT, can be an effective intervention when used with parents. Research with adults has shown positive benefits when using mindfulness, including reduced stress and anxiety, improved immune functioning, and improved emotional regulation and overall mental health (Hanson & Mendius, 2009). Some research links the physical and mental benefits from mindfulness practices to structural changes in brain functioning. For example, the practice of mindfulness in adults has been found to alter the organization and action of neural circuitry that is associated with changes in stress reactivity and immune functioning (Davidson et al., 2003), including structural changes in the brain in the prefrontal and parietal cortices and hippocampus (Lazar et al., 2000). These changes in brain functioning, along with decreased sympathetic nervous system reactivity, contribute to an overall sense of calm and well-being for the individual practicing mindfulness, including reduced internalizing symptoms such as anxiety and depression (Hanson & Mendius, 2009; Vollestad et al., 2012).

Emerging research suggests that mindfulness teachings may be effectively adapted for children (Zelazo & Lyons, 2012). Meditation, for example, when practiced by children between the ages of 9 and 17 with internalizing symptoms, academic problems, ADHD, and learning disabilities may help to improve attention and academic performance, and decrease anxiety, depression, and externalizing behavior problems (Beauchemin, Hutchins, & Patterson, 2008; Raes et al., 2014; Semple et al., 2009). In addition, there is evidence that meditation and relaxation may be effective in treating childhood PTSD with school-age children (Catani et al., 2009). Yoga may also lead to reduced anxiety in elementary age children (Stueck & Gloeckner, 2005), with one study finding decreased cortisol levels and improved behaviors in second graders after participating in a 10-week yoga intervention (Butzer et al., 2014). Moreover, a study found that a mindfulness program for fourth through seventh graders resulted in improved self-reported optimism, positive affect, student attention, social–emotional competence, and fewer externalizing behaviors (Schonert-Reichl & Lawlor, 2010). Harnett and Dawe (2012) in their review of several dozen studies concluded that mindfulness-based interventions are an important addition to the repertoire of existing therapies when working with the childhood population, particularly if parents can also participate. When parents are also involved in their own mindfulness work, improvements in the parent–child relationship are evident, including increased parental executive functioning, more active listening, and a reduction in parental stress (see Chapter 3).

Promising results have also emerged from research on the use of mindfulness specifically with young children. In a study by Flook, Goldberg, Pinger, and Davidson (2015), preschool students who participated in a mindfulness-based kindness curriculum showed greater improvements in social competence and earned higher report card grades in domains of health, learning, and social–emotional development than the control group. These results were evident after only 12 weeks of intervention and support the use of mindfulness in promoting prosocial behavior and self-regulation in young children.

When doing mindfulness work with young children, it is important to adjust the interventions to make them developmentally appropriate. Expectations of the participants will also need to be modified as typically young children cannot sit still and maintain focus for long periods of time. The use of postures and poses to keep the child engaged both in body and mind can be helpful. For example, incorporating some yoga movements while directing the child on breathing techniques is often indicated. A sampling of interventions follows.

4 × 6 BREATHS

This technique involves practicing mindful breathing. The child is instructed to breathe in slowly to the count of 4 through the nose, and then out to the count of 6 through the mouth. The clinician can count off for the child how long the measured breaths should last, and model the correct breathing pace. If the younger child has a challenge in exhaling slowly, the child can imagine that he or she is blowing bubbles, with the goal of blowing as many bubbles as possible (if the breath is too quick, no bubbles will be created). Actual bubbles could be made available if this helps, or blowing on a pinwheel could be an alternative activity ("How long will the pinwheel spin?"; Altman, 2014). Another activity could be having the child lay down and placing an object on his or her stomach, with the goal being to watch the object rise and fall as the child practices deep belly breathing (as opposed to shallow breaths only through the lungs). If the count of 6 on the outbreath is too long, modify this to an outbreath of 4.

LISTEN TO THE BELL

This activity is an easy way for young children to practice being mindful. This technique involves using a bell or chime (even a phone app will work), making the sound, and telling the child that he or she should listen carefully until he or she no longer hears it. The clinician can have the child raise his or her hand when the sound can no longer be heard. Hanson and Mendius (2009) call this "sustained attention" in mediation practice. This technique can be used individually or classroom-wide.

FIVE SENSES

In this exercise the child is educated about the five senses (tasting, hearing, seeing, touching, smelling) including the fact that the senses are the means through which we take in information about our world, and the fact that "thinking" is not a sense (though we often run all of our experiences through our thoughts, which leads us to not being in the moment). This exercise has been referred to as the power of "single tasking" (Willard, 2014). The clinician would ask the child to begin by taking in deep 4 × 6 breaths, and then have the child close his or her eyes and focus only on what sounds are in the room. The clinician can point out some possible sounds nearby that he or she might hear (e.g., people talking in the halls, the sound of a clock, birds outside the window). Next the child should be instructed to notice how the chair underneath him or her feels, how the floor feels under his or her feet, and how hot or cold the temperature of the room feels on his or her skin. The clinician can tell the child to notice if he or she can smell any scents in the room, or if there is any taste on his or her tongue that is noticeable. Finally, the child is told to open his or her eyes and look at the room. The clinician can suggest that colors may seem brighter than before, or that maybe the child sees things that he or she did not notice before. The clinician can talk with the child about becoming much more observant about what is around us if we use our five senses. A twist on this meditation is to discuss how superheroes have super senses to tell them about their world. For example, the clinician can suggest the child activate his or her "spidey-senses" or "bionic powers," focusing on what he or she can taste, smell, see, feel, and hear in the present moment.

MINDFUL WALKS

Walking with the child outdoors (if possible) and having him or her notice things that perhaps he or she has not noticed before can be another effective mindful activity. The clinician can have the child use the above Five Senses method to tune into his or her world as he or she is walking about. Commentary from the child should be limited, and the clinician should request that the child simply pay attention to what is going on around him or her (Germer, 2009).

THOUGHT-GLOBE

In this exercise, the analogy of a snow globe is used to explain how thoughts are often like the snow in the globe, flying about and capturing our attention. The child would start by taking in some deep breaths and then imagining that the snow in the globe is settling; any thoughts that the child is having simply float to the bottom of the globe, and calm and peace are returned to the mind. Noticing thoughts without attachment is a key component of mindfulness and teaches the child that just because he or she is having a thought does not mean that attention must be given to it (Willard, 2014). An actual snow globe, or glass jar with the child's thoughts written on small pieces of paper, can be used to illustrate this idea with the child. Shake the globe or jar with the child, then notice how the thoughts fall to the bottom. An alternative to this exercise is to have the child imagine that his or her thoughts are put into bubbles, and have the bubble just float away, without attachment to the thought.

MINDFUL EATING

Eating something mindfully is a popular technique for introducing mindfulness to a child. Kabat-Zinn (1990) recommends that clinicians use clear instructions, focused on awareness and nonjudgmental experience to savor the food object. Form 4.7 is a sample script for mindful eating.

There are several formalized programs available for mindfulness practices when working with children. Some of these programs can be implemented by the clinician working with children directly (e.g., MindUP at *http://thehawnfoundation.org*), whereas others may involve a representative from that particular mindfulness organization to come and implement the program (e.g., *MindfulSchools.org*), or both (e.g., the Inner Kids Program at *www.susankaisergreenland.com*; the Mind–Body Awareness Project at *www.mbaproject.org*). Although outcome data are limited on these programs to date, they do incorporate validated mindfulness techniques.

CHAPTER SUMMARY

Although the treatment of internalizing disorders in young children has traditionally been overlooked by mental health professionals, more attention has been brought to this important area over the last few years. This chapter provided an overview of commonly used prevention methods and treatment modalities for use with preschool- and kindergarten-age children experiencing internalizing problems. A growing body of literature attests to the effectiveness of cognitive-behavioral techniques and mindfulness with children in general, though more research is needed when focusing specifically on young children. By simplifying the language used, involving parents and teachers in the treatment plan, and using concrete examples, these same techniques can be helpful for this young population.

FORM 4.1

Parent Handout: Treatment of Anxiety

Many young children have fears. Typical fears exhibited by preschool- and kindergarten-age children include fear of the dark, fear of specific animals, and fear of separation from parents (or other caregivers). Fears are not unusual in young children, but when a fear begins to interfere with the child's functioning (e.g., the child refuses to attend school) or the family's functioning (e.g., parents argue about how to address a fear), then treatment should be considered. Some common intervention techniques for fears and the ways you, as a parent, can assist with treatment are discussed below. Make sure first to discuss your use of these techniques with your child's clinician.

Systematic Desensitization

This technique involves gradually exposing your child to a feared object, while having your child engage in an activity that is incompatible with fear. Relaxation is used as the incompatible response with older children. Relaxation may be used with young children, but other fun activities, such as blowing bubbles, running around the yard, or playing a short game also can be used.

It is important not to rush the exposure exercises but to start with exposure to situations in which the child is unlikely to exhibit a high level of fear. For example, for a child with a fear of dogs, the child might first look at pictures of a dog, then observe a dog outside, then be in the same room as a dog, then touch the dog.

Your child's clinician will help you set up a systematic desensitization program. The clinician may work with your child on exposure exercises during sessions and also may have you conduct some exposure exercises at home.

Positive Self-Talk

Pay attention to what your child says and help him/her replace negative thoughts with more positive ones. For example, if your child says, "I can't go outside because there might be a dog and dogs are scary," you can respond with, "Dogs can be scary, but most dogs outside are nice and you're brave. Tell yourself that you're brave, and that you'll be OK outside." When using this approach, make sure you do not minimize or belittle your child's fear. The goal is to acknowledge the fear while putting a more positive "spin" on your child's thoughts.

Modeling

Make sure to model appropriate (nonfearful) interactions for your child. If your child is afraid of dogs and the friendly neighbor dog comes along while you are outside with your child, talk out loud to the dog, saying such things as, "You're a nice, friendly dog—I'd like to pet you."

Contingency Management

Using this approach, you would reinforce your child for gradually interacting with the feared object. For example, if your child is afraid of dogs, you might initially reinforce your child for looking out the window at the neighbor's dog, then standing in the yard with the dog for a brief period of time, then standing in the yard for a longer period of time, etc. You can use stickers or candy as reinforcers, but also make sure to provide your child with verbal praise (e.g., "Great job hanging out in the yard with Rufus. You're so brave").

From Melissa L. Holland, Jessica Malmberg, and Gretchen Gimpel Peacock. Copyright © 2017 The Guilford Press. Permission to photocopy this form is granted to purchasers of this book for personal use or use with individual students (see copyright page for details). Purchasers can download additional copies of this material (see box at the end of the table of contents).

FORM 4.2

Visual Aid for Children Self-Assessing Their Current Anxiety Level

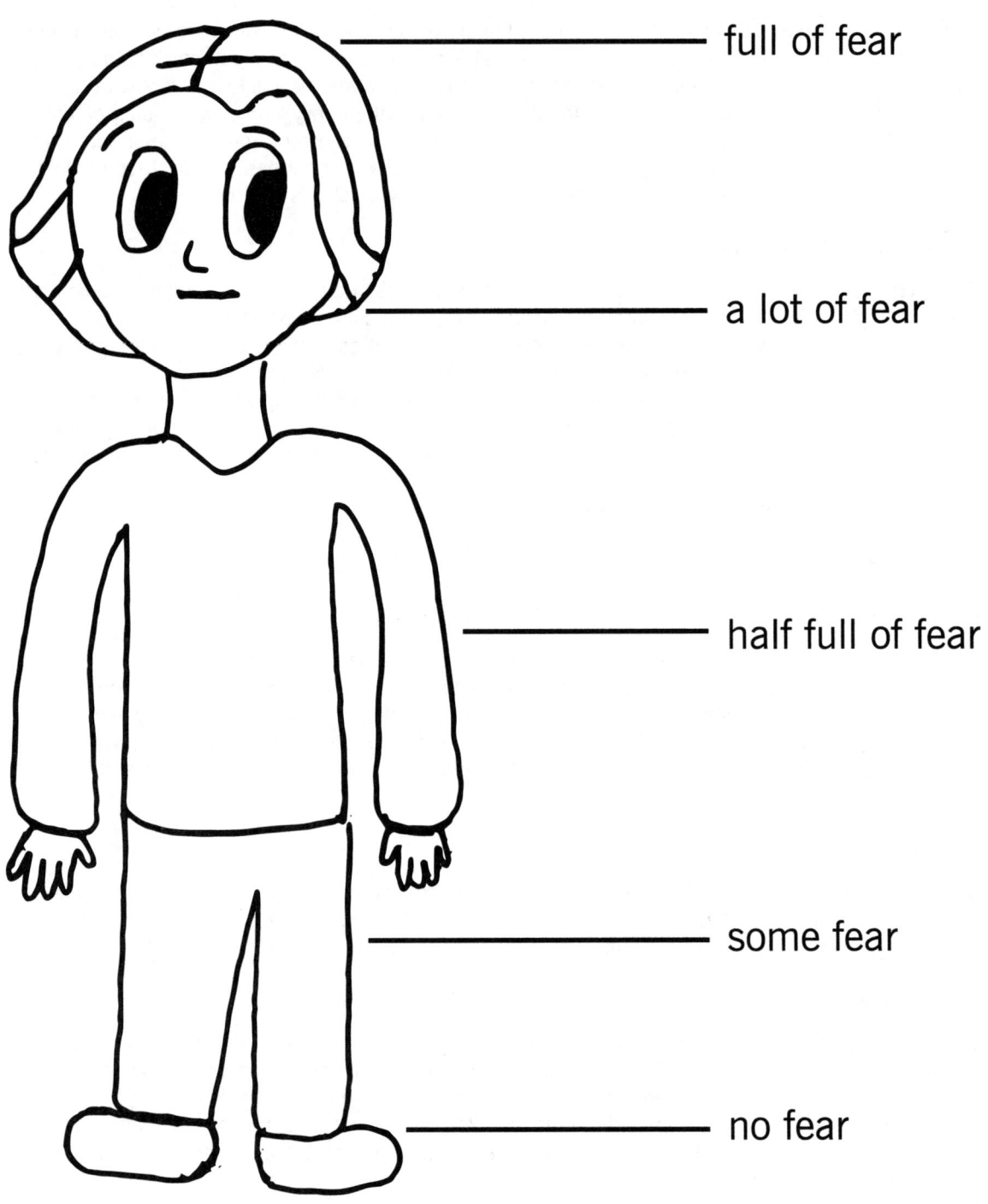

- full of fear
- a lot of fear
- half full of fear
- some fear
- no fear

From Melissa L. Holland, Jessica Malmberg, and Gretchen Gimpel Peacock. Copyright © 2017 The Guilford Press. Permission to photocopy this form is granted to purchasers of this book for personal use or use with individual students (see copyright page for details). Purchasers can download additional copies of this material (see box at the end of the table of contents).

FORM 4.3

Relaxation Script for Young Children

Begin with breathing exercises.

Feet: "Great job on your breathing. Now we are going to curl up our toes into tight little balls, just like this. They are like roly-polies [potato bugs] curled up! Good. And hold it, and hold it [8–10 seconds]. Now release. Feel how warm and tingly your toes and feet feel. They are very relaxed now."

Legs: "Now we are going to point our toes up and back toward our shins, like this. Feel how tight the backs of your legs feel? Kitty cats do this when they have just gotten up from a nap to stretch. Good, and hold it [8–10 seconds], and relax. Your legs feel so warm and good now."

Thighs: "Now we are going to press our knees together and hold them really tight so that our legs feel really tight, like you are squishing something in between your knees. Good, and press them harder, and hold it, and hold it [8–10 seconds], and release. Feel that warm, relaxed feeling now going down our legs and into our feet and toes."

Stomach: "OK, now we are going to tighten our tummies really hard, like an elephant was going to step on our tummy, so we need it to be really tight, and hold it [8–10 seconds], and release. Feel how nice and comfortable that is?"

Hands: "Good, now we are going to curl our hands up into two tight balls by making tight fists, like we are squeezing lemons with our hands. And hold it, and make them tighter [8–10 seconds], and release. Feel that warm, tingly feeling in your fingers and hands?"

Arms/Chest: "Now we are going to put our hands together and press the palms of our hands into one another [model a praying position, with the hands over our midchest]. And press harder, and hold it [8–10 seconds], and release."

Shoulders: "Let's put our shoulders up like we are trying to touch our shoulders to our ears. We look like monkeys when we do this! And hold them up, and up [8–10 seconds], and release. Feel that warm, relaxed feeling go down your shoulders, into your arms and hands, down through your stomach, and out your legs and toes. How warm and relaxed and calm our bodies feel."

Face: "Now we will scrunch up our faces . . . tighten all of the muscles of your face—the cheeks, mouth, and nose muscles, the muscles of your forehead. How funny a scrunched-up face can you make? Good! And hold it like that, hold it [8–10 seconds], and let go. Feel how good that feels."

End with breathing exercises.

From Melissa L. Holland, Jessica Malmberg, and Gretchen Gimpel Peacock. Copyright © 2017 The Guilford Press. Permission to photocopy this form is granted to purchasers of this book for personal use or use with individual students (see copyright page for details). Purchasers can download additional copies of this material (see box at the end of the table of contents).

FORM 4.4

Parent Handout: Separation Anxiety and School Refusal

Young children often have difficulty separating from their parents. When separation is anticipated, they may engage in behaviors such as clinginess, crying, and throwing tantrums. Refusal to go to school is frequently seen as part of separation anxiety disorder. However, school refusal also can be due to other problems, such as fear of the school or a specific individual at the school. In children with separation anxiety disorder, fear of separating from the caregiver is the main anxiety, and this is expressed in any situation in which separation is anticipated (e.g., at school, with a babysitter). Although some anxiety is typical when children are first introduced to a new situation (e.g., when they begin school), it is important to intervene if these symptoms do not go away.

Prevention of Separation Anxiety

To help prevent distress upon separation and to decrease the chances that separation anxiety will develop, the following steps can be taken when your child is introduced to a new situation, such as day care or preschool:

1. Select a day care or preschool with which you are comfortable and familiar.
2. Discuss with your child positive activities that will take place in the new setting (e.g., playing games, meeting new people).
3. Accompany your child to the new setting and stay with him/her for a *short* period of time.
4. After you pick up your child, praise him/her for doing well in school and allow your child to talk about what happened during the day.

Treatment of Separation Anxiety/School Refusal

Children with separation anxiety typically engage in behaviors in an attempt to prevent separation from occurring. The child may directly state his/her refusal to attend school, but more frequently this refusal is communicated through indirect methods, such as complaints of stomachaches or headaches in the morning or throwing temper tantrums when you are getting the child ready to leave for day care/preschool. Typically the child also becomes quite clingy when you attempt to leave him/her at day care/preschool. If your child is exhibiting such behaviors, it is important to address the problem immediately.

1. Do not reinforce the child's anxious and avoidant behaviors. *This is very important.* Do not allow your child to stay home from school unless he/she truly is sick. Do not give in to whining and crying and allow your child to stay home.
2. If you have been allowing your child to stay home, immediately return your child to school and do not allow him/her to miss future days of school.
3. Give your child a "transitional object" to help him/her get through the day. A transitional object is an item given by a parent to remind the child of the parent. Some examples of objects include a locket with a photograph of the parent in it, a "lucky penny," a "power ring," or a note or picture drawn by the parent to help the child feel special, loved, and powerful.
4. Forewarn the day care provider or teacher about your child's separation anxiety.
5. Reinforce your child for having attended day care/school.

Consistency is key to resolving your child's school refusal behavior. If you have allowed your child to stay out of school for a long time or if your child has severe anxiety symptoms, a more gradual exposure to the school setting may be necessary. For example, you might first have your child go to school for an hour each day and gradually work up to having him/her there for the whole school day. However, in most cases immediate and full return to the school setting is best.

From Melissa L. Holland, Jessica Malmberg, and Gretchen Gimpel Peacock. Copyright © 2017 The Guilford Press. Permission to photocopy this form is granted to purchasers of this book for personal use or use with individual students (see copyright page for details). Purchasers can download additional copies of this material (see box at the end of the table of contents).

FORM 4.5

Feelings Chart for Preschoolers and Kindergartners

Nervous   Sad

Happy   Excited

Angry

From Melissa L. Holland, Jessica Malmberg, and Gretchen Gimpel Peacock. Copyright © 2017 The Guilford Press. Permission to photocopy this form is granted to purchasers of this book for personal use or use with individual students (see copyright page for details). Purchasers can download additional copies of this material (see box at the end of the table of contents).

FORM 4.6

Daily Feelings Chart for Preschoolers and Kindergartners

CIRCLE HOW YOU ARE FEELING

Monday	Nervous	Sad	Happy	Excited	Angry
Tuesday	Nervous	Sad	Happy	Excited	Angry
Wednesday	Nervous	Sad	Happy	Excited	Angry
Thursday	Nervous	Sad	Happy	Excited	Angry
Friday	Nervous	Sad	Happy	Excited	Angry
Saturday	Nervous	Sad	Happy	Excited	Angry
Sunday	Nervous	Sad	Happy	Excited	Angry

From Melissa L. Holland, Jessica Malmberg, and Gretchen Gimpel Peacock. Copyright © 2017 The Guilford Press. Permission to photocopy this form is granted to purchasers of this book for personal use or use with individual students (see copyright page for details). Purchasers can download additional copies of this material (see box at the end of the table of contents).

FORM 4.7

Script for Mindful Eating

This exercise can be used individually or classroomwide. After handing out the food object, tell the child/children to not eat the food object right away and to pretend he/she/they are "discovering the object" for the very first time, like an alien from a different planet, not knowing what the object is. The example used here is a foil-wrapped chocolate candy, though raisins are also often used in mindful eating exercises. Read the following script to the child/children in a calm, slow voice after giving out the food item, and model the actions you are suggesting to the child as you move through the script.

"Bring your attention to the object. Do not eat the object until I tell you to. Pretend you have never seen an object like it before. Pick up the object and notice what it feels like between your fingers. Maybe it feels bumpy, or smooth, soft or hard. Notice whether the light catches on the object and makes it shiny in some places. Notice the color of the object. Now slowly unwrap your object, and notice if you hear any sound as you unwrap it. Now look at it again. Notice the color of it now. Notice if it feels smooth or rough. Now lift the object to your nose and take in a deep breath through your nose. Notice if the object has any smell. Do this again, taking in a deep breath, and noticing the smell. Now place the object on your tongue, but don't bite it yet. Notice what your mouth does with the object on your tongue. Notice any taste in your mouth. Now slowly chew the object. Notice any taste left on your tongue after you have swallowed your object."

After you are done with the activity, ask the child/children what that was like. Ask what he/she/they noticed as they ate the chocolate, and if that is different from how he/she/they normally eat(s). Point out the fact that all five senses were used and review the senses. Talk about trying out this way of eating at mealtime for the first bite of each meal. Encourage the child/children to review what was learned with members of his/her/their family.

From Melissa L. Holland, Jessica Malmberg, and Gretchen Gimpel Peacock. Copyright © 2017 The Guilford Press. Permission to photocopy this form is granted to purchasers of this book for personal use or use with individual students (see copyright page for details). Purchasers can download additional copies of this material (see box at the end of the table of contents).

CHAPTER 5

Managing and Preventing Everyday Problems

Some of the problems that cause the most stress and concern for parents of preschool- and kindergarten-age children are behaviors related to routines that are part of everyday life, such as eating, sleeping, and using the bathroom appropriately. Although these problems are often transitory and may not be severe enough to warrant a formal diagnosis, providing treatment can alleviate significant parental and child stress and potentially foster a more positive parent–child relationship. Moreover, management of such problems while the child is young may prevent later adverse outcomes in those situations in which the problem is not transitory. This chapter provides a detailed description of common effective treatments for these everyday problems.

TOILETING

Toilet Training

Toilet training is an important developmental milestone for preschool-age children; unfortunately, there is little scientific literature regarding how to toilet-train or how to address the problems associated with toilet training. For most children this task is accomplished with relatively little difficulty; however, many parents have questions and/or concerns regarding this process. A question parents commonly ask is when they should begin toilet training their child. Although there are no clear guidelines to follow, toilet training should not be initiated until the child is both physiologically and psychologically ready for it. Parents who overestimate their child's readiness may face prolonged training or toileting problems (Choby & George, 2008). In infancy, the bladder empties as a reflex; the infant has no control over this action. In the toddler years, children begin to become aware of when their bladders are full. By age 3, most children are able to control their sphincter muscles voluntarily and inhibit urination during the day; nighttime control comes a year or two later. Children are typically considered to have achieved bladder control when they can remain dry for several hours, empty their bladders completely when urinating, and demonstrate some realization that they need to urinate (Kuhn, Marcus, & Pitner, 1999; Rogers, 2013). For most children, toilet training starts between 21 and 36 months (Choby & George, 2008).

In addition to physiological readiness, children must exhibit other aspects of readiness before toilet training can be successful. For example, children must be able to perform the motor movements required for toileting, such as walking to the bathroom, removing the appropriate clothing, and sitting on the toilet (Rogers, 2013). They must have some basic language skills and be able to understand and communicate the words related to toileting. In addition, the ability to follow parental instructions is important to successful toilet training. Children who are noncompliant and exhibit disruptive behaviors will be difficult to toilet train. In fact, children with easy temperaments have been shown to be 33 times more likely to be easily toilet trained in comparison to those children with difficult temperaments (Schonwald, 2004). If a parent is having difficulty toilet training his or her child, behavioral characteristics of the child need to be assessed and, if necessary, behavioral parent training (see Chapter 3) should be implemented prior to toilet training, so that the child first learns to comply with parental commands (Kuhn et al., 1999).

There are two basic approaches to toilet training: the child-oriented approach advocated by Brazelton (1962) and the structured behavioral approach pioneered by Azrin and Foxx (1974). Despite limited empirical evidence, the American Academic of Pediatrics recommends the child-oriented approach based on expert opinion (Kiddoo, 2012). Although few outcome studies have been published, one large, prospective, cohort study found that 61% of children trained with the Brazelton method were continent by 36 months and 98% by 48 months (Taubman, 1997). In Brazelton's child-oriented approach, toilet training is gradually introduced to the child beginning at the age of 18 months. First, the child is provided with a potty chair; the child sits on the chair, fully clothed, for a few minutes each day. Next, the child sits on the potty chair without diapers. As the child becomes more interested in and comfortable with the potty chair, the child may be taken to the potty chair when his or her diaper is soiled. The diaper is then dropped into the potty chair to help the child learn the purpose of the chair. Next, the chair is placed in the child's play area, and he or she is told to use the potty, if need be. Once the child begins to use the potty chair, he or she is "graduated" to training pants or cotton underwear. Potty chair use is continued and encouraged. If the child does not make progress with the training, Brazelton recommends that training be stopped and resumed at a later time. Children who are ready for toilet training will progress faster and be easier to train than those who are not yet ready.

Schroeder and Gordon (2002) outlined a somewhat modified approach to the child-oriented method. After determining that the child is ready for toilet training, parents begin tracking their child's toileting habits by checking his or her diaper on a regular basis. This helps the parents know when the child is most likely to need to use the toilet. The child is then placed on the toilet at times when he or she is most likely to urinate or have a bowel movement. (See the section "Treatment of Retentive Encopresis" for more detailed information on "toilet sits.") If the child does urinate or defecate in the toilet, he or she is given a reinforcer. During this training time, diapers are not used and accidents are handled in a matter-of-fact manner. Schroeder and Gordon indicate that when such a program is used, most children are successfully toilet trained within 2 to 4 weeks.

Parents who desire a quicker method of toilet training may want to try Azrin and Foxx's (1974) *Toilet Training in Less Than a Day* program. As the title of the program suggests, this training method is designed to be implemented over the course of a single day. The training is parent-oriented and intensive and involves providing the child with numerous opportunities to experience successful toileting. Although no recent research that empirically evaluates this method has been published, several earlier cohort studies evaluating the Azrin and Foxx method have demonstrated success rates from 74 to 100% in children less than 25 months of age and from 93 to 100% in older toddlers (Butler, 1976). Despite the method's demonstrated success, pediatricians are generally less inclined to recommend it. A study of 103 pediatricians revealed that only 29% would recommend intensive training, although typically without all components (e.g. would not recommend using consequences for accidents or overcorrection techniques; Polaha, Warzak, & Dittmer-McMahon, 2002). This method may be useful for motivated parents who want their child toilet trained relatively quickly, but parents must be prepared for an intense, regimented routine, which may not be appropriate for every child's temperament.

When using the Azrin and Foxx method, parents use a toy doll that wets to model to the child the process of drinking and then urinating in the toilet. The child is encouraged to drink a large amount of liquids so that he or she will have repeated opportunities to practice using the toilet. Initially, parents prompt their child to sit on the potty every 15 minutes and decrease the frequency as their child has several successful potty trials. Parents should provide immediate and varied positive reinforcement for every instance of a correct toileting skill. Dry pants checks are conducted every 5 minutes. If the child does have an accident during the training day, a mildly aversive consequence for wetting (verbal reprimand, helping clean up) is provided. This is followed by 10 rapid "positive practice" sessions using the doll to imitate toileting. Given the potential for problems and side effects such as temper tantrums, particularly for those children with difficult temperaments, it is recommended that this program be used only in consultation with a professional (Schroeder & Gordon, 2002).

Most parents make it through the toilet-training phase without any assistance from a medical or mental health professional. Typically, it is only when a child continues to wet or have soiling accidents into the later preschool years, or when a child who was toilet trained resumes wetting or soiling, that a parent seeks professional help. Often parents will first seek assistance from their pediatrician (rather than a psychologist or other mental health professional). If a parent does first seek help from a mental health professional and has not consulted with his or her pediatrician, the mental health professional should refer the parent to a physician prior to initiating treatment. Although enuresis and encopresis are rarely due to physical problems, such problems must be ruled out before implementing any behavioral treatment.

Enuresis

As noted in Chapter 1, enuresis can involve repeated daytime (diurnal) or nighttime (nocturnal) wetting. Given that children need to be at least 5 years of age to receive a diagnosis, many preschool-age children will be ineligible for a diagnosis, but treatment may still be warranted depending on the presenting situation. Before treatment for either diurnal or nocturnal enuresis is initiated, it is important to obtain a thorough understanding of the problem. Following a medical evaluation to rule out an organic cause, mental health professionals should obtain a full history of the child's wetting problems and any related toileting issues. In addition, the child's developmental history should be obtained. Parents should also be encouraged to track the child's wetting both initially, as part of the assessment process, as well as during treatment. (See Forms 5.1, 5.2, 5.3, and 5.4 for sample tracking sheets.)

Treatment of Diurnal Enuresis

Although significant research on the treatment of nocturnal enuresis has been conducted, less research has been conducted on the treatment of diurnal enuresis. Several studies suggest that behavioral strategies (e.g., timed voiding, modification of fluid intake, positive reinforcement) are particularly effective in treating diurnal enuresis (Mulders, Cobussen-Boekhorst, de Gier, Feitz, & Kortmann, 2011; Wiener et al., 2000). If the child has never been dry during the day, it is likely that the child was never fully toilet trained. In this case, parents should consider reinstituting toilet-training procedures. If the child has been dry for some time but has begun to wet again, it is imperative that a thorough assessment be completed in order to identify any contextual, social, or psychological contributing factors. If such factors are identified, they should be directly addressed in treatment. A modified version of Schroeder and Gordon's (2002) toilet-training approach also is recommended. In addition to the toilet sits, parents should institute "dry-pant checks," in which they check the child's pants at certain times throughout the day and provide the child with a reinforcer if he or she is dry. When the child does wet, he or she should be required to assist with the cleanup, as appropriate for his or her age. Likely this will involve changing clothes and putting the wet clothes in a laundry hamper or other appropriate place. Schroeder and Gordon also suggest that children engage in "positive practice" activities, in which they practice walking to the bathroom and using the toilet from different locations (e.g., yard, different rooms in the house).

Treatment of Nocturnal Enuresis

Most parents will not implement treatment for nocturnal enuresis until early elementary school, so the discussion of this treatment applies more to kindergarten-age and older children. Recently published practical consensus guidelines endorsed by the American Academy of Pediatrics noted two first-line treatment options: the urine alarm and medication (specifically desmopressin; Vande Walle et al., 2012). Treatment selection should be guided by family motivation and child characteristics (e.g., reduced bladder capacity, excessive urine output). Research has shown that the urine alarm, which is discussed shortly, is the most effective long-term treatment method for most cases of nocturnal enuresis. However, the antidiuretic medication desmopressin may also be useful, particularly for families exhibiting low motivation, parents who are at risk of using excessive punishment after bedwetting episodes, and children with nocturnal polyuria (e.g., overproduction of urine at night; Campbell, Cox, & Borowitz, 2009; Vande Walle et al., 2012). Desmopressin decreases urine production and concentrates urine. Children generally respond quickly to this medication, making it an ideal option for sleepovers, but symptoms tend to resume once treatment has been discontinued. Although desmopressin is not curative, there is some recent evidence that structured withdrawal of the medication may reduce relapse rates following its discontinuation (Vande Walle et al., 2012).

The most well-established and empirically supported treatment for nocturnal enuresis is the urine alarm (Campbell et al., 2009). Children with normal nighttime urine output and families that are highly motivated are most likely to benefit from this treatment approach. Parents should be advised that improvement is typically not seen for several weeks or months, and families often report that the disruptive nature of the alarm affects their child's sleep (and often that of the entire household), which increases the risk of poor adherence and early withdrawal from treatment (Vande Walle et al., 2012). Treatment adherence is critical in order to see symptom improvement. For families who are adherent to the use of the urine alarm, symptoms do improve in nearly two thirds of children during its use and almost half of children are successful in remaining dry after therapy is stopped (Robson, 2009).

The original alarm consisted of a large pad that was connected to an alarm covering the bed; when the child began to wet, the moisture would set off sensors in the pad that caused the alarm to sound. The alarms in use today are more compact and typically consist of snaps or a clip that are attached to the child's underwear. The snaps are then connected to a small alarm box that can be worn on the child's wrist or shoulder. When the child wets, a connection is made between the snaps and the alarm sounds. The urine alarm is presumed to be effective by improving arousal from sleep either by classical conditioning and/or operant conditioning (e.g. avoidance) effects (Axelrod, Tornehl, & Fontanini-Axelrod, 2014). For example, the noise of the alarm may be aversive to the child, so the child learns to wake up to the sensation of a full bladder, rather than wetting the bed. However, it appears that when children stop wetting the bed, many of them sleep through the night instead of waking to use the bathroom (Harari, 2013), so the mechanism of action is still unclear.

The urine alarm is typically never used in isolation. Other treatment components, such as reinforcement for following the alarm procedures and cleanliness training (having the child assist with changing sheets and clothing following a wetting incident), are commonly part of a complete intervention package. In addition, methods such as *retention-control training*, in which the child drinks a large quantity of fluid and attempts to avoid urination as long as possible, and *overlearning*, in which the child consumes fluids prior to bedtime, also have been studied as added components to the alarm procedures. One manualized multicomponent treatment approach, full-spectrum home training, has been empirically evaluated and found to have an average success rate of 79%, occurring within 2 to 4 months (Brown, Pope, & Brown, 2011). This treatment involves use of the urine alarm in conjunction with retention-control training with monetary rewards, cleanliness training, self-monitoring of wet/dry nights, and a graduated overlearning procedure. Using the urine alarm in conjunction with other treatment components is intended to reduce treatment time and relapse rates. Although success rates do increase as more components are added, the urine alarm continues to be the most critical element in these treatment packages (Brown et al., 2011).

Urine alarms can be purchased from a variety of different companies and cost approximately $50 to $150. A prescription is not required when purchasing a urine alarm, but insurance companies may cover the cost if the alarm is recommended by a doctor. Although parents can use the alarm without professional assistance, it is helpful for parents to consult with a mental health professional when first setting up an alarm-based program. Following an initial consultation, parents should continue to check in with the professional on an as-needed basis.

Upon initiating treatment, the use of the urine alarm should be discussed with both the parent and child present, and handouts on the use of the alarm should be provided. (See Form 5.5 for a parent handout describing the use of the alarm and Form 5.6 for a child handout that can be given to older children to read themselves or be read aloud to younger children.) It is important that both the parent and their child agree to the use of the alarm because both of them need to be active in the treatment procedures. Both parent and child should be shown how to attach the alarm, but the child should be responsible for attaching the alarm every night before he or she goes to bed. The parent may want to check to make sure the alarm is attached appropriately, especially when the child first uses the alarm. When the alarm sounds, the parent should immediately wake up and go to the child's room. Placing a baby monitor in the child's room and/or leaving the bedroom doors of both rooms open in order for the parent to hear the alarm can help facilitate this process. When the alarm is first used, children should be instructed to listen for the alarm and to awaken if they hear it. Children often do not awaken, so it will be necessary for the parent to wake the child if he or she has not awakened on his or her own. Once the child is fully awake, he or she should detach the alarm, get up, go to the bathroom, and attempt to urinate in the toilet. Even if the child insists he or she no longer needs to go, this step should still be included. Afterward, the child should assist with any necessary cleanup (e.g., changing pajamas, changing the sheets). If the wet spot on the sheets is small, it is not necessary to change them during the night; instead, a towel can be placed over the spot. If the wet area is large (which is typical, at first), then the sheets should be changed. When the bed has been remade, the child should reattach the alarm and return to bed. If the alarm sounds again during the night, these same procedures should be repeated. During these nighttime proceedings it is essential that the parent not become angry with, or punish, the child. The parent should assist the child matter-of-factly with the alarm procedures.

In the morning, the child should receive a small reward if he or she stayed dry during the night or if he or she followed the alarm procedures correctly. Given that it will take some time for the child to begin to have dry nights consistently, the child should be rewarded simply for following the procedures correctly. If these procedures are followed on a nightly basis, the child should become dry. The child should also track his or her wet and dry nights on a chart so that progress can be seen. If the child was dry during the night, the parent should praise him or her for staying dry, but if the child was wet, the parent should not be discouraging or negative. Instead the parent should simply praise the child for following the alarm procedures (if the child did so) and perhaps make a matter-of-fact comment such as, "Even though you wet last night, you did a great job following the alarm procedures. Maybe you'll be dry tonight."

The urine alarm does not produce immediate effects; in fact, it is not unusual for it to take several months for the child to become consistently dry during the night. One of the first indicators of progress is that the wet spots in the bed become smaller because the child begins to awaken more quickly to the alarm and stops voiding until he or she gets to the bathroom. The alarm should continue to be used until the child has 14 dry nights in a row. Following this accomplishment, the use of the alarm can be discontinued. However, if the child begins to wet again, use of the alarm should be reinstated immediately and should continue until the child again has 14 consecutive dry nights.

Encopresis

As noted in Chapter 1, encopresis involves fecal soiling in inappropriate places, such as clothing. In children with retentive encopresis, the most common type, the encopresis is a result of extreme constipation. Children may not have regular bowel movements for a variety of reasons including various behavioral/dietary factors, reduced colonic motility, and fecal retention (Friman, Hofstadter, & Jones, 2006). When a child does not have a bowel movement in response to the need to do so, the fecal material returns to the colon. This fecal material then becomes hardened, which makes it more difficult and painful for the child to pass. Loss of appetite, early satiety, nausea, and vomiting may also occur. As the child becomes more and more constipated, fecal material becomes impacted in the colon. In addition, the muscles around the colon become stretched; as a result, the child is unable to feel the need to have a bowel movement and is unable to pass bowel movements effectively. Typically, fluid leaks out around the impaction (e.g. overflow incontinence), producing some soiling. Children with retentive encopresis often do not know when this leaking occurs and therefore are not aware of the soiling. Occasionally, large fecal masses are expelled along with leakage (Friman et al., 2006; Schroeder & Gordon, 2002). In contrast, children with nonretentive encopresis are not constipated, so impaction of feces is not a problem for them. They typically have consistent bowel movements and stools that are normal in size. In addition, whereas children with retentive encopresis may complain of abdominal pain, such complaints are not typical in children with nonretentive encopresis (Boles et al., 2008; Bongers, Tabbers, & Benninga, 2007).

Treatment of Retentive Encopresis

The typical treatment program for retentive encopresis, which has been demonstrated to be effective (Campbell et al., 2009; Friman et al., 2006), involves a combination of medical procedures and behavioral interventions. It is important that children with encopresis receive a medical evaluation prior to treatment in order to rule out the possibility of any organic etiology (e.g., medical condition, malformation of the intestines). Coexisting symptoms that would suggest possible organic etiology include fever, nausea, vomiting, abdominal distention, and weight loss (Montgomery & Navarro, 2008). However, encopresis rarely has an organic cause. About 95% of the cases of retentive encopresis and 99% of the cases of nonretentive encopresis do not have an organic etiology (Kuhn et al., 1999); but it is important to confirm this absence before proceeding. In addition to ruling out an organic etiology, the physician can discuss with the parents any medical interventions that should occur. Often, because the child's colon is very impacted with fecal material, it is necessary to administer a series of enemas to clear out this material. Enemas should be administered under the direction of a physician and before behavioral interventions are implemented, as they will likely be less successful if the child is still severely impacted. The physician may also recommend stool softeners or laxatives to help ensure regular bowel movements.

Additionally, parents should receive instruction regarding appropriate dietary modifications. Children with encopresis need to consume an appropriate amount of fiber. The consumption of fruits and vegetables should be encouraged. In addition, wheat germ or bran may be sprinkled on food as a supplement. Parents should also be encouraged to increase their child's water intake and to reduce the child's consumption of dairy products, if it is high. It may be beneficial for the parents to consult with a nutritionist who can assist them in making appropriate dietary modifications.

The behavioral component of an encopresis treatment program involves the implementation of scheduled toilet sits, as well as rewards for producing a bowel movement in the toilet. Toilet sits encourage the child to use the toilet and also help the child establish a routine of using the toilet when he or she is most likely to have a bowel movement. Toilet sits are a key component to treatment programs; children who do not engage in the prescribed toilet sits are more likely to show little or no improvement (Brooks et al., 2000). Children should engage in two to four toilet sits per day, at times when they are most likely to have a bowel movement (e.g., soon after waking up in the morning, after mealtimes). During a toilet sit, the child remains on the toilet for 5–10 minutes. Toilet sits should be fun and enjoyable; the child should be given a book or toy with which to play or be allowed to listen to music while in the bathroom. Obviously, the child needs to be comfortable on the toilet, and his or her feet should reach the floor (parents can use either a potty chair or provide a stool on which the child can rest his or her feet). If the child is successful at having a bowel movement, he or she receives a reward. In addition, parents should also complete "clean pants checks" several times a day and give a reward to the child if he or she has not had a soiling accident. Soiled pants should be treated matter-of-factly; the child (with assistance from a parent as needed) should be required to wash his or her underwear in the sink or bathtub, then clean him- or herself and get redressed. Parents should make sure not to verbally reprimand or punish their child for soiling; a matter-of-fact tone is far more effective (Friman et al., 2006). (See Form 5.7 for a parent handout detailing the treatment of encopresis, and Form 5.8 for a treatment log for parents to use in tracking treatment progress.)

Treatment of Toileting Refusal/Nonretentive Encopresis

As noted above, retentive encopresis is the more common type of encopresis. However, children may also be encopretic for reasons other than constipation. In young children, refusal to use the toilet may be a particularly salient problem. Toilet refusal is a fairly common behavior encountered by parents during the toilet training process, in which approximately 20% of children in the general population engage in a period of stool toileting refusal, with only a fourth of these children requiring later intervention due to ongoing toileting refusal problems (van Dijk et al., 2007). Children who overtly refuse to sit on the toilet may have a stubborn temperament or other behavioral/emotional difficulties, may have negative associations with the bathroom/toilet due to past painful bowel movements, or may have had other negative toileting experiences (e.g., harsh or punitive parenting approach to toileting; Friman et al., 2006). The mechanism underlying nonretentive encopresis is largely unknown. Current consensus suggests that it most likely is a multifactorial disorder. Some factors that may contribute to this diagnostic presentation include never having been successfully toilet trained, emotional/behavioral difficulties, and/or denying or neglecting their normal and appropriate physiological signals to go to the bathroom (Bongers et al., 2007).

If the child is fearful about using the bathroom or toileting, more positive stimuli need to be associated with toileting procedures. One way to help the child learn to associate the bathroom and toileting with positive stimuli is through the use of planned, positive toilet sits (Boles et al., 2008). These sits are similar to those previously described; however, the initial purpose of these sits is not to encourage the child to have a bowel movement in the toilet but to simply help reduce the child's anxiety about the toilet. Thus, during these initial sits, the child can wear a diaper or other clothing. Initially these sits should be fairly brief in time (perhaps less than 1 minute), but the time should be increased as the child becomes more comfortable. As with the toilet sits described above, the child should be comfortable on the toilet, and the setting and atmosphere should be fun; the child should be encouraged to listen to music, bring books into the bathroom, and so forth. In addition, these sits should be associated with positive parent–child interactions. Parents should make sure not to nag or scold their child during this time but instead should interact with him or her in a positive, child-directed manner.

In some instances, the child may be so resistant to scheduled toilet sits that they will have to be shaped more gradually. In this situation, Kuhn and colleagues (1999) recommend that parents begin by modeling appropriate toileting behavior. After this step, parents should engage their child in fun activities in the bathroom (or close to the bathroom). For example, parents may play the child's favorite game with him or her in the doorway to the bathroom. These fun activities are then gradually moved closer to the toilet, and eventually the parent has the child engage in these activities while sitting on the toilet. See Chapter 4 for additional information regarding treatment of anxiety- or fear-related symptoms (e.g. systematic desensitization).

Once the child has overcome his or her toileting "fear," parents can shift to working on training their child to have bowel movements in the toilet. A rigorously scheduled toileting program is also the cornerstone of treatment for children with nonretentive encopresis (Bongers et al., 2007). Parents should institute regular toilet sits (in which the child is no longer wearing a diaper) two to four times a day, as already described. It is important that the positive activities initiated during the toilet sits be continued and that the child be provided with incentives for having a bowel movement in the toilet (Boles et al., 2008).

FEEDING/EATING PROBLEMS

Although there are a variety of feeding/eating disorders young children may have (some of which are due to complex medical complications), this chapter focuses on the more common difficulties that parents may encounter with their preschool- and kindergarten-age children. First, we discuss how to promote healthy eating behaviors and prevent childhood obesity. Next, we address how to intervene with "picky" eaters who eat only a limited number of food items, as well as with children who refuse to eat. Treatments for pica and rumination, inappropriate behavior at mealtimes (e.g., throwing temper tantrums), and more severe eating disorders are also briefly discussed. For children who behave inappropriately at mealtimes or have severe eating problems, the guidelines covered in Chapter 3 (for the treatment of externalizing problems) should also be followed.

Promoting Healthy Eating Habits

Social learning theory is heavily implicated in young children's developing patterns of eating and physical activity, since children often learn by observing the behaviors modeled by their parents. For example, if parents are observed eating a healthy diet and engaging in regular physical activity, their children are more likely to imitate similar behaviors. Additionally, parents are responsible for structuring their children's environment and providing them with varying degrees of opportunities for physical activity, the use of electronics, and the consumption of certain foods. Thus, children are dependent on their parents to provide them with a home environment that promotes the development of a healthy lifestyle.

A critical first step in promoting healthy eating habits is to ensure that a child has ready access to a variety of healthy foods and limited access to junk food. Young children who are provided with regular opportunities to eat healthy foods are more likely to continue to prefer and consume these foods (Anzman, Rollins, & Birch, 2010). Recent data suggest that even young children are consuming diets too high in added sugar, fat, and salt, while consuming too few fruits, vegetables, and complex carbohydrates (Institute of Medicine, 2011). Parents should limit access to nutrient-poor foods such as candy, potato chips, and sugar-sweetened beverages. Instead, children should be offered whole grain foods, fruits, vegetables, and low-fat dairy products. Children should also be supported in developing the habit of drinking water when thirsty, rather than consuming high- sugar beverages such as fruit juice or soda.

Parents should also be encouraged to establish responsive feeding practices at mealtime, which helps to support children in self-regulating their eating behaviors in response to their internal hunger and fullness cues (Black & Aboud, 2011). Research indicates that young children have some ability to regulate their food intake (Institute of Medicine, 2011). Parents who strictly limit access to junk food, offer large portions of palatable foods, or insist that a child eat everything on his or her plate may interfere with their child's ability to learn to self-regulate food intake. In responsive feeding, parents offer their child access to appropriately sized portions of healthy foods and allow their child to control the amount he or she eats. Children should be kept on a regular eating schedule, which typically consists of three meals and two to three snacks per day, which prevents children from becoming too hungry and overeating. Parents are encouraged to sit and eat with their child so that they can observe their child's eating behaviors and remind the child of his or her hunger and fullness cues. Use of child-sized plates, utensils, and food portions (e.g. sandwiches cut in quarters) can also help children learn to self-regulate their food intake. Children can be supported in serving themselves, with parents guiding their child as to how much food can be taken at one time (e.g. "You can take one spoonful and then you can have more if you are still hungry").

Parents should also ensure that their child is getting adequate daily physical activity, as a strong relationship has been established between physical activity and the risk of childhood obesity. The Institute of Medicine (2011) recommends that toddlers and preschoolers should be physically active for at least 3 hours per day. To assist with this goal, children's access to electronics should also be limited. Limiting electronic use will not only decrease children's sedentary behaviors, it will also help to limit their exposure to food and beverage marketing. It is currently estimated that preschool-age children are exposed to approximately 4 hours of screen time per day, while current recommendations are that children's access to screen time should be limited to 1–2 hours per day (Pooja, Zhou, Lozano, & Christakis, 2010). Parents should be encouraged to develop a family culture that embodies all of the above lifestyle recommendations, as this will increase children's receptiveness to these changes, as well as increase their sustainability.

Typical Feeding Problems

The primary interventions for feeding problems involve behavioral methods. No matter what the initial cause of the problem, children with feeding difficulties are often reinforced for their inappropriate feeding behaviors. For example, parents may comment on or attempt to correct their child's spitting out of food (although this attention is typically negative, it is often reinforcing to the child); parents may give their child the foods he or she prefers if the child becomes upset when presented with nonpreferred foods; or parents may allow their child to leave the feeding situation when he or she misbehaves (Adamson et al., 2013). Given that the reinforcement of inappropriate eating behaviors often either causes or exacerbates feeding problems, it is logical that behavioral methods should be the most common and effective interventions for these difficulties. The behavioral principles used are fairly straightforward and empirically based: positive reinforcement for appropriate feeding behaviors, the removal of reinforcers, and/or the application of mildly aversive consequences for inappropriate behaviors.

Since some feeding disorders can have an organic component, a child with an ongoing feeding problem should first receive a medical evaluation. Behavioral interventions may still be part of the treatment package, but other interventions may also be appropriate. For the typically developing child, feeding problems often have a strong environmental component, and assessment should focus on determining the antecedents and consequences for both appropriate and inappropriate feeding behaviors (assuming that the child has received a medical evaluation and has been found to have no medical problems). Specific behaviors that the child engages in and the settings in which these behaviors occur should be identified and operationally defined. The clinician also should inquire about parental responses to the child's behaviors, foods the child likes/does not like, and other eating-related issues (Babbitt et al., 1994; Kedesdy & Budd, 1998; Linscheid, 2006). (See Table 5.1 for interview questions for parents.) This assessment information helps the clinician develop an intervention program that targets the contingencies that are maintaining the feeding difficulties.

Environmental changes regarding mealtime are perhaps the most basic and easily implemented of the behavioral interventions needed to improve the child's eating patterns. Parents should create a consistent feeding environment (e.g., all meals at the dining room

TABLE 5.1. Interview Questions for Parents Regarding Their Child's Eating Problems

1. Describe the specific problem behaviors your child exhibits in relation to eating.
2. How long have these problems been going on?
3. What have you tried previously to decrease these problem behaviors? What has been the most successful? What has not worked?
4. How long does your child engage in eating (e.g., how long does your child stay at the dinner table)? What portion of a meal does your child generally eat?
5. Does your child feed him/herself? If not, who does? If so, are there any problems with this?
6. What times of day does your child eat? (Include all instances of eating—snacks and meals.)
7. What does your child typically eat in these instances? Where does the eating occur?
8. What foods does your child like/dislike? Are there certain textures, types of foods, etc., for which your child has a preference? What foods are routinely not eaten, spit out, etc.?
9. Are there certain settings, foods, etc., that are likely to prompt your child's feeding problems? Please describe them.
10. When your child engages in problem eating behaviors, what do you do?
11. Give an example of a recent interaction you had with your child related to feeding. Describe the setting, your child's behaviors, and your actions.
12. Describe a typical mealtime in your house.
13. Do you have any other behavioral concerns about your child?

Note. Based on Kedesdy and Budd (1998) and Silverman and Tarbell (2009).

or kitchen table), use a comfortable and secure seat for their child (e.g., highchair or booster seat with a strap), and should eliminate distractions (such as electronics and toys; Kedesdy & Budd, 1998; Silverman & Tarbell, 2009). Portions that are appropriately sized to the child's developmental level and weight should be served. The child's feeding schedule should be purposefully constructed to facilitate promotion of appetite and reduce the child's motivation to engage in food refusal. For example, mealtimes should occur on a regular schedule, and children should be prevented from grazing between scheduled meals. Research has demonstrated a significant correlation between feeding difficulties and mealtimes that are longer than 30 minutes (Benjasuwantep, Chaithirayanon, & Eiamudomkan, 2013); thus, meals should generally last 30 minutes or less. When mealtime is over, parents should prevent their child from eating again until the next scheduled snack/mealtime, regardless of the amount of food the child consumed. This allows a child to experience the natural consequence of hunger after a "failed" meal and increases his or her motivation to eat at the next meal (Silverman & Tarbell, 2009).

Giving positive attention for appropriate feeding behaviors is one of the most common behavioral interventions recommended for feeding problems. When the child is eating appropriately, the parent provides praise and social attention. Parents should also provide positive reinforcement to siblings, if they are present, for engaging in appropriate mealtime behaviors. When the child is not eating correctly, the parent is instructed to ignore him or her for a brief period of time, attending to the child again only when he or she resumes appropriate eating behaviors. At the initial stages of the intervention, positive reinforcement may be given for each instance of appropriate eating behavior. As the child begins to engage in more and more appropriate eating behaviors, the reinforcement should gradually be decreased (Linscheid, 2006).

Preferred foods also may be used as rewards to encourage eating. This intervention, based on the Premack principle (using a high probability behavior to reinforce a low probability behavior), is commonly recommended along with use of contingent praise and social attention. In such an intervention, the child would be allowed to have several bites of pizza (a highly preferred food) after eating several bites of carrots (a nonpreferred food). Tangible reinforcers can also be used to help shape appropriate eating behaviors. For example, children may earn special privileges (e.g., inviting a friend over, staying up later) for engaging in appropriate eating behavior.

In addition to contingently providing positive reinforcement for a child's appropriate eating behaviors, mild punishment, such as a brief time-out procedure, may be used for inappropriate eating behaviors (e.g., spitting out food, refusing food, throwing a tantrum). However, for children who find eating to be aversive, time-out may simply be seen as a method of escaping something they do not want to do in the first place (i.e., eat). Thus, it is important that time-out be used in conjunction with strategies aimed at promoting the child's appetite (e.g., feeding schedule, restriction of food between snacks/mealtimes) and providing the child with strong positive reinforcement for appropriate eating behaviors (Kedesdy & Budd, 1998; Linscheid, 2006). Other common negative consequences for inappropriate eating behaviors include the removal of preferred food items or the loss of desired privileges. (See Form 5.9 for a parent handout that summarizes these treatment options.)

In typically developing children, providing positive reinforcement for appropriate eating behaviors and negative consequences for inappropriate eating behaviors likely will be sufficient to overcome any problems. However, in children with developmental delays and some children with more severe feeding problems, additional methods may be necessary. These methods include physical guidance, such as jaw prompting, in which the clinician or parent puts food in the child's mouth while holding the chin with his or her thumb and index finger. After the child chews and swallows the food, the child's jaw is released (Williams, Field, & Seiverling, 2010). One negative reinforcement procedure termed "contingency contacting" has also been proposed, in which a parent holds the eating utensil, food, or drink to the child's mouth until it is accepted, with all inappropriate behaviors blocked and ignored (Linscheid, 2006; Williams et al., 2010). Additional punishment techniques may include spraying lemon juice into a child's mouth following inappropriate eating behaviors, and overcorrection (e.g., having a child repeatedly clean up after spitting out food). These more aversive techniques are not recommended, unless the positive reinforcement and milder versions of punishment (e.g., time-out) are not successful (Kedesdy & Budd, 1998; Williams & McAdam, 2013). With the vast majority of typically developing children, these aversive techniques will not be needed.

Pica

As noted in Chapter 1, pica refers to the eating of nonfood, nonnutritive substances. Given that pica can be dangerous to the child (e.g., ingestion of lead paint), it should always be treated. As with other feeding problems, behavioral interventions are the most recommended form of treatment. Discrimination training may be needed (i.e., teaching the child to be able to identify food and nonfood items), especially for children with developmental delays. When treating pica, children should earn reinforcers for eating appropriate food substances and receive a mild punishment for eating nonfood substances. Time-out can be an effective punishment. In addition, spraying water mist on a child's face or lemon juice into the child's mouth has been found useful (Kedesdy & Budd, 1998; Motta & Basile, 1998; Williams & McAdam, 2013). Overcorrection procedures have also been successfully used in several treatment programs. For example, after a pica incident, the child would be required to brush his or her teeth for several minutes with a soft toothbrush soaked in a strong antiseptic mouthwash. This may be followed by a period of face washing, as well as time spent tidying up the room (Stiegler, 2005).

Rumination

As noted in Chapter 1, rumination involves repeatedly regurgitating food. Although rumination disorder is generally considered a "benign" condition, significant negative outcomes have been identified. Children with rumination are at risk for experiencing significant functional disability, including social difficulties and school absences, as well as health related problems including dental issues, malnutrition, weight loss, and dehydration (Chial, Camilleri, Williams, Litzinger, & Perrault, 2003). Given these concerns, early recognition of the clinical features of rumination and referral for treatment are imperative.

As with the other feeding disorders, rumination disorder is generally responsive to behavioral interventions, which include reinforcing nonruminating eating behaviors or reinforcing a response that does not allow the child to engage in the ruminating behavior. For example, if a child uses his or her finger to induce rumination, the child can be reinforced for engaging in another activity that requires his or her hands (e.g., drawing, building with blocks, holding a utensil correctly). Additionally, diaphragmatic breathing and other relaxation strategies have been shown to be effective competing responses (Chial et al., 2003). A recent study has also demonstrated the utility of having a child chew gum after meals, as it increases the frequency of the swallowing response (Green, Alioto, Mousa, & Di Lorenzo, 2011). Punishment procedures also can be incorporated into behavioral treatment plans, although they have become far less commonly used or studied in recent years because of a failure to maintain treatment gains, negative side effects, and the potential to exacerbate internal injuries (e.g., gastrointestinal bleeding; Lang et al., 2011). Useful techniques have included mild punishments, such as time-out or spraying lemon juice into the child's mouth. Altering the feeding rate by giving repeated smaller portions of food, rather than one larger portion all at once, as well as satiation (allowing the child to eat unlimited amounts of food during mealtimes) have also been used to treat rumination (Lang et al., 2011). Although all of these techniques have received some empirical support, the research supporting their effectiveness (particularly with young children without developmental delays) is still quite limited.

SLEEP PROBLEMS

As noted in Chapter 1, sleep problems are commonly reported by parents of preschool-age children. Treatment is often warranted, not only because the sleep problems themselves are distressing, but also because of other problems children may experience due to lack of appropriate sleep. One recent study highlighted the vital function that sleep has on a child's neurological development, and in turn, on his or her cognitive and self-regulatory skills (Turnbull, Reid, & Morton, 2013). Other research has demonstrated that sleep problems are associated with emotional/behavioral problems (e.g., anxiety, impulsivity, reactivity); social difficulties (e.g. initiating negative interactions, reduced social engagement/motivation, lower social competence); and cognitive impairment (e.g. impaired school performance, decreased executive functioning, impaired creativity/abstract reasoning) (Reid, Hong, & Wade, 2009; Stores, 2001; Turnbull et al., 2013; Vaughn, Elmore-Staton, Shin, & El-Sheikh, 2015). Childhood sleep problems can also be a significant source of distress for parents, affecting the quality and quantity of their sleep, and leading to less effective parenting (Owens, 2008). Additionally, childhood sleep problems can lead to marital conflict and family dysfunction (Kelly & El-Sheikh, 2011). Consequently, treating sleep problems may also be helpful in reducing other behavioral/emotional problems, improving school performance, and enhancing relationships with peers and family members. Given the significant connection between early childhood sleep problems and other behavioral and emotional problems mentioned earlier, clinicians should routinely ask about sleep-related issues in any initial interview with the parents of a referred child.

A thorough assessment of a child's sleep-related problems should be conducted before developing an intervention. An interview with the child's parents (see Table 5.2), as well as logs of the child's sleep problems (see Forms 5.10 and 5.11), are important to obtain. Information about the child's bedtime routine and the parents' response to the child if he or she awakens during the night is particularly salient. Often parents unwittingly reinforce their child's sleep problems by immediately responding when the child awakens during the night. Thus, the child learns (and comes to expect) that when he or she cries, his or her parents will respond. Nighttime wakings are normal and occur approximately two to six times every night, and sometimes even more often in younger children (Meltzer & Crabtree, 2015). If parents immediately respond when the child awakens and stay with the child until he or she

TABLE 5.2. Interview Questions for Parents Regarding Their Child's Sleep Behaviors

1. Describe your child's current sleep pattern and sleep difficulties (e.g., what occurs and when).
2. How long have these difficulties been present?
3. Did anything (e.g., birth of a sibling, starting day care, marital arguments) precipitate these problems?
4. Is there anything that makes your child's sleep problems better or worse?
5. What do you do in response to your child's wakings/difficulties falling asleep?
6. Describe your typical bedtime routine with your child, including who puts your child to bed, when, where (e.g., child's room, parents' room), how long you stay with your child, etc.
7. What happens before beginning the bedtime routine?
8. When does your child wake up in the morning? Does your child wake up on his/her own? If not, who awakens your child and how?
9. Does your child awaken during the night? If so, describe what happens (how often your child awakens, what you do, etc.).
10. Does your child have nightmares, engage in sleepwalking, wet the bed, or have any other sleep-related problems? If so, describe.

Note. Based on Stores (2001) and Meltzer and Crabtree (2015).

falls back asleep, the child never learns to self-soothe and instead becomes dependent on his or her parents to return to sleep. For most children who have sleep problems involving nighttime wakings, the problem is not that of staying asleep but a problem of initiating sleep (Thomas, Moore, & Mindell, 2014).

Problems Initiating Sleep

Difficulty initiating sleep is a significant concern for parents and has been the focus of much of the literature on sleep problems in children. Typically children with this problem refuse to go to bed or engage in lengthy stalling behaviors, and if they awaken during the night, they often have difficulty getting back to sleep. Although problems with initiating sleep and night wakings generally decrease from the infant/toddler years to the preschool years, they still cause difficulties for a number of preschool-age children, with prevalence estimates ranging from 20–30% (Honaker & Meltzer, 2014). Behavioral interventions for these issues have proved to be highly effective and include establishing bedtime routines, extinction, and scheduled awakenings. These procedures, which are described in the next sections, all have strong empirical support (Meltzer & Crabtree, 2015). A parent handout summarizing these interventions is included in Form 5.12.

Developing Bedtime Routines

Developing and implementing consistent bedtime routines can be effective in reducing problematic sleep-related behaviors because these routines help to provide environmental cues that assist with maintaining the circadian rhythm (Meltzer & Crabtree, 2015). When first developing a routine, parents are instructed to move the child's bedtime gradually to the time when the child naturally becomes sleepy. In addition, parents are instructed to create a bedtime routine (usually no more than three to five steps) that is simple and relaxing, while also preparing their child for bed (Meltzer & Crabtree, 2015). The bedtime routine may include taking a bath, brushing teeth, reading a story, and/or listening to soft music. Parents should be encouraged to have the end of this routine occur in the child's bedroom (e.g., reading a bedtime story, saying prayers) in order to facilitate the transition to bed. This bedtime routine, as well as the child's bedroom/sleeping environment, should help set the stage for sleep to occur, and the routine should assist the child in associating his or her bed with nonstimulating, restful behaviors (Stores, 2001). Once the child is going to bed without significant problems, the child's bedtime and its associated routine can be gradually moved back to the time desired by the parents (Kuhn & Weidinger, 2000; Mindell, 1999).

Although it is important for the child to associate bedtime with relaxing activities, clinicians should ensure that parents do not inadvertently establish routines that impede a child's ability to fall asleep independently. For example, parents should be discouraged from rocking their child to sleep, laying with the child on his or her bed, providing the child with a bottle until he or she falls asleep, etc. If such activities become routine, it may become difficult for the child to fall back to sleep without them. Reducing these parent-dependent cues at bedtime will also make it more likely that a child will fall back asleep on his or her own after waking during the night (Meltzer & Crabtree, 2015; Stores, 2001). Parents also should ensure that the child's sleep environment is conducive to sleep. The bedroom should be quiet and the temperature adequately controlled (not too hot or too cold). The child's bed should be comfortable and age appropriate and a night-light should be allowed, if desired by the child. All technology should be removed from the bedroom, and parents should restrict access to electronic devices starting at least 1 hour before bedtime. Discontinuing use of electronics at bedtime not only allows for a period of relaxation and reduced stimulation, it also avoids exposure to the light emitted from electronics, which has been shown to suppress melatonin secretion (Wood, Rea, Plitnick, & Figueiro, 2013).

Extinction-Based Interventions

Extinction-based interventions are some of the most common strategies recommended to parents of children with sleep problems. These interventions work particularly fast, with treatment success occurring in about 3–5 days when using the standard extinction method described below (Meltzer & Crabtree, 2015). A recent meta-analysis revealed that behavioral interventions, such as extinction-based strategies, have strong empirical support and result in significant improvements for sleep-onset latency, night-waking frequency, and night-waking duration in young children (Meltzer & Mindell, 2014). In extinction-based strategies parents are instructed to consistently ignore their child's cries and protests at bedtime and throughout the night. Extinction techniques are based on the idea that the child exhibiting sleep problems is positively reinforced (through parental attention, game playing, etc.) for crying/throwing a tantrum at bedtime or when he or she awakens during the night. As previously stated, many children with sleep problems may have learned to expect that their parents will respond when they cry; because of this association, they are unable to initiate sleep on their own. Thus, removal of that positive reinforcement (i.e., by ignoring the child) should result in a decrease in the problem behavior and will help the child learn to fall asleep independently.

Several extinction-based methods are available for addressing early childhood sleep problems. In a standard extinction program (oftentimes referred to as the "cry it out" method), parents are instructed to put their child to bed at a specified time and not return to the child until the next morning at a specified time. Parents are to ignore all screaming, crying, and other protests. When the child first cries, the parent can check that the child is safe, but this checking should be done in a straightforward manner, with little attention given to the child. Thereafter the parent should ignore any crying or tantrum throwing. Use of extinction can produce quick results (a significant decrease in crying within several days) and is generally easy for parents to understand. However, extinction can be difficult for parents to put into practice because they often have a difficult time ignoring their child's crying, particularly during the likely extinction burst that will occur during the first few nights, and may end up attending to this behavior. This attention can be counterproductive, as parents may intermittently reinforce their child's crying behaviors, thereby making them more difficult to extinguish. Thus, when recommending this approach, it is imperative that clinicians inform parents about what to expect (e.g., an extinction burst) and reassure parents that no long-term negative effects will occur for the child and/or in the parent–child relationship (Price, Wake, Ukoumunne, & Hiscock, 2012).

Although the standard extinction method is highly effective, some parents will have difficulty tolerating the amount of crying experienced with this approach. Additionally, for certain children a standard extinction approach is contraindicated (e.g., children with complex medical conditions, children with severe anxiety or history of trauma; Meltzer & Crabtree, 2015). In these cases, variations to the standard extinction method also can be utilized. Graduated extinction programs are based on the same principle (i.e., not responding to the undesired behavior will result in a decrease in this behavior), but instead of completely ignoring the child, parents are instructed to modify how they attend to the child; generally, instead of completely ignoring their crying child, parents gradually reduce the attention they give in response to the crying. This approach is generally better accepted and tolerated by parents, as children often have less intense emotional reactions; however, this approach is also likely to take a longer period of time (e.g. several weeks) to achieve treatment success.

Graduated extinction is typically accomplished in one of two ways. In one method, the parent ignores the child's tantrums and crying, but checks on the child at set time intervals (e.g., every 10 minutes). When the parent checks on the child, the parent should briefly comfort him or her (e.g., give the child a pat on the back, say "good-night"—no extended attention) and then leave. Parents should generally be discouraged from picking their child up during these checks. Typically, the time period that the parent waits before returning to comfort the child is gradually increased. For example, initially the parent may check on the child every 10 minutes, then every 15, then every 20 minutes, as the child develops better self-soothing skills (Honaker & Meltzer, 2014). This method may be more acceptable to parents than complete attention withdrawal, even though having the parent come back into the child's room may have the adverse effect of prolonging the crying, which is ultimately counterproductive for self-soothing and sleep initiation (Meltzer & Crabtree, 2015).

In another method of graduated attention withdrawal, the parent immediately responds to the child but gradually decreases the amount of time spent with the child (Meltzer & Mindell, 2014; Thomas et al., 2014). For example, perhaps prior to treatment the parent was spending 30 minutes helping his or her child return to sleep. During treatment, initially the parent would spend 20 minutes with the child, then 15 minutes, then 10, eventually reducing this time to a brief interaction as part of the bedtime routine. Depending on how gradually the time the parent spends with the child is reduced, this approach may take longer than other extinction programs. Still, parents may find this approach more acceptable because it allows for a gradual withdrawal of attention, while enabling them to spend time with their child.

A graduated extinction approach can also be used to fade out parental presence. In this approach, a parent gradually moves away from his or her child's bed. For example, a parent may start by sitting on the bed next to the child, then move to sitting on a chair next to the child's bed, and then move the chair incrementally further away until the parent is sitting outside the bedroom door (Honaker & Meltzer, 2014). For the first few nights, parents may provide verbal reassurance and minimal physical interactions, but this attention should be decreased over time. Another variant of this approach involves having a parent set-up a bed for him- or herself in the child's room. This method ought to be used in the child's bedroom, not the parents', for obvious reasons. If the child cries after being put in bed, the parent lies down on his or her own bed and pretends to be asleep. The parent then leaves when the child falls asleep but returns and repeats this procedure if the child awakens and cries during the night. The parent continues doing this for 1 week and then proceeds to completely withdraw attention. This program may be particularly useful for children who are accustomed to having their parents present as they fall asleep and for children who may have some separation anxiety related to bedtime (Kuhn & Weidinger, 2000).

Parents can stop using extinction methods once the child is regularly sleeping through the night. If the child does cry or has awakened because of an illness or bad dream, the parent should pay attention to the child, as appropriate; otherwise the parent's attention should be very brief. If sleep problems recur after the intervention has been discontinued, parents should immediately resume using it. As a supplement to the extinction procedures, parents may also want to consider using a positive reinforcement program for the child, in which he or she would receive a reinforcer in the morning if the child stays in his or her bed all night. Alternatively, a "sleep fairy" can visit once a child falls asleep and leave a small treat under the child's pillow (Honaker & Meltzer, 2014).

Finally, parents should be informed about what to expect in terms of child behaviors when using extinction-based interventions. The "extinction burst" is one of the most crucial concepts for parents to be aware of. With all methods that incorporate ignoring of a child's problem behaviors, it is common for a child's behaviors to increase in duration and intensity before they decrease. A "spontaneous recovery" of the problem behavior after a seemingly successful intervention is also common. In this situation, the child improves initially but then reverts to exhibiting the same problem behaviors. When such a regression occurs, parents should continue with the program they are using and not return to attending to the child's crying, as this attention will only serve to delay and complicate extinction of the problem behavior (Meltzer & Crabtree, 2015).

Scheduled Wakings

Scheduled wakings have also been recommended for children who have difficulties falling back to sleep after waking during the night. In order to utilize this strategy, parents must first record when their child typically awakens during the night, then awaken their child 15–30 minutes prior to this time. After waking the child, the parent comforts the child, as was done when the child awoke on his or her own. Gradually the parent lengthens the time he or she waits before waking the child so that the child learns to sleep for longer periods of time. Although this treatment method may seem somewhat counterintuitive, the parent is essentially shaping the child's sleep time by gradually teaching the child to sleep longer. Thus, the child's sleep time gradually increases, and spontaneous wakings are eliminated (Honaker & Meltzer, 2014; Kuhn & Weidinger, 2000).

Bedtime Pass

Another treatment option for children who awaken and also leave the bedroom is the use of a "bedtime pass," as described by Friman and colleagues (1999). When using this method, the child is given a bedtime pass (created from an index card or some other form of paper) before going to sleep. The child is informed that he or she can use the pass for one out-of-bedroom experience per night. The child must use the pass for a specific activity (e.g., getting a drink, going to the bathroom) and must surrender the pass to his or her parents after using it. Once the child has used the pass, all other crying and/or additional requests are ignored. Parents whose children awaken frequently during the night should consider initially giving their child several passes and gradually reducing the number of passes allowed over time. If the child still has passes left in the morning, they can then be exchanged for an immediate small reward (Honaker & Meltzer, 2014).

Arousal Disorders

Sleep terrors and sleepwalking are types of arousal disorders that may be seen in young children. These disorders share similar features, including disorientation, difficulty being aroused, and failure to recall the episode. These behaviors occur at a specific time during the sleep cycle, when a child is transitioning out of slow-wave sleep, which generally occurs approximately 1 to 3 hours after the onset of sleep. There appears to be a developmental progression to these disorders, in that they often disappear or significantly decrease once adolescence is reached, most likely because slow-wave sleep also decreases with age (Meltzer & Crabtree, 2015). A summary of these problems and suggested intervention methods is presented in the next sections, and a handout for parents is provided in Form 5.13.

Sleep Terrors

Sleep terrors or night terrors are very common in early childhood, with an estimated prevalence rate of 40% for children ages 2½–6 years (Petit, Touchette, Tremblay, Boivin, & Montplaisir, 2007). A child having a sleep terror will commonly suddenly sit upright, with his or her eyes open, and scream or cry. The child will frequently appear frightened, as well as dazed and confused. Despite this dramatic presentation, the child will be unresponsive to a parent's attempts to provide consolation. In fact, some children will become physically violent during these night terrors, particularly if soothing attempts are made (Modi, Camacho, & Valerio, 2014). Attempts to provide comfort and/or wake the child up during a night terror may also make the event last longer (Meltzer & Crabtree, 2015). These episodes typically resolve spontaneously within a few minutes, and the child will quickly fall back to sleep. Children will generally have no recollection of these events in the morning.

As children typically outgrow sleep terrors, and because these episodes have no negative impact on the child, minimal intervention is needed. However, these events can be disruptive to the household and can be frightening for parents. Thus, parents can make some modifications that may reduce the occurrence of sleep terrors. A lack of sleep or unusual stress can exacerbate sleep terrors (and other arousal disorders). Thus, parents should ensure that their child is following a regular sleep routine and is getting an adequate amount of sleep. In addition, any unusual stressors in the child's life should be addressed, if possible. Educating parents (and the child, too) about the nature of sleep terrors is appropriate, and parents should be assured that the sleep terrors are not a sign of an underlying psychological problem. Because attempting to awaken and reassure a child having a sleep terror can result in increased agitation and physical aggression, parents should be instructed to avoid intervening unless the child's safety becomes an issue (Modi et al., 2014). Scheduled awakenings may also help to reduce the frequency of night terrors. Parents should be instructed when using this strategy to monitor their child's sleep patterns for at least 2 weeks to determine if there is a consistent pattern to their child's night terrors. If so, parents should gently awaken their child each night approximately 15–30 minutes before the anticipated event and then allow him or her to return to sleep. These scheduled awakenings should continue every night for 2–4 weeks (Meltzer & Crabtree, 2015).

Sleep terrors should be differentiated from nightmares, which are frightening dreams that may awaken the child. Nightmares typically occur during the second half of the night, and children are often able to recall the dream content. As many as 75% of young children have occasional nightmares (American Academy of Sleep Medicine, 2014). As with the arousal disorders, nightmares tend to decrease as the child ages (Meltzer & Crabtree, 2015). Nightmares can be exacerbated by stress but, in general, are seen as a typical part of development (Schroeder & Gordon, 2002). In extreme cases, children may develop a fear or anxiety about bedtime because of nightmares. If this reaction occurs, the interventions discussed in Chapter 4 for treating anxiety disorders should be used. For example, desensitization may be used to depotentiate the content of the child's nightmare. Obviously, if the child is having nightmares due to exposure to frightening stimuli during the day, the child's exposure to these stimuli should be reduced (Schroeder & Gordon, 2002). In general, the only "treatment" recommended for nightmares is reassurance by the parents at the time of the nightmare. For children who are having frequent nightmares that are becoming disruptive to their sleep, use of imagery rehearsal therapy should be considered. This therapy helps the child in rescripting his or her dream (often with drawings) into a more benign or pleasant image and then rehearsing the new dream both during the day and immediately following a nightmare (Meltzer & Crabtree, 2015). This allows the child to focus on more pleasant images and to develop a sense of control over his or her dreams.

Sleepwalking

Sleepwalking is estimated to occur in approximately 17–40% of children (Meltzer & Crabtree, 2015). Children who sleepwalk may only engage in simple movements, such as gesturing, or may perform complex behaviors such as walking around the house or getting dressed. Given the potential for harm when a child sleepwalks, parents should safeguard against potential safety concerns. For example, outside doors and windows should be shut and locked, and the child's bedroom should be on the first floor (or floor without stairs leading down), if possible. In addition, parents may want to consider installing some type of mechanism that will alert them to when their child has awakened. For example, bells may be attached to the child's door. When parents interact with their sleepwalking child, they should not yell at or shake the child but gently lead him or her back to the bedroom. Scheduled awakenings (discussed previously) may also be used to attempt to reduce the incidence of sleepwalking (Modi et al., 2014).

CHAPTER SUMMARY

This chapter provided a review of interventions for common problems with daily routines such as toileting, feeding, or sleeping frequently exhibited by young children that are sources of stress and concern for parents. Although many parents do not initially consult mental health professionals about these problems, professionals trained in behavioral interventions can be an excellent resource to call on. The empirically supported interventions for these disorders are all based on behavioral methods of reinforcing appropriate behaviors (e.g., attending to appropriate eating behaviors, giving praise and tangible reinforcers for having a bowel movement in the toilet) and ignoring or providing a mildly aversive consequence for inappropriate behaviors (e.g., ignoring crying at bedtime, using time-out for inappropriate eating behaviors). Although the problems discussed in this chapter are often not indicative of later psychopathology, providing treatment in the early years can significantly reduce problematic parent–child interactions and potentially preclude stressful social and emotional experiences for the child.

FORM 5.1

Daytime Wetting Log

Date	Time of wetting accident	Situation (what was happening)	Parent response to wetting

From Melissa L. Holland, Jessica Malmberg, and Gretchen Gimpel Peacock. Copyright © 2017 The Guilford Press. Permission to photocopy this form is granted to purchasers of this book for personal use or use with individual students (see copyright page for details). Purchasers can download additional copies of this material (see box at the end of the table of contents).

FORM 5.2

Daytime Wetting Treatment Log

Date	Pant checks			Wetting accidents		
	Time	Dry (yes or no)	Reward (yes or no)	Time	Situation	Response

From Melissa L. Holland, Jessica Malmberg, and Gretchen Gimpel Peacock. Copyright © 2017 The Guilford Press. Permission to photocopy this form is granted to purchasers of this book for personal use or use with individual students (see copyright page for details). Purchasers can download additional copies of this material (see box at the end of the table of contents).

FORM 5.3

Nighttime Wetting Log

	Bedtime	Wet? (yes or no) Record time(s) if known	Size of wet area	Parent response to wetting	Time awake
Sunday					
Monday					
Tuesday					
Wednesday					
Thursday					
Friday					
Saturday					

From Melissa L. Holland, Jessica Malmberg, and Gretchen Gimpel Peacock. Copyright © 2017 The Guilford Press. Permission to photocopy this form is granted to purchasers of this book for personal use or use with individual students (see copyright page for details). Purchasers can download additional copies of this material (see box at the end of the table of contents).

FORM 5.4

Nighttime Wetting and Alarm Use Log

	Bedtime	Wet? (yes or no) Record time(s)	Size of wet area	Alarm procedures followed? (yes or no)	Reward given for following procedures or staying dry? (yes or no)	Time awake
Sunday						
Monday						
Tuesday						
Wednesday						
Thursday						
Friday						
Saturday						

From Melissa L. Holland, Jessica Malmberg, and Gretchen Gimpel Peacock. Copyright © 2017 The Guilford Press. Permission to photocopy this form is granted to purchasers of this book for personal use or use with individual students (see copyright page for details). Purchasers can download additional copies of this material (see box at the end of the table of contents).

FORM 5.5

Treatment of Bed-Wetting—Use of the Enuresis Alarm: Instructions for Parents

The enuresis/moisture alarm can be an effective treatment for children who wet the bed. Most alarms today are small and consist of a sensor, worn in the child's underwear, which is hooked to a small alarm unit worn on the child's shoulder or wrist. When the child begins to wet, the sensor detects the moisture and the alarm sounds. For the alarm method to be successful, parents need to take an active role in treatment. Below are important guidelines.

At Night/During the Night

1. Make sure your child appropriately attaches the alarm each night before bed.
2. When the alarm sounds, immediately go to your child's room. Often the child will not awaken to the alarm at first, and he/she will need to be awakened by you.
3. Once your child is fully awake, have him/her detach the alarm and walk to the bathroom to finish urinating in the toilet. Even if your child says he/she no longer needs to urinate, he/she must at least try.
4. If the wet spot on the bed is large, assist your child in changing the bedding. (If the spot is small, consider placing a towel over it until the morning.) Your child also should change his/her clothing and place the wet clothing in an appropriate place (e.g., laundry hamper).
5. Have your child reattach the alarm and return to bed.
6. Repeat above procedures, as needed, throughout the night.

In the Morning

1. If your child did not wet, praise him/her for having a dry night.
2. If your child did not wet or if your child wet but he/she followed the alarm procedures appropriately, provide him/her with a small reward. It is important that rewards are given not just for staying dry but also for following the alarm procedures.
3. Record data on the progress chart.

Things to Remember

1. It is very important to remain neutral when your child wets. Do not become angry with your child or punish him/her for having a wet night. This program will work, but it takes time and patience.
2. When you first begin using the alarm, your child may not wake up when the alarm goes off. This is not unusual and should not be cause for concern. However, it is important that you wake your child if this occurs. Thus, you need to be in a location where you can hear the alarm or use baby monitors (or a similar system) to allow you to hear the alarm.
3. Eventually your child will start waking on his/her own to the alarm. You will also begin to notice that the amount of urine in the bed has decreased until eventually there is just enough to set the alarm off. Dry nights will then begin to appear more frequently.
4. Your child should continue to wear the alarm until he/she has had 14 dry nights in a row. Following this you may discontinue use of the alarm. However, if your child resumes wetting the bed, immediately reinstate the use of the alarm and, again, continue using it until your child has 14 dry nights in a row.

From Melissa L. Holland, Jessica Malmberg, and Gretchen Gimpel Peacock. Copyright © 2017 The Guilford Press. Permission to photocopy this form is granted to purchasers of this book for personal use or use with individual students (see copyright page for details). Purchasers can download additional copies of this material (see box at the end of the table of contents).

FORM 5.6

Treatment of Bed-Wetting—Use of the Enuresis Alarm: Instructions for Children

The enuresis/moisture alarm can help you learn to stop wetting the bed. The alarm does not shock you or hurt you in any way but will make a loud noise if you begin to wet the bed. The alarm will help you wake up during the night and use the toilet. For the alarm to work, it is important that you listen for it and wake up immediately when it goes off. Following the instructions below will help make using the alarm successful and help you stop wetting the bed.

1. Hook up the alarm yourself each night. (If it is difficult to hook up, ask your mother, father, or other adult for help.)
2. When the alarm sounds, wake up and stop wetting. It is important to do this as soon as you hear the alarm.
3. After you wake up, disconnect the alarm.
4. Go to the bathroom and try to go in the toilet.
5. Put on clean underwear and pajamas, change your sheets (with your parents' help, if needed) and reconnect the alarm.
6. If the alarm goes off again during the night, repeat these same steps.
7. In the morning, mark on your chart whether you were wet or dry throughout the night.
8. Use the alarm every night until you are dry for 14 nights in a row.

It may take a little while for you to stop wetting the bed completely. Don't become discouraged—just keep using the alarm!

From Melissa L. Holland, Jessica Malmberg, and Gretchen Gimpel Peacock. Copyright © 2017 The Guilford Press. Permission to photocopy this form is granted to purchasers of this book for personal use or use with individual students (see copyright page for details). Purchasers can download additional copies of this material (see box at the end of the table of contents).

FORM 5.7

Treatment Guidelines for Children with Encopresis

Encopresis involves a child who is at least 4 years old having a bowel movement in inappropriate places (e.g., clothing). Encopresis is most often the result of chronic constipation. Children who become severely constipated will have leakage of fecal material but be unaware of it. It is important to remember that, in most cases, the child is not soiling intentionally and cannot control the soiling response. By following the guidelines below, you should see results within 1–2 months.

1. Prior to implementing other treatment procedures, take your child to his/her physician for an examination. The following steps will not be successful if the child is still severely constipated and has impacted fecal material. Your child's physician may suggest administering an enema to "clean out" your child's bowels. The physician also may instruct you to give your child mineral oil and/or laxatives to keep material moving through the intestinal system. It is important to follow your physician's recommendations carefully.

2. Have your child engage in regular toilet sits. Approximately two to four times a day, schedule 5- to 10-minute toilet sits at times when your child is most likely to have a bowel movement (e.g., soon after waking in the morning, 15 to 20 minutes after meals). Make sure that the bathroom and the toilet are comfortable for the child. Your child's feet should be able to rest flat on the floor or a stool, and the toilet seat should be sized appropriately. Allow your child to bring a favorite toy or book into the bathroom so that he/she can engage in a pleasant activity while sitting on the toilet.

3. Reward your child for appropriate bowel movements. If your child has a bowel movement in the toilet, provide a small reward to him/her. It is a good idea to have different rewards available, so that your child does not tire of the same reward. Allowing your child to draw a reward coupon out of a bag or spin a game-wheel to determine what reward he/she gets can be fun for the child. Rewards do not have to be large and can include extra time with a parent, a special dessert, being allowed to watch extra TV, etc. You should give rewards to your child as immediately as possible (and at least within the same day).

4. Conduct pants checks. Several times throughout the day, check your child's pants. If he/she has soiled, he/she should be responsible for cleanup as much as possible. Your child should rinse and wash out his/her underwear and pants, bathe quickly, and put on clean clothes. (You may assist with these steps if your child is not able to complete the cleanup process on his/her own.) If your child has not soiled when these pant checks are conducted, give him/her a small reward.

5. Ensure that your child is getting adequate nutrition and physical activity. For regular bowel movements to occur, it is important that your child's diet include adequate amounts of fiber. Make sure your child eats plenty of fruits and vegetables, and consider sprinkling bran or wheat germ on foods. In addition, dairy products should be limited (although not cut out completely). The combination of fiber, water, and regular exercise will promote regular bowel movements. You may find it helpful to consult with a nutritionist who can help you modify your child's diet.

6. Record your child's progress. You and your child should keep a chart of your child's bowel movements, toilet sits, and pant checks. Keeping a chart will help you both see progress, as well as stick to the treatment plan.

From Melissa L. Holland, Jessica Malmberg, and Gretchen Gimpel Peacock. Copyright © 2017 The Guilford Press. Permission to photocopy this form is granted to purchasers of this book for personal use or use with individual students (see copyright page for details). Purchasers can download additional copies of this material (see box at the end of the table of contents).

FORM 5.8

Encopresis Treatment Log

Date	Toilet sits			Pant checks		
	Time	Bowel movement (yes or no)	Reward (yes or no)	Time	Clean (yes or no)	Reward (yes or no)

From Melissa L. Holland, Jessica Malmberg, and Gretchen Gimpel Peacock. Copyright © 2017 The Guilford Press. Permission to photocopy this form is granted to purchasers of this book for personal use or use with individual students (see copyright page for details). Purchasers can download additional copies of this material (see box at the end of the table of contents).

FORM 5.9

Solutions to Mealtime Problems: Guidelines for Parents

Difficult behaviors at mealtimes are common in young children. Typically these problems are not long-lasting and are not an indicator of more serious problems. "Picky" eating is the most common eating problem exhibited by young children. Picky eaters include children who eat only a limited number of foods and/or very small portions of foods. These children also frequently exhibit problem behaviors at mealtimes.

The guidelines below will help you increase your child's appropriate eating behaviors.

- **Have regular, set mealtimes and snack times.**
  - Do not allow your child to "graze" throughout the day.
- **Create a pleasant mealtime environment.**
  - Seat child comfortably.
  - Reduce distractions (e.g., turn off the TV).
  - Give child age-appropriate foods and portions (if unsure, consult with a pediatrician or dietician).
- **Provide positive verbal attention for appropriate eating behaviors.**
  - Example: "I really like how you're eating the food on your plate and talking nicely to us."
- **Use preferred foods as reinforcers.**
  - Pair a desirable food with a less-desirable food.
  - Example: If your child really likes grapes but does not like peas, let him/her know that he/she can have some grapes after he/she eats some peas.
- **Set up a reward program.**
  - Establish rules for mealtimes.
    - Example: "No whining about the food, eat at least half of what is on your plate [assuming portion size is correct], and no spitting out food."
  - Reward child for following rules.
    - Treat jar
      - Contains reinforcing items (e.g., small toys, stickers, passes for special time with Mom or Dad).
      - Add in new rewards regularly.
  - Have reasonable expectations.
    - Example: Do not expect a child who is eating one-eighth of the meal to start eating all of the meal right away.
- **Provide consequences for inappropriate eating behaviors.**
  - Use consequences if positive approach does not work or if child is engaging in several acting-out behaviors (beyond refusing to eat).
  - Consequences may include:
    - Loss of a certain privilege for the rest of the day (e.g., no watching TV).
    - Not receiving preferred food items.
    - Time-out (but be careful that time-out does not reinforce inappropriate behavior by allowing the child to escape mealtime).

From Melissa L. Holland, Jessica Malmberg, and Gretchen Gimpel Peacock. Copyright © 2017 The Guilford Press. Permission to photocopy this form is granted to purchasers of this book for personal use or use with individual students (see copyright page for details). Purchasers can download additional copies of this material (see box at the end of the table of contents).

FORM 5.10

Sleep Chart

	Wake-up time	Nap time(s)	Time begins bedtime routine	Time in bed	Time asleep	Times wakes up during night
Sunday						
Monday						
Tuesday						
Wednesday						
Thursday						
Friday						
Saturday						

From Melissa L. Holland, Jessica Malmberg, and Gretchen Gimpel Peacock. Copyright © 2017 The Guilford Press. Permission to photocopy this form is granted to purchasers of this book for personal use or use with individual students (see copyright page for details). Purchasers can download additional copies of this material (see box at the end of the table of contents).

FORM 5.11

Nighttime Wakings Chart

Day	Time awake	Your response	Time back to sleep
Example:			
Sunday	11:00 P.M.	Rocked, gave drink	11:30 P.M.
Sunday	2:00 A.M.	Ignored	2:15 A.M.
Sunday	4:00 A.M.	Got in bed with	4:20 A.M.

From Melissa L. Holland, Jessica Malmberg, and Gretchen Gimpel Peacock. Copyright © 2017 The Guilford Press. Permission to photocopy this form is granted to purchasers of this book for personal use or use with individual students (see copyright page for details). Purchasers can download additional copies of this material (see box at the end of the table of contents).

FORM 5.12

Solutions to Sleep Problems

If your child seems to be resistant to going to bed (he/she cries, whines, asks for one more drink, etc.), or if your child frequently awakens during the night and cries until you comfort him/her, there are several treatment options that can reduce these problems.

Establish Bedtime Routine

- DO THIS FIRST BEFORE IMPLEMENTING ANYTHING ELSE.
- Establish a standard bedtime.
- Begin bedtime routine 15–30 minutes before bedtime.
- Engage in relaxing activities (e.g., reading a book).

Total Ignoring of Inappropriate Behaviors

- Put your child to bed following his/her bedtime routine.
- Do not respond when child cries after being put to bed.

Gradual Ignoring of Inappropriate Behaviors

- Put your child to bed following his/her bedtime routine.
- Check on your child if he/she cries after being put to bed or awakens later in the night.
- Decrease the amount of time spent with your child when you check on him/her.
  - Example: If you had been spending an average of 30 minutes with your child, reduce that to 25 minutes initially.
- Leave and do not return once the preset attending time is up (e.g., 25 minutes in the above example).
- Repeat the procedure if the child awakens later in the night.
- Gradually (over days) reduce the amount of time you spend with your child before leaving.

Brief Checks

- Put your child to bed following his/her bedtime routine.
  - Check on your child every 5–10 minutes if he/she cries after being put to bed or awakens during the night.
- Continue to check on your child every 5–10 minutes until he/she stops crying.
- Do not give extended attention to your child when you check on him/her.
  - Example: Pat on back, retuck blankets, say "good night."
- Over time, increase the time between checks.

Gradual Withdrawal of Parent

- Put a bed (or chair) for yourself in your child's room.
- Consider gradually moving yourself away from your child's bed a little each night with the goal of being outside your child's bedroom by the end of the week.
- Put your child to bed following his/her bedtime routine.
- Lie down on your bed or sit in your chair and ignore your child's crying.
- Leave the room once your child has fallen asleep.

(continued)

From Melissa L. Holland, Jessica Malmberg, and Gretchen Gimpel Peacock. Copyright © 2017 The Guilford Press. Permission to photocopy this form is granted to purchasers of this book for personal use or use with individual students (see copyright page for details). Purchasers can download additional copies of this material (see box at the end of the table of contents).

Solutions to Sleep Problems *(page 2 of 2)*

- Repeat the procedure if your child awakens.
- After 1 week of this procedure, return to your own room and ignore your child's crying.

Scheduled Wakings

- Keep a chart noting when your child typically awakens during the night.
- Put your child to bed following his/her bedtime routine.
- Awaken your child 15–30 minutes before he/she typically awakens during the night.
- Interact with him/her as you would if he/she awoke on his/her own during the night.
- Gradually lengthen the amount of time you wait before awakening your child.

Remember, it might get worse before it gets better!

FORM 5.13

Sleep Terrors/Sleepwalking/Nightmares: Information for Parents

Sleep Terrors

Definition: The child suddenly screams, appears fearful, and is unresponsive to parental attempts to soothe. If the child is awakened, he/she may appear more agitated and disoriented. These episodes can be upsetting for parents, but the child typically returns to sleep within 5 minutes and has no memory of the incident later. Sleep terrors typically occur 1–3 hours after the child falls asleep.

What to do: Do not attempt to awaken your child—simply make sure he/she is safe. Because sleep terrors can be related to lack of sleep, make sure your child is getting an adequate amount of sleep and following an appropriate bedtime routine. Sleep terrors also may occur more in times of stress, so stressors should be identified and reduced, if possible.

Sleepwalking

Definition: The child actually gets out of bed and walks around the house. This behavior typically occurs 1–3 hours after the child falls asleep.

What to do: As with sleep terrors, do not attempt to awaken your child—simply lead him/her back to bed in a calm manner. Because sleepwalking can be dangerous for the child, prevention of injury is essential. Parents should ensure that windows and doors are shut and locked. If your child's bedroom is not on the first floor, install a gate at the top of the stairs. Parents also may consider rigging some type of alarm system that will notify them when their child is out of his/her room. Bells, tin cans, or some other noise-making device may be tied to the child's door so that when it is opened, the parents are awakened. As with sleep terrors, it is important that your child is getting enough sleep and that stress is reduced, if possible.

Nightmares

Definition: Nightmares are frightening dreams that may awaken the child and typically occur in the second half of the night. The child likely will remember these dreams in the morning.

What to do: Provide comfort to your child at the time the nightmare occurs. Give the child an opportunity to talk about the nightmare but do not pressure him/her to do so. Parents should also consider using a technique called imagery rehearsal therapy (IRT). This involves supporting your child in rescripting the dream (often with drawings) and then rehearsing the new dream both during the day and immediately following a nightmare. This helps your child focus his/her attention on more benign thoughts and in developing a sense of control over his/her own dreams.

From Melissa L. Holland, Jessica Malmberg, and Gretchen Gimpel Peacock. Copyright © 2017 The Guilford Press. Permission to photocopy this form is granted to purchasers of this book for personal use or use with individual students (see copyright page for details). Purchasers can download additional copies of this material (see box at the end of the table of contents).

CHAPTER 6

Academic and Behavioral Interventions and Supports in the Classroom

The number of young children who attend daycare and preschool facilities has markedly increased over the past several decades. According to Census Bureau data from 2011, approximately 4.8 million children attend an organized daycare or preschool facility (Laughlin, 2013). Children enter these settings with a range of behavioral and preacademic skills. In regular daycare/preschool settings (i.e., not special education preschool settings), behavioral issues are often more of a concern than academic issues, although increasingly researchers and educators are attending to the preacademic/preliteracy skills that will promote academic success upon beginning formal schooling. Young children are disproportionately suspended and expelled from their early childhood learning settings, with preschool-age children being 3.2 times more likely to be expelled than students in K–12 educational programs (Gilliam, 2005). Young students who are suspended or expelled are at risk for numerous negative life events, many of which are related to later schooling/academic problems, including being 10 times more likely to drop out of high school, experience academic failure and grade retention, and become incarcerated (Lamont et al., 2013). Taken together, it is critical that early childhood educators be adequately trained, supported, and prepared to effectively work with young children who have preacademic and behavioral issues. One model that can be helpful in conceptualizing the prevention of and intervention for these concerns is that of the multi-tiered system of support (MTSS). When addressing academic issues, this model is often referred to as response to intervention (RTI) and when addressing behavioral issues, this model is referred to as Positive Behavioral Interventions and Supports (PBIS). The RTI and PBIS models have more recently been integrated into the MTSS model, in part due to increased understanding and awareness that both academic and behavioral difficulties must be addressed in order to afford students the best opportunities to succeed (Eagle, Dowd-Eagle, Snyder, & Holtzman, 2015). The MTSS framework is focused on providing high-quality instruction and evidence-based interventions that are matched to a student's needs across academic and behavioral domains. A student's progress is then monitored on an ongoing basis in order to make decisions about changes to instructions and/or goals. This chapter discusses RTI and PBIS separately in order to differentiate the approaches used with both academic and behavioral difficulties; however, readers should be aware of the merit of integrating these approaches into a broader MTSS framework. First, we overview the tiered system of support, and discuss RTI for early literacy/academic issues in preschool-age children. PBIS is then discussed as a framework for addressing behavioral concerns within preschool and kindergarten classrooms. Finally, an overview of social–emotional learning programs for young children, which are often included as part of a tiered system of support, is provided.

Within a tiered system of support (see Figure 6.1; *www.pbis.org*), it is generally expected that 80% of children will be performing/behaving as expected. These children are considered to be at Tier 1 and require no extra support above and beyond effective instruction and behavior management within the classroom setting. Universal prevention methods such as classwide and schoolwide systems of support are implemented at the Tier 1 level. Universal prevention programs target a whole population that has not been identified on the basis of individual risk (O'Connell, Boat, & Warner, 2009). The focus of universal prevention programs is on providing positive, proactive services independent of risk status, with the

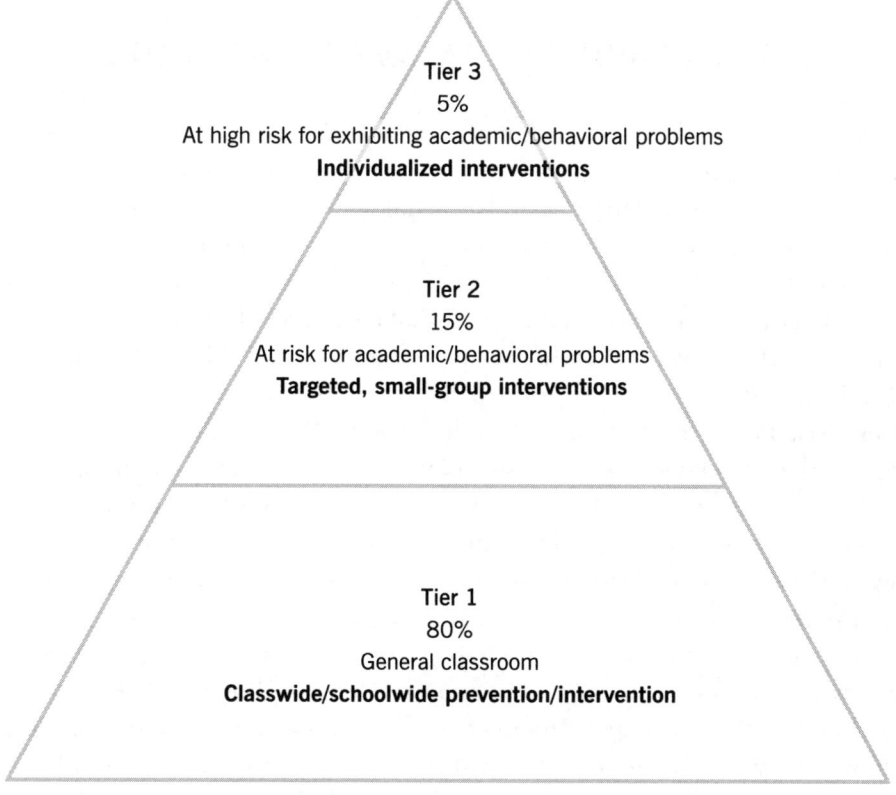

FIGURE 6.1. Tiered systems of support.

understanding that the entire population (e.g., an entire school, a whole class) could benefit from the content of the program. At the Tier 2 level, children are considered to be at risk for academic and/or behavioral difficulties. The approximately 15% of children at this level are provided with more targeted prevention/intervention efforts, often in a small group setting. At the Tier 3 level, consisting of approximately 5% of youth, children are at high risk for or are exhibiting academic and/or behavioral problems. Interventions at this level are typically individualized to the child's presenting problem(s).

While academic and behavioral interventions delivered at the first two tiers within an MTSS framework will meet the needs of most children, at the upper end of the intervention tier (Tier 3), more intensive interventions are needed. The National Center on Intensive Intervention (*www.intensiveintervention.org*) contains a variety of information and resources on data-based individualization (DBI) to intensify instruction. As explained here, the DBI process involves the following five steps: (1) implementation of current evidenced-based intervention program with increased intensity; (2) collection of frequent progress monitoring data; (3) if struggles continue, collection of diagnostic information to aid in identification of specific deficits/concerns; (4) use of diagnostic data to better meet a student's needs; and (5) continued collection of progress monitoring data and additional intervention adaptations as needed. Thus, this process is an extension of the MTSS process and makes greater use of continuous progress monitoring, as well as more comprehensive assessment (including functional assessment, covered in Chapter 2).

RTI FOR EARLY LITERACY/ACADEMIC SKILLS

The RTI framework for addressing academic concerns has been gaining momentum in the K–12 schools for some time. RTI gained prominence in the research literature and applied fields of psychology (in particular, school psychology) and education following the reauthorization of the Individuals with Disabilities Education Improvement Act (IDEIA) in 2004. This reauthorization permitted the use of an RTI model in classifying children with specific learning disabilities (SLD) and stated that a significant discrepancy between intellectual abilities and achievement abilities was no longer required for a classification of SLD. Although RTI had been discussed prior to this time, the passage of IDEIA 2004 set the stage for increased research and interest in this model.

Although the preschool years (before the beginning of formal schooling) may seem to be premature for addressing academic concerns, from a prevention standpoint, it is an ideal time. Various researchers have noted the importance of early literacy skills and the connection between these skills and later academic achievement. Children who enter kindergarten with more limited early reading skills typically do not "catch up" with other children when beginning formal instruction; in fact, this gap between students who enter school with good preliteracy skills and those who do not may grow over time (Bingham & Patton-Terry, 2013; Greenwood et al., 2014). Although the preschool years may be an ideal time for academic intervention, until recently, there had been little research evaluating curricula for promoting early literacy skills in preschool children. To address this need, the Preschool Curriculum Evaluation Research (PCER) initiative was funded by the Institute of Education

Sciences (IES) in 2002 to evaluate preschool curricula. The PCER evaluated 14 curricula using a variety of student and classroom measures. Student outcomes included early literacy and mathematical skills/knowledge. Classroom-level measures included classroom quality, teacher–child interactions, and instructional practices. Child outcomes were measured at the end of prekindergarten and at the end of the child's kindergarten year. Only 2 of the 14 programs evaluated had a positive impact on student outcomes during the prekindergarten years, although four had a positive impact on student outcomes in the kindergarten year, and eight had a positive impact on prekindergarten classroom-level outcomes (Preschool Curriculum Evaluation Research Consortium, 2008). Likewise, an evaluation of the Early Reading First Program, which focused on teacher development to better address early-literacy skills in the school years, had disappointing results, in that the program had a positive impact on children's print and letter knowledge but not on their phonological awareness or oral language skills (Jackson et al., 2007). Rather than conclude that these results indicate that preschool interventions do not work, researchers have called for a more individualized approach to addressing early academic concerns that can be met through an RTI model (Greenwood et al., 2014).

The Center for Response to Intervention in Early Childhood (CRTIEC; *www.crtiec.org*) was developed by Greenwood and colleagues (2014) with support from IES to develop tools that could be used within an RTI model for preschool-age children. Researchers identified three early literacy targets on which to focus: (1) oral language and comprehension, (2) phonological awareness, and (3) alphabet knowledge. At the Tier 2 and Tier 3 levels, both phonological awareness and alphabet knowledge are emphasized—but with differing curricula. At Tier 2 the emphasis is on "more challenging academic vocabulary and inferential questions" and at Tier 3 the emphasis is on "more basic, core vocabulary and elaborating utterances" (p. 254). Other researchers and clinicians have proposed variations on the RTI model but, in general, these three core literacy skills have been the focus of intervention.

Buysse and colleagues' (2013) Recognition and Response RTI model developed for preschool-age children has been shown to be feasible to implement and to have promising child outcomes, although more research is needed due to the pilot nature of the initial outcome studies. As with other RTI models, assessment of student progress and a tiered service delivery model with evidence-based interventions is essential. Within this program, formative assessments are conducted by teachers three times per year to help determine what supports are needed and to monitor progress. As with all multi-tiered systems, at Tier 1, an effective core curriculum is in place. Buysse and colleagues note that all teachers should be implementing the core curriculum in an effective manner before progressing to other components of the program. They also recommend that dialogic reading be incorporated into Tier 1 instruction. This is an interactive shared reading method in which the adult engages the child through a variety of prompts, allowing the child to be involved in the book reading. At the Tier 2 level, children who are identified as needing additional supports based on universal screening measures are given small group lessons and "embedded learning activities," which also are incorporated into other classroom activities outside of the small learning groups. At Tier 3, specific, individual "scaffolding" methods are used. These include modeling (teacher demonstrating a response), prompting (teacher using cues to elicit a response), peer supports, and corrective feedback.

Gettinger and Stoiber (2007) also developed an RTI model (Exemplary Model of Early Reading Growth and Excellence [EMERGE]) for use with preschool-age children. Their program focused on low-income children in center-based early childhood programs, and had four key components that are consistent with the RTI model: (1) evidence-based early literacy instruction; (2) screening, monthly progress monitoring, and outcome assessment; (3) high-quality classroom environments; and (4) ongoing professional development. Family involvement was also a key feature. As with the Recognition and Response program, at Tier 1 the utilization of correctly implemented research-based literacy instruction was emphasized. Small group instruction was provided at Tier 2, and individual tutoring was offered at Tier 3. Although the tiers differed in their intensity of supports to students, they all followed a similar curriculum sequence. Thus, Tier 2 and 3 instruction was not qualitatively different but instead was a more intense version of the instruction provided at Tier 1. Preliminary outcome data presented show that children in the EMERGE program had higher performance on early literacy and language tasks than did children in control classrooms. Although all children made gains throughout the school year, for the children in the EMERGE classrooms the gains were greater.

Specific to more intensive interventions, Kaminski, Powell-Smith, Hommel, McMahon, and Bravo Aguayo (2014) outlined the development and assessment of a Tier 3 intervention for preschool-age children that focused on the alphabetic principle and the connection between letters and speech sounds. Their program, Reading Ready Early Literacy Intervention (RRELI), focused on increasing children's ability to recognize and name letters as well as on producing the initial sounds in words and matching of sounds to letters (p. 319). Their intervention package consisted of 30 lessons that covered the practice, review, and introduction of new skills. The program is mastery based in that children pass a "check-out" before moving on to the next lesson. While this study was focused on development of the intervention, the authors did note that positive outcomes were obtained from children who took part in the RRELI program as part of this iterative development process. The authors also noted variability in responses in that children who had individualized education plans (IEPs), made fewer gains than those not on IEPs, suggesting the need for more intensive interventions for these children.

An important aspect of the RTI model is having appropriate assessment tools that can be used to determine which children are in need of interventions beyond Tier 1 as well as for ongoing progress monitoring. At the Tier 1 level, assessment tools must be brief enough to be administered for universal screening of all children multiple times a year. One such tool is the Preschool Early Literacy Indicators (PELI) that can be used for both screening and progress monitoring of children receiving interventions (Kaminski, Abbott, Bravo Aguayo, Latimer, & Good, 2014). The PELI is a storybook format assessment that assesses Alphabet Knowledge, Listening Comprehension, Phonological Awareness, and Vocabulary–Oral Language. Studies to date have indicated support for the tool's psychometric properties and diagnostic utility (in terms of preliminary benchmark goals) (Kaminski, Abbott, et al., 2014). The PELI was developed by the Dynamic Measurement Group (the same group that developed the DIBELS commonly used in elementary school RTI models) and was in early release for research partners in the 2015–2016 school year (see *dibels.org/peli.html*). Another tool is the Preschool Individual Growth and Development Indicators

(IGDIs; *igdis.umn.edu*) that evaluate early literacy skills in preschool-age children within an RTI framework. The IGDIs 2.0 consists of four measures of phonological awareness: sound blending, syllable sameness, rhyming, and alliteration (Wackerle-Hollman, Schmitt, Bradfield, Rodriguez, & McConnell, 2015). In an overview of the development and evaluation of these IGDIs, Wackerle and colleagues (2015) indicate support for their utility and psychometric adequacy when used with young children. In addition, in a review of the technical adequacy of earlier IGDIs, Moyle, Hielmann, and Berman (2013) summarize data supporting their reliability and validity. A third tool that has been used with preschool-age children is the Phonological Awareness and Literacy Screening (PALS; *pals.virginia.edu*)—PreK (Invernizzi, Sullivan, Meier, & Swank, 2004), which was developed to identify children struggling with early literacy concepts. The PALS–PreK measures the early literacy skills of alphabet knowledge, phonological awareness, print concepts, and writing. Reviews of the PALS–PreK psychometric properties indicate that the measure has good internal consistency and test–retest reliability as well as good predictive validity of reading difficulties at a later age (Invernizzi, Landrum, Teichman, & Townsend, 2010; Moyle et al., 2013). In a comparison of the PALS–PreK and IGDIs Moyle and colleagues (2013) noted more of a floor effect with the IGDIs, suggesting that they may not be as useful with lower-performing preschoolers or younger preschoolers. However, additional data are needed, especially given the recent development of the IGDIs 2.0.

Summary of RTI

As more research is conducted on RTI models and interventions in the preschool years, it is likely that a growing body of literature on best-practice models, including best practices in both assessment and intervention for young children, will emerge. The advantage of the RTI is that it can be tailored to individual students—targeting those children who need additional supports while ensuring that the whole class receives adequate instruction. While preschool RTI may be less broadly used than RTI models in K–12 schools, it is certainly a model that shows promise for children who are receiving preschool instruction, and when applied more widely, may increase the number of children who are ready for kindergarten instruction upon school entry.

POSITIVE BEHAVIORAL INTERVENTIONS AND SUPPORTS

As noted earlier, PBIS (Horner et al., 2009) is a multi-tiered prevention and intervention approach to promoting prosocial behaviors and reducing disruptive behaviors and academic failure among students. Historically, school systems have taken a reactive and punishment-based approach to managing students' misbehaviors. Although punishment-based strategies can be effective in reducing a child's disruptive behaviors, when they are applied inconsistently and in the absence of other positively based strategies, they become ineffective and result in unintended negative side effects (e.g. aggression, apathy, escape/avoidance; Chance, 2013). PBIS takes a proactive and positive approach to behavior management by teaching, modeling, and reinforcing positive/prosocial behaviors. By reinforcing positive behaviors (e.g., keeping hands and feet to self) that are incompatible with disruptive behaviors (e.g., hitting/kicking a peer), students learn that engaging in these positive behaviors is more efficient and functional. Research has demonstrated that the implementation of PBIS in preschool and elementary school settings has a significant impact on reducing disruptive behaviors, suspensions, and expulsions, as well as on increasing academic performance and teachers' self-efficacy (Bradshaw, Mitchell, & Leaf, 2010; Muscott et al., 2004; Reinke et al., 2013). Although PBIS supports can be created and implemented at a schoolwide, classroom, small-group, and individualized level, this section will specifically focus on classroom-based supports. A summary of these techniques is provided in Table 6.1.

Efforts to disseminate PBIS supports at a universal level in elementary schools have primarily focused on schoolwide PBIS (Bradshaw, Koth, Thornton, & Leaf, 2009). While these efforts have been largely successful in improving the overall school climate (Bradshaw et al., 2010), research has indicated that early childhood and elementary school teachers continue to struggle with managing students' classroom misbehaviors (Benedict, Horner, & Squires, 2007; Reinke et al., 2013). They have consistently indicated that classroom behavior management is the most challenging aspect of their job, while commenting that this is also the aspect of teaching for which they get the least amount of training (Reinke et al., 2011). Thus, in order to optimize student outcomes, PBIS supports must also be present at the classroom level.

Initial Considerations

While there is strong empirical evidence that behavioral interventions in the classroom are effective (Reinke et al., 2013), poor treatment integrity can result in little or no behavioral change. Unfortunately, the literature suggests that the implementation of evidence-based interventions in the schools is often completed with low fidelity (Forman, Olin, Hoagwood, Crowe, & Saka, 2009). Thus, it is critical that purposeful efforts be made to persuade and motivate teachers to use PBIS. The Classroom Check-Up, a variation of the Family Check-Up (see Chapter 3), has been developed as a classroom-level consultation model that provides support, while also minimizing treatment integrity problems (Reinke et al., 2008). As with the Family Check-Up, the Classroom Check-Up utilizes motivational interviewing techniques to engage and motivate teachers. Specific strategies can include providing personalized feedback to teachers on changes to classroom behaviors based on implemen-

---

TABLE 6.1. Summary of PBIS Classroom Intervention Techniques

- Establishing classroom rules
- Developing a classroom schedule
- Providing effective instruction
- Utilizing selective attention/verbal praise
- Reward-based behavior management programs, including token economies
- Precorrection
- Response cost (e.g., removal of tokens)
- Home–school notes
- Time-out

tation of behavioral strategies, developing a menu of intervention options, offering suggestions when solicited while empowering teachers to make decisions, supporting teacher self-efficacy while highlighting their existing strengths, and providing examples of teachers' successful efforts at changing their students' behaviors (Reinke et al., 2008).

Establishing Classroom Rules

The first step in implementing universal PBIS supports in the classroom is to establish effective classroom management strategies. One of the most important and fundamental features of a classroom should be a list of rules that clearly communicate to the students what behaviors are expected and considered appropriate in the classroom setting. Rules should be kept to a minimum (typically three to five) in order to avoid overwhelming the teacher or the students, and they should be focused on the most important aspects of classroom behavior. Rules should be stated in a positive manner, in which the students are told what *to do* rather than what *not* to do. For example, instead of posting "No running in the hallway," the rule might be worded "Always walk in the hallway." Rules should be posted (with pictorial reminders for nonreaders) and reviewed with the class periodically. Rules that may be appropriate to the preschool classroom include "Keep hands and feet to self," and "Stay seated during teacher-directed activities." Teachers should be mindful to develop classroom rules that closely align with schoolwide expectations (e.g., Be Kind, Be Safe, Be Responsible) in order to promote generalization in all school settings (Reinke et al., 2013). For example, a classroom rule that would align with the schoolwide expectation of "Be Safe" is "Keep hands, feet, and objects to yourself." It is also helpful for teachers to regularly engage students in brief lessons on positive behavior expectations and to provide reminders of expectations throughout the day.

Developing a Classroom Schedule

In addition to establishing classroom rules, teachers should develop a structured schedule and well-defined routines in order to promote an efficient and proactive learning environment. This strategy may be particularly beneficial during times of transition when student misbehaviors are more likely to occur (Hemmeter, Ostrosky, & Corso, 2012). When developing a classroom schedule, teachers should be consistent in their application of the schedule, minimize wait times during transitions, and teach students the steps of routines, including behavioral expectations. In developing classroom routines, a task analysis should be completed for each activity in order to determine the discrete steps that must be completed. Teachers should begin a task analysis by listing all activities and transitions that occur throughout the school day. A lesson plan should then be created in which students are effectively taught the steps of the routine. Teachers often miss this critical step in the mistaken assumption that children already know what is expected of them during classroom activities/routines (Hemmeter et al., 2012). Teachers also should explain and model the routine's steps and expectations, as well as give students time to practice and receive teacher feedback. For example, when teaching students how to line up to leave the classroom, a teacher should start by describing the correct way to line up and then modeling the correct way for the class. The students would then be supported in role playing this skill, with the teacher praising individual students who are lining up correctly.

Students can also be engaged in practice activities such as "Correct the Teacher" and "Lining Up Right Game" to further solidify their understanding of the targeted skill (McIntosh, Herman, Sanford, McGraw, & Florence, 2004). In the "Correct the Teacher" activity, students use a thumbs-up or thumbs-down signal to evaluate the teacher's behavior. If students signal a thumbs-down, the teacher calls on a student to explain the correct expectation and models it for the class. When playing the "Lining Up Right Game," the class practices lining up correctly. If the class performs this targeted skill appropriately, it gets one point. If the class does not line up correctly, the teacher gets one point, and the class practices the skill again. This game is continued until the class gets three points in a row, at which time the teacher can consider providing a reward (e.g., 5 extra minutes of playtime). Once students have demonstrated mastery of a targeted skill, the teacher should continue to review and practice these routines and behavioral expectations on a regular basis. A similar "game" could also be used when teaching a variety of other behavioral skills.

Providing Effective Instruction

Another critical classroom management strategy is effective instruction. When students are effectively engaged in academic instruction (e.g., listening to the teacher, answering questions), they are less likely to be off task and drawn to disruptive behaviors. Research has demonstrated that in order for instruction to be effective and engaging, it must be rigorous, relevant, and delivered at an appropriate pace (Simonsen, Fairbanks, Briesch, Myers, & Sugai, 2008). One particularly salient way of ensuring that instruction is effective is by increasing the frequency with which students are given the opportunity to respond (OTR). An OTR is defined as teacher behavior that invites a student response (Simonsen, Myers, & Deluca, 2010). The positive effects of increasing an OTR have been well documented in kindergarten through third-grade classrooms and include a reduction in student disruptive behaviors and improvement in on-task behavior, academic engagement, and academic achievement (Reinke et al., 2013). It is recommended that teachers elicit a minimum of 3.5 responses from students per minute of active instruction based on research that has demonstrated this number is a "tipping point" for increasing student engagement and achievement (Stichter et al., 2009). However, this research was completed with children in kindergarten through eighth grade, and it is likely that preschool-age children would require even more engagement opportunities. Teachers should invite student responses through a variety of modalities including verbal responses, gestures, written responses, and interactive technology tools.

Utilizing Selective Attention

The literature consistently demonstrates that teachers who are successful at delivering specific and contingent praise in their classrooms have students who engage in lower rates of disruptive behaviors (Dufrene et al., 2012). Despite this finding, teachers commonly overuse reprimands and underutilize praise, particularly when specific training has not been provided (Gable, Hester, Rock, & Hughes, 2009). Accordingly, teachers should be trained on how to use selective attention effectively in the classroom on a regular basis to reinforce their students for appropriate, on-task behaviors. When the teacher notices that a child is following a classroom rule or otherwise behaving appropriately, she or he should deliver a behavior-specific praise statement (e.g., "Jennifer, I like how you're sitting in your seat and listening to my instructions."). Conversely, teachers should ignore minor and infrequent misbehaviors (e.g., talking, out of seat) and should provide immediate positive feedback once the student is no longer misbehaving and is engaging in appropriate behaviors (e.g., stops talking, sits back in seat). This allows the teacher to differentially reinforce the student for engaging in desirable behaviors. Similar to the ratio of positive to negative interactions between a parent and child that was recommended in Chapter 3, researchers have recommended that teachers aim for a ratio of four positive interactions for every one negative interaction with their students (Reinke et al., 2013).

Reward-Based Behavior Management Programs

In addition to using praise, teachers may also want to consider implementing a classroom-wide reward-based behavior management program, such as the Good Behavior Game (Tingstrom, Sterling-Turner, & Wilczynski, 2006). In this "game" the class is divided into two teams. Every time a child breaks a classroom rule or engages in an inappropriate behavior, a mark is made for that child's team. The team with the lowest number of points "wins," but both teams can earn reinforcers or special privileges if the number of marks received is below a certain amount. There are a number of variations of this group contingency program. For example, rather than receiving marks for inappropriate behaviors, teams can earn points for appropriate behaviors, or a combination of the two may be implemented. In addition, rather than splitting the class into teams, the class as a whole could work toward a reinforcer. When working with young children, it is helpful to use pictures or simple charts so that students can see how many more points they still need to earn a reinforcer. For example, a teacher could post a chart with a picture of the reward to be earned. Each time that the team (or class as a whole) earns a point, a marker on the chart is moved a step closer to the picture of the reinforcer.

An alternative classroomwide behavior management program is the Mystery Motivator (Kowalewicz & Coffee, 2014). This intervention relies on an interdependent group contingency, whereby students work toward a common goal, and reinforcement depends on the performance of the entire class. The Mystery Motivator also uses a variable schedule of reinforcement, reinforcement uncertainty (e.g., reward is unknown to students), and immediate performance feedback by the teacher. In the original Mystery Motivator program, the teacher first develops a chart showing a period of time (e.g., a week or month) and then randomly selects the days during which students may earn an unknown reward for exhibiting previously agreed upon behaviors. The teacher marks an "M" on randomly selected days and then covers each square with paper that can later be removed (e.g., a sticky note). The chart is placed in a visible location. At the end of each designated period for which students meet the behavioral goal, the paper is removed to reveal whether an "M" is present for that day. If an "M" is present, the students are given a reward selected by the teacher but unknown to the students. If an "M" is not present, the students are praised for meeting their behavioral goal and reminded they will have another opportunity to earn a reward the following school day.

When using this program with young children, several modifications have been suggested. Rules with accompanying pictures should be posted in a visible area of the classroom. The delay between children engaging in the required behavior and receiving the reward should be reduced, and a continuous schedule of reinforcement is recommended, wherein children earn a motivator each time they reach the goal. Murphy, Theodore, Aloiso, Alric-Edwards, and Hughes (2007) empirically evaluated a modified Mystery Motivator program for preschoolers. This intervention involved a 15-minute large group activity, wherein students could earn a reward if the group obtained a total of five or fewer checks (e.g., rule violations). At the end of each activity, one reward was randomly selected from a mystery motivator box (12 cards with pictures of possible rewards) if the class met the criterion. If the criterion was not met, the teacher explained the reason why and informed the class that another chance to earn a mystery motivator would occur the next day. Results show that this procedure substantially reduced disruptive behaviors in the classroom.

Teachers can also use a classwide token reinforcement system to increase the likelihood of appropriate behaviors, although this strategy has been less widely researched and implemented because of a lower level of cognitive readiness in young children. To ensure that this behavioral strategy is effective with young children, the token economy must be developmentally sensitive. Thus, it must be structured (e.g., clear behavioral targets and schedule of token delivery); simple (e.g., require minimal math skills); and use visually engaging tokens (e.g., brightly colored, stickers, animal shapes). Children must be able to exchange their tokens on a regular basis for tangible reinforcers. For younger children, this exchange should occur on a daily basis, at least when the program is first initiated. It is also important to vary the tangible reinforcers so that the children do not become bored and disinterested. For example, if students receive stickers every day they have a certain number of tokens remaining, eventually they will become tired of stickers and the stickers will lose their reinforcing properties. Allowing children to choose from a variety of rewards (e.g., stickers, small toys, special privileges) will help items maintain their reinforcing value.

School-based behavioral interventions that are complex can require a good deal of time and effort for teachers to implement; some research has found that teachers are generally more accepting of those interventions or strategies that are less complex and require less time to put into practice (Briesch, Briesch, & Chafouleas, 2015). For example, when a teacher sees a child engaging in an appropriate behavior, the teacher could simply place a pompom, marble, or other visually engaging token into a glass jar at the front of the classroom and offer a brief praise statement. Once the jar is filled, the class is awarded a tangible reinforcer (e.g., extra recess time, stickers, small toys, etc.). Another example of a simple, yet effective behavioral intervention was described in a study by Bahl, McNeil, Cleavenger, Blanc, and Bennett (2000), in which preschool students were provided with labeled praise and happy faces for engaging in appropriate behaviors and were given a warning and sad faces for inappropriate behaviors. Students were randomly assigned to groups of 4 to 5 children, and rewards were given to groups who earned more happy, than sad, faces. Results of this study demonstrated that the frequency of children's engagement in appropriate behaviors increased, and teachers rated high satisfaction with this program.

Responding to Behavioral Violations and Severe Problem Behaviors

Although PBIS emphasizes the importance of prioritizing the use of environmental changes and reinforcement-based strategies to promote appropriate and prosocial behaviors, a continuum of strategies for responding to inappropriate behaviors has also been advocated; these include planned ignoring (discussed above), precorrection, punishment-based procedures (such as response cost), and other more intensive application of standard behavioral techniques. These strategies will typically not be used as Tier 1 interventions, but they may be implemented as more intensive interventions at Tier 2 and/or Tier 3. In addition, given the individualized nature of Tier 3 interventions, interventions discussed in previous chapters may be implemented at this level in the school system by qualified individuals (e.g., school psychologists). It is important to note that while punishment-based procedures can be effective in reducing the occurrence of problematic behaviors, they should never be used in isolation. In fact, as previously discussed, using punishment-based procedures in isolation is rarely an effective strategy and also results in negative side effects (Chance, 2013). Thus, these strategies are best used as a component of a more comprehensive behavior management package, including effective classroom management strategies and reinforcement-based procedures.

Noncontingent Reinforcement

Although attention is used contingently as part of an intervention program most frequently, the use of noncontingent attention/noncontingent reinforcement, has also been evaluated, especially as part of an intervention for more serious problem behaviors. Single-case design studies are generally used to evaluate this technique, given the focus on more severe problem behaviors. Noncontingent reinforcement is used to negate the function of the behavior if the inappropriate behavior is being used to gain access to a reinforcer (e.g., attention, stimulation). Noncontingent reinforcement has been found to be effective in addressing problematic behaviors, including physically aggressive behaviors and self-injurious behaviors in an adopted child (Nolan & Filter, 2012) and in addressing the aggressive behavior of a young adult with autism (Gerhardt, Weiss, & Delmolino, 2004). In both of these studies, noncontingent reinforcement was not the only intervention applied but was used in combination with other methods (e.g., response cost and functional communication training).

Precorrection Strategies

Precorrection strategies are antecedent manipulations aimed at preventing the predictable problematic behaviors and at prompting engagement in appropriate behaviors (Ennis, Schwab, & Jolivette, 2012). The first step in this process is for a teacher to identify the context in which the problematic behavior is likely to occur (e.g., time of day, location, activity) and to define the expected behavior. For example, students may consistently jump up from their seats and rush to the door when the teacher asks students to form a line for recess. The teacher should first ensure that the students have been adequately taught the procedure and behavioral expectations for lining up for recess. This should include allowing the students an opportunity to practice engaging in the expected behaviors. Moving forward, the teacher can call on a few students to demonstrate the procedure and then provide a verbal reminder to the class regarding the expected behaviors (e.g., "Remember to wait for your table to be called, push your chair underneath your desk, and walk to the door to form a line"). The teacher should then praise individual students and the class as a whole each time they successfully engage in this procedure.

Response Cost

Adding a response–cost component to group-based reward programs may increase the efficacy of classroom interventions. Studies of preschool-age children who have ADHD have shown that providing only positive reinforcement for appropriate behaviors is not enough to change behavior on a consistent basis (Barkley et al., 2000; Jurbergs, Palcic, & Kelley, 2007). Instead, a response–cost program, in which children lose points/tokens/access to other reinforcers for inappropriate behavior, is also needed. Although reinforcement and response–cost systems can be used independently, teachers can also combine the two. In a combined system, children would earn tokens for appropriate behavior (as in the token reinforcement program) and lose them for inappropriate behavior (as in the response–cost system). For example, in a classwide token economy wherein the students are earning pompoms for appropriate behaviors, the teacher would remove a previously earned pompom when a student breaks a classroom rule or engages in another inappropriate behavior. The teacher would note which classroom rule the child broke and remove the pompom from the glass jar. In another classroom-based response–cost system, buttons could be placed on a chart and used as tokens. Children start each classroom activity (10–15 minutes in duration) with five small buttons and one big button. When a child breaks a rule, one of his or her small buttons is removed from the chart. If the child has at least three buttons at the end of the activity, he or she is allowed to keep the big button. At the end of the day, children who have at least three big buttons earn a tangible reward (McGoey & DuPaul, 2000). Tiano, Fortson, McNeil, and Humphreys (2005) implemented a response–cost system in a Head Start classroom. In this study, the response cost system consisted of a board with four levels. The first three levels had sunshine and were the "sunny zone," and the bottom level had clouds and was the "cloudy zone." A shape was assigned to each child. The teacher provided one verbal warning when a child engaged in an inappropriate behavior and, if the behavior continued, the child's shape was moved down one level. However, if a behavior involved destruction or aggression, the shape was moved down without warning. At specified times throughout the day, each child whose shape was in the "sunny zone" received a reward. Although successfully implemented, conclusions regarding the effectiveness of the response–cost component could not be made, due to increases in appropriate behavior across all conditions over time.

Home–School Notes/Check-In/Check-Out

Home–school notes, which are commonly used with school-age children, can also be implemented at the preschool level. This system utilizes positive reinforcement for appropriate behavior and may contain a response cost (e.g., loss of home privileges) for inappropriate behaviors. This intervention has been shown to have high acceptability and feasibility with preschool teachers given the limited time and effort required (Briesch et al., 2015). The purpose of the home–school note is to enhance communication between the parents and the school while developing contingencies for school-based behaviors. In a typical home–school note system, the teacher evaluates the child on certain behaviors (e.g., raises hand before speaking) throughout the day, and the note is then taken home to the parents, who provide consequences for appropriate or inappropriate behavior (Cox, 2005). When developing a home–school note system, it is important that it be manageable for everyone involved. This means that the note cannot be overly time consuming or complicated. The most salient behaviors should be targeted first. Thus, if the child is having difficulties in play settings due to inappropriate sharing skills, one behavior to target on the home–school note might be, "Shares with other children during playtime." The behaviors included on the note should be behaviors that can be easily observed by the teacher, and they should be stated in positive terms.

The actual design of a home–school note can vary a great deal. An example of one such note is displayed in Figure 6.2, and a blank home–school note is displayed in Form 6.1. In the example home–school note, the day is divided into time categories. Activity categories (e.g., circle time, recess, lunch) can also be used. Three target behaviors are listed down the side of the note. The teacher then checks "Yes" or "No" for each behavior during each time period to indicate whether the child performed the target behaviors. When teachers are marking the note, they should also provide the child with qualitative feedback. For example, the teacher might say, "Joel, you did a great job sharing your toys and following directions. You still need to work on keeping your hands and feet to yourself."

Instead of a yes/no system, a rating system (e.g., 1–3, where 1 = *never*, 2 = *sometimes*, and 3 = *always*) can be used or, with preschool children, a method using smiley/frowny faces can be effective. A criterion is set for how many "points" (in the Figure 6.2 example, how many "Yes" marks) a child needs to receive in order to obtain a reward at home. It is important that this number be relatively low at first so that the child experiences success. Over time, the number of points needed for a reward can be increased. It is extremely important that parents follow through with providing the reward at home, when the child receives the required number of points. It is also important that the home–school note actually make it home. For school-age children, a response–cost component is often included so that the child loses certain privileges for that evening if he or she does not bring the note home (or receives an extremely low number of points). With preschool- and kindergarten-age children, teachers will likely need to be more proactive in making sure the note reaches the parents. Notes can be placed in the folders or backpacks that go home on a daily basis. Parents should also be proactive in asking for the note or checking the child's backpack when the child arrives home. Parents should praise the child liberally if his or her goal has been met for the day and then give the child the earned reinforcer as soon as possible. In some situations the reinforcer may not be appropriate immediately (e.g., the child earned a special dessert following dinner), but the parent should praise the child and mention that the child will receive it later. As children improve on certain behaviors, these behaviors may be removed from the note and replaced with new behaviors.

Child's name: John Smith

Target Behaviors	9 A.M.–10 A.M.		10 A.M.–11 A.M.		11 A.M.–12 P.M.		12 P.M.–1 P.M.		1 P.M.–2 P.M.	
	Yes	No	Yes	No	Yes	No	Yes	No	Yes	No
Shares toys	✓		✓		✓		✓		✓	
Keeps hands and feet to self		✓	✓			✓	✓		✓	
Follows directions	✓		✓			✓	✓		✓	

Number of "yes" marks needed for reward: __10__

Number of "yes" marks earned: __12__

Identified reward: _Choose what is for dinner._

Comments: _John had a great day today!_

Teacher signature: _Mrs. Anderson_

FIGURE 6.2. Sample home–school note.

Check-In/Check-Out is a specific program that has been developed to address more intensive problems and makes use of a daily point card (similar to a home–school note system). In this intervention, students check in at the beginning of school and are encouraged to meet daily goals. Teachers use a behavior point card to provide feedback throughout the day. An afternoon checkout occurs, and the card is reviewed before being taken home for review by the child's parents. In a review of the literature on Check-In/Check-Out (Maggin, Zurheide, Pickett, & Baillie, 2015) the authors concluded that this method is effective in addressing child problem behaviors, particularly behaviors that are maintained by attention.

Time-Out

Time-out is an additional discipline strategy that is sometimes used in early education classrooms. Although teachers are often reluctant to implement time-out, and there are some ethical/legal issues to consider (e.g., least restrictive environment; excluding the child from the classroom; leaving the child in time-out for long periods of time), it can be used effectively in preschool classrooms. Before implementing an exclusionary time-out, teachers should clarify whether least restrictive behavioral intervention procedures need to be followed, which may involve obtaining permission from parents or a school committee to use this approach. Ritz, Noltemeyer, and Green (2014) provide an overview of behavior management strategies used in the preschool classroom setting, including the use of time-out. Allowing a child to remain in the classroom should be a top priority, and thus, an isolation time-out in which the child is removed from the classroom is not recommended. Time-outs in which the child is removed from the current activity but not the classroom setting are considered to be the most appropriate. Such time-outs may involve complete exclusion, in which the child cannot participate in or view the activity, or partial exclusion, in which the child is removed from the activity but can still view it. In general, the least-intrusive form possible should be used each time (Ritz et al., 2014).

Before time-out is used in the classroom, the teacher should first explain it to the children. This explanation should be kept brief, but it should also be made clear that when a child misbehaves (as defined by existing classroom rules), then the child will be sent to time-out. The teacher should model for the class what is involved in time-out and how one must behave to be allowed out of time-out. Time-out, should be used consistently when children do not follow the classroom rules. In some situations, this may involve stopping ongoing teaching in order to place a child in time-out (Turner & Watson, 1999). Obviously, implementing this method is easier with at least two adults in the classroom; if an aide is present, both the teacher and the aide should follow the same guidelines and procedures for time-out use.

The time-out location selected in the classroom should be a place where the child is removed from ongoing activity but can be easily monitored by the teacher or aide. Results have varied on the optimal duration of a time-out; however, it is generally recommended that the time-out not be an extensively long period of time (Ritz et al., 2014). Thus, the "1 minute per year of age, not to exceed 5 minutes" guideline discussed in Chapter 3 is appropriate for classroom time-outs. If a child repeatedly attempts to leave the time-out location, he or she should be returned to it. This will only work, realistically, if an aide (or other second adult) is present in the classroom. A barrier to keep the child in time-out may also be used, but this solution has logistical and equipment problems (e.g., what will be used for a barrier) that make it less than ideal (Turner & Watson, 1999). Once the time-out period has ended, the adult, rather than the child, should release the child from time-out (Ritz et al., 2014).

Summary of PBIS

Addressing early childhood disruptive school behaviors is critical to the long-term outcomes of students. Without adequate behavioral supports, these children are more likely to be suspended or expelled, demonstrate poor academic achievement, and experience a variety of negative life outcomes. While schools have historically utilized a punitive approach to behavior management, this has proven ineffective. PBIS is an evidence-based approach to addressing student misbehaviors through use of positively based antecedent and consequence strategies aimed at promoting prosocial and appropriate behaviors in students. Although classroom implementation of PBIS has been given less attention in the literature compared to schoolwide use, the classroom can be a highly effective setting in which to apply these strategies. Teachers are encouraged to utilize the strategies discussed in order to increase students' engagement in desirable behaviors.

SOCIAL AND EMOTIONAL LEARNING

Social and emotional learning (SEL) has been defined as systematic instruction designed to teach students social and emotional skills both as a preventive measure and as an early intervention for mental health problems from PreK to 12th grade (Greenberg et al., 2003). SEL programs are primarily used as Tier 1 and Tier 2 interventions in the schools to help support five core social–emotional competencies: self-management, social awareness, relationship skills, self-awareness, and responsible decision making (CASEL, 2008). Self-management refers to a child's ability to regulate behaviors and emotions to achieve goals; social awareness involves understanding and empathizing with others; relationship skills include the child's ability to cooperate, manage conflict, and develop relationships; self-awareness refers to the ability to identify personal emotions, as well as strengths and challenges; and, responsible decision making involves making ethical, constructive decisions about personal and social behavior and interactions. The premise of SEL programs is that these skills must be taught, just like other subjects in school, and that these skills are critical to the emotional, behavioral, and academic success and health of the child. Additionally, the Common Core State Standards (CCSS), adopted by most states in the United States, embed standards that address the social and emotional health of students in order for them to be college and career ready in today's society, both academically and socially–emotionally. In the preschool and kindergarten years, SEL skills include learning how to listen to others and take turns speaking, how to ask and answer questions in seeking help or information, and how to express thoughts, feelings, and ideas clearly. As students progress in school, taking another's perspective, working with peers collaboratively, and resolving disagreements are all expected standards requiring social and emotional competencies (Common Core State Standards Initiative, 2015).

Given the fact that children spend the major part of their day in the school setting, classrooms can be an ideal setting in which children can learn social and emotional skills (Jones & Bouffard, 2012). Consistent with the multi-tiered model of services, Shastri (2009) notes that schools can use a multidisciplinary approach to widely treat and prevent milder mental health issues and identify those students who have greater mental health challenges. These classroom or schoolwide SEL programs reach every child in the school, benefiting children at every tier and reaching those students at risk for or currently experiencing problems.

Benefits of SEL Programs

Copious research supports the use of SEL programs in the schools, particularly in the K–12 grades. A meta-analysis of 213 universal school-based SEL programs found that, compared to students not in SEL programs, K–12 students in SEL programs had significantly improved social and emotional skills, behaviors, and attitudes. Of note is that students in the SEL groups also demonstrated academic performance gains, with an overall 11-percentile-point gain in achievement (Durlak, Weissberg, Dymnicki, Taylor & Schellinger, 2011). Dymnicki, Sambolt, and Kidron (2013) found that student participants in SEL programs develop skills such as better communication, effectively working on a team, organization, problem solving, and conflict resolution, in addition to increasing their resiliencies. Additionally, decreases in problematic behaviors, as measured by rating scales, have also been evidenced after implementation of an SEL program with preschool-age children, along with increases in desirable social and emotional behaviors (Schultz, Richardson, Barber, & Wilcox, 2011).

Common SEL Programs

A wide variety of SEL programs are currently available for use in the schools. Those that include, or are specifically designed for, the preschool, kindergarten and early elementary years are briefly reviewed.

The Incredible Years

The Incredible Years (IY; 2013; *incredibleyears.com*) is a series of comprehensive training programs for parents, teachers, and children. The primary goals of this program are to improve social and emotional functioning in children and to reduce challenging behaviors. The parent programs are overviewed in Chapter 3. The in-school portion (the Dinosaur School program) is used by teachers as a classroomwide social and emotional learning and prevention program. The Dinosaur School program is composed of 60 lessons that are implemented two to three times a week and contains three levels geared to the child's development (Level 1: ages 3–5, Level 2: ages 5–6, Level 3: ages 7–8). The program focuses on the development of empathy, social skills, and problem solving. Goals include improving parent–child interactions, preventing/reducing behavioral or emotional problems of children, and promoting children's competencies, including problem solving and emotional regulation (IY; 2013).

Research supports the effectiveness of the Dinosaur School program. A school-based study of preschool, kindergarten, and first- grade students in the program found that students had improved social skills, emotional regulation, and concentration postintervention as compared to students in the control group. Greatest improvements were found with those students deemed to be "high-risk" (Webster-Stratton, Reid, & Stoolmiller, 2008). Positive effects on classroom climate and teacher behaviors in preschool settings have also been found when using the Dinosaur School program (Raver et al., 2008).

Teacher training is necessary to ensure the most successful outcome from using the Dinosaur School program. Ideally, teachers should receive both formalized training and coaching during program implementation (Reinke et al., 2012). Cresswell (2014) recommends active participation from parents, school staff, and children to aid program success. Ongoing teacher support and buy-in, as well as resources devoted to teacher training and supervision, are recommended. The Dinosaur School program, therefore, requires both teacher dedication to the trainings, as well as a high level of participation and buy-in from school staff, parents, and students in order to be most effective. Both the teacher training modules and the materials needed to implement the program are available for individual purchase.

Second Step

Second Step (*www.cfchildren.org/second-step*) is a social skills program that can be used in the classroom for children ages 4–14 (preschool through junior high). Each grade has a distinct curriculum designed to improve children's resiliencies and social competencies, while reducing impulsive, high-risk, and aggressive behaviors. The program is based on cognitive-behavioral principles integrated with social information processing, social learning theory, and empathy research. Second Step focuses on three units (Empathy Training, Impulse Control and Problem Solving, and Anger Management), with approximately five to nine lessons per unit being taught once or twice per week. In the Early Learning Program (ages 4–5) the Skills for Learning, Empathy, Emotion Management, Friendship Skills and Problem Solving, and Transition to Kindergarten skills are taught. Each lesson typically starts by introducing a weekly concept (e.g., how to understand how others are feeling) and presenting a story about that concept using various strategies, such as story cards, videos, and sample discussion questions. The preschool and kindergarten curriculum includes 28 weeks of lessons with targeted objectives for each week, such as demonstrating listening skills, identifying feelings, demonstrating relaxation skills, and inviting others to play.

Sprague and colleagues (2001) examined whether general schoolwide behavioral practices along with exposure to the Second Step curriculum would lead to increases in prosocial behavior and safety in children in grades K–8 across nine treatment schools and six control schools. The nine treatment elementary schools reported greater decreases in office discipline referrals than comparison schools, and each grade across schools showed improvements on knowledge of Second Step principles after a year of treatment (Sprague et al., 2001). Research by Hart and colleagues (2009) examining social and emotional knowledge found the Second Step program's Impulse Control and Problem Solving unit to be effective with elementary grade students, with increases in knowledge found from pre- to postintervention. However, for children classified as having an emotional disturbance, there have not been any studies to date regarding the effectiveness of the Second Step curriculum and, therefore, additional research is needed (U.S. Department of Education, 2013).

Promoting Alternative Thinking Strategies

Promoting Alternative Thinking Strategies (PATHS; Channing Bete Company, 2015) is a comprehensive SEL program for preschool through sixth grades, which is implemented by teachers, with separate curricula available for each grade. The materials cover social skills, conflict resolution, emotional awareness, and self-control.

The PATHS program has been found to increase emotional awareness and problem-solving skills in elementary-age students, along with reducing externalizing behaviors (Greenberg, Kusché, Cook, & Quamma, 1995). Additionally, research has provided support for the PATHS curriculum in promoting impulse control and increasing verbal fluency in elementary school children (Riggs, Greenberg, Kusche, & Pentz, 2006). At the preschool level, children who were exposed to the PATHS intervention had higher emotion knowledge and were rated by teachers as being less socially withdrawn and more socially competent than children in the control group (Domitrovich, Cortes, & Greenberg, 2007). Teacher training and support, however, is crucial. Teachers need to attend two workshops in order to best implement the materials in their classrooms. Effects also were stronger when teachers implemented the program with fidelity and when strong administrator support was present (Kam, Greenberg, & Walls, 2003).

Connecting With Others: Lessons for Teaching Social and Emotional Competence

The Connecting With Others (Richardson, 1996) curriculum is an SEL curriculum available for use in the schools. The curriculum is broken down by age groups, with the kindergarten to second- grade materials designed to help students learn to resolve conflicts, respect differences, and learn tolerance and acceptance of others. The curriculum includes 30 lessons divided into five skill areas: Concept of Self and Others, Socialization, Problem Solving and Conflict Resolution, Communication, Sharing, Empathy and Caring. Instructional strategies include the use of relaxation techniques, storytelling, modeling, coaching, behavioral rehearsal, reinforcement, creative expression, and self-instruction.

Research has found that the Connecting with Others curriculum is effective at increasing children's social and emotional competencies. A pre/post study conducted by Schultz and colleagues (2011) using the BASC-2 and the Connecting with Others research scale found that, postintervention, preschool-age children exposed to the K–2 curriculum demonstrated improvements in emotional and behavioral symptoms, as measured by the BASC rating scale, with medium-sized effects (d values ranging from 0.45 to 0.63). Increases in social–emotional knowledge was also evidenced via a Connecting with Others research scale given to teachers. Further investigation is needed to better understand the outcome research for this curriculum with young children.

Strong Start

The Strong Start PreK (Merrell, Whitcomb, & Parisi, 2009) and K–2 (Merrell, Parisi, & Whitcomb, 2007) curricula are SEL programs that can be easily implemented with minimal training by teachers, school psychologists, or mental health care professionals in the schools. They are designed to be both prevention and early intervention programs, targeting those students who are typically developing, those who are at risk, and those who have emotional disturbance. The entire series contains five different sets of materials dependent on grade level: Strong Start for PreK, Strong Start for Grades K–2, Strong Kids Grades 3–5, Strong Kids Grades 6–8, and Strong Teens for Grades 9–12. The Strong Kids/Strong Start programs focus on building social–emotional and coping skills and promoting resilience.

The Strong Start PreK (Merrell et al., 2009) and K–2 (Merrell et al., 2007) programs can be effectively implemented into a variety of settings, such as general and special education schools, group counseling, and youth treatment facilities that have an educational component. The materials are easy to use and inexpensive. Both the PreK and the K–2 curricula contain similar lessons, including topics related to understanding feelings, anger management, coping with anxiety, empathy training, and conflict resolution. Beyond recommending that a stuffed animal be used as the "mascot" to contribute to scenarios and role plays, all other materials are either contained in the book or are typical classroom materials likely to be already on hand (e.g., pens, paper). The lessons are highly structured, short, and partially scripted to address specific goals covering social and emotional health topics. Repetition and review of previously learned materials help to solidify knowledge learned.

Research has evidenced significant support for the Strong Kids program, including increased emotional knowledge and reduced negative behavioral and emotional symptoms for participating students (Marchant, Brown, Caldarella, & Young, 2010). Kramer, Caldarella, Christensen, and Shatzer (2011) found, after implementing the Strong Start K–2 SEL program with 67 kindergarteners, that students exhibited significant increases in prosocial behaviors and decreases in internalizing behaviors via teacher and parent pre/post comparison on rating scales and interview information. These gains were maintained at a 6-week follow-up rating. Both teachers and parents rated meaningful changes in their student's prosocial behavior, with very large and moderate effect sizes, respectively. Similar results have been found in studies of the Strong Start PreK curriculum. In a control group study examining the curriculum, the treatment group evidenced great reductions in internalizing behaviors postintervention, with the greatest reduction in symptoms over time exhibited by the treatment-plus-booster-sessions group ($d = 1.43$). There was no statistically significant change in internalizing scores for the control group ($d = .023$). It was concluded that interventions such as the Strong Start PreK program could provide help for at-risk preschool students without having to identify and treat them individually (Gunther, Caldarella, Kerth, & Young, 2012).

Summary of SEL Programs

All SEL programs reviewed in this section achieve their goals of increasing social and emotional knowledge and awareness, and often decreasing negative behavior or internalizing symptoms. Some curricula do require more training, support, or materials than others, so it is important for the clinician to select the SEL program that will work best within the parameters of the environment in which it is to be implemented. Given the importance of addressing social and emotional needs of children in the schools, the research on these curricula offer encouraging initial data to support their use in group or school settings when working with young children, though more research is warranted with the preschool population.

CHAPTER SUMMARY

This chapter included an overview of early academic and behavioral supports for students in the classroom. RTI models for early literacy and academic issues for preschool-age children were discussed, along with the research support for such interventions. The need for approaches such as PBIS within preschool and kindergarten classrooms was also examined. Finally, SEL programs for preschool and kindergarten-age children were summarized, along with related research that validates the use of these programs with this age group. To conclude, early academic and behavioral interventions, although relatively new, are thus far supported in the literature and are recommended as prevention and early intervention methods.

FORM 6.1

Home–School Note

Child's name: _____

Target Behaviors	Yes	No	Yes	No	Yes	No	Yes	No	Yes	No

Number of "yes" marks needed for reward: _____

Number of "yes" marks earned: _____

Identified reward: _____

Comments: _____
_____
_____

Teacher signature: _____

From Melissa L. Holland, Jessica Malmberg, and Gretchen Gimpel Peacock. Copyright © 2017 The Guilford Press. Permission to photocopy this form is granted to purchasers of this book for personal use or use with individual students (see copyright page for details). Purchasers can download additional copies of this material (see box at the end of the table of contents).

CHAPTER 7

Referral Issues and Conclusion

This book was designed to be a practical guide focused on assessment and evidence-based interventions for use with young children. All interventions are based on best practice and are practical in nature, offering mental health providers the tools they need to address the most common problems these children face. However, there are times when a youth's problem necessitates different or more intensive interventions than can be provided by a certain individual or in a certain setting, and a referral to another provider is required. This chapter overviews the situations in which additional assistance for the child should be considered and summarizes the steps for referral.

REFERRAL PROCEDURES

It should be self-evident that all mental health professionals should work within their areas of competence/professional training and recognize when a referral might be in the best interest of the child or family. Referrals may be made for many reasons, including the need for a non–mental health professional or for a more specialized mental health professional to be involved in treatment or if there is a need for more intensive services than can be obtained in the current setting. When considering whether or not to refer a child to another provider, it can be helpful to consult with all individuals involved in that child's care. Teachers, special education staff, daycare providers, and others who work with the child on a regular basis can give their observations and insights about how the child is functioning. If treatment has already been started, the most recent outcome data would also be important to consider. In addition, and most important, the child's parents should be brought in for consultation; ultimately, the parents are often the ones who make the call to initiate a referral to an outside expert.

REFERRAL SOURCES

A variety of professionals can offer helpful services to a child experiencing significant emotional or behavioral challenges. During the referral process, it is important to ensure that both the child's physical and mental well-being are taken into account. Common referral sources are listed in the following sections; other referrals to professionals such as physical therapists, speech pathologists, or occupational therapists may also be considered, depending on the presenting concern.

Primary Care Provider

When working with young children who have behavioral issues, a referral to or consultation with the child's primary care provider (PCP) is often necessary. This PCP may be a medical doctor (MD or DO) who specializes in pediatrics or family practice medicine. Increasingly, individuals other than medical doctors, such as nurse practitioners or advanced practice nurses who have master's or doctoral degrees, also provide primary care services. In most states, these providers can perform most of the outpatient functions, including prescribing medications, of a medical doctor. If a child is experiencing any neurological or physical complaints or is exhibiting behaviors that may have a medical component, it is important to evaluate and rule out medical causes for a problem before proceeding with behavioral interventions. Often when a young child is feeling anxious or depressed, he or she may begin to exhibit somatic complaints along with psychological symptoms. These symptoms may include headaches, stomachaches, leg pains, sleep and appetite disturbance (Domènech-Llaberia et al., 2004), and, in more extreme cases, self-injurious behaviors (de Zulueta, 2007). Also, the link between stress and anxiety and lowered immune functioning and chronic physical illness is well documented (Burgess & Roberts, 2005); therefore, a PCP visit to rule out or control for any physical reactions the child may be experiencing could be warranted to stave off any long-term physical complications or effects.

Consultation with PCPs also may be needed when a child is taking psychotropic medications. Progress monitoring data available to mental health clinicians may enable them to provide important information on the child's behavior (particularly in the school context) that can help the PCP know if the medication is having the desired effect.

Child Psychiatrist

For children with more complex psychiatric medical needs, a referral to a child psychiatrist may be warranted. A child psychiatrist is a medical doctor (MD or DO) who specializes in psychiatry and is certified in treating mental health disorders. All psychiatrists are trained in diagnostic evaluation and psychotherapy, although often their primary role is to prescribe psychiatric medication. Children who are experiencing intense psychiatric reactions may benefit from both therapy and medication. Symptoms such as severe anxiety, sleeplessness, inattention, mood instability, and depression can all be treated with psychotropic medications, in addition to intensive mental health therapy. In fact, studies have shown that children who are experiencing severe psychological symptoms can better benefit from therapy when a combination approach is used (Varley, 2006). Therefore, it can be helpful to consult with a child psychiatrist, as well as with other physicians and mental health providers. In addition to child psychiatrists, psychiatric mental health nurse practitioners (PMHNP) may also be an appropriate referral source for children with more complex mental health/psychiatric concerns.

Master's-Level Therapist

A master's-level therapist, such as an MFT (Marriage and Family Therapist), an LCSW (Licensed Clinical Social Worker), or an LPCC (Licensed Professional Clinical Counselor) are other mental health providers to consider when looking to refer a child for emotional support. MFTs and LPCCs have received master's degrees in psychology or counseling, with an emphasis on private counseling, whereas an LCSW has received a master's degree in social work, called an MSW. All three can be equally qualified to work with children who are experiencing emotional distress; however, the professional's background, training, and expertise should be carefully investigated when choosing a provider. The therapist should be specialized in working with young children and have the proper training and experience in treating the presenting problem.

Licensed Clinical Psychologist

A licensed clinical psychologist has a doctorate degree in Clinical Psychology (PhD or PsyD). In addition to providing therapeutic services, psychologists are also trained to provide psychoeducational and social–emotional assessment, which can be an important component in ensuring accurate diagnosing and subsequent treatment. For children who have particularly complex presentations of a disorder, are not responding to current treatment efforts, or simply present with a problem outside a provider's scope of competence, referral to a licensed clinical psychologist may be indicated.

A referral to a pediatric psychologist may be warranted when working with a medically complex child, particularly if the child is experiencing comorbid psychological symptoms, is having difficulty coping with a medical diagnosis/treatment, or has not been adherent to his or her medical regimen. In addition, pediatric psychologists often develop specializations and, particularly in larger cities, universities and/or medical schools may have specialty clinics that address a particular problem area. Some examples of these specialty clinics are the child anxiety clinics at universities, including Temple University (*childanxiety.org/wps*), Yale School of Medicine (*childstudycenter.yale.edu/clinics/anxiety*), and UCLA (*www.semel.ucla.edu/caap*). Knowing local referral options for specialty services is an important part of being an effective clinician.

HOSPITALIZATION AND OTHER INPATIENT SETTINGS

If the child is evidencing behaviors that are dangerous to him- or herself or others, a hospitalization at an inpatient psychiatric facility may be indicated. Although it is extremely rare for young children to need hospitalization, it is important to note that some facilities do treat this age group. The mental health professional or physician who is working with the child can help with this referral and transition the child into inpatient care; however, if the child is actively dangerous to him- or herself or others, an emergency call (e.g., calling 911) may be indicated by any adult who has serious concerns regarding the safety of the child. Children who are not an acute danger to themselves or others but are experiencing serious emotional and behavioral challenges that cannot be adequately addressed in an outpatient clinic can also be referred to a partial hospitalization/day treatment program. Intensive mental health services, such as inpatient and partial hospitalization programs, can aid in stabilizing the child by administering and adjusting any medications and by providing intensive therapy and other interventions to help both the child and the family prepare for the release of the child back to the home and/or school setting.

REFERRAL AVENUES

For many school psychologists, counselors, and parents the task of determining how to find a referral to a mental health provider or psychiatrist can seem overwhelming and confusing. There are several avenues to finding a referral that are outlined in the following sections.

Medical Insurance

If the family will be using their medical insurance to pay for the mental health assessment and treatment, a call to the family's medical insurance provider is necessary. The goal of this call is for the family to secure a list of eligible providers in their geographic region who specialize in both the assessment and treatment of young children. It is imperative that the family ensure that the provider they select is a preferred provider on their medical insurance, or coverage may not be guaranteed and the family would then be fully financially responsible for the services rendered. Similarly, families who have Medicaid may be required to receive services at a specific facility (typically a community mental health agency) in order for the services to be covered by Medicaid. Most communities also have low-cost options if families elect not to use a preferred insurance provider or cannot afford the related costs (e.g., a deductible or co-pay). Many universities have training clinics that provide services at low cost or even no cost (especially if the services are part of a research study).

Primary Care Provider

The child's PCP often has knowledge of the young child's history and has a working relationship with the parents. Many PCPs have lists of mental health referrals, and the provider's staff can help parents navigate the referral process to ensure services are secured. In addition, some insurance companies require that the initial referral for mental health assessment and treatment come from the PCP, so this is often a good, logical first step.

Therapist Associations and Online Searches

Local, statewide, and national, therapist organizations can also be valuable sources of information when searching for a mental health provider. They frequently have information on the specialization of the mental health provider and what populations he or she treats. The American Psychological Association maintains a webpage with links to all state associations (*www.apa.org/about/apa/organizations/associations.aspx*). Different state associations list different information about providers, but all include some information on providers in that state. Other professional organizations often maintain lists of therapists that have a specific focus that fits with that organization (e.g., the Association for Behavioral and Cognitive Therapies has a searchable site—*www.findcbt.org/xFAT/index.cfm*—listing therapists who utilize cognitive and/or behavioral techniques). Online resources may be a starting place for professionals (and parents) to find out more about effective treatments and identify professionals who offer them. Two such websites include *effectivechildtherapy.org* and *infoaboutkids.org* and have resources for both parents and professionals.

Word of Mouth

One of the best approaches to locating a good mental health provider is via word of mouth. A referral from a family member, school staff person, or friend who has knowledge about the skills and demeanor of a particular mental health provider is invaluable. In addition, nothing replaces personal experience. Parents will likely be very involved with a mental health provider who is working with their child, and it is essential that the parents feel comfortable with that provider. Therefore, careful "shopping" for a mental health provider who can properly assess the child for his or her mental health needs and provide the best subsequent treatment, if needed, is highly encouraged. Of utmost importance is that the provider be experienced and trained in working with young children, who have significantly different needs in a therapy relationship than do adults, including the need to effectively build rapport with this age group. Ensuring a good fit between the mental health provider, the child, and the family is critical in the outcome and success of the service. Therefore, parents may want to visit several mental health professionals before making a choice for their child to ensure a good fit.

CONCLUSION AND BEST-PRACTICE RECOMMENDATIONS

In general, the best practice for assessing and intervening with a young child who is exhibiting emotional, social, or behavioral concerns is a multifaceted approach. Integrating information from various sources and assessments in order to gain the most complete and accurate diagnostic picture of the child without stigmatizing or overpathologizing normal childhood behaviors is the first step. From there, integrating evidence-based interventions into the home and school environments is essential. This book overviewed these best practices, along with next steps to pursue if the child's challenges extend beyond the interventions that can be provided in a regular school, home, or outpatient clinic setting.

References

Achenbach, T. M., & Rescorla, L. A. (2000). *Manual for ASEBA Preschool Forms and Profiles.* Burlington: University of Vermont.

Achenbach, T. M., & Rescorla, L. A. (2001). *Manual for the ASEBA School-Age Forms and Profiles.* Burlington: University of Vermont.

Achenbach, T. M., & Rescorla, L. A. (2009). *Multicultural supplement to the Manual for the ASEBA Preschool Forms and Profiles.* Burlington: University of Vermont.

Adamson, M., Morawska, A., & Sanders, M. R. (2013). Childhood feeding difficulties: A randomized controlled trial of a group-based parenting intervention. *Journal of Developmental and Behavioral Pediatrics, 34,* 293–302.

Altman, D. (2014). *The mindfulness toolbox: 50 practical tips, tools and handouts for anxiety, depression, stress and pain.* Eau Claire, WI: PESI Publishing and Media.

American Academy of Child and Adolescent Psychiatry. (2007). Practice parameters for the assessment and treatment of children and adolescents with anxiety disorders. *Journal of the American Academy of Child and Adolescent Psychiatry, 46,* 922–937.

American Academy of Sleep Medicine. (2014). *International classification of sleep disorders: Diagnostic and coding manual* (3rd ed.). Darien, IL: Author.

American Psychiatric Association. (2013). *Diagnostic and statistical manual of mental disorders* (5th ed.). Arlington, VA: Author.

Anderson, S. E., & Whitaker, R. C. (2010). Household routines and obesity in US preschool-aged children. *Pediatrics, 12),* 420–428.

Angold, A., & Egger, H. L. (2004). Psychiatric diagnosis in preschool children. In R. DelCarmen-Wiggens & A. Carter (Eds.) *Handbook of infant, toddler and preschool mental health assessment* (pp. 123–139). New York: Oxford University Press.

Anzman, S. L., Rollins, B. Y., & Birch, L. L. (2010). Parental influence on children's early eating environments and obesity risk: Implications for prevention. *International Journal of Obesity, 34,* 1116–1124.

Armstrong, A. B., & Field, C. E. (2012). Altering positive/negative interaction ratios of mothers and young children. *Child and Family Behavior Therapy, 34,* 231–242.

Arndorfer, R. E., Allen, K. D., & Aliazireh, L. (1999). Behavioral health needs in pediatric medicine and the acceptability of behavioral solutions: Implications for behavioral psychologists. *Behavior Therapy, 30,* 137–148.

Axelrod, M. I., Tornehl, C., & Fontanini-Axelrod, A. (2014). Enhanced response using a multicomponent urine alarm treatment for nocturnal enuresis. *Journal for Specialists in Pediatric Nursing, 19,* 172–182.

Azrin, N. H., & Foxx, R. M. (1974). *Toilet training in less than a day.* New York: Simon & Schuster.

Babbitt, R. L., Hoch, T. A., Coe, D. A., Cataldo, M. F., Kelly, K. J., Stackhouse, C., et al. (1994). Behavioral assessment and treatment of pediatric feeding disorders. *Developmental and Behavioral Pediatrics, 15,* 278–291.

Bahl, A. B., McNeil, C. B., Cleavenger, C. J., Blanc, H. M., & Bennett, G. M. (2000). Evaluation of a whole-classroom approach for the management of disruptive behavior. *Proven Practice, 2,* 62–71.

Baird, D. C., Seehusen, D. A., & Bode, D. V. (2014). Enuresis in children: A case- based approach. *American Family Physician, 90,* 560–568.

Barkley, R. A. (2013). *Defiant children: A clinician's manual for assessment and parent training* (3rd ed.). New York: Guilford Press.

Barkley, R. A., & Murphy, K. R. (2006). *Attention-deficit hyperactivity disorder: A clinical workbook* (3rd ed.). New York: Guilford Press.

Barkley, R. A., Shelton, T. L., Crosswait, C., Moorehouse, M., Fletcher, K., Barrett, S., et al. (2000). Multi-method psychoeducational intervention for preschool children with disruptive behavior: Preliminary results at posttreatment. *Journal of Child Psychology and Psychiatry and Allied Disciplines, 41,* 319–332.

Barlow, J., Smailagic, N., Huband, N., Roloff, V., & Bennett, C. (2014). Group-based parent training programmes for improving parental psychosocial health. *Cochraine Database of Systematic Reviews, 5,* CD002020.

Barnes, J. C., Boutwell, B. B., Beaver, K. M., & Gibson, C. L. (2013). Analyzing the origins of childhood externalizing behavioral problems. *Developmental Psychology, 49,* 2272–2284.

Bauermeister, J. J., Canino, G., Polanczyk, G., & Rohde, L. A. (2010). ADHD across cultures: Is there evidence for a bidimensional organization of symptoms? *Journal of Clinical Child and Adolescent Psychology, 39,* 362–372.

Beauchemin, J., Hutchins, T. L., & Patterson, F. (2008). Mindfulness meditation may lessen anxiety, promote social skills, and improve academic performance among adolescents with learning difficulties. *Complementary Health Practice Review, 13,* 34–35.

Beckwith, L. (2000). Prevention science and prevention programs. In C. H. Zeanah (Ed.), *Handbook of infant mental health* (2nd ed., pp. 439–456). New York: Guilford Press.

Benedict, E. A., Horner, R. H., & Squires, J. K. (2007). Assessment and implementation of positive behavior support in preschools. *Topics in Early Childhood Special Education, 27,* 174–192.

Benham, A. L. (2000). The observation and assessment of young children including use of the infant–toddler mental status exam. In C. H. Zeanah (Ed.), *Handbook of infant mental health* (2nd ed., pp. 249–265). New York: Guilford Press.

Benjasuwantep, B., Chaithirayanon, S., & Eiamudomkan, M. (2013). Feeding problems in healthy young children: Prevalence, related factors and feeding practices. *Pediatric Reports, 5,* 38–42.

Berkovitz, M. D., O'Brien, K. A., Carter, C. G., & Eyberg, S. M. (2010). Early identification and intervention for behavior problems in primary care: A comparison of two abbreviated versions of Parent–Child Interaction Therapy. *Behavior Therapy, 41,* 375–387.

Bingham, G. E., & Patton-Terry, N. (2013). Early language and literacy achievement of early reading first students in kindergarten and 1st grade in the United States. *Journal of Research in Childhood Education, 27,* 440–453.

Black, M. M., & Aboud, F. E. (2011). Responsive feeding is embedded in a theoretical framework of responsive parenting. *Journal of Nutrition, 141,* 490–494.

Blissett, J., Meyer, C., & Haycraft, E. (2011). The role of parenting in the relationship between childhood eating problems and broader behaviour problems. *Child: Care, Health and Development, 37*(5), 642–648.

Bluth, K., & Wahler, R. G. (2011). Parenting preschoolers: Can mindfulness help? *Mindfulness, 2,* 282–285.

Bohnert, K. M., & Breslau, N. (2008). Stability of psychiatric outcomes of low birth weight: A longitudinal investigation. *Archives of General Psychiatry, 65,* 1080–1086.

Bogels, S., & Restifo, K. (2014). *Mindful parenting: A guide for mental health practitioners.* New York: Norton.

Boles, R. E., Roberts, M. C., & Vernberg, E. M. (2008). Treating non-retentive encopresis with rewarded scheduled toilet visits. *Behavior Analysis in Practice, 1,* 68–72.

Bongers, M. E., Tabbers, M. M., & Benninga, M. A. (2007). Functional nonretentive fecal incontinence in children. *Journal of Pediatric Gastroenterology and Nutrition, 44,* 5–13.

Bor, W., Sanders, M. R., & Markie-Dadds, C. (2002). The effects of the Triple P-Positive Parenting Program on preschool children with co-occurring disruptive behavior and attentional/hyperactive difficulties. *Journal of Abnormal Child Psychology, 30,* 571–587.

Bornstein, M. (2013). Parenting and child mental health: A cross-cultural perspective. *World Psychiatry, 12,* 258–265.

Bornstein, M. H., Hahn, C., & Suwalsky, J. D. (2013). Language and internalizing and externalizing behavioral adjustment: Developmental pathways from childhood to adolescence. *Development and Psychopathology, 25,* 857–878.

Bosquet, M., & Egeland, B. (2006). The development and maintenance of anxiety symptoms from infancy through adolescence in a longitudinal sample. *Development and Psychopathology, 18,* 517–550.

Boylan, K., Vaillancourt, T., Boyle, M., & Szatmari, P. (2007). Comorbidity of internalizing disorders in children with oppositional defiant disorder. *European Child and Adolescent Psychiatry, 16,* 484–494.

Bradshaw, C. P., Koth, C. W., Thornton, L. A., & Leaf, P. J. (2009). Altering school climate through school-wide positive behavioral interventions and supports: Findings from a group-randomized effectiveness trial. *Prevention Science, 10,* 100–115.

Bradshaw, C. P., Mitchell, M. M., & Leaf, P. J. (2010). Examining the effects of schoolwide positive behavioral interventions and supports on student outcomes: Results from a randomized controlled effectiveness trial in elementary schools. *Journal of Positive Behavior Interventions, 12,* 133–148.

Bradstreet, L. E., Juechter, J. I., Kamphaus, R. W., Kerns, C. M., & Robins, D. L. (2016). Using the BASC-2 parent rating scales to screen for autism spectrum disorder in toddlers and preschool-aged children. *Journal of Abnormal Child Psychology.* [EPub ahead of print]

Bratton, S. C., Ray, D., Rhine, T., & Jones, L. (2005). The efficacy of play therapy with children: A meta-analytic review of treatment outcomes. *Professional Psychology: Research and Practice, 36,* 376–390.

Brazelton, T. B. (1962). A child-orientated approach to toilet training. *Pediatrics, 29,* 121–128.

Breaux, R. P., Harvey, E. A., & Lugo-Candelas, C. I. (2014). The role of parent psychopathology in the development of preschool children with behavior problems. *Journal of Clinical Child and Adolescent Psychology, 43,* 777–790.

Brennan, L. M., Shaw, D. S., Dishion, T. J., & Wilson, M. (2012). Longitudinal predictors of school-age academic achievement: Unique contributions of toddler-age aggression, oppositionality, inattention, and hyperactivity. *Journal of Abnormal Child Psychology, 40,* 1289–1300.

Briesch, A. M., Briesch, J. M., & Chafouleas, S. M. (2015). Investigating the usability of classroom management strategies among elementary schoolteachers. *Journal of Positive Behavior Interventions, 17*(1), 5–14.

Brooks, R. C., Copen, R. M., Cox, D. J., Morris, J., Borowitz, S., & Sutphen, J. (2000). Review of the treatment literature for encopresis, functional constipation, and stool-toileting refusal. *Annals of Behavioral Medicine, 22,* 260–267.

Brown, F. L., Whittingham, K., Boyd, R. N., McKinlay, L., & Sofronoff, K. (2014). Improving child and parenting outcomes following paediatric acquired brain injury: A randomised controlled trial of stepping stones triple P plus acceptance and commitment therapy. *Journal of Child Psychology and Psychiatry, 55,* 1172–1183.

Brown, H. E., Pearson, N., Braithwaite, R. E., Brown, W. J., & Biddle, S. J. (2013). Physical activity interventions and depression in children and adolescents. *Sports Medicine, 43,* 195–206.

Brown, M. L., Pope, A. W., & Brown, E. J. (2011). Treatment of primary nocturnal enuresis in children: A review. *Child: Care, Health and Development, 37,* 153–160.

Bub, K. L., McCartney, K., & Willett, J. B. (2007). Behavior problem trajectories and first-grade cognitive ability and achievement skills: A latent growth curve analysis. *Journal of Educational Psychology, 99,* 653–670.

Bufferd, S. J., Dougherty, L. R., Carlson, G. A., & Klein, D. N. (2011). Parent-reported mental health in preschoolers: Findings using a diagnostic interview. *Comprehensive Psychiatry, 52,* 359–369.

Bulotsky-Shearer, R. J., Dominguez, X., & Bell, E. R. (2012). Preschool classroom behavioral context and school readiness outcomes for low-income children: A multilevel examination of child- and classroom-level influences. *Journal of Educational Psychology, 104,* 421–438.

Burgers, R., Reitsma, J. B., Bongers, M. J., de Lorijn, F., & Benninga, M. A. (2013). Functional nonretentive fecal incontinence: Do enemas help? *Journal of Pediatrics, 162,* 1023–1027.

Burgess, A. W., & Roberts, A. R. (2005). Crisis intervention for persons diagnosed with clinical disorders based on the stress-crisis continuum. In A. R. Roberts (Ed.), *Crisis intervention handbook: Assessment, treatment and research* (pp. 120–140). New York: Oxford University Press.

Burlaka, V., Bermann, E. A., & Graham-Bermann, S. A. (2015). Internalizing problems in at-risk preschoolers: Associations with child and mother risk factors. *Journal of Child and Family Studies, 24*, 2653–2660.

Butler, J. F. (1976). The toilet training success of parents after reading *Toilet Training in Less Than a Day*. *Behavior Therapy, 7*, 185–191.

Butler, R. J., Golding, J., Northstone, K., & The ALSPAC Study Team. (2005). Nocturnal enuresis at 7.5 years old: Prevalence and analysis of clinical signs. *BJU International, 96*, 404–410.

Butzer, B., Day, D., Potts, A., Ryan, C., Coulombe, S. Davies, B., et al. (2014). Effects of a classroom-based yoga intervention on cortisol and behavior in second-and third-grade students: A pilot study. *Journal of Evidence-Based Complementary andAlternative Medicine, 20*, 41–49.

Buyse, E., Verschueren, K., & Doumen, S. (2011). Preschoolers' attachment to mother and risk for adjustment problems in kindergarten: Can teachers make a difference? *Social Development, 20*, 33–50.

Buysse, V., Peisner-Feinberg, E. S., Soukakou, E., LaForett, D. R., Fettig, A., & Schaaf, J. M. (2013). Recognition and response: A model of response to intervention to promote academic learning in early education. In V. Buysse & E. S. Peisner-Feinberg (Eds.), *Handbook of response to intervention in early childhood* (pp. 69–84). Baltimore: Brookes.

Campbell, L. K., Cox, D. J., & Borowitz, S. M. (2009). Elimination disorders: Enuresis and encopresis. In M. C. Roberts & R. G. Steele (Eds.), *Handbook of pediatric psychology* (4th ed., pp. 481–490). New York: Guilford Press.

Campbell, S. B. (1995). Behavior problems in preschool children: A review of recent research. *Child Psychology and Psychiatry and Allied Disciplines, 36*, 113–149.

Campbell, S. B. (2002). *Behavior problems in preschool children: Clinical and developmental issues* (2nd ed.). New York: Guilford Press.

Carballo, J. J., Baca-Garcia, E., Blanco, C., Perez-Rodriguez, M. M., Jimenez Arriero, M. A., Artes-Rodriguez, et al. (2010). Stability of childhood anxiety disorder diagnoses: A follow-up naturalistic study in psychiatric care. *European Child and Adolescent Psychiatry, 19*, 395–403.

Carter, A. S., Wagmiller, R. J., Gray, S. O., McCarthy, K. J., Horwitz, S. M., & Briggs-Gowan, M. J. (2010). Prevalence of DSM-IV disorder in a representative, healthy birth cohort at school entry: Sociodemographic risks and social adaptation. *Journal of the American Academy of Child and Adolescent Psychiatry, 49*, 686–698.

CASEL. (2008). Social and emotional learning (SEL) and student benefits: Implications for the safe schools/healthy students core elements. Retrieved from *https://safesupportivelearning.ed.gov/resources/social-and-emotional-learning-and-student-benefits-implications-safe-schoolhealthy*.

Catani, C., Mahendren, K., Ruf, M., Schauer, E., Elbert, T., & Neuner, F. (2009). Treating children traumatized by war and tsunami: A comparison between exposure therapy and meditation-relaxation in North-East Sri Lanka. *BMC Psychiatry, 9*, 1–11.

Chacko, A., Wymbs, B. T., Chimiklis, A., Wymbs, F. A., & Pelham, W. E. (2012). Evaluating a comprehensive strategy to improve engagement to group-based behavioral parent training for high-risk families of children with ADHD. *Journal of Abnormal Child Psychology, 40*, 1351–1362.

Chance, P. (2013). *Learning and Behavior* (7th ed.). Belmont, CA: Thomson Wadsworth.

Chang, H., Shaw, D. S., Dishion, T. J., Gardner, F., & Wilson, M. N. (2014). Direct and indirect effects of the family check-up on self-regulation from toddlerhood to early school-age. *Journal of Abnormal Child Psychology, 42*, 1117–1028.

Channing Bete Company. (2015). PATHS program results. Retrieved from *www.channing-bete.com/prevention-programs/paths/results-recognition.html*.

Chaste, P., & Leboyer, M. (2012). Autism risk factors: Genes, environment, and gene-environment interactions. *Dialogues in Clinical Neuroscience, 14*, 281–292.

Chawarska, K., Klin, A., & Volkmar, F. R. (Eds.) (2010). *Autism spectrum disorder in infants and toddlers: Diagnosis, assessment, and treatment*. New York: Guilford Press.

Chial, H. J., Camilleri, M., Williams, D. E., Litzinger, K., & Perrault, J. (2003). Rumination syndrome in children and adolescents: Diagnosis, treatment, and prognosis. *Pediatrics, 111*, 158–162.

Child Welfare Information Gateway. (2014). *Mandatory reporters of child abuse and neglect*. Washington, DC:

U.S. Department of Health and Human Services, Children's Bureau. Retrieved from *www.childwelfare.gov/pubPDFs/manda.pdf*.

Choby, B. A., & George, S. (2008). Toilet training. *American Family Physician, 78*, 1059–1064.

Chorpita, B. F., & Southam-Gerow, M. A. (2006). Fears and Anxieties. In E. J. Mash & R. A. Barkley (Eds.), *Treatment of childhood disorders* (3rd.ed., pp. 271–335). New York: Guilford Press.

Christakis, D. A., & Zimmerman, F. J. (2007). Violent television viewing during preschool is associated with antisocial behavior during school age. *Pediatrics, 120*, 993–999.

Christensen D. L., Baio J., Braun K. V., Bilder, D., Charles, J., Constantino, J. N., et al. (2016). Prevalence and characteristics of autism spectrum disorder among children aged 8 years—Autism and Developmental Disabilities Monitoring Network, 11 sites, United States, 2012. *MMWR Surveillance Summaries, 65*, 1–23.

Chronis, A. M., Chacko, A., Fabiano, G. A., Wymbs, B. T., & Pelham, W. E. (2004). Enhancements to the behavioral parent training paradigm for families of children with ADHD: Review and future directions. *Clinical Child and Family Psychology Review, 7*, 1–27.

Clark, R., Tluczek, A., & Gallagher, K. C. (2004). Assessment of parent-child early relational disturbances. In R. DelCarmen-Wiggens & A. Carter (Eds.) *Handbook of infant, toddler and preschool mental health assessment* (pp. 25–60). New York: Oxford University Press.

Coatsworth, J. D., Duncan, L. G., Greenberg, M. T., & Nix, R. L. (2010). Changing parent's mindfulness, child management skills and relationship quality with their youth: Results from a randomized pilot intervention trial. *Journal of Child and Family Studies, 19*, 203–217.

Cohen, J. A., Mannarino, A. P., Berliner, L., & Deblinger, E. (2000). Trauma-focused cognitive behavioral therapy for children and adolescents: An empirical update. *Journal of Interpersonal Violence, 15*, 1202–1223.

Combs-Ronto, L., Olson, S., Lunkenheimer, E., & Sameroff, A. (2009). Interactions between maternal parenting and children's early disruptive behavior: Bidirectional associations across the transition from preschool to school entry. *Journal of Abnormal Child Psychology, 37*, 1151–1163.

Common Core State Standards Initiative. (2015). Development process. Retrieved from *www.corestandards.org/about-the-standards/development-process*.

Conduct Problems Prevention Research Group. (1999a). Initial impact of the Fast Track prevention trial for conduct problems: I. The high-risk sample. *Journal of Consulting and Clinical Psychology, 67*, 631–647.

Conduct Problems Prevention Research Group. (1999b). Initial impact of the Fast Track prevention trial for conduct problems: II. Classroom effects. *Journal of Consulting and Clinical Psychology, 67*, 648–657.

Conduct Problems Prevention Research Group. (2010). Effects of a multiyear universal social-emotional learning program: The role of student and school characteristics. *Journal of Consulting and Clinical Psychology, 78*, 156–168.

Conners, C. K. (2008). *Conners Rating Scales manual*. North Tonawanda, NY: Multi-Health Systems.

Conners, C. K. (2009). *Conners Early Childhood*. North Tonawanda, NY: Multi-Health Systems.

Cooper, S., Valleley, R. J., Polaha, J., Begeny, J., & Evans, J. H. (2006). Running out of time: Physician management of behavioral health concerns in rural pediatric primary care. *Pediatrics, 118*, e132–e138.

Cowart, M., & Ollendick, T. H. (2013). Specific phobias. In C. A. Essau & T. H. Ollendick (Eds.), *The Wiley-Blackwell handbook of the treatment of childhood and adolescent anxiety* (pp. 353–368). West Sussex, UK: Wiley.

Cox, D. D. (2005). Evidence-based interventions using home–school collaboration. *School Psychology Quarterly, 20*, 473–497.

Coyne, L. W., & Murrell, A. R. (2009). *The joy of parenting: An acceptance and commitment therapy guide to effective parenting in the early years*. Oakland, CA: New Harbinger.

Coyne, L. W., & Wilson, K. G. (2004). The role of cognitive fusion in impaired parenting: An RFT analysis. *International Journal of Psychology and Psychological Therapy, 4*, 468–486.

Crane, J., Mincic, M. S., & Winsler, A. (2011). Parent-teacher agreement and reliability on the Devereux Early Childhood Assessment (DECA) in English and Spanish for ethnically diverse children living in poverty. *Early Education and Development, 22*, 520–547.

Cresswell, A. (2014). Delivering Incredible Years programmes: A practice perspective 2. *International Journal of Birth and Parent Education, 2*, 36–38.

Crossen-Tower, C. (2014). *Understanding child abuse and neglect* (9th ed.). Upper Saddle River, NJ: Pearson.

Cyr, M., Pasalich, D. S., McMahon, R. J., & Spieker, S. J. (2014). The longitudinal link between parenting and child aggression: The moderating effect of attachment security. *Child Psychiatry and Human Development, 45,* 555–564.

Dasari, M., & Knell, S. M. (2015). Cognitive-behavioral play therapy for children with anxiety and phobias. In H. G. Kaduson & C. E. Schaefer (Eds.), *Short-term play therapy for children* (3rd ed., pp. 25–52). New York: Guilford Press.

Davidson, R. J., Kabat-Zinn, J., Schumacher, J., Rosenkranz, M., Muller, D., Santorelli, S. F., et al. (2003). Alternations in brain and immune function produced by mindfulness meditation. *Psychosomatic Medicine, 65,* 564–570.

Davis, S., Votruba-Drzal, E., & Silk, J. S. (2015). Trajectories of internalizing symptoms from early childhood to adolescence: Associations with temperament and parenting. *Social Development, 24,* 501–520.

de Wolf, M. S., Theunissen, M. H., Vogels, A. G., & Reijneveld, S. A. (2013). Three questionnaires to detect psychosocial problems in toddlers: A comparison of the BITSEA, ASQ:SE, and KIPPPI. *Academic Pediatric Association, 13,* 587–592.

De Young, A. C., Kenardy, J. A., & Cobham, V. E. (2011). Diagnosis of posttraumatic stress disorder in preschool children. *Journal of Clinical Child and Adolescent Psychology, 40,* 375–384.

de Zulueta, F. (2007). The treatment of psychological trauma from the perspective of attachment research. In A. Hosin (Ed.), *Responses to traumatized children* (pp. 105–121). New York: Palgrave Macmillan.

Dishion, T. J., & Patterson, G. R. (1992). Age effects in parent training outcome. *Behavior Therapy, 23,* 719–729.

Domènech-Llaberia, E., Jané, C., Canals, J., Ballespí, S., Esparó, G., & Garralda, E. (2004). Parental reports of somatic symptoms in preschool children: Prevalence and associations in a Spanish sample. *Journal of the American Academy Of Child and Adolescent Psychiatry, 43,* 598–604.

Domitrovich, C. E., Cortes, R. C., & Greenberg, M. T. (2007). Improving young children's social and emotional competence: A randomized trial of the Preschool PATHS curriculum. *Journal of Primary Prevention, 2,* 67–91.

Doobay, A. (2008). School refusal behavior associated with separation anxiety disorder: A cognitive-behavioral approach to treatment. *Psychology in the Schools, 45,* 261–272.

Dowdy, E., Chin, J. K., & Quirk, M. P. (2013). An examination of the Behavioral and Emotional Screening System Preschool Teacher Form (BESS Preschool). *Journal of Psychoeducational Assessment, 31,* 578–584.

Dufrene, B. A., Parker, K. M., Menousek, K., Zhou, Q., Harpole, L. L., & Olmi, D. J. (2012). Direct behavioral consultation in Head Start to improve teacher use of praise and effective instruction delivery. *Journal of Educational and Psychological Consultation, 22,* 159–186.

Dumas, J. E. (2005). Mindfulness-based parent training: Strategies to lessen the grip of automaticity in families with disruptive children. *Journal of Clinical Child and Adolescent Psychology, 34,* 779–791.

Dumenci, L., McConaughy, S. H., & Achenbach, T. M. (2004). A hierarchical three-factor model of inattention–hyperactivity–impulsivity derived from the attention problems syndrome of the Teacher's Report Form. *School Psychology Review, 33,* 287–301.

Duncombe, M. E., Havighurst, S. S., Holland, K. A., & Frankling, E. J. (2012). The contribution of parenting practices and parent emotion factors in children at risk for disruptive behavior disorders. *Child Psychiatry and Human Development, 43,* 715–733.

DuPaul, G. J., Power, T. J., Anastopoulos, A. D., & Reid, R. (1998). *ADHD Rating Scale–IV: Checklists, norms, and clinical interpretation.* New York: Guilford Press.

DuPaul, G. J., Power, T. J., Anastopoulos, A. D., & Reid, R. (2016). *ADHD Rating Scale–5: Checklists, norms, and clinical interpretation.* New York: Guilford Press.

Durand, V. M. (2014). *Autism spectrum disorder: A clinical guide for general practitioners.* Washington, DC: American Psychological Association.

Durlak, J. A., Weissberg, R. P., Dymnicki, A. B., Taylor, R. D., & Schellinger, K. B. (2011). The impact of enhancing students' social and emotional learning: A meta-analysis of school-based universal interventions. *Child Development, 82,* 405–432.

Dymnicki, A., Sambolt, M., & Kidron, Y. (2013). *Improving college and career readiness by incorporating social and emotional learning.* Washington DC: American Institutes for Research. Retrieved from www.ccrscenter.org/sites/default/files/1528%20CCRS%20Brief%20d9_lvr.pdf.

Eagle, J. W., Dowd-Eagle, S. E., Snyder, A., & Holtzman, E. G. (2015). Implementing a multi-tiered system of support (MTSS): Collaboration between school psychologists and administrators to promote systems-level change. *Journal of Educational and Psychological Consultation, 25,* 160–177.

Egger, H. L., & Angold, A. (2004). The Preschool Age Psychiatric Assessment (PAPA): A structured parent interview for diagnosing psychiatric disorders in preschool children. In R. DelCarmen-Wiggins & A. Carter (Eds.), *Handbook of infant, toddler, and preschool mental health assessment* (pp. 223–243). New York: Oxford University Press.

Egger, H. L., Erkanli, A., Keeler, G., Potts, E., Walter, B. K., & Angold, A. (2006). Test–retest reliability of the Preschool Age Psychiatric Assessment (PAPA). *Journal of the American Academy of Child and Adolescent Psychiatry, 45,* 538–549.

Ehrenreich-May, J., & Chu, B. C. (2014). Overview of transdiagnostic mechanisms and treatments for youth psychopathology. In J. Ehrenreich-May & B. C. Chu (Eds.), *Transdiagnostic treatments for children and adolescents: Principles and practice* (pp. 3–14). New York: Guilford Press.

Eisenstadt, T. H., Eyberg, S., McNeil, C. B., Newcomb, K., & Funderburk, B. (1993). Parent-child interaction therapy with behavior problem children: Relative effectiveness of two stages and overall treatment outcome. *Journal of Clinical Child Psychology, 22,* 42–51.

Elliott, S. N., & Gresham, F. M. (2008). *Social Skills Improvement System (SSIS).* San Antonio, TX: Pearson.

Ennis, R. P., Schwab, J. R., & Jolivette, K. (2012). Using precorrection as a secondary-tier intervention for reducing problem behaviors in instructional and noninstructional settings. *Beyond Behavior, 22,* 40–47.

Essau, C., Olaya, B., & Ollendick, T. H. (2013). Classification of anxiety disorders in children and adolscents. In C. A. Essau & T. H. Ollendick (Eds.), *Wiley–Blackwell handbook of the treatment of childhood and adolescent anxiety* (pp. 1–21). Malden, MA: Wiley.

Eyberg, S. M., Nelson, M. M., & Boggs, S. R. (2008). Evidence-based psychosocial treatments for children and adolescents with disruptive behavior. *Journal of Clinical Child and Adolescent Psychology, 37,* 215–237.

Eyberg, S. M., & Pincus, D. (1999). *Eyberg Child Behavior Inventory and Sutter–Eyberg Student Behavior Inventory—Revised: Professional manual.* Odessa, FL: Psychological Assessment Resources.

Ezpeleta, L., Granero, R., Osa, N., Trepat, E., & Doménech, J. M. (2016). Trajectories of oppositional defiant disorder irritability symptoms in preschool children. *Journal of Abnormal Child Psychology, 44,* 115–128.

Fabiano, G. A., Pelham, W. E., Coles, E. K., Gnagy, E. M., Chronis-Tuscano, A., & O'Connor, B. C. (2009). A meta-analysis of behavioral treatments for attention-deficit/hyperactivity disorder. *Clinical Psychology Review, 29,* 129–140.

Fearon, R. P., Bakermans-Kranenburg, M. J., van IJzendoorn, M. H., Lapsley, A., & Roisman, G. I. (2010). The significance of insecure attachment and disorganization in the development of children s externalizing behavior: A meta-analytic study. *Child Development, 81,* 435–456.

Feil, E. G., Severson, H. H., & Walker, H. M. (1998). Screening for emotional and behavioral delays: Early screening project. *Journal of Early Intervention, 21,* 252–266.

Feil, E. G., Walker, H. M., & Severson, H. H. (1995). The early screening project for young children with behavioral problems. *Journal of Emotional and Behavioral Disorders, 3,* 194–202.

Ferguson, C. (2005). *Reaching out to diverse populations: What can schools do to foster family–school connections?* Austin, TX: Southwest Educational Development Laboratory. Retrieved from *www.sedl.org/pubs/catalog/items/fam103.html.*

Fergusson, D. M., Horwood, L. J., & Ridder, E. M. (2005). Show me the child at seven: The consequences of conduct problems in childhood for psychosocial functioning in adulthood. *Journal of Child Psychology and Psychiatry, 46,* 837–849.

Finkelhor, D. (2007). Developmental victimology: The comprehensive study of childhood victimization. In R. C. David, A. J. Lurigio, & S. Herman (Eds.), *Victims of crime* (3rd ed., pp. 9–34). Thousand Oaks, CA: SAGE.

Flook, L., Goldberg, S., Pinger, L., & Davidson, R. (2015). Promoting prosocial behavior and self-regulatory skills in preschool children through a mindfulness-based kindness curriculum. *Developmental Psychology, 51,* 44–51.

Flora, S. R. (2000). Praise's magic reinforcement ratio: Five to one gets the job done. *Behavior Analyst Today, 1,* 64–69.

Forman, S. G., Olin, S. S., Hoagwood, K. E., Crowe, M., & Saka, N. (2009). Evidence-based interventions in schools: Developers' views of implementation barriers and facilitators. *School Mental Health, 1,* 26–36.

Franz, L., Angold, A., Copeland, W., Costello, E. J., Towe-Goodman, N., & Egger, H. (2013). Preschool anxiety disorders in pediatric primary care: Prevalence and comorbidity. *Journal of the American Academy of Child and Adolescent Psychiatry, 52,* 1294–1303.

Frey, J. R., Elliott, S. N., & Gresham, F. M. (2011). Preschoolers' social skills: Advances in assessment for intervention using social behavior ratings. *School Mental Health, 3,* 179–190.

Frick, P. J., Barry, C. T., & Kamphaus, R. W. (2010). *Clinical assessment of child and adolescent personality and behavior* (3rd ed.). New York: Springer.

Friedberg, R., Gorman, A., Hollar Witt, L., Biuckian, A., & Murray, M. (2011). *Cognitive behavioral therapy for the busy child psychiatrist and other mental health professionals: Rubrics and rudiments.* New York: Routledge.

Friedman-Krauss, A. H., Raver, C. C., Morris, P. A., & Jones, S. M. (2014). The role of classroom-level child behavior problems in predicting preschool teacher stress and classroom emotional climate. *Early Education and Development, 25,* 530–552.

Friman, P. C., Hoff, K. E., Schnoes, C., Freeman, K. A., Woods, D. W., & Blum, N. (1999). The bedtime pass: An approach to bedtime crying and leaving the room. *Archives of Pediatric and Adolescent Medicine, 153,* 1027–1029.

Friman, P. C., Hofstadter, K. L., & Jones, K. M. (2006). A biobehavioral approach to the treatment of functional encopresis in children. *Journal of Early and Intensive Behavior Intervention, 3,* 263–272.

Funderburk, B. W., Eyberg, S. M., Rich, B. A., & Behar, L. (2003). Further psychometric evaluation of the Eyberg and Behar rating scales for parents and teachers of preschoolers. *Early Education and Development, 14,* 67–81.

Gable, R., Hester, P., Rock, M., & Hughes, K. (2009). Back to basics: Rules, praise, ignoring, and reprimands revisited. *Intervention in School and Clinic, 44,* 195–205.

Garbarino, J., Stott, F., & Faculty of the Erikson Institute. (1992). *What children can tell us.* San Francisco: Jossey-Bass.

Garber, S. W., Garber, M. D., & Spizman, R. F. (1992). *Good behavior made easy handbook.* Glastonbury, CT: Great Pond.

Gerhardt, P. F., Weiss, M. J., & Delmolino, L. (2004). Treatment of severe aggression in an adolescent with autism: Non-contingent reinforcement and functional communication training. *Behavior Analyst Today, 4,* 386–394.

Germer, C. (2009). *The mindful path to self-compassion: Freeing yourself from destructive thoughts and emotions.* New York: Guilford Press.

Gettinger, M., & Stoiber, K. (2007). Applying a response-to-intervention model for early literacy development in low-income children. *Topics in Early Childhood Special Education, 27,* 198–213.

Gil, E. (2010). *Working with children to heal interpersonal trauma: The power of play.* New York: Guilford Press.

Gilliam, J. E. (2013). *GARS-3: Gilliam Autism Rating Scale—Third edition.* Austin, TX: PRO-ED.

Gilliam, W. S. (2005). *Prekindergartners left behind: Expulsion rates in state prekindergarten systems.* New York: Foundation for Child Development.

Gottman, J. M., & Levenson, R. W. (1992). Marital processes predictive of later dissolution: Behavior, physiology, and health. *Journal of Personality and Social Psychology, 63,* 221–233.

Gray, S. O., Carter, A. S., Briggs-Gowan, M. J., Jones, S. M., & Wagmiller, R. L. (2014). Growth trajectories of early aggression, overactivity, and inattention: Relations to second-grade reading. *Developmental Psychology, 50,* 2255–2263.

Green, A. D., Alioto, A., Mousa, H., & Di Lorenzo, C. (2011). Severe pediatric rumination syndrome: Successful interdisciplinary inpatient management. *Journal of Pediatric Gastroenterology and Nutrition, 52,* 414–418.

Greenberg, M. T., Kusché, C. A., Cook, E. T., & Quamma, J. P. (1995). Promoting emotional competence in school-aged children: The effects of the PATHS curriculum. *Development and Psychopathology, 7,* 117–136.

Greenberg, M. T., Weissberg, R. P., O'Brien, M. U., Fredericks, L., Resnick, H., & Elias, M. J. (2003). Enhancing school-based prevention and youth development through coordinated social, emotional, and academic learning. *American Psychologist, 58,* 466–474.

Greenhill, L., Kollins, S., Abikoff, H., McCracken, J., Riddle, M., Swanson, J., et al. (2006). Efficacy and safety of immediate-release methylphenidate treatment for preschoolers with ADHD. *Journal of the American Academy of Child and Adolescent Psychiatry, 45,* 1284–1293.

Greenspan, S. I., & Greenspan, N. T. (2003). *Clinical interview of the child* (2nd ed.). Washington, DC: American Psychiatric Press.

Greenwood, C. R., Carta, J. J., Goldstein, H., Kaminski, R. A., McConnell, S. R., & Atwater, J. (2014). The center for response to intervention in early childhood: Developing evidence-based tools for a multi-tier approach to preschool language and early literacy instruction. *Journal of Early Intervention, 36,* 246–262.

Gregory, A. M., & O'Connor, T. G. (2002). Sleep problems in childhood: A longitudinal study of developmental change and association with behavioral problems. *Journal of the American Academy of Child and AdolescentPsychiatry, 41,* 964–971.

Gresham, F. M., & Elliott, S. N. (2008). *The Social Skills Rating System.* Circle Pines, MN: American Guidance.

Gresham, F. M., Elliott, S. N., Vance, M. J., & Cook, C. R. (2011). Comparability of the social skills rating system to the social skills improvement system: Content and psychometric comparisons across elementary and secondary age levels. *School Psychology Quarterly, 26,* 27–44.

Gresham, F. M., Elliott, S. N., Cook, C. R., Vance, M. J., & Kettler, R. (2010). Cross-informant agreement for ratings for social skill and problem behavior ratings: An investigation of the Social Skills Improvement System—Rating Scales. *Psychological Assessment, 22,* 157–166.

Gresham, F. M., & Lambros, K. M. (1998). Behavioral and functional assessment. In T. S. Watson & F. M. Gresham (Eds.), *Handbook of child behavior therapy* (pp. 3–22). New York: Plenum Press.

Griest, D. L., Forehand, R., Rogers, T., Breiner, J., Furey, W., & Williams, C. A. (1982). Effects of parent enhancement therapy on the treatment outcome and generalization of a parent training program. *Behaviour Research and Therapy, 20,* 429–436.

Groh, A. M., Roisman, G. I., van IJzendoorn, M. H., Bakermans-Kranenburg, M. J., & Fearon, R. P. (2012). The significance of insecure and disorganized attachment for children's internalizing symptoms: A meta-analytic study. *Child Development, 83,* 591–610.

Gross, D., Fogg, L., Young, M., Ridge, A., Cowell, J., Sivan, A., et al. (2007). Reliability and validity of the Eyberg Child Behavior Inventory with African American and Latino parents of young children. *Research in Nursing and Health, 30,* 213–223.

Gunther, L., Caldarella, P., Kerth, B., & Young, K. R. (2012). Promoting social and emotional learning in preschool students: A study of Strong Start Pre-K. *Early Childhood Journal of Education, 40,* 151–159.

Hanf, C. (1969, June). *A two-stage program for modifying maternal controlling during mother–child (M-C) interaction.* Paper presented at the annual meeting of the Western Psychological Association, Vancouver, British Columbia, Canada.

Hanson, R., & Mendius, R. (2009). *Buddha's brain: The practical neuroscience of happiness, love, and wisdom.* Oakland, CA: New Harbinger.

Harari, M. D. (2013). Nocturnal enuresis. *Journal of Paediatrics and Child Health, 49,* 264–271.

Hardy, K. K., Kollins, S. H., Murray, D. W., Riddle, M. A., Greenhill, L., Cunningham, C., et al. (2007). Factor structure of parent- and teacher-rated attention-deficit/hyperactivity disorder symptoms in the Preschoolers with Attention-Deficit/Hyperactivity Disorder Treatment Study (PATS). *Journal of Child and Adolescent Psychopharmacology, 17,* 621–633.

Harnett, P. H., & Dawe, S. (2012). Review: The contribution of mindfulness-based therapies for children and families and proposed conceptual integration. *Child and Adolescent Mental Health, 17,* 195–208.

Harrell-Williams, L. M., Raines, T. C., Kamphaus, R. W., & Denver, B. V. (2015). Psychometric analysis of the BASC-2 Behavioral and Emotional Screening System (BESS) student form: Results from high school student samples. *Psychological Assessment, 27,* 738–743.

Hart, S. R., Dowdy, E., Eklund, K., Renshaw, T. L., Jimerson, S. R., Jones, C., et al. (2009). A controlled study assessing the effects of the impulse control and problem solving unit of the Second Step curriculum. *California School Psychologist, 14,* 105–110.

Hastings, P. D., Helm, J., Mills, R. L., Serbin, L. A., Stack, D. M., & Schwartzman, A. E. (2015). Dispositional and environmental predictors of the development of internalizing problems in childhood: Testing a multilevel model. *Journal of Abnormal Child Psychology, 43,* 831–845.0

Hayes, S. C., Strosahl, K. D., & Wilson, K. G. (1999). *Acceptance and commitment therapy: An experiential approach to behavior.* New York: Guilford Press.

Hayes, S. C., Strosahl, K. D., & Wilson, K. G. (2012). *Acceptance and commitment therapy: The process and practice of mindful change* (2nd ed.). New York: Guilford Press.

Heberle, A. E., Krill, S. C., Briggs-Gowan, M. J., & Carter, A. S. (2015). Predicting externalizing and internalizing behavior in kindergarten: Examining the buffering role of early social support. *Journal of Clinical Child and Adolescent Psychology, 44,* 640–654.

Heinrichs, N., Kliem, S., & Hahlweg, K. (2014). Four-year follow-up of a randomized controlled trial of triple P group for parent and child outcomes. *Prevention Science, 15,* 233–245.

Hemmeter, M. L., Ostrosky, M. M., & Corso, R. M. (2012). Preventing and addressing challenging behavior: Common questions and practical strategies. *Young Exceptional Children, 15,* 32–46.

Henricsson, L., & Rydell, A. (2006). Children with behaviour problems: The influence of social competence and social relations on problem stability, school achievement and peer acceptance across the first six years of school. *Infant and Child Development, 15,* 347–366.

Heo, K., & Squires, J. (2012). Adaptation of a parent-completed social emotional screening instrument for young children: Ages and Stages Questionnaires–Social Emotional. *Early Human Development, 88,* 151–158.

Hess, R. S., Pejic, V., & Castejon, K. S. (2014). Best practices in delivering culturally responsive, tiered-level supports for youth with behavioral challenges. In P. L. Harrison & A. Thomas (Eds.), *Best practices in school psychology: Student-level services* (pp. 321–334). Bethesda, MD: National Association of School Psychologists.

Higa-McMillan, C. K., Francis, S. E., & Chorpita, B. F. (2014). Anxiety disorders. In E. J. Mash & R. A. Barkley (Eds.), *Child psychopathology* (3rd ed., pp. 345–428). New York: Guilford Press.

Higa-McMillan, C. K., Francis, S., Rith-Najarian, L., & Chorpita, B. F. (2016). Evidence base update: 50 years of research on treatment for child and adolescent anxiety. *Journal of Clinical Child and Adolescent Psychology, 45,* 91–113.

Hirschland, D. (2008). *Collaborative intervention in early childhood: Consulting with parents and teachers of 3- to 7-year-olds.* New York: Oxford University Press.

Hirshfeld-Becker, D. R., Biederman, J., Henin, A., Faraone, S. V., Davis, S., Harrington, K., et al. (2007). Behavioral inhibition in preschool children at risk is a specific predictor of middle childhood social anxiety: A five-year follow-up. *Journal of Developmental and Behavioral Pediatrics, 28,* 225–233.

Hirshfeld-Becker, D. R., Masek, B., Henin, A., Blakely, L. R., Pollock-Wurman, R. A., McQude, J., et al. (2010). Cognitive-behavioral therapy for 4- to 7-year-old children with anxiety disorders: A randomized clinical trial. *Journal of Consulting and Clinical Psychology, 78,* 498–510.

Hofstra, M. B., van der Ende, J., & Verhulst, F. C. (2002). Child and adolescent problems predict DSM-IV disorders in adulthood: A 14-year follow-up of a Dutch epidemiological sample. *Journal of the American Academy of Child and Adolescent Psychiatry, 41,* 182–189.

Honaker, S., & Meltzer, L. (2014). Bedtime problems and night wakings in young children: An update of the evidence. *Paediatric Respiratory Reviews, 15,* 333–339.

Hong, J. S., Tillman, R., & Luby, J. L. (2015). Disruptive behavior in preschool children: Distinguishing normal misbehavior from markers of current and later childhood conduct disorder. *Journal of Pediatrics, 166,* 723–730.

Horner, R., Sugai, G., Smolkowski, K., Todd, A., Nakasato, J., & Esperanza, J. (2009). A randomized control trial of school-wide positive behavior support in elementary schools. *Journal of Positive Behavior Interventions, 11,* 113–144.

Huberty, T. J. (2008). Best practices in school-based interventions for anxiety and depression. In A. Thomas & J. Grimes (Eds.), *Best practices in school psychology V* (pp. 1473–1486). Bethesda, MD: National Association of School Psychologists.

Huberty, T. J. (2010). Anxiety and anxiety disorders in children. In A. Canter, L. Paige, & S. Shaw (Eds.), *NASP Helping Children at Home and School III: Handouts for families and educators* (p. S5H2). Bethesda, MD: National Association of School Psychologists.

Huberty, T. J. (2013). Best practices in school-based interventions for anxiety and depression. In P. Harrison & A. Thomas (Eds.), *Best practices in school psychology: Student-level services* (pp. 349–363). Bethesda, MD: National Association of School Psychologists.

Hughes, J. N., & Baker, D. B. (1990). *The clinical child interview.* New York: Guilford Press.

Hurlburt, M. S., Nguyen, K., Reid, J., Webster-Stratton, C., & & Zhang, J. (2013). Efficacy of the Incredible Years group parent program with families in Head Start who self-reported a history of child maltreatment. *Child Abuse and Neglect, 37,* 531–543.

The Incredible Years. (2013). The incredible year series: Parents, teachers, and children training series. Retrieved from *http://incredibleyears.com/about/incredible-years-series.*

Institute of Medicine. (2011). *Early childhood obesity prevention policies.* Washington, DC: National Academies Press.

Invernizzi, M., Landrum, T. J., Teichman, A., & Townsend, M. (2010). Increased implementation of emergent literacy screening in pre-kindergarten. *Early Childhood Education Journal, 37,* 437–446.

Invernizzi, M., Sullivan, A., Meier, J., & Swank, L. (2004). *Phonological awareness and literacy screening: Preschool (PALS–PreK).* Charlottesville: University of Virginia Press.

Ireland, J., Sanders, M., & Markie-Dadds, C. (2003). The impact of parent training on marital functioning: A comparison of two group versions of the Triple P Positive Parenting Program for parents of children with early-onset conduct problems. *Behavioural and Cognitive Psychotherapy, 31,* 127–142.

Jackson, R., McCoy, A., Pistorino, C., Wilkinson, A., Burghardt, J., Clark, M.,et al. (2007). *National evaluation of Early Reading First: Final report.* Washington, DC: U.S. Government Printing Office. Available at *http://ies.ed.gov/ncee/pdf/20074007.pdf.*

James, S., & Mennen, F. (2001). Treatment outcome research: How effective are treatments for abused children? *Child and Adolescent Social Work Journal, 18,* 73–95.

Jones, S. M., & Bouffard, S. M. (2012). Social and emotional learning in schools: From programs to strategies. *Social Policy Report, 26,* 3–22.

Juntunen, V. R. (2013). *Child abuse sourcebook* (3rd ed). Detroit, MI: Omnigraphics.

Jurbergs, N., Palcic, J., & Kelley, M. L. (2007). School-home notes with and without response cost: Increasing attention and academic performance in low-income children with attention-deficit/hyperactivity disorder. *School Psychology Quarterly, 22,* 358–379.

Kabat-Zinn, J. (1990). *Full catastrophe living: Using the wisdom of your body and mind to face stress, pain, and illness.* New York: Bantam Dell.

Kabat-Zinn, M. (1994). *Wherever you go, there you are: Mindfulness meditation in everyday life.* New York: Hyperion.

Kam, C. M., Greenberg, M. T., & Walls, C. T. (2003). Examining the role of implementation quality in school-based prevention using the PATHS curriculum. *Prevention Science, 4,* 55–63.

Kaminski, J. W., Valle, L. A., Filene, J. H., & Boyle, C. L. (2008). A meta-analytic review of components associated with parent training effectiveness. *Journal of Abnormal Child Psychology, 36,* 567–589.

Kaminski, R. A., Abbott, M., Bravo Aguayo, K., Latimer, R., & Good, R. I. (2014). The Preschool Early Literacy Indicators: Validity and benchmark goals. *Topics in Early Childhood Special Education, 34,* 71–82.

Kaminski, R. A., Powell-Smith, K. A., Hommel, A., McMahon, R., & Bravo Aguayo, K. (2014). Development of a tier 3 curriculum to teach early literacy skills. *Journal of Early Intervention, 36,* 313–332.

Kamphaus, R. W., & Reynolds, C. R. (2015). *BASC-3 Behavioral and Emotional Screening System, 3rd ed. (BESS-3).* San Antonio, TX: Pearson.

Katzmarzyk, P. T., Barreira, T. V., Broyles, S. T., Champagne, C. M., Chaput, J., Fogelholm, M., et al. (2015). Relationship between lifestyle behaviors and obesity in children ages 9–11: Results from a 12-country study. *Obesity, 23,* 1696–1702.

Kazdin, A. E. (2010). Problem-solving skills training and parent management training for oppositional defiant disorder and conduct disorder. In J. R. Weisz & A. E. Kazdin (Eds.), *Evidence-based psychotherapies for children and adolescents* (2nd ed., pp. 211–226). New York: Guilford Press.

Kazdin, A. E. (2012). *Behavior modification in applied settings* (7th ed.). Long Grove, IL: Waveland Press.

Kearney, C. (2006). Dealing with school refusal behavior: A primer for family physicians. *Journal of Family Practice, 55,* 685–692.

Kearney, C. A., & Spear, M. (2013). Assessment of selective mutism and school refusal behavior. In D. McKay & E. A. Storch (Eds.), *Handbook of assessing variants and complications in anxiety disorder* (pp. 29–42). New York: Springer.

Kedesdy, J. H., & Budd, K. S. (1998). *Childhood feeding disorders: Biobehavioral assessment and intervention.* Baltimore: Brookes.

Kehle, T., Bray, M., & Theodore, L. (2010). Selective mutism: A primer for parents and educators. In A. Canter, L. Paige, & S. Shaw (Eds.), *NASP Helping Children at Home and School II: Handouts for families and educators* (p. S8H36). Bethesda, MD: National Association of School Psychologists.

Keith, L. K., & Campbell, J. M. (2000). Assessment of social and emotional development in preschool children. In B. A. Bracken (Ed.), *The psychoeducational assessment of preschool children* (3rd ed., pp. 364–382). Boston: Allyn & Bacon.

Kelly R., & El-Sheikh M. (2011). Marital conflict and children's sleep: Reciprocal relations and socioeconomic effects. *Journal of Family Psychology, 25,* 412–422.

Kiddoo, D. A. (2012). Toilet training children: When to start and how to train. *Canadian Medical Association Journal, 184,* 511–511.

Kim-Cohen, J., Arseneault, L., Newcombe, R., Adams, F., Bolton, H., Cant, L., et al. (2009). Five-year predictive validity of DSM-IV conduct disorder research diagnosis in 4½–5-year-old children. *European Child and Adolescent Psychiatry, 18,* 284–291.

King, N., Heyne, D., Gullone, E., & Molloy, G. (2001). Usefulness of emotive imagery in the treatment of childhood phobias: Clinical guidelines, case examples and issues. *Counseling Psychology Quarterly, 14,* 95–101.

King, N., Tonge, B. J., Mullen, P., Myseron, N., Heyne, D., Rollings, S., et al. (2000). Sexually abused children and post-traumatic stress disorder. *Counselling Psychology Quarterly, 13,* 365–375.

Knell, S. M. (2000). Cognitive-behavioral play therapy for childhood fears and phobias. In H. G. Kaduson & C. E. Schaefer (Eds.), *Short-term play therapy for children* (pp. 3–27). New York: Guilford Press.

Kolko, D. J., & Lindhiem, O. (2014). Introduction to the special series on booster sessions and long-term maintenance of treatment gains. *Journal of Abnormal Child Psychology, 42,* 339–342.

Kollins, S., Greenhill, L., Swanson, J., Wigal, S., Abikoff, H., McCracken, J., et al. (2006). Rationale, design, and methods of the Preschool ADHD Treatment Study (PATS). *Journal of the American Academy of Child and Adolescent Psychiatry, 45,* 1275–1283.

Kowalewicz, E. A., & Coffee, G. (2014). Mystery motivator: A tier 1 classroom behavioral intervention. *School Psychology Quarterly, 29,* 138–156.

Kramer, T., Caldarella, P., Christensen, L., & Shatzer, R. (2011). Social and emotional learning in the kindergarten classroom. Evaluation of the Strong Start curriculum. *Early Childhood Education Journal, 37,* 303–309.

Kuhn, B. R., Marcus, B. A., & Pitner, S. L. (1999). Treatment guidelines for primary nonretentive encopresis and stool toileting refusal. *American Family Physician, 59,* 2171.

Kuhn, B. R., & Weidinger, D. (2000). Interventions for infant and toddler sleep disturbance: A review. *Child and Family Behavior Therapy, 22,* 33–50.

Kwon, K., Kim, E., & Sheridan, S. (2012). Behavioral competence and academic functioning among early elementary children with externalizing problems. *School Psychology Review, 41,* 123–140.

Lahey, B. B., Pelham, W. E., Loney, J., Lee, S. S., & Willcutt, E. (2005). Instability of the DSM-IV subtypes of ADHD from preschool through elementary school. *Archives of General Psychiatry, 62,* 896–902.

Lamont, J. H., Devore, C. D., Allison, M., Ancona, R., Barnett, S. E., Gunther, R., et al. (2013). Out-of-school suspension and expulsion. *Pediatrics, 131,* e1000–e1007.

Lane, B., Paynter, J., & Sharman, R. (2013). Parent and teacher ratings of adaptive and challenging behaviors in young children with autism spectrum disorders. *Research in Autism Spectrum Disorders, 7,* 1196–1203.

Lang, R., Mulloy, A., Giesbers, S., Pfeiffer, B., Dulaune, E., Didden, R., et al. (2011). Behavioral interventions for rumination and operant vomiting in individuals with intellectual disabilities: A systematic review. *Research in Developmental Disabilities, 32,* 2193–2205.

Laughlin, L. (2013). *Who's minding the kids?: Child care arrangements: Spring 2011* (Current Population Reports, P70–135). Washington, DC: U.S. Census Bureau.

Lavigne, J. V., Bryant, F. B., Hopkins, J., & Gouze, K. R. (2015). Dimensions of oppositional defiant disorder in young children: Model comparisons, gender and longitudinal invariance. *Journal of Abnormal Child Psychology, 43,* 423–439.

Lavigne, J. V., LeBailly, S. A., Gouze, K. R., Binns, H. J., Keller, J., & Pate, L. (2010). Predictors and correlates of completing behavioral parent training for the treatment of oppositional defiant disorder. *Behavior Therapy, 41,* 198–211.

Lavigne, J. V., LeBailly, S. A., Hopkins, J., Gouze, K. R., & Binns, H. J. (2009). The prevalence of ADHD,

ODD, depression, and anxiety in a community sample of 4-year-olds. *Journal of Clinical Child and Adolescent Psychology, 38,* 315–328.

Lazar, S. W., Bush, G., Gollub, R. L., Fricchione, G. L., Khalsa, G., Benson, H. (2000). Functional brain mapping of the relaxation response and meditation. *NeuroReport, 11,* 1581–1585.

LeBeauf, I., Smaby, M., & Maddux, C. (2009). Adapting counseling skills for multicultural and diverse clients. In G. R. Walz, J. C. Bleuer, & R. K. Yep (Eds.), *Compelling counseling interventions: VISTA 2009* (pp. 33–42). Alexandria, VA: American Counseling Association.

LeBuffe, P. A., & Naglieri, J. A. (2012). *Devereux early childhood assessment for preschoolers, second edition.* Lewisville, NC: Kaplan Early Learning Company.

Lenze, S. N., Pautsch, J., & Luby, J. (2011). Parent-child interaction therapy emotion development: A novel treatment for depression in preschool children. *Depression and Anxiety, 28,* 153–159.

Levitt, J. M., Saka, N., Romanelli, L. H., & Hoagwood, K. (2007). Early identification of mental health problems in schools: The status of implementation. *Journal of School Psychology, 45,* 63–191.

Lewin, A. B. (2011). Parent training for childhood anxiety. In D. M. McKay & E. A. Storch (Eds.), *Handbook of child and adolescent anxiety disorders* (pp. 405–418). New York: Springer.

Lewis, G., Rice, F., Harold, G., Collishaw, S., & Thapar, A. (2011). Investigating environmental links between parent depression and child depressive/anxiety symptoms using an assisted conception design. *Journal of the American Academy of Child and Adolescent Psychiatry, 50,* 451–459.

Lin, Y., & Bratton, S. C. (2015). A meta-analytic review of child-centered play therapy approaches. *Journal of Counseling and Development, 93,* 45–58.

Linscheid, T. R. (2006). Behavioral treatments for pediatric feeding disorders. *Behavior Modification, 30,* 6–23.

Loeber, R., & Burke, J. D. (2011). Developmental pathways in juvenile externalizing and internalizing problems. *Journal of Research on Adolescence, 21,* 34–46.

Lord, C., Rutter, M., DiLavore, R., Gotham, K., & Bishop, S. (2012). *Autism diagnostic observation schedule, 2nd edition.* Torrance, CA: Western Psychological Services.

Lowenstein, L. (2011). The complexity of investigating possible sexual abuse of a child. *American Journal of Family Therapy, 39,* 292–298.

Luby, J. (2013). Treatment of anxiety and depression in the preschool period. *Journal of the American Academy of Child and Adolescent Psychiatry, 52,* 346–358.

Luby, J. L. (2000). Depression. In C. H. Zeanah (Ed.), *Handbook of infant mental health* (2nd ed., pp. 382–396). New York: Guilford Press.

Lucas, C., Fisher, P., & Luby, J. (1998). *Young-Child DISC-IV Research Draft: Diagnostic Interview Schedule for Children.* New York: Columbia University, Division of Child Psychiatry, Joy and William Ruane Center to Identify and Treat Mood Disorders.

Lundahl, B., Risser, H. J., & Lovejoy, C. (2006). A meta-analysis of parent training: Moderators and follow-up effects. *Clinical Psychology Review, 26,* 86–104.

Lundahl, B. W., Kunz, C., Brownell, C., Tollefson, D., & Burke, B. L. (2010). A meta-analysis of motivational interviewing: Twenty-five years of empirical studies. *Research on Social Work Practice, 20,* 137–160.

Luoma, J. B., Hayes, S. C., & Walser, R. D. (2007). *Learning ACT: An acceptance and commitment therapy skills-training manual for therapists.* Oakland, CA: New Harbinger.

Maggin, D. M., Zurheide, J., Pickett, K. C., & Baillie, S. J. (2015). A systematic evidence review of the check-in/check-out program for reducing student challenging behaviors. *Journal of Positive Behavior Interventions, 17,* 197–208.

Manassis, K. (2013). Empirically supported psychosocial treatments. In C. A. Essau & T. H. Ollendick (Eds.) *Wiley–Blackwell handbook of the treatment of childhood and adolescent anxiety* (pp. 207–228). Malden, MA: Wiley.

Manikam, R., & Perman, J. A. (2000). Pediatric feeding disorders. *Journal of Clinical Gastroenterology, 30,* 34–46.

Marakovitz, S. E., Wagmiller, R. L., Mian, N. D., Briggs-Gowan, M. J., & Carter, A. S. (2011). Lost toy? Monsters under the bed?: Contributions of temperament and family factors to early internalizing problems in boys and girls. *Journal of Clinical Child and Adolescent Psychology, 40,* 233–244.

Marchant, M., Brown, M., Caldarella, P., & Young, E. (2010). Effects of Strong Kids curriculum on students with internalizing behaviors: A pilot study. *Journal of Evidence-Based Practices for Schools, 11,* 123–143.

Marchant, R. (2013). How young is too young? The evidence of children under five in the English criminal justice system. *Child Abuse Review, 22,* 432–445.

Marks, I. (2013). *Fears and phobias.* New York: Academic Press.

Martel, M. M., von Eye, A., & Nigg, J. T. (2010). Revisiting the latent structure of ADHD: Is there a 'g' factor? *Journal of Child Psychology and Psychiatry, 51,* 905–914.

Mattila, M., Hurtig, T., Haapsamo, H., Jussila, K., Kuusikko-Gauffin, S., Kielinen, M., et al. (2010). Comorbid psychiatric disorders associated with Asperger syndrome/high-functioning autism: A community- and clinic-based study. *Journal of Autism and Developmental Disorders, 40,* 1080–1093.

Maughan, D. R., Christiansen, E., Jenson, W. R., Olympia, D., & Clark, E. (2005). Behavioral parent training as a treatment for externalizing behaviors and disruptive behavior disorders: A meta-analysis. *School Psychology Review, 34,* 267–286.

Mazza, J. (2014). Best practices in clinical interviewing parents, teachers and students. In P. L. Harrison & A. Thomas (Eds.), *Best practices in school psychology: Data-based and collaborative decision making* (pp. 317–330). Bethesda, MD: National Association of School Psychologists.

McCarney, S. B. (1995a). *The Early Childhood Attention Deficit Disorders Evaluation Scale, home version, technical manual.* Columbia, MO: Hawthorne.

McCarney, S. B. (1995b). *The Early Childhood Attention Deficit Disorders Evaluation Scale, school version, technical manual.* Columbia, MO: Hawthorne.

McCarney, S. B., & Arthaud, T. (2013a). *The Attention Deficit Disorders Evaluation Scale-Fourth Edition, home version, technical manual.* Columbia, MO: Hawthorne.

McCarney, S. B., & Arthaud, T. (2013b). *The Attention Deficit Disorders Evaluation Scale-Fourth Edition, school version, technical manual.* Columbia, MO: Hawthorne.

McCart, M. R., Priester, P. E., Davies, W. H., & Azen, R. (2006). Differential effectiveness of behavioral parent-training and cognitive-behavioral therapy for antisocial youth: A meta-analysis. *Journal of Abnormal Child Psychology, 34,* 525–541.

McConaughy, S. (2013). *Clinical interviews for children and adolescents* (2nd ed.). New York: Guilford Press.

McGinnis, E. (2011). *Skillstreaming in early childhood: A guide for teaching social skills* (3rd ed.). Champaign, IL: Research Press.

McGoey, K. E., & DuPaul, G. J. (2000). Token reinforcement and response cost procedures: Reducing the disruptive behavior of preschool children with attention-deficit/hyperactivity disorder. *School Psychology Quarterly, 15,* 330–343.

McGoey, K. E., DuPaul, G. J., Haley, E., & Shelton, T. L. (2007). Parent and teacher ratings of attention-deficit/hyperactivity disorder in preschool: The ADHD-Rating Scale–IV Preschool Version. *Journal of Psychopathological Behavioral Assessment, 29,* 269–276.

McIntosh, K., Herman, K., Sanford, A., McGraw, K., & Florence, K. (2004). Teaching transitions: Techniques for promoting success between lessons. *Teaching Exceptional Children, 37,* 32–38.

McMahon, R. J., & Forehand, R. L. (2003). *Helping the noncompliant child: Family-based treatment for oppositional behavior* (2nd ed.). New York: Guilford Press.

McNeil, C. B., & Kembree-Kigin, T. L. (2011). *Parent–child interaction therapy: Issues in clinical child psychology* (2nd ed.). New York: Springer.

McWayne, C., & Cheung, K. (2009). A picture of strength: Preschool competencies mediate the effects of early behavior problems on later academic and social adjustment for Head Start children. *Journal of Applied Developmental Psychology, 30,* 273–285.

Meiser-Stedman, R., Smith, P., Glucksman, E., Yule, W., & Dalgleish, T. (2008). The posttraumatic stress disorder diagnosis in preschool- and elementary school-age children exposed to motor vehicle accidents. *American Journal of Psychiatry, 165,* 1326–1337.

Meltzer, H., Vostanis, P., Dogra, N., Doos, L., Ford, T., & Goodman, R. (2009). Children's specific fears. *Child: Care, Health and Development, 35,* 781–789.

Meltzer, L. J., & Crabtree, V. M. (2015). *Pediatric sleep problems: A clinician's guide to behavioral interventions.* Washington, DC: American Psychological Association.

Meltzer, L. J., & Mindell, J. A. (2006). Sleep and sleep disorders in children and adolescents. *Psychiatric Clinics of North America, 29,* 1059–1076.

Meltzer, L. J., & Mindell, J. A. (2014). Systematic review and meta-analysis of behavioral interventions for pediatric insomnia. *Journal of Pediatric Psychology, 39,* 932–948.

Menting, A. T., de Castro, B. O., & Matthys, W. (2013). Effectiveness of the Incredible Years parent training to modify disruptive and prosocial child behavior: A meta-analytic review. *Clinical Psychology Review, 33*(8), 901–913.

Merrell, K. W. (2003). *Preschool and Kindergarten Behavior Scales, 2nd Edition.* Austin, TX: PRO-ED.

Merrell, K. W. (2008a). *Behavioral, social, and emotional assessment of children and adolescents* (3rd ed.). Mahwah, NJ: Erlbaum.

Merrell, K. W. (2008b). *Helping students overcome depression and anxiety: A practical guide* (2nd ed.). New York: Guilford Press.

Merrell, K. W., & Holland, M. L. (1997). Social-emotional behavior of preschool-age children with and without developmental delays. *Research in Developmental Disabilities, 18*(6), 393–405.

Merrell, K. W., Parisi, D. M., & Whitcomb, S. A. (2007). *Strong start: Grades K–2: A social and emotional learning curriculum.* Baltimore: Brookes.

Merrell, K. W., Whitcomb, S. A., & Parisi, D. M. (2009). *Strong Start: Pre-K: A social and emotional learning curriculum.* Baltimore: Brookes.

Mian, N. D., Godoy, L., Briggs-Gowan, M. J., & Carter, A. S. (2012). Patterns of anxiety symptoms in toddlers and preschool-age children: Evidence of early differentiation. *Journal of Anxiety Disorders, 26*(1), 102–110.

Michelson, D., Davenport, C., Dretzke, J., Barlow, J., & Day, C. (2013). Do evidence-based interventions work when tested in the "real world?" A systematic review and meta-analysis of parent management training for the treatment of child disruptive behavior. *Clinical Child and Family Psychology Review, 16*(1), 18–34.

Miller-Lewis, L. R., Baghurst, P. A., Sawyer, M. G., Prior, M. R., Clark, J. J., Arney, et al. (2006). Early childhood externalising behaviour problems: Child, parenting, and family-related predictors over time. *Journal of Abnormal Child Psychology, 34*(6), 891–906.

Mindell, J. A. (1999). Empirically supported treatments in pediatric psychology: Bedtime refusal and night wakings in young children. *Journal of Pediatric Psychology, 24*, 465–481.

Modi, R. R., Camacho, M., & Valerio, J. (2014). Confusional arousals, sleep terrors, and sleepwalking. *Sleep Medicine Clinics, 9*(4), 537–551.

Montgomery, D. F., & Navarro, F. (2008). Management of constipation and encopresis in children. *Journal of Pediatric Health Care, 22*(3), 199–204.

Morris, R. J., Kratochwill, T. R., Schoenfield, G., & Auster, E. R. (2008). Childhood fears, phobias, and related anxieties. In R. J. Morris & T. R. Kratochwill (Eds.), *The practice of child therapy* (4th ed., pp. 93–141). Mahwah, NJ: Erlbaum.

Moss, E., Cyr, C., & Dubois-Comtois, K. (2004). Attachment at early school age and developmental risk: Examining family contexts and behavior problems of controlling-caregiving, controlling-punitive, and behaviorally disorganized children. *Developmental Psychology, 40*(4), 519–532.

Motta, R. W., & Basile, D. M. (1998). Pica. In L. Phelps (Ed.), *Health-related disorders in children and adolescents: A guidebook for understanding and educating* (pp. 524–527). Washington, DC: American Psychological Association.

Moyle, M. J., Heilmann, J., & Berman, S. S. (2013). Assessment of early developing phonological awareness skills: A comparison of The Preschool Individual Growth and Development Indicators and the Phonological Awareness and Literacy Screening—PreK. *Early Education and Development, 24*(5), 668–686.

Mulders, M. M., Cobussen-Boekhorst, H., de Gier, R. P., Feitz, W. F., & Kortmann, B. B. (2011). Urotherapy in children: Quantitative measurements of daytime urinary incontinence before and after treatment. *Journal of Pediatric Urology, 7*(2), 213–218.

Muris, P., & Ollendick, T. H. (2015). Children who are anxious in silence: A review on selective mutism, the new anxiety disorder in DSM-5. *Clinical Child and Family Psychology Review, 18*(2), 151–169.

Murphy, K. A., Theodore, L. A., Aloiso, D., Alric-Edwards, J. M., & Hughes, T. L. (2007). Interdependent group contingency and mystery motivators to reduce preschool disruptive behavior. *Psychology in the Schools, 44*(1), 53–63.

Muscott, A. J., Muscott, H. S., Mann, E., Benjamin, T. B., Gately, S., & Bell, K. E. (2004). Positive behavioral interventions and supports in New Hampshire: Preliminary results of a statewide system for implementing schoolwide discipline practices. *Education and Treatment of Children, 27*(4), 453–475.

Myers, C. L., Bour, J. L., Sidebottom, K. J., Murphy, S. B., & Hakman, M. (2010). Same constructs, different results: Examining the consistency of two behavior-rating scales with referred preschoolers. *Psychology in the Schools, 47,* 205–216.

Nadler, C. B., & Roberts, M. W. (2013). Parent-collected behavioral observations: An empirical comparison of methods. *Child and Family Behavior Therapy, 35,* 95–109.

National Association of School Psychologists. (2009). *Early childhood assessment* [Position Statement]. Bethesda, MD: Author. Retrieved from *www.nasponline.org/assets/documents/Research%20and%20 Policy/Position%20Statements/EarlyChildhoodAssessment.pdf.*

Neece, C. L. (2013). Mindfulness-based stress reduction for parents of young children with developmental delays: Implications for parental mental health and child behavior problems. *Journal of Applied Research in Intellectual Disabilities, 27,* 174–186.

Nickerson, A., & Fishman, C. (2009). Convergent and divergent validity of the Devereux Student Strengths Assessment. *School Psychology Quarterly, 24,* 48–59.

Nickerson, A., Reeves, M., Brock, S., & Jimerson, S. (2009). *Identifying, assessing and treating PTSD at school.* New York: Springer.

Nock, M. K., & Kazdin, A. E. (2005). Randomized controlled trial of a brief intervention for increasing participation in parent management training. *Journal of Consulting and Clinical Psychology, 5,* 872–879.

Nolan, J. D., & Filter, K. J. (2012). A function-based classroom behavior intervention using non-contingent reinforcement plus response cost. *Education and Treatment of Children, 35,* 419–430.

Normand, S., Flora, D. B., Toplak, M. E., & Tannock, R. (2012). Evidence for a general ADHD factor from a longitudinal general school population study. *Journal of Abnormal Child Psychology, 40,* 555–567.

Norris, M., & Lecavalier, L. (2010). Screening accuracy of Level 2 autism spectrum disorder rating scales: A review of selected instruments. *Autism, 14,* 263–284.

O'Connell, M. E., Boat, T. F., & Warner, K. E. (Eds.). (2009). *Preventing mental, emotional, and behavioral disorders among young people: Progress and possibilities.* Washington, DC: National Academies Press.

Olino, T. M., Dougherty, L. R., Bufferd, S. J., Carlson, G. A., & Klein, D. N. (2014). Testing models of psychopathology in preschool-aged children using a structured interview-based assessment. *Journal of Abnormal Child Psychology, 42,* 1201–1211.

Ollendick, T. H., Davis III, T. E., & Muris, P. (2004). Treatment of specific phobia in children and adolescents. In P. Barrett & T. H. Ollendick (Eds.), *The handbook of interventions that work with children and adolescents: From prevention to treatment* (pp. 273–299). West Sussex, UK: Wiley.

Ollendick, T. H., & King, N. J. (1998). Empirically supported treatments for children with phobic and anxiety disorders: Current status. *Journal of Clinical Child Psychology, 27,* 156–167.

Olson, S. L., Tardif, T. Z., Miller, A., Felt, B., Grabell, A. S., Kessler, D., et al. (2011). Inhibitory control and harsh discipline as predictors of externalizing problems in young children: A comparative study of U.S., Chinese, and Japanese preschoolers. *Journal of Abnormal Child Psychology, 39,* 1163–1175.

Owens, J. (2008). Classification and epidemiology of childhood sleep disorders. *Primary Care: Clinics in Office Practice, 35,* 533–546.

Pandolfi, V., Magyar, C. I., & Dill, C. A. (2009). Confirmatory factor analysis of the child behavior checklist 1.5–5 in a sample of children with autism spectrum disorders. *Journal of Autism and Developmental Disorders, 39,* 986–995.

Parent, J., Forehand, R., Merchant, M. J., Edwards, M. C., Conners-Burrow, N. A., Long, N., et al. (2011). The relation of harsh and permissive discipline with child disruptive behaviors: Does child gender make a difference in an at-risk sample? *Journal of Family Violence, 26,* 527–533.

Parker, S. K., Schwartz, B., Todd, J., & Pickering, L. K. (2004). Thimerosal-containing vaccines and autistic spectrum disorder: A critical review of published original data. *Pediatrics, 114,* 793–804.

Parlakian, R., & Lerner, C. (2007). Promoting healthy eating habits right from the start. *Young Children, 62,* 1–3.

Patterson, G. R. (1982). *Coercive family process.* Eugene, OR: Castalia.

Patterson, G. R., Chamberlain, P., & Reid, J. B. (1982). A comparative evaluation of a parent-training program. *Behavior Therapy, 13,* 638–650.

Paulus, F. W., Backes, A., Sander, C. S., Weber, M., & von Gontard, A. (2015). Anxiety disorders and behavioral inhibition in preschool children: A population-based study. *Child Psychiatry and Human Development, 46,* 150–157.

Perry, N. B., Nelson, J. A., Calkins, S. D., Leerkes, E. M., O'Brien, M., & Marcovitch, S. (2014). Early physiological regulation predicts the trajectory of externalizing behaviors across the preschool period. *Developmental Psychobiology, 56,* 1482–1491.

Petit, D., Touchette, E., Tremblay, R. E., Boivin, M., & Montplaisir, J. (2007). Dyssomnias and parasomnias in early childhood. *Pediatrics, 119,* e1016–e1025.

Piaget, J. (1983). Piaget's theory. In P. H. Mussen (Series Ed.) & W. Kessen (Vol. Ed.), *Handbook of child psychology: Vol. 1. History, theory, and methods* (4th ed., pp. 103–128). New York: Wiley.

Pidano, A. E., & Allen, A. R. (2015). The Incredible Years series: A review of the independent research base. *Journal of Child and Family Studies, 24,* 1898–1916.

Pihlakoski, L., Sourander, A., Aromaa, M., Rautava, P., Helenius, H., & Sillanpää, M. (2006). The continuity of psychopathology from early childhood to preadolescence: A prospective cohort study of 3–12-year-old children. *European Child and Adolescent Psychiatry, 15,* 409–417.

Piotrowska, P. J., Stride, C. B., Croft, S. E., & Rowe, R. (2015). Socioeconomic status and antisocial behaviour among children and adolescents: A systematic review and meta-analysis. *Clinical Psychology Review, 35,* 47–55.

Plotts, C. A., & Lasser, J. (2013). *School psychologist as counselor: A practitioner's handbook.* Bethesda, MD: National Association of School Psychologists.

Polaha, J., Warzak, W. J., & Dittmer-McMahon, K. (2002). Toilet training in primary care: Current practice and recommendations from behavioral pediatrics. *Journal of Developmental and Behavioral Pediatrics, 23,* 424–429.

Pooja, S. T., Zhou, C., Lozano, P., & Christakis, D. A. (2010). Preschoolers' total daily screen time at home and by type of child care. *Journal of Pediatrics, 158,* 297–300.

Posthumus, J., Raaijmakers, M., Maassen, G., Engeland, H., & Matthys, W. (2012). Sustained effects of Incredible Years as a preventive intervention in preschool children with conduct problems. *Journal of Abnormal Child Psychology, 40,* 487–500.

Prelock, P. A., & McCauley, R. J. (Eds.). (2012). *Treatment of autism spectrum disorders: Evidence-based interventions strategies for communication and social interaction.* New York: Brookes.

Preschool Curriculum Evaluation Research Consortium. (2008). *Effects of preschool curriculum programs on school readiness* (NCER 2008–2009). Washington, DC: National Center for Education Research, Institute of Education Sciences, U.S. Department of Education. Available at *www.ies.ed.gov/ncer/pubs/.*

Price, A. M., Wake, M., Ukoumunne, O. C., & Hiscock, H. (2012). Five-year follow-up of harms and benefits of behavioral infant sleep intervention: Randomized trials. *Pediatrics, 130,* 643–651.

Raes, F., Griffith, J. W., Van der Gucht, K., & Williams, M. G. (2014). School-based prevention and reduction of depression in adolescents: A cluster randomized controlled trial of a mindfulness group program. *Mindfulness, 5,* 477–486.

Ramakrishnan, K. (2008). Evaluation and treatment of enuresis. *American Family Physician, 78*(4), 489–496.

Raver, C., Jones, S. M., Li-Grining, C., Metzger, M., Champion, K. M., & Sardin, L. (2008). Improving preschool classroom processes: Preliminary findings from a randomized trial implemented in Head Start settings. *Early Childhood Research Quarterly, 23,* 10–26.

Reedtz, C., Handegard, B. H., & Morch, W. T. (2011). Promoting positive parenting practices in primary care: Outcomes and mechanisms of change in a randomized controlled risk reduction trial. *Scandinavian Journal of Psychology, 52,* 131–137.

Reich, W., Welner, Z., & Herjanic, B. (1997). *Diagnostic Interview for Children and Adolescents-IV (DICA-IV).* North Tonawanda, NY: Multi-Health Systems.

Reichow, B. (2012). Overview of meta-analyses on early intensive behavioral intervention for young children with autism spectrum disorders. *Journal of Autism and Developmental Disorders, 42,* 512–520.

Reid, G. J., Hong, R. Y., & Wade, T. J. (2009). The relation between common sleep problems and emotional and behavioral problems among 2- and 3-year-olds in the context of known risk factors for psychopathology. *Journal of Sleep Research, 18,* 49–59.

Reid, M. J., Webster-Stratton, C., & Baydar, N. (2004). Halting the development of conduct problems in head start children: The effects of parent training. *Journal of Clinical Child and Adolescent Psychology, 33,* 279–291.

Reigada, L. C., Fisher, P. H., Cutler, C., & Warner, C. M. (2008). An innovative treatment approach for children with anxiety disorders and medically unexplained somatic complaints (2008). *Cognitive and Behavioral Practice, 15,* 140–147.

Reinke, W. M., Herman, K. C., & Stormont, M. (2013). Classroom-level positive behavior supports in schools implementing SW-PBIS: Identifying areas for enhancement. *Journal of Positive Behavior Interventions, 15*, 39–50.

Reinke, W. M., Lewis-Palmer, T., & Merrell, K. (2008). The classroom check-up: A classwide teacher consultation model for increasing praise and decreasing disruptive behavior. *School Psychology Review, 37*, 315–332.

Reinke, W. M., Stormont, M., Herman, K. C., Puri, R., & Goel, N. (2011). Supporting children's mental health in schools: Teacher perceptions of needs, roles, and barriers. *School Psychology Quarterly, 26*, 1–13.

Reinke, W. M., Stormont, M., Webster-Stratton, C., Newcomer, L., & Herman, K. C. (2012). The Incredible Years teacher classroom management program: Using coaching to support generalization to real-world classroom settings. *Psychology in the Schools, 49*, 416–428.

Rellini, E., Tortolani, D., Carbone, S., Trillo, S., & Montecchi, F. (2004). Childhood Autism Rating Scale (CARS) and Autism Behavior Checklist (ABC) correspondence and conflicts with DSM-IV criteria in diagnosis of autism. *Journal of Autism and Developmental Disorders, 34*, 703–708.

Reynolds, C. R., & Kamphaus, R. W. (2015). *Behavior Assessment System for Children, Third Edition.* San Antonio, TX: Pearson.

Reynolds, L. K., & Kelley, M. L. (1997). The efficacy of a response cost-based treatment pacakage for managing aggressive behavior in preschoolers. *Behavior Modification, 21*, 216–230.

Richardson, R. C. (1996). *Connecting with others: Lessons for teaching social and emotional competence grades K–2.* Champaign, IL: Research Press.

Riddle, M. A., Yershova, K., Lazzaretto, D., Paykina, N., Yenokyan, G., Greenhill, L., et al. (2013). The Preschool Attention-deficit/hyperactivity disorder Treatment study (PATS) 6-year follow-up. *Journal of the American Academy of Child and Adolescent Psychiatry, 52*, 264–278.

Riggs, N. R., Greenberg, M. T., Kusche, C. A., & Pentz, M. A. (2006). The mediational role of neurocognition in the behavioral outcomes of a social-emotional prevention program in elementary school students: Effects of the PATHS curriculum. *Prevention Science, 71*, 91–102.

Rinaldi, C. M., & Howe, N. (2012). Mothers' and fathers' parenting styles and associations with toddlers' externalizing, internalizing, and adaptive behaviors. *Early Childhood Research Quarterly, 27*, 266–273.

Ritz, M., Noltemeyer, D. D., & Green, J. (2014). Behavior management in preschool classrooms: Insight revealed through systematic observation and review. *Psychology in the Schools, 51*, 181–197.

Robins, D., Casagrande, K., Barton, M., Chen, C., Dumont-Mathieu, T., & Fein, D. (2014). Validation of the Modified Checklist for Autism in Toddlers, Revised With Follow-Up (M-CHAT-R/F). *Pediatrics, 133*, 37–45.

Robins, D., Fein, D., & Barton, M. (2009). Modified Checklist for Autism in Toddlers, Revised with Follow-Up (M-CHAT-R/F). Retrieved from *www.m-chat.org*.

Robson, W. L. M. (2009). Evaluation and management of enuresis. *New England Journal of Medicine, 360*, 1429–1436.

Rogers, J. (2013). Daytime wetting in children and acquisition of bladder control. *Nursing Children and Young People, 25*, 26–33.

Rogers, S. J., & Vismara, L. A. (2008). Evidence-based comprehensive treatments for early autism. *Journal of Clinical Child and Adolescent Psychology, 37*, 8–38.

Rolon-Arroyo, B., Arnold, D. H., & Harvey, E. A. (2014). The predictive utility of conduct disorder symptoms in preschool children: A 3-year follow-up study. *Child Psychiatry and Human Development, 45*, 329–337.

Rowe, R., Costello, E. J., Angold, A., Copeland, W. E., & Maughan, B. (2010). Developmental pathways in oppositional defiant disorder and conduct disorder. *Journal of Abnormal Psychology, 119*, 726–738.

Saklofske, D. H., Janzen, H. L., Hildebrand, D. K., & Kaufmann, L. (1998). Depression in children: Handouts for parents and teachers. In A. S. Canter & S. A. Carroll (Eds.), *Helping children at home and school: Handouts from your school psychologist* (pp. 237–244). Bethesda, MD: National Association of School Psychologists.

Salazar, F., Baird, G., Chandler, S., Tseng, E., O'Sullivan, T., & Howlin, P. (2015). Co-occurring psychiatric disorders in preschool and elementary school-aged children with autism spectrum disorder. *Journal of Autism and Developmental Disorders, 45*, 2283–2294.

Sameroff, A., Seifer, R., & McDonough, S. C. (2004). Contextual contributors to the assessment of infant mental health. In R. DelCarmen-Wiggins & A. Carter (Eds.), *Handbook of infant, toddler, and preschool mental health assessment* (pp. 61–76). New York: Oxford University Press.

Sanders, M. R. (1999). Triple P–Positive Parenting Program: Towards an empirically validated multilevel parenting and family support strategy for the prevention of behavior and emotional problems in children. *Clinical Child and Family Psychology Review, 2,* 71–90.

Sanders, M. R. (2010). Community-based parenting and family support interventions and the prevention of drug abuse. *Addictive Behaviors, 25,* 929–942.

Sattler, J. M. (1998). *Clinical and forensic interviewing of children and families.* San Diego, CA: Author.

Saywitz, K. J., Mannarino, A. P., Berliner, L., & Cohen, J. A. (2000). Treatment for sexually abused children and adolescents. *American Psychologist, 55,* 1040–1049.

Scaramella, L. V., & Leve, L. D. (2004). Clarifying parent-child reciprocities during early childhood: The early childhood coercion model. *Clinical Child and Family Psychology Review, 7,* 89–107.

Scheeringa, M. S., & Gaensbauer T. J. (2000). Posttraumatic stress disorder. In C. H. Zeanah (Ed.), *Handbook of infant mental health* (2nd ed., pp. 369–381). New York: Guilford Press.

Scheeringa, M. S., Zeanah, C. H., & Cohen, J. A. (2011). PTSD in children and adolescents: Toward an empirically based algorithm. *Depression and Anxiety, 28,* 770–782.

Schoenfield, G., & Morris, R. (2009). Cognitive-behavioral treatment for childhood anxiety disorders. In M. J. Mayer, R. Van Acker, J. E. Lochman, & F. M. Gresham (Eds.), *Cognitive-behavioral interventions for emotional and behavioral disorders: School-based practice* (pp. 204–232). New York: Guilford Press.

Schonert-Reichl, K., & Lawlor, M. S. (2010). The effects of mindfulness-based education program on pre and early adolescents' well-being and social and emotional competence. *Mindfulness, 1,* 137–151.

Schonwald, A. (2004). Difficult toilet training. *Pediatrics for Parents, 21,* 3, 12.

Schopler, M., Van Bourgondien, G., Wellman, G., & Love, S. (2010). *Childhood Autism Rating Scale* (2nd ed.). Los Angeles, CA: Western Psychological Services.

Schroeder, C. S., & Gordon, B. N. (2002). *Assessment and treatment of childhood problems: A clinician's guide* (2nd ed.). New York: Guilford Press.

Schultz, B. L., Richardson, R. C., Barber, C. R., & Wilcox, D. (2011). A preschool pilot study of "Connecting with Others: Lessons for Teaching Social and Emotional Competence." *Early Childhood Education Journal, 39,* 143–148.

Schwarz, S. M., Corredor, J., Fisher-Medina, J., Cohen, J., & Rabinowitz, S. (2001). Diagnosis and treatment of feeding disorders in children with developmental disabilities. *Pediatrics, 108,* 671–676.

Semple, R. J., Lee, J., Rosa, D., & Miller, L. F. (2009). A randomized trial of mindfulness-based cognitive therapy for children: Promoting mindful attention to enhance social-emotional resiliency in children. *Journal of Child and Family Studies, 19,* 218–229.

Serra Giacobo, R., Jané, M. C., Bonillo, A., Ballespí, S., & Díaz-Regañon, N. (2012). Somatic symptoms, severe mood dysregulation, and aggressiveness in preschool children. *European Journal of Pediatrics, 171,* 111–119.

Sharma-Patel, K., Filton, B., Brown, E., Zlotnik, D., Campbell, C., & Yedlin, J. (2011). Pediatric posttraumatic stress disorder. In D. McKay & E. A., Storch (Eds.), *Handbook of child and adolescent anxiety disorders* (pp. 303–321). New York: Springer.

Shastri, P. C. (2009). Promotion and prevention in child mental health. *Indian Journal of Psychiatry, 51,* 88–95.

Shaw, D. S., Dishion, T. J., Supplee, L., Gardner, F., & Arnds, K. (2006). Randomized trial of a family-centered approach to the prevention of early conduct problems: 2-year effects of the family check-up in early childhood. *Journal of Consulting and Clinical Psychology, 74,* 1–9.

Shaw, D. S., Keenan, K., Vondra, J. I., Delliquadri, E., & Giovannelli, J. (1997). Antecedents of preschool children's internalizing problems: A longitudinal study of low-income families. *Journal of the American Academy of Child and Adolescent Psychiatry, 36,* 1760–1767.

Shaw, D. S., Leijten, P., Dishion, T. J., Wilson, M. N., Gardner, F., & Matthys, W. (2014). The family check-up and service use in high-risk families of young children: A prevention strategy with a bridge to community-based treatment. *Prevention Science, 16,* 397–406.

Shea, S., & Coyne, L. W. (2011). Maternal dysphoric mood, stress, and parenting practices in mothers of Head Start preschoolers: The role of experiential avoidance. *Child and Family Behavior Therapy, 33,* 231–247.

Shelleby, E. C., & Kolko, D. J. (2015). Predictors, moderators, and treatment parameters of community and clinic-based treatment for child disruptive behavior disorders. *Journal of Child and Family Studies, 24,* 734–748.

Shelleby, E. C., Shaw, D. S., Cheong, J., Chang, H., Gardner, F., Dishion, T. J., et al. (2012). Behavioral control in at-risk toddlers: The influence of the family check-up. *Journal of Clinical Child and Adolescent Psychology, 41,* 288–301.

Shelton, T. L., Barkley, R. A., Crosswait, C., Moorehouse, M., Fletcher, K., Barrett, S., et al. (2000). Multimethod psychoeducational intervention for preschool children with disruptive behavior: Two-year post-treatment follow-up. *Journal of Abnormal Child Psychology, 28,* 253–266.

Shonkoff, J. P., & Meisels, S. J. (1990). Early childhood intervention: The evolution of a concept. In S. J. Meisels & J. P. Shonkoff (Eds.), *Handbook of early childhood intervention* (pp. 3–31). New York: Cambridge University Press.

Silverman, A. H., & Tarbell, S. (2009). Feeding and vomiting problems in pediatric populations. In M. C. Roberts & R. G. Steele (Eds.), *Handbook of pediatric psychology* (4th ed., pp. 429–445). New York: Guilford Press.

Silverstein, D. M. (2004). Enuresis in children: Diagnosis and management. *Clinical Pediatrics, 43,* 217–221.

Simonoff, E., Pickles, A., Charman, T., Chandler, S., Loucas, T., & Baird, G. (2008). Psychiatric disorders in children with autism spectrum disorders: Prevalence, comorbidity, and associated factors in a population-derived sample. *Journal of the American Academy of Child and Adolescent Psychiatry, 47,* 921–929.

Simonsen, B., Fairbanks, S., Briesch, A., Myers, D., & Sugai, G. (2008). Evidence-based practices in classroom management: Considerations for research to practice. *Education and Treatment of Children, 31,* 351–380.

Simonsen, B., Myers, D., & DeLuca, C. (2010). Teaching teachers to use prompts, opportunities to respond, and specific praise. *Teacher Education and Special Education, 33,* 300–318.

Singh, N., Lancioni, G., Winton, A., Fisher, B., Wahler, R., McAleavey, K., et al. (2006). Mindful parenting decreases aggression, noncompliance, and self-injury in children with autism. *Journal of Emotional and Behavioral Disorders, 14,* 169–177.

Singh, N., Lancioni, G., Winton, A., Singh, J., Curtis, W., Wahler, R., et al. (2007). Mindful parenting decreases aggression and increases social behavior in children with developmental disabilities. *Behavior Modification, 31,* 749–771.

Skalická, V., Stenseng, F., & Wichstrøm, L. (2015). Reciprocal relations between student–teacher conflict, children's social skills and externalizing behavior: A three-wave longitudinal study from preschool to third grade. *International Journal of Behavioral Development, 39,* 413–425.

Slemming, K., Sørensen, M. J., Thomsen, P. H., Obel, C., Henriksen, T. B., & Linnet, K. M. (2010). The association between preschool behavioural problems and internalizing difficulties at age 10–12 years. *European Child and Adolescent Psychiatry, 19,* 787–795.

Smith, J. D., Stormshak, E. A., & Kavanagh, K. (2015). Results of a pragmatic effectiveness-implementation hybrid trial of the Family Check-up in community mental health agencies. *Administration and Policy in Mental Health and Mental Health Services Research, 42,* 265–278.

Spence, S. H., Rapee, R., McDonald, C., & Ingram, M. (2001). The structure of anxiety symptoms among preschoolers. *Behaviour Research and Therapy, 39,* 1293–1316.

Sprague, J., Walker, H., Golly, A., White, K., Myers, D. R., & Shannon, T. (2001). Translating research into effective practice: The effects of a universal staff and student intervention on indicators of discipline and safety. *Education and Treatment of Children, 24,* 495–511.

Squires, J., Bricker, D., & Twombly, E. (2015). *The ASQ:SE2 user's guide: For the Ages & Stages Questionnaires: Social–emotional, 2nd Edition.* Baltimore: Brookes.

Steege, M. W., & Watson, T. S. (2009). *Conducting school-based functional behavioral assessments: A practitioner's guide* (2nd ed.). New York: Guilford Press.

Sterba, S., Egger, H. L., & Angold, A. (2007). Diagnostic specificity and nonspecificity in the dimensions of preschool psychopathology. *Journal of Child Psychology and Psychiatry, 48,* 1005–1013.

Stichter, J. P., Lewis, T. J., Whittaker, T. A., Richter, M., Johnson, N. W., & Trussell, R. P. (2009). Assessing teacher use of opportunities to respond and effective classroom management strategies: Comparisons among high- and low-risk elementary schools. *Journal of Positive Behavior Interventions, 11,* 68–81.

Stiegler, L. N. (2005). Understanding pica behavior: A review for clinical and education professionals. *Focus on Autism and Other Developmental Disabilities, 20,* 27–38.

Strain, P. S., Young, C. C., & Horowitz, J. (1981). An examination of child and family demographic variables related to generalized behavior change during oppositional child training. *Behavior Modification, 5,* 15–26.

Strickland, J., Keller, J., Lavigne, J. V., Gouze, K., Hopkins, J., & LeBailly, S. (2011). The structure of psychopathology in a community sample of preschoolers. *Journal of Abnormal Child Psychology, 39,* 601–610.

Stringaris, A., & Goodman, R. (2009). Three dimensions of oppositionality in youth. *Journal of Child Psychology and Psychiatry, 50,* 216–223.

Stores, G. (2001). *A clinical guide to sleep disorders in children and adolescents.* Cambridge, UK: Cambridge University Press.

Stueck, M., & Gloeckner, N. (2005). Yoga for children in the mirror of the science: Working spectrum and practice fields of the training of relaxation with elements of yoga for children. *Early Child Development and Care, 175,* 371–377.

Suarez, M., & Mullins, S. (2008). Motivational interviewing and pediatric health behavior interventions. *Journal of Developmental and Behavioral Pediatrics, 29,* 417–428.

Tan, T. X., Dedrick, R. F., & Marfo, K. (2006). Factor structure and clinical implications of Child Behavior Checklist/1.5–5 ratings in a sample of girls adopted from China. *Journal of Pediatric Psychology, 32,* 807–818.

Taubman, B. (1997). Toilet training and toileting refusal for stool only: A prospective study. *Pediatrics, 99,* 54–58.

Taylor, L. E., Swerdfeger, A. L., & Eslick, G. D. (2014). Vaccines are not associated with autism: An evidence-based meta-analysis of case-control and cohort studies. *Vaccine, 32,* 3623–3629.

Thomas, J. H., Moore, M., & Mindell, J. A. (2014). Controversies in behavioral treatment of sleep problems in young children. *Sleep Medicine Clinics, 9,* 251–259.

Thomas, R., & Zimmer-Gembeck, M. J. (2007). Behavioral outcomes of parent–child interaction therapy and Triple-P-Positive Parenting Program: A review and meta-analysis. *Journal of Abnormal Child Psychology, 35,* 475–495.

Thome, M., & Skuladottir, A. (2005). Changes in sleep problems, parents distress and impact of sleep problems from infancy to preschool age for referred and unreferred children. *Scandinavian Journal of Caring Sciences, 19,* 86–94.

Tiano, J. D., Fortson, B. L., McNeil, C. B., & Humphreys, L. A. (2005). Managing classroom behavior of Head Start children using response cost and token economy procedures. *Journal of Early and Intensive Behavior Intervention, 2,* 28–39.

Tingstrom, D. H., Sterling-Turner, H. E., & Wilczynski, S. M. (2006). The good behavior game: 1969–2002. *Behavior Modification, 30,* 225–253.

Tonge, B., Brereton, A., Kiomall, M., Mackinnon, A., King, N., & Rinehart, N. (2006). Effects on parental mental health of an education and skills training program for parents of young children with autism: A randomized controlled trial. *Journal of the American Academy of Child and Adolescent Psychiatry, 45,* 561–569.

Toplak, M. E., Sorge, G. B., Flora, D. B., Chen, W., Banaschewski, T., Buitelaar, J., et al. (2012). The hierarchical factor model of ADHD: Invariant across age and national groupings? *Journal of Child Psychology and Psychiatry, 53,* 292–303.

Turnbull, K., Reid, G. J., & Morton, J. B. (2013). Behavioral sleep problems and their potential impact on developing executive function in children. *Sleep, 36,* 1077–1084.

Turner, H. S., & Watson, T. S. (1999). Consultants guide for the use of time-out in the preschool and elementary classroom. *Psychology in the Schools, 36,* 135–148.

Ullebø, A. K., Breivik, K., Gillberg, C., Lundervold, A. J., & Posserud, M. (2012). The factor structure of ADHD in a general population of primary school children. *Journal of Child Psychology and Psychiatry, 53,* 927–936.

U.S. Department of Education. (2013). Second Step. Retrieved from *http://ies.ed.gov/ncee/wwc/interventionreport.aspx?sid=623.*

van Dijk, M., Benninga, M. A., Grootenhuis, M. A., Nieuwenhuizen, A. O., & Last, B. F. (2007). Chronic childhood constipation: A review of the literature and the introduction of a protocolized behavioral intervention program. *Patient Education and Counseling, 67,* 63–77.

Vande Walle, J., Rittig, S., Bauer, S., Eggert, P., Marschall-Kehrel, D., & Tekgul, S. (2012). Practical consensus guidelines for the management of enuresis. *European Journal of Pediatrics, 171*, 971–983.

van Oort, F. A., van der Ende, J., Wadsworth, M. E., Verhulst, F. C., & Achenbach, T. M. (2011). Cross-national comparison of the link between socioeconomic status and emotional and behavioral problems in youths. *Social Psychiatry and Psychiatric Epidemiology, 46*, 167–172.

Varley, C. K. (2006). Treating depression in children and adolescents: What options now? *CNS Drugs, 20*, 1–13.

Vaughn, B. E., Elmore-Staton, L., Shin, N., & El-Sheikh, M. (2015). Sleep as a support for social competence, peer relations, and cognitive functioning in preschool children. *Behavioral Sleep Medicine, 13*, 92–106.

Vaughan, C. (2011). Test review: Childhood Autism Rating Scale (2nd ed). *Journal of Psychoeducational Assessment, 29*, 489–493.

Vollestad, J., Nielson, M. B., & Nielson, G. H. (2012). Mindfulness and acceptance based interventions for anxiety disorders: A systematic review and meta-analysis. *British Journal of Clinical Psychology, 51*, 239–260.

Wacker, D. P., Cooper, L. J., Peck, S. M., Derby, K. M., & Berg, W. K. (1999). Community-based functional assessment. In A. C. Repp & R. H. Horner (Eds.), *Functional analysis of problem behavior: From effective assessment to effective support* (pp. 32–56). Belmont, CA: Wadsworth.

Wackerle-Hollman, A. K., Schmitt, B. A., Bradfield, T. A., Rodriguez, M. C., & McConnell, S. R. (2015). Redefining individual growth and development indicators: Phonological awareness. *Journal of Learning Disabilities, 48*, 495–510.

Walker, H. M., Severson, H. H., & Feil, E. G. (1995). *The Early Screening Project: A proven child find process.* Longmont, CO: Sopris West.

Walker, H. M., Severson, H. H., & Feil, E. G. (2014). *Systematic Screening for Behavior Disorders, 2nd Edition.* Eugene, OR: Pacific Northwest.

Warner, C. M., Colognori, D., Re, K., Reigada, L., Kelin, R., Browner-Elhanan, K., et al. (2011). Cognitive-behavioral treatment of persistent functional somatic complaints and pediatric anxiety: An initial controlled trial. *Depression and Anxiety, 28*, 551–559.

Warner, C. M., Fisher, P. H., & Reigada, L. (2006). Feeling Good: Pediatric anxiety treatment manual. Unpublished Manuscript. In L. C., Reigada, P. H. Fisher, C. Cutler, & C. M. Warner (2008). An innovative treatment approach for children with anxiety disorders and medically unexplained somatic complaints (2008). *Cognitive and Behavioral Practice, 15*, 140–147.

Warren, S. L., & Sroufe, L. A. (2004). Developmental issues. In T. H. Ollendick & J. S. March (Eds.), *Phobic and anxiety disorders in children and adolescents: A clinician's guide to effective psychosocial and pharmacological interventions* (pp. 92–115). New York: Oxford University Press.

Webster-Stratton, C. (2009). Affirming diversity: Multi-cultural collaboration to deliver the Incredible Years parent programs. *International Journal of Child Health and Human Development, 2*, 17–32.

Webster-Stratton, C. (2011). *The Incredible Years parents, teachers, and children's training series: Program content, methods, research and dissemination 1980–2011.* Seattle, WA: Incredible Years.

Webster-Stratton, C., & Hancock, L. (1998). Training for parents of young children with conduct problems: Content, methods, and therapeutic procedures. In J. M. Briesmesiter & C. E. Schaefer (Eds.), *Handbook of parent training: Helping parents prevent and solve problem behaviors* (2nd ed., pp. 98–152). New York: Wiley.

Webster-Stratton, C., & Herman, K. (2009). Disseminating Incredible Years series early-intervention programs: Integrating and sustaining services between school and home. *Psychology in the Schools, 47*, 36–54.

Webster-Stratton, C., & Reid, M. (2003). The Incredible Years parents, teachers, and children training series: A multifaceted treatment approach for young children with conduct problems. In A. E. Kazdin & J. R. Weisz (Eds.), *Evidence-based psychotherapies for children and adolescents* (pp. 224–240). New York: Guilford Press.

Webster-Stratton, C., Reid, M., & Hammond, M. (2004). Treating children with early-onset conduct problems: Intervention outcomes for parent, child, and teacher training. *Journal of Clinical Child and Adolescent Psychology, 33*, 105–124.

Webster-Stratton, C., Reid, M. J., & Stoolmiller, M. (2008). Preventing conduct problems and improving school readiness: Evaluation of the Incredible Years Teacher and Child Training Programs in high-risk schools. *Journal of Child Psychology and Psychiatry, and Allied Disciplines, 49*, 471–488.

Weis, R., Lovejoy, M. C., & Lundahl, B. W. (2005). Factor structure and discriminative validity of the Eyberg Child Behavior Inventory with young children. *Journal of Psychopathology and Behavioral Assessment, 27,* 269–278.

Whittingham, K., Sanders, M., McKinlay, L., & Boyd, R. N. (2014). Interventions to reduce behavioral problems in children with cerebral palsy: An RCT. *Pediatrics, 133,* e1249–e1257.

Wichstrøm, L., Berg-Nielsen, T. S., Angold, A., Egger, H. L., Solheim, E., & Sveen, T. H. (2012). Prevalence of psychiatric disorders in preschoolers. *Journal of Child Psychology and Psychiatry, 53,* 695–705.

Wiener, J. S., Scales, M. T., Hampton, J., King, L. R., Surwit, R., & Edwards, C. L. (2000). Long-term efficacy of simple behavioral therapy for daytime wetting in children. *Journal of Urology, 164,* 786–790.

Willard, C. (2014). *Mindfulness for teen anxiety: A workbook for overcoming anxiety at home, at school and everywhere else.* Oakland, CA: New Harbinger.

Williams, D. E., & McAdam, D. (2012). Assessment, behavioral treatment, and prevention of pica: Clinical guidelines and recommendations for practitioners. *Research in Developmental Disabilities, 33,* 2050–2057.

Williams, K. E., Field, D. G., & Seiverling, L. (2010). Food refusal in children: A review of the literature. *Research in Developmental Disabilities, 31,* 625–633.

Willoughby, M. T., Pek, J., & Greenberg, M. T. (2012). Parent-reported attention deficit/hyperactivity symptomatology in preschool-aged children: Factor structure, developmental change, and early risk factors. *Journal of Abnormal Child Psychology, 40,* 1301–1312.

Wolff, J. C., & Ollendick, T. H. (2010). Conduct problems in youth: Phenomenology, classification, and epidemiology. In R. C. Murrihy, A. D. Kidman, & T. H. Ollendick (Eds.), *Clinical handbook of assessing and treatment conduct problems in youth* (pp. 3–20). New York: Springer.

Wolff, N., Darlington, A., Hunfeld, J., Verhulst, F., Jaddoe, V., Hofman, A., et al. (2010). Determinants of somatic complaints in 18-month-old children: The generation R study. *Journal of Pediatric Psychology, 35,* 306–316.

Wood, B., Rea, M., Plitnick, B., & Figueiro, M. (2013). Light level and duration of exposure determine the impact of self-luminous tablets on melatonin suppression. *Applied Ergonomics, 44,* 237–240.

Yule, W., Smith, P., Perrin, S., & Clark, D. M. (2013). Post-traumatic stress disorder. In C. A. Essau & T. H. Ollendick (Eds.), *Wiley–Blackwell handbook of the treatment of childhood and adolescent anxiety* (pp. 451–470). Malden, MA: Wiley.

Zakrzweski, V. (2014). How social–emotional learning transforms classrooms: The Greater Good Science Center. Retrieved from *http://greatergood.berkeley.edu/article/item/how_social_emotional_learning_transforms_classrooms*.

Zelazo, P. D., & Lyons, K. E. (2012). The potential benefits of mindfulness training in early childhood: A developmental social cognitive neuroscience perspective. *Child Development Perspectives, 6,* 154–160.

Zhang, S., Faries, D. E., Vowles, M., & Michelson, D. (2005). ADHD Rating Scale IV: Psychometric properties from a multinational study as a clinician administered instrument. *International Journal of Methods in Psychiatric Research, 14,* 186–201.

Zhang, X., & Sun, J. (2011). The reciprocal relations between teachers' perceptions of children's behavior problems and teacher–child relationships in the first preschool year. *Journal of Genetic Psychology: Research And Theory On Human Development, 172,* 176–198.

Zimmerman, F. J., & Christakis, D. A. (2007). Associations between content types of early media exposure and subsequent attentional problems. *Pediatrics, 120,* 986–992.

Zisenwine, T., Kaplan, M., Kushnir, J., & Sadeh, A. (2013). Nighttime fears and fantasy–reality differentiation in preschool children. *Child Psychiatry and Human Development, 44,* 186–199.

Index

Page numbers followed by *f* indicate figure, *t* indicate table.

ABC log, 64
ABCs of behavior, 97–98
Academic performance, interviews about, 32
Academic problems, prevention of, 186–189
Acceptance and commitment therapy (ACT)
    acceptance and, 88
    cognitive defusion in, 84–85
    committed action and, 88–89
    core processes in, 83, 83*f*
    evidence-based clinical application in, 89–90
    mindfulness in, 85–87
    overview of, 82–83
    self as context and, 87
    values of, 83–84
Acting-out problems. *See* Externalizing problems
"Adapted Zen Koan for Parents, An," 84
ADHD, 3–4
    ASD and, 15
    behavioral parent training and, 67
    comorbid ODD/CD and, 20
    defined, 3
    diagnostic criteria for, 3
    and positive versus negative reinforcement, 196
    subtypes of, 3–4
ADHD Rating Scale–5, 45–46
Adjustment disorder, with depressed mood, 10
Ages and Stages Questionnaires: Social-Emotional (ASQ:SE-2), 43–44
American Psychological Association, online resources of, 211
Anxiety disorders, 5–8, 110–123
    assessment tools for, 17
    fears and specific phobias, 111–119
    handouts for parents, 140–141
    self-assessment handout, 142

    separation anxiety, 7, 119–123, 144
    treatment of, 110–123
Asperger syndrome, 14
Assessment, 25–55
    with child interviews, 33–36
    with direct observation, 47–54
    with parent and teacher interviews, 26–32
    with rating scales, 36–47
    See also Direct observation; Interviews; Rating scales
Assessment forms
    ABC log, 65
    behavior log, 64
    behavior/interval recording, 63
    child intake, 57–62
    Consent to Obtain or Release Confidential Information, 57
Association for Behavioral and Cognitive Therapies, online resources of, 211
Attention
    positive, 72
    strategic, 72, 87, 99–100
Attention Deficit Disorders Evaluation Scale—4th Ed (ADDES-4), 45
Attention-deficit/hyperactivity disorder (ADHD). *See* ADHD
Autism and Developmental Disabilities Monitoring (ADDM) Network, 14
Autism Diagnostic Observation Schedule, 2nd Edition (ADOS-2), 43, 54
Autism-spectrum disorder (ASD), 13–15
    categories of, 14
    causes and risk factors, 15
    prevalence of, 14–15
Avoidant/restrictive food intake disorder, 12
Azrin-Foxx toilet training method, 150

BASC-3 Behavioral and Emotional Screening System (BASC-3 BESS), 38
Bedtime routines, developing, 163–164
Bed-wetting, forms pertaining to, 170–175
Behavior Assessment System for Children, 3rd Edition (BASC-3), 39–40, 39t
Behavior Basics form, 97–98
Behavior log, 64
Behavior management
    in public places, 109
    reward-based, PBIS and, 193–195
    using privileges for, 107
Behavior problems
    rating scales for, 37–47
    teacher/daycare worker interviews and, 31–32
Behavior rating scales, for preschool- and kindergarten-age children, 25–26
Behavior record cards, 54
Behavioral interventions, punishment-based, 189. *See also* Behavioral violations/severe problem behaviors
Behavioral interventions/supports, positive. *See* Positive behavioral interventions and supports (PBIS)
Behavioral parent training for externalizing problems, 66–82
    with acceptance and commitment therapy, 82–90, 83f
    additional reinforcement/discipline methods in, 79–80
    ADHD and, 67
    behavioral principles in, 71
    conducting, 71–81, 71t
    discipline techniques in, 75–79
    effective commands in, 74–75
    forms pertaining to, 97–109
    group, 81–82
    and implementation of "Child's Game," 73–74
    initial considerations, 68–71
    motivational interviewing and, 69–70
    overview, 67–68
    prevention and early intervention programs for, 92–96
    skill generalization and maintenance in, 80–81
    social skills interventions, 90–92, 91t
    strategic attention in, 72
Behavioral problems
    impacts in school settings, 18–19
    predictors of, 21–24, 21t, 23t
    stability of, 19–21
Behavioral violations/severe problem behaviors, responding to, 195–200
    with home–school notes/check-in/check-out, 196–197, 198f, 199
    with noncontingent reinforcement, 195
    with precorrection strategies, 195–196
    with response cost program, 196
    with time-out, 199–200
Behavior/interval recording form, 63
Bell technique, in treatment of depression, 138
Best-practice recommendations, 211
Brazelton toilet-training method, 149
Breathing, mindful, 86–87
Breathing techniques, for treatment of specific phobias/fears, 114
Broadband rating scales, 39–42

Caregivers. *See* Parents/caregivers
Center for Response to Intervention in Early Childhood (CRTIEC), 187
Centers for Disease Control and Prevention (CDC), ADDM Network and, 14
Check-In/Check-Out program, 199
Child abuse and neglect
    detection of, 128
    prevention of, 131–133, 132t
    reporting requirements for, 127
Child Behavior Checklist (CBCL), 20, 40–41, 41t
Child intake assessment forms, 57–62
Child interests/strengths, teacher/daycare worker interviews and, 30
Child psychiatrist, referrals to, 208–209
Child strengths/talents, teacher/daycare worker interviews and, 32
Child Symptom Inventory (CSI), 17
Childhood Autism Rating Scale—2nd Edition (CARS-2), 46
Child's Game, 73–74, 87
    form for, 101
    homework sheet for, 102
Classroom, establishing rules and schedule in, 191–192
Classroom Check-up, 190
Clinical psychologist, licensed, referrals to, 209
Coercive parenting cycle, 21–22, 72, 85–86
Cognitive behavioral therapy (CBT), PTSD and, 129–130
Cognitive defusion, 84–85
Cognitive-behavioral therapy (CBT), for specific phobia/fear treatment, 117–118
Cognitive/school functioning, parental interviews and, 28–29, 28t
Commands, effective, 74–75
    form for, 103
Common Core State Standards (CCSS), 200
Conduct disorder (CD), 4–5, 93
    ADHD and, 20
    stability of, 20–21
Confidentiality form, 56
Connecting with Others curriculum, 203–204
Conners Rating Scales, 41–42, 42t
Constipation, encopresis and, 154–155
Contingency contracting, 79
Contingency management
    handout for parents, 141
    for treatment of specific phobias/fears, 118
"Correct the Teacher," 192
Cultural background/beliefs, parental interviews and, 28

Daycare facilities, numbers attending, 184
Daycare refusal. *See* Separation anxiety
Daycare workers. *See* Teachers/daycare workers
Depression, 10, 133–139
    prevention of, 133
    treatment of, 134–139
        with five senses exercise, 138–139
        with 4 × 6 breaths technique, 138
        with listening to bell technique, 138
        with mindful eating, 139
        with mindful walks, 139
        mindfulness in, 136–138
        with thought-globe, 139

Desensitization, systematic, for treatment of specific phobias/fears, 112–114
Desmopressin, for nocturnal enuresis, 151–152
Developmental issues, child interviews and, 33–34
Devereux Early Childhood Assessment for Preschoolers, 2nd Edition (DECA-P2), 44
Diagnostic and Statistical Manual of Mental Disorders (DSM-5)
    ADHD in, 3
    autism spectrum disorders in, 14
    conduct disorder in, 5
    controversies over tools based on, 16
    depressive disorders in, 10
    externalizing problem diagnoses and, 66
    fears in, 6
    feeding/eating disorders in, 12
    ODD in, 4–5
    PTSD in, 8–9
    sleep disorders in, 13
    somatic symptom and related disorders in, 10
    specific phobias in, 6–7
Diagnostic Interview Schedule for Children—Young Child (DISC-YC), 16–17
Diagnostic tools
    direct observations as, 48–54
    rating scales as, 38–47
Diet, encopresis and, 155
Dinosaur School program, 201–202
Direct observation, 47–54
    data recording methods for, 49–50, 50*t*, 51*f*
    as diagnostic/evaluation tools, 48–54
    formal, 53–54
    functional assessment and, 52–53
    informal
        by parents or teachers, 52
        structured, 48–52, 50*t*, 51*f*
    as progress monitoring tool, 54
    as screener, 48
Discipline
    additional methods for, 79–80
    appropriate techniques for, 75–79
    cultural practices for, 127
Duration recording procedure, 49

Early childhood
    evidence-based interventions during, 1–2
    interviews during, 33–36
    rapport building and, 34–35
    See also Kindergartners; Preschoolers
Early intervention, 25
Early intervention programs, for behavioral parent training, 92–96. *See also* Behavioral parent training for externalizing problems
Early Screening Project (ESP), 53–54
Eating problems. *See* Feeding/eating problems
effectivechildtherapy.org, 211
Emergency calls, 210
Emotional/behavioral problems
    best-practice recommendations for, 211
    externalizing, 2–5, 2*t*
    impacts in school settings, 18–19
    internalizing, 2*t*, 5–10
    other, 2*t*, 10–15
    overview of, 2–16, 2*t*
    rating scales for, 37–47
    See also Autism-spectrum disorder (ASD); Externalizing problems; Internalizing problems
Emotive imagery, for treatment of specific phobias/fears, 115–117
Encopresis, 11–12, 154–156
    forms pertaining to, 176–177
    refusal/nonretentive, 155–156
    retentive, 154–155
Enuresis, 11, 154–156
    diurnal, 151
    forms pertaining to, 170–175
    nocturnal, 151–154
Enuresis alarm, forms pertaining to, 173–175
Evaluation tools
    direct observations as, 48–54
    rating scales as, 38–47
Event recording procedure, 49
Everyday problems, 148–183
    feeding/eating, 156–161
    forms for, 170–183
    sleep, 161–168
    toileting, 148–156
    See also specific problems
Evidence-based interventions, overview of, 1–2
Exemplary Model of Early Reading Growth and Excellence (EMERGE), 188
Externalizing problems, 2–5, 2*t*, 66–109
    ADHD, 3–4
    oppositional defiant disorder/conduct disorder, 4–5
    parental versus child factors in, 21–23, 21*t*
    predictors of, 21–23, 21*t*
    prevalence of, 66
    prevention and early intervention programs for, 92–96
    social skills interventions for, 90–92
    stability of, 19–20
    See also Behavioral parent training for externalizing problems
Eyberg Child Behavior Inventory (ECBI), 43, 95

Family Check-Up, 70
Family relationships, parental interviews and, 28
Fast Track program, 93
Fears, 5–6
    age differences in, 6
    hierarchy of, 113*t*
    See also Specific phobias/fears
Feeding/eating problems, 12–13, 156–161
    forms pertaining to, 178
    interview questions for parents, 159*t*
    pica, 160–161
    and promotion of healthy eating habits, 157–158
    rumination disorder, 161
    typical types, 158–160
Feelings charts, for preschoolers and kindergartners, 145–146
5:1 rule, 72, 99
Five senses exercise, in treatment of depression, 138–139
4 × 6 breaths technique, in treatment of depression, 138
Frequency recording procedure, 49
Functional assessment, direct observation and, 52–53

Generalized anxiety disorder (GAD), 7–8
  ASD and, 15
Gilliam Autism Rating Scale—3rd Edition (GARS-3), 46–47
Good behaviors, catching, 99
Group behavioral parent training, 81–82

Hanf model of parental training, 67–68, 81
Home–school notes, 197, 198*f*
  form for, 206
Hospitalization, referrals for, 209–210

Ignoring, planned, 100, 195
Imagery, for treatment of specific phobias/fears, 115. *See also* Emotive imagery
Incredible Years Program, 81–82, 94–95, 201–202
Individuals with Disabilities Education Improvement Act (IDEIA), RTI and, 186
infoaboutkids.org, 211
Inpatient settings, referrals for, 209–210
Instruction, effective, PBIS and, 192
Insurance, selection and procedures, 210
Internalizing problems, 2*t*, 5–10, 110–147
  anxiety disorders, 6–8, 110–123
  depression, 133–139
  fears and anxieties, 5–6
  forms for use with, 141–147
  parental versus child-related predictors of, 23–24, 23*t*
  PTSD and traumatic experience/abuse, 8–10, 127–133
  selective mutism, 124–126
  somatic complaints, 126–127
  stability of, 20
  treatment of, 110–147
  See also specific disorders
Interval recording procedure, 50
Intervention, early, 25
Interviews
  as diagnostic/evaluation tools, 26–32
  parent. *See* Parent/caregiver interviews
  as progress monitoring tools, 32
  as screeners, 26
  with young children, 33–36

Kindergartners
  evidence-based interventions and, 1–2
  suspension and expulsion of, 184

Learning disabilities, specific, RTI and, 186
"Leaves on the stream" exercise, 85
Licensed clinical psychologist, referrals to, 209
"Lining Up Right Game," 192
Literacy/academic skills, RTI for, 186–189

Medical history, parental interviews and, 29
Medical insurance, selection and procedures, 210
Mental health issues
  assessment of, 25–55. *See also* Assessment
  prevalence of, 16–18
Methylphenidate, use in preschoolers, 3
"Milk exercise," 85
Mindful breathing exercise, 86–87

Mindful eating
  handout for, 147
  in treatment of depression, 139
Mindful walks, in treatment of depression, 139
Mindfulness practices
  ACT and, 85–87
  programs for, 139
  for specific phobias/fears, 111
  in treatment of depression, 136–138
Modeling
  handout for parents, 141
  for treatment of specific phobias/fears, 118
Modified Checklist for Autism in Toddlers, Revised with Follow-Up, 38
Momentary time sampling procedure, 50
Motivational interviewing, central tenets and therapeutic skills in, 69–70
Multi-tiered system of support (MTSS), 184–186, 185*f*
Mutism, selective, 8
  prevention and treatment of, 124–126
Mystery Motivator program, 193–194

Narrow-Band Rating Scales, 43–47
National Center on Intensive Intervention, website for, 186
Naturalistic observations, 48–49
Negative social behaviors, formal observations of, 54
Nightmares
  forms pertaining to, 183
  versus sleep terrors, 168
Noncontingent reinforcement, 195

Obesity, prevalence of, 13
Observations. *See* Direct observation
Obstructive sleep apnea, 13
Opportunity to respond (OTR), 192
Oppositional-defiant disorder (ODD), 4–5, 93
  ADHD and, 20
  ASD and, 15

Parent Rating Scale—Preschool version, 39, 39*t*
Parent training, behavioral. *See* Behavioral parent training for externalizing problems
Parental factors
  in externalizing problems, 21–22, 21*t*
  in internalizing problems, 23–24, 23*t*
Parent/caregiver interviews, 26–30, 26–-30, 28*t*
  for eating problems, 159*t*
  for sleep problems, 162*t*
Parent–child interaction therapy (PCIT), 89–90, 95
Parent–child interactions, magical ratio for, 72
Parenting cycle, coercive, 21–22, 72, 85–86
Parenting interventions, for externalizing problems, 66–67
Parents/caregivers
  of child with anxiety, handout for, 141
  of child with depression, 134–136
  of child with PTSD, 129–130
  information observations by, 52
  motivation of, 69
Peer relationships, parental interviews and, 28*t*, 29
Phobias, specific. *See* Specific phobias
Phonological Awareness and Literacy Screening (PALS), 189

Physical development, parental interviews and, 29
Pica, 12, 160–161
Play therapy, PTSD and, 128–129, 129f
Positive behavioral interventions and supports (PBIS), 184–186, 189–200
- developing classroom schedule, 191–192
- effective instruction, 192
- establishing classroom rules, 191
- responding to behavioral violations and severe problems, 195–197, 198f, 199–200
- and reward-based behavior management programs, 193–195
- summary, 200
- techniques for, 190, 190t
- utilizing selective attention, 192–193

Positive reinforcement systems, 79–80, 99–100
Positive self-talk, handout for parents, 141
Precorrection strategies, 195–196
Preschool ADHD Treatment Study (PATS), 3
Preschool Age Psychiatric Assessment (PAPA), 16–18
Preschool and Kindergarten Behavior Scales—2nd Edition (PDBS-2), 42
Preschool Curriculum Evaluation Research (PCER) initiative, 186–187
Preschool Early Literacy Indicators (PELI), 188
Preschool facilities, numbers attending, 184
Preschool Individual Growth and Development Indicators (IGDIs), 188–189
Preschoolers
- evidence-based interventions and, 1–2
- methylphenidate use in, 3
- prevalence of mental health concerns in, 16–18
- and prevention of academic problems, 186–189
- suspension and expulsion of, 184

Prevention programs, for behavioral parent training, 92–96
Primary care provider
- referrals to, 208
- role of, 210

Privileges
- behavior management and, 107
- removal of, 79
- worksheet for, 108

Problem-solving skills training, 91–92
Progress monitoring
- with direct observation, 54
- with interviews, 32
- rating scales for, 47

Progressive muscle relaxation
- handout for young children, 143
- for treatment of specific phobias/fears, 114–115

Promoting Alternative Thinking Strategies (PATHS), 203
Prosocial behaviors, formal observations of, 54
Psychiatric history, parental interviews and, 29
Psychiatrist, child, referrals to, 208–209
Psychological testing, parental interviews and, 30
PTSD, 8–10
- treatment of, 128–131

Public places, behavior management in, 109
Put-back technique, 76–77

Questions, for child interviews, 35–36

Rapport, with young children, 34–35
Rating scales, 36–47
- advantages and limitations of, 36–37
- broadband, 39–42
- narrow-band, 43–47
- social, emotional, and behavioral, 37–47
  - as diagnostic/evaluation tools, 38–47
  - as progress monitoring tools, 47
  - as screeners, 37–38

Reading Ready Early Literacy Intervention (RRELI), 188
Recognition and Response RTI model, 187
Referrals
- avenues of, 210–211
- to child psychiatrist, 208–209
- to licensed clinical psychologist, 209
- to master's-level therapist, 209
- online searches and, 210–211
- to primary care provider, 208
- procedures for, 207
- therapist associations and, 210–211
- word of mouth, 211

Reinforcement, noncontingent, 195
Relaxation techniques. *See* Progressive muscle relaxation
Response cost program, 196
Response to intervention (RTI), 184–185
- for early literacy/academic skills, 186–189

Response–cost system, 196–197
Rett's disorder, 14
Rumination, 12, 161

School refusal. *See* Separation anxiety
Schroeder-Gordon toilet training method, 149–150
Screening
- interviews for, 26
- with rating scales, 37–38

Second Step program, 202–203
Selective attention, PBIS and, 192–193
Selective mutism, 8
- prevention and treatment of, 124–126

Self-as-context, versus self-as-content, 87
Self-soothing, sleep problems and, 165
Self-statements, positive, for treating specific phobias/fears, 118
Self-talk, handout for parents, 141
Separation anxiety, 7, 119–123
- handout for parents, 144

Skills, parental, generalization and maintenance of, 80–81
Skillstreaming program, 90–91
Sleep apnea, obstructive, 13
Sleep problems, 13, 161–168
- arousal disorders, 167–168
- assessment of, 162–163, 162t
- bedtime pass for, 166–167
- extinction-based interventions for, 164–165
- forms pertaining to, 179–183
- impacts of, 162
- problem initiating sleep, 163–167
- scheduled wakings for, 166
- solutions for, 181–182

Sleep terrors, 167–168
  versus nightmares, 168
  forms pertaining to, 183
  prevalence of, 167
Sleepwalking, 168
  forms pertaining to, 183
Social and emotional learning (SEL), 200–205
  benefits of, 201
  common programs, 201–204
  defined, 200
  skills in, 200–201
  summary of, 205
Social anxiety disorder (SAD), 8
Social behaviors, formal observations of, 54
Social problems
  impacts in school settings, 18–19
  rating scales for, 37–47
Social skills, teacher/daycare worker interviews and, 32
Social Skills Improvement System Performance Screening Guide, 38
Social Skills Improvement System Rating Scales (SSIS-RS), 44–45
Social skills interventions, in behavioral parent training, 90–92, 91t
Social-emotional development, parental interviews and, 30
Somatic complaints, 10
  treatment of, 126–127
Specific learning disabilities (SLD), RTI and, 186
Specific phobias/fears, 6–7
  prevention of, 111
  treatment of, 111–119
    with cognitive approaches, 117–118
    with contingency management, 118–119
    with deep breathing, 114
    with emotive imagery, 115–117
    with imagery, 115
    with modeling, 118
    with progressive muscle relaxation, 114–115
    with slow breathing, 114
    with systematic desensitization, 112–114
Strategic attention, 72, 87
  forms pertaining to, 99–100
Strengths and Difficulties Questionnaire (SDQ), 17

Strong Start program, 204
Systematic desensitization
  handout for parents, 141
  for treatment of specific phobias/fears, 112–114
Systematic Screening for Behavior Disorders, 2nd Edition (SSBD-2), 38

Teacher Rating Scale—Preschool version, 39, 39t
Teachers, information observations by, 52
Teacher's Report Form (TRF), 40–41, 41t
Teachers/daycare workers
  of child with depression, 136
  interviews with, 26–32
Temperament, parental interviews and, 30
Testing history, in teacher/daycare worker interviews, 30
Therapist, master's-level, referrals to, 209
Therapist associations, 210–211
Thought-globe, in treatment of depression, 139
Time-in technique, 73–74, 99
Time-out technique, 76–79
  ethical/legal issues in, 199–200
  FAQs about, 105
  homework sheet for, 106
  using effectively, 104
Toilet training, 148–150
  child-oriented approach to, 149–150
  parent-oriented approach to, 150
Toileting problems, 11–12, 148–156
  encopresis, 154–156
  enuresis, 150–154
  forms pertaining to, 170–177
Token economy systems, 79
Trauma, parental interviews and, 30
Traumatic circumstances, in teacher/daycare worker interviews, 30
Treatment for Anxiety and Physical Symptoms (TAPS), 126–127
Triple P—Positive Parenting Program, 94

Urine alarms, 151–154

Values clarification, ACT and, 84

Youth Self-Report (YSR), 20